BULGARIA

CZECHOSLOVAKIA

EAST GERMANY

HUNGARY

POLAND

ROMANIA

SOVIET UNION

The Warsaw Pact:

Political Purpose & Military Means

Edited by Robert W. Clawson and Lawrence S. Kaplan

 *Scholarly Resources Inc.*
Wilmington, Delaware

First published 1982
Printed and bound in the United States of America

Scholarly Resources Inc.
104 Greenhill Avenue
Wilmington, Delaware 19805

Library of Congress Cataloging in Publication Data
Main entry under title:

The Warsaw Pact.

    Papers originally presented at a conference
held at Kent, Ohio, Apr. 22–23, 1981, sponsored
by the Center for NATO Studies at Kent State
University.
    Includes index.
    1. Warsaw Treaty Organization—Congresses.
I. Clawson, Robert W.   II. Kaplan, Lawrence S.
III. Kent State University. Center for NATO
Studies.
UA646.8.W367   355'.031'0947   81-86387
ISBN 0-8420-2198-1   AACR2
ISBN 0-8420-2199-X (pbk.)

CONTENTS

THE WEAPONS

DOCTRINE AND CAPABILITIES

PREFACE

This volume, like its predecessor *NATO After Thirty Years* (1981), grew out of a conference held at Kent, Ohio. That meeting, entitled "The Warsaw Pact after Twenty-five Years," was sponsored by the Center for NATO Studies at Kent State University on 22–23 April 1981 with the support of the NATO Information Service and the American Association for the Advancement of Slavic Studies. In addition to the papers presented by the authors of individual chapters, Stephen M. Millett of the Battelle Laboratories contributed a study on Soviet perceptions of nuclear strategy. The conference was the beneficiary of the views of honored guests General Lyman L. Lemnitzer, former Supreme Allied Commander Europe, and Colonel Charles E. Thomann (ret.), executive director of the National Military Intelligence Association. Ambassador Robert M. Komer drew from his long experience with NATO problems in presenting a memorable banquet address.

The conference also benefited from scholars and officials knowledgeable in Warsaw Pact matters who served as commentators on the papers: Carl G. Anthon of American University; Robert Brown of Rochester Institute of Technology; Morris Honick, deputy SHAPE historian; Bernard Reiner of Fairleigh Dickinson University; T. Michael Ruddy of St. Louis University; and Anders Stephanson of Columbia University. Lieutenant Colonel Harold M. Beardslee, USA, director of the Military Science Program at Kent State University, and Colonel Nicholas M. Keck, USAF, former director of Aerospace Studies at Kent State University, were moderators of the sessions.

To all these participants the authors wish to express their appreciation for comments on and criticisms of their respective papers. Many of their viewpoints have been incorporated into this volume.

The infrastructure for the conference was built by members of the staff of the Center for NATO Studies. For conference management and preparation of the manuscript James Carlton, Deborah Clawson, Marjorie Evans, Mike Hicks, and Wilda Lunceford deserve special recognition. Student associates of the center—Roger Freeman, Tim Fleshman, Lynne Dunn Jurkovic, Whitt Miller, Don Theiss, David Tschantz, and Patrick Tulp—provided a variety of services to the conference, which the editors wish to acknowledge with thanks.

Robert W. Clawson and Lawrence S. Kaplan
Kent State University

INTRODUCTION

A great deal of western scholarly literature has been produced on the Warsaw Pact, particularly in the last few years. However, when compared with the substantial volume of historical and analytic material available on NATO and various related aspects of western defense policy, the literature on the Soviet-sponsored alliance in East Europe is modest. This relative imbalance in both quantity and quality of scholarly analysis can be partly explained by the Soviet-imposed compulsion for comprehensive secrecy about even the most ordinary phenomena. Moreover, information from the Soviet Union and East Europe generally is produced in languages that are not widely accessible to scholars from outside the region. For those westerners who can read the appropriate languages or who have access through translation to the necessary journals, newspapers, books, and reports, the analysis of that available data is still somewhat of an arcane skill. But the fact is that there is a great deal of relevant data available both from western defense sources as well as from Soviet and East European publications and contacts, and there are substantial numbers of western specialists trained in the languages and unique analytic skills necessary to provide meaningful interpretation of data from the Warsaw Pact.

The scholarly publication gap, therefore, must result at least partially from a relative lack of demand for information and analysis about NATO's principal potential adversary. The reasons for this comparative disinterest on the part of the consumer of western scholarly analysis are also not hard to uncover. The Warsaw Pact is still a mysterious organization, not least of all to its own members. It has had no single easily comprehensible *raison d'être*. It appears to be the sum total not only of Soviet power considerations but also of geographic location, foreign policy objectives, and domestic conditions of virtually all the East European members. Thus, simply postulating the right questions has proved uncomfortably difficult for interested westerners. In all too many instances it has been far easier to assume either that the term Warsaw Pact was synonymous with the Soviet Union, hence reducing the complexity of the variables—and true enough in some cases—or that the Pact constituted a massive prima facie threat to the West and therefore needed no further explication.

The participants in the Warsaw Pact conference have sought to help close the gap by bringing together in this volume the historical, analytic, and linguistic skills necessary to ask the right questions and to explain the complexities of the Warsaw Pact and its component parts. In order to address this task, their contributions are arranged under five principal topics: the Warsaw Pact's principal political relationships, NATO and the Warsaw Pact, the armed forces of the member states, weapons deployment within the Pact, and the combat doctrines dominant within the alliance.

THE PRINCIPAL POLITICAL RELATIONSHIPS

In an overview of the role and performance of the Warsaw Pact from a perspective of twenty-five years, Andrzej Korbonski tests the long-term performance of the alliance against its initial goals and objectives. He finds that from a military security perspective the operation of the treaty has provided an unimpressive record, playing a function more symbolic than real. From a diplomatic standpoint, the alliance at first appeared to be a potentially useful international actor to be manipulated by Soviet policymakers in order to obtain concessions from the West, but in practice its diplomatic utility has proved to be quite limited. And the East European allies have been less than docile and at times even troublesome on the international diplomatic stage. Korbonski contends that it is only as an instrument of political-military integration that the Warsaw Pact has played a useful and effective role, minimizing defection and open discontent in concert with other organizations, particularly COMECON. While the external failures of the Pact hardly qualify it as an entangling alliance, its successes in the realm of internal bloc control make it more than an empty shell.

Focusing on the three northern members—Poland, Czechoslovakia, and the German Democratic Republic—Jörg Hoensch argues that military-political factors affecting the founding and maintenance of the Pact have not been sufficiently investigated in western analysis. While the important variables in the Soviet decision to form the Pact may have included gaining bargaining leverage with NATO, providing a means for exercising comprehensive discipline and control over its neighbors, and having an additional transmission belt in East Europe, it is important not to ignore the very real role that the military implications of West German accession to NATO played in that Soviet decision. Hoensch also finds that West German admission to NATO in 1955 was persuasive to secure unconditional support for the formation of the Pact by Poland and Czechoslovakia, both having been recent victims of German military aggression. In contradiction to Korbonski, Hoensch contends that the formation of the Warsaw Pact was accompanied from the very beginning by the diffusion of new military manpower policies, equipment deployment, and principles of command and control. This early military focus, coupled with the Pact's organizational changes of the late 1960s and Soviet modernization of equipment and streamlining of doctrine during the 1970s, has been especially important in the Northern Tier. In the final analysis, though, he agrees that today the Pact not only serves vital military purposes but also is an important instrument in Soviet bloc management.

Considering the three southern members of the Pact—Bulgaria, Hungary, and Romania—Edgar O'Ballance demonstrates that widely held assumptions about the secondary value of the southern flank in Soviet conventional strategic thinking have been repeatedly confirmed by events and policies in the area. The manifest Soviet conclusion that neither Hungary nor Romania is particularly trustworthy and that the expeditionary potential of the three armed forces is extremely modest has resulted in the southern members being given very limited Pact contingency defense assignments. Offensively, the troublesome southern members likely would have only the supplementary assignments of reaching the Aegean Sea and helping to seize and hold the Turkish Straits. O'Ballance concludes that as long as the East-West strategic balance persists essentially as it is today, the status quo in the south is apt to exist until perhaps the onset of the twenty-first century, with only a gradual loosening of tight Moscow control. That trend should continue at least until the USSR has become more deeply involved in its confrontation with China.

NATO AND THE WARSAW PACT

In his research on the historical evolution of NATO's perception of the Warsaw Pact, Lawrence Kaplan finds that when the Warsaw Pact was created in 1955, NATO and the western leadership could not take it seriously as an authentic alliance. The new organization was regarded as a diversion to prevent West Germany's entry into NATO and as a transparent charade to dress up Soviet domination of East Europe while insultingly disguised to look like NATO. After the Warsaw Treaty was signed and made public, NATO leaders perceived no new military threat from the East. They only feared the propaganda effect of the USSR's promise to dissolve the Pact if NATO were abolished. Kaplan concludes that it was the occupation of Czechoslovakia in 1968 that changed NATO's basic perception of the eastern alliance. In the 1970s the Pact's participation in the MBFR negotiations and Helsinki talks implied full bloc-to-bloc equality with NATO; by the late 1970s it had taken on more than the equality of a diplomatic actor. The massive quantitative growth and surprising qualitative modernization of the Pact's military forces in the 1970s have produced a firm and convincing military image among the NATO allies; the Warsaw Pact is now seen as a permanent feature, a true counter-NATO.

Analyzing the contemporary relationship between NATO and the Warsaw Pact, Boleslaw Boczek observes that NATO's current perception of the growing imbalance in both Soviet long-range theater nuclear missiles and conventional forces has caused substantial anxiety among the NATO political leadership. However this perception is not shared by large numbers of West Europeans, who either do not believe that there is an imbalance or do not support countermeasures to redress the situation. NATO's response to Soviet superiority in long-range theater nuclear weapons has been a dual policy (adopted in 1979) to change the balance, starting in 1983, and to promote negotiations on arms control, which are now likely to begin at the end of 1981. The Soviets regard the NATO missile program as destabilizing and are especially concerned about NATO plans for stationing new missiles on the territory of their traditional German enemy. Moreover, the growing antinuclear movement in Europe is threatening to frustrate western efforts to catch up with the Soviets in long-range theater nuclear weapons. At the same time the Vienna arms limitation talks on mutual and balanced force reductions are foundering because of very fundamental differences.

THE FORCES

In his essay on the military configurations, strengths, and capabilities of the Soviet armed forces, James Reitz maintains that the specifics of western estimates of the USSR's actual military power have been consistently suspect. But the broad outlines of historical trends can be seen, and to ignore them is to risk missing insights critical to the security of Europe and the West. Between 1960 and 1980 the Soviets undoubtedly have made astonishing progress toward building massive modern military power. Most remarkable is their seemingly inexorable advancement in virtually every major armed forces component. In some cases the numbers are smaller over the twenty-year period, but almost invariably such reductions have been accompanied by significant increases in technology, thus substituting quality for quantity. In other cases, however, the gains have been in both quality and quantity.

In evaluating the military capabilities of the non-Soviet members of the Warsaw Pact, Thomas Cason focuses on each individual East European member's armed forces, assessing qualitative as well as quantitative variables that contribute to or detract from their utility to the Pact. The East European armed forces, particularly those of Poland, Czechoslovakia, and East Germany, certainly represent overall military assets to the Warsaw Pact and the USSR. However, the utility of those forces will vary significantly with the different potential conflicts in which they might be used. Considering subjective qualitative factors it seems clear that in the cases of Bulgaria, Romania, and Hungary, even with across-the-board infusions of new Soviet equipment, prospects for any real contribution to a Warsaw Pact aggressive war are doubtful. Czechoslovakia is still very much a question mark, largely due to the lingering effects of 1968, while East Germany remains the most trustworthy and least trusted member of the Pact. The Polish armed forces, which are certainly the most capable Soviet allied army, are large, well equipped, and proficiently trained, but their reliability is suspect due to persistent Polish nationalism and that nation's unique self-image.

THE WEAPONS

In his essay on Soviet battlefield weapons, James Carlton points out that the Soviets are continuing a tradition of developing and deploying durable and workable weapons to complement their employment doctrine. Yet they also have shown great flexibility in adapting their doctrine to fit available weapons. This pragmatic and innovative spirit has produced a steady flow of new and effective tanks, personnel carriers, self-propelled artillery, bridging equipment, and mechanized antiaircraft weapons. Typical of Soviet designed weapons, these systems possess relatively sophisticated technology in their essential firepower, mobility, and protective features. However, it is obvious that much less concern is devoted to ease of maintenance, crew comfort, or appearance. Nevertheless, their very best equipment is usually as good as that available to NATO armies and is produced in far larger numbers. Naturally, their major weapons systems display identifiable weaknesses and vulnerabilities, but any major technical vulnerabilities, as in the West, are the subject of continuing design efforts to eliminate such flaws; subsequent models rarely display them. Their continued indifference to crew comfort is important but probably would not prove crucial if the Warsaw Pact could fight the kind of short, intense war for which they continue to plan.

Recognizing that the USSR reserves the sole right within the Pact to develop and produce combat aircraft, Bill Sweetman examines the dramatic advances that have been made in the present generation of Soviet types, including substantially increased war load, operational radius, survivability, and lethality. The changes are mainly evolutionary, but they do contribute to closing the quality gap. In the next step forward, the Soviet Union probably will be following western examples much more closely. Sweetman argues that the West should learn to anticipate technical surprises from the Soviet Union based on known technology but built in an innovative manner. Such designs can be tested, manufactured, and deployed quickly while the West is still anticipating Soviet development of a system equivalent to a western type. Improvements in the near future, particularly in long-range interdiction fighters, serve as a reminder that the Soviets are able to produce the high-quality aircraft to fill anticipated needs. The author believes that in developing their own air capabilities, western planners should analyze their programs more carefully for opportunities they may present to the Soviets. Sweetman also maintains that while the Soviet aircraft development watchword has been conservatism, it has been in the best sense: an appreciation of the value of proven success and the need to reinforce it.

Louis Andolino, focusing primarily on the Soviet naval building program, analyzes past and present ship construction and finds that dramatic periodic shifts in emphasis have characterized the development of the postwar Soviet fleet. The primary results have been to produce a highly capable force for the prosecution of antisubmarine and anticarrier warfare. Centering on submarines—almost entirely a Soviet monopoly within the Pact—he states that prolonged emphasis on both strategic and attack craft has produced a formidable force that is currently being augmented by the development and deployment of several extraordinary new underwater craft. Andolino concludes that the Soviets also have made a massive, if somewhat more recent, commitment to the surface fleet and the concept of a well-balanced ocean-going navy that, along with its other tasks, can help to project Soviet national power on a global scale.

John Erickson argues that the commonly held western view of the Pact as a vast monolith is especially inaccurate in the field of alliance military economics. The Soviet production monopoly for major weapons systems has not prevented proliferation of many secondary systems designed and built by individual East European member states. On the other hand, Soviet secrecy and control, especially over tank and fighter aircraft production, probably has impeded a more rational approach to modernization. As the Soviets are shifting from selective reequipment of certain East European armed forces to overall modernization within the Pact, especially in the Northern Tier, national resentment over the Soviet main weapons monopoly can be expected to assume a more pronounced and troublesome form.

DOCTRINE AND CAPABILITIES

John Binder and Robert Clawson conclude that there can be little doubt that the Soviet Union possesses one of the finest conventional ground forces in existence today and that the ground armies of the other Warsaw Pact allies significantly augment Soviet capabilities in Europe. Soviet ground forces provide the standard for Pact organization, training, doctrine, and equipment. Their emphasis on vigorous offensive action, deep objectives, mass echelon attack, and modernized combined arms warfare, along with excellent infantry fighting vehicles, tanks, and a growing stock of modern self-propelled artillery, has produced a first-class European and Asian theater army. That army also has provided the Soviet Union with the basis for air delivered long-range power projection. However, the ground forces of the Pact do have serious vulnerabilities, some of which derive from the very characteristics that augment their power. But Binder and Clawson also stress that some characteristics commonly assumed to be serious liabilities to Warsaw Pact fighting performance do not hold up under closer examination.

Robert Clawson finds that all of the Warsaw Pact air forces, standardized to the Soviet model, recently have been receiving significant new stocks of modern Soviet fighter aircraft designed specifically for important tactical and air defense missions. Eastern Europe and the USSR are integrated into a single Moscow-directed Warsaw Pact strategic air defense system continually undergoing modernization, and air combat doctrine is being made less rigid in order to take greater advantage of the more capable new aircraft and the higher levels of integration in both air defense and tactical aviation. Soviet military air transport and the naval air arm still have significantly lower priorities, but as modernization programs in the other forces mature, it is probable that transport and naval aviation will undergo modernization on an impressive scale. Only long-range bomber aviation, temporarily revived by the addition of modest numbers of *Backfires*, is likely to receive no significantly increased resources. It is important to note that the whole system of Soviet air combat forces is presently undergoing comprehensive reform and that even the main outlines of these changes are still relatively obscure.

In his essay on the navies of the Warsaw Pact, Steve Kime states that while the non-Soviet navies of the alliance do have important missions, they have no responsibility for major strategic operations in wartime, nor do they act as vital instruments of peacetime policy. Only the Soviet navy has global pretensions. The position of the non-Soviet Pact navies reflects the political and military realities governing relations between East Europe and the Soviet Union. The East European navies are designed to operate close to their own shores, and even in war they would perform tasks close to home or in the wake of their senior ally. In a future war the East European navies are to help seize the Turkish Straits, the Danish Narrows, and other targets. However, none of those operations relies critically on East European assistance, and nothing about those navies would allow them to stand in the way of Soviet offensive action.

———

The authors have provided a wealth of data as well as analyses on the history, politics, and economics of the Warsaw Pact. They also have addressed Soviet and East European military capabilities in a detailed and sustained effort to explain the major strengths and vulnerabilities of the Pact and its individual members. Inevitably, this has required focusing special attention on the military services and doctrine of the USSR. However, the sum of all the analyses inevitably must fall short of being comprehensive. Nor could every topic of related interest be thoroughly explored, even to the extent of available public sources. Thus, for instance, no attempt has been made to focus special attention on the Soviet Strategic Rocket Forces. That independent service devotes the vast bulk of its capabilities to targets outside the primary venue of the Warsaw Pact and no other Pact country possesses strategic capabilities. Its principal dimensions have been included in subsidiary portions of other essays.

It is also clear that the Soviet system of military organization is currently undergoing one of its periodic transformations. But military reform in the unique atmosphere of Russia and the Soviet Union always has been a great deal more evolutionary than in the West. Russian and Soviet military tradition amount to much more than ceremony, uniforms, or even doctrinal predelictions. There is a bedrock ethos that remains secure no matter how the services are divided and compartmentalized, and that dampens the effects of paper reorganizations on the essential nature of the armed forces. The fact that some of their Ground Forces' academies are named after naval heroes, or that their naval pilots are trained in Air Forces' flying schools, should be adequate warning to the westerner, especially the North American, that western-made organizational charts are likely to yield only modest insights into the real nature of the Soviet military. The imposition of Soviet military standards on the East European armies has created partial, but recognizable, similarities in most of them.

The current military reforms will leave more unchanged than changed and will become perceptible to the West only after a prolonged period, perhaps not until the Soviets are ready for their next reorganization. These periodic reshuffles inevitably reflect careful planning and response to what the Soviets perceive as significant innovations in enemy weapons or strategies and are military measures based on political policy. The authors of these essays have written history and analysis and provided data and interpretations in an attempt to provide insights into understanding the complex phenomena of Soviet bloc military power and the Warsaw Pact.

CONTRIBUTORS

LOUIS J. ANDOLINO is associate professor of political science at Rochester Institute of Technology and an associate of the Center for NATO Studies. His graduate work was done at Kent State University. An interest in naval affairs dates from his own years of service with the U.S. Navy; his teaching and research interests focus on Soviet foreign policy, Soviet-American relations, and the Warsaw Pact.

JOHN J. BINDER is assistant dean for student life at Kent State University, where he received his Ph.D. He served as a cannoneer with division artillery, 45th Infantry Division, in Korea in 1953–54. Dr. Binder holds the rank of LTC U.S. Army Reserve and is currently assistant commandant of the 2077 USAR School, Cleveland, Ohio. He has taught Soviet tactics at various locations in the United States as a nonresident instructor of the Command and Staff College, Ft. Leavenworth, Kansas.

BOLESLAW ADAM BOCZEK is professor of political science at Kent State University and an associate of the Center for NATO Studies. He holds a doctorate in international law from Jagiellonian University and a Ph.D. in political science from Harvard University. Author of *Flags of Convenience* (1962) and *Taxation in Switzerland* (1976), he also has written numerous articles, monographs, and reviews dealing with international law and organization. He has a special interest in NATO, the Warsaw Pact, and international security in Europe.

JAMES R. CARLTON is a research associate with the Center for NATO Studies at Kent State University. He served with U.S. forces in Europe in an 8th Infantry Division armor battalion, mainly in Germany. His special interest is in armored fighting vehicles, and he is currently working on a long-term project focusing on decision making in NATO weapons systems acquisition. He is a contributor to the center's recent publication, *NATO After Thirty Years* (1981).

THOMAS O. CASON has served as politico-military affairs officer in the Directorate of Concepts, Headquarters USAF, where he participated in major net assessment studies on Soviet vulnerabilities in Central Europe. While assigned to the University of Maryland as assistant professor of Aerospace Studies, he worked independently with John Erickson on studies of the Soviet military district system and the Warsaw Pact. He holds a M.A. degree from Auburn University and is currently completing his doctorate in political science at George Washington University.

ROBERT W. CLAWSON is associate professor of political science, director of the Center for International and Comparative Programs, and administrative coordinator of the Center for NATO Studies at Kent State University. His doctorate is from UCLA. He is a graduate of the Defense Language Institute in Russian and has been an exchange scholar at the State University of Moscow. He has traveled widely throughout Eastern Europe and the USSR. Author of articles on Soviet-sponsored international organizations as well as domestic politics, he is coeditor of *NATO After Thirty Years* (1981).

JOHN ERICKSON is professor of politics and director of defense studies at the University of Edinburgh. He is the author of many articles, monographs, and books on Soviet and East European military affairs. Among his best known works are *The Soviet High Command* (1972), *The Road to Stalingrad* (1975), and *Soviet Military Power and Performance* (1979). He was a research fellow at St. Antony's College, Oxford, and in 1971–72 was Lees-Knowles lecturer at Trinity College, Cambridge. He is also a consultant to the U.S. Strategic Institute's *Strategic Review*.

JÖRG K. HOENSCH has been professor of history at the University of the Saarland since 1972, specializing in post-World War II Eastern Europe. He has visited and engaged in research in almost all the countries of the Warsaw Pact, most notably in Czechoslovakia and Poland. He has studied at the universities of Marburg, Vienna, and Bristol and received a M.A. from the University of California at Berkeley. His doctorate is from Tübingen. In 1976–77 he was a visiting professor at Columbia's Institute on East Central Europe and is currently a fellow of the German UNESCO Commission. He is the author of *Sowjetische Osteuropapolitik, 1945–1975* (1977).

LAWRENCE S. KAPLAN is university professor of history and director of the Center for NATO Studies at Kent State University. Prior to coming to Kent State in 1954 he was with the Historical Office, Office of the Secretary of Defense. He has written numerous articles, monographs, and books on U.S. diplomatic history and NATO affairs, including *A Community of Interests: NATO and the Military Assistance Program, 1948–1951* (1980). He is editor of the center's recent publication, *NATO After Thirty Years* (1981).

STEVE F. KIME is associate dean of faculty and academic programs at the National War College and holds adjunct professorships at the American University and Georgetown University. He received a MPA and Ph.D. from Harvard University. He has served on three U.S. Navy submarines and spent several years in Moscow as a naval attaché. Commander Kime served in the Defense Intelligence Agency and after graduation from the National War College in 1977 became director of Soviet studies there. He is the author of numerous reviews, monographs, and articles on the Soviet navy, Soviet foreign policy, and the Warsaw Pact.

ANDRZEJ KORBONSKI is a leading authority on Soviet participation in international organizations and the Warsaw Pact. He holds a M.A. degree in economics and a Ph.D. in public law and government, both from Columbia University. His publications include many monographs, books, and articles on East-West relations as well as the economic politics of the Soviet Union and Eastern Europe. He also has maintained a special interest in Polish domestic affairs.

EDGAR O'BALLANCE is an author, free-lance journalist, and commentator who presently lives in Derbyshire, England. He has written extensively on military affairs, including more than twenty books and countless articles, and is particularly well known to the international military community through the columns he regularly writes for journals such as *Ground Forces International*. He is a member of the International Institute for Strategic Studies and the Foreign Affairs Research Institute, both of which are in London.

JAMES T. REITZ is a senior staff member with the BDM Corporation, where he is responsible for projects primarily dealing with the Soviet Union. His graduate study was at Columbia University's Russian Institute. He served more than twenty years in the U.S. Army, including intelligence assignments with the Department of the Army and the Defense Intelligence Agency. His multifaceted service career also involved extensive travel throughout the Soviet bloc and a two-year appointment as assistant U.S. Army attaché in Moscow.

BILL SWEETMAN is a free-lance author and commentator specializing in aviation and air power. He was educated at Queen Mary's College in Great Britain, served as a staff member on the British aviation weekly *Flight International*, especially as analyst-commentator on Soviet military aviation, and presently is air correspondent for the London *Observer*. While he is perhaps best known for his book *Soviet Air Power* (1978), Sweetman is also the author of the recently published *Concise Guide to Soviet Military Aircraft* (1981). As an aviation affairs analyst, he has been heard on the BBC domestic and world service.

NOTE ON FOREIGN
AND TECHNICAL TERMS

For the purposes of this volume it was decided to employ a minimum number of foreign terms in the text itself. Only where western usage has adopted a particular abbreviation, word, or phrase has a foreign language term been retained, and then mainly without italics. Hence, BMP has been included, whereas *Dalnaya aviatsia* has not. Nor have English language abbreviations for Soviet or East European terms been employed; in such cases the full English translation has been used. Thus, *Dalnaya aviatsia* has been referred to as Long-Range Aviation, rather than LRA as is sometimes seen.

Russian-English transliteration systems abound; the editors' goal has been to use one of them consistently. For this purpose the table employed by the *Current Digest of the Soviet Press* was chosen. Where Russian sources are cited, translations have been provided for the reader's convenience. German or other West European source titles have not been translated.

When discussing Soviet-built aircraft, the NATO system has been used in an effort to avoid confusion that might result from differences between Soviet service and design bureau designations as well as inaccuracies arising from incomplete intelligence about new types. The NATO system, administered by the Air Standards Coordinating Committee (ASCC), provides a discrete set of references for all aircraft of Soviet manufacture. It has not always been foolproof but is presently more reliable than Soviet designations.

With reference to Soviet-built ships, in the absence of complete and detailed data from the USSR, western designations remain a curious mixture of Russian names and diverse western-imposed identification systems. Conventional western usage is employed because no useful alternative presently exists.

ABBREVIATIONS

AASW	airborne antisubmarine warfare
AAW	antiair warfare
ABC (NBC)	atomic (nuclear), biological, and chemical weapons
ABM	antiballistic missile (system)
ACW	anticarrier warfare
AOR	replenishment oiler
APC	armored personnel carrier
APFDS	armor-penetrating, fin-stabilized, discarding sabot
ASCC	Air Standards Coordinating Committee
ASM	air-to-surface missile
ASW	antisubmarine warfare
ATGM	antitank guided missile
ATWG	antitank wire-guided missile
AWACS	airborne warning and control system
BMP	fighting vehicle, infantry
BRDM	combat reconnaissance patrol vehicle
BTR	armored transporter
BVP	Czech BMP
BWP	Polish BMP
CEP	circular error probable
CG	guided-missile cruiser
COMECON	(CMEA) Council on Mutual Economic Assistance
COMINFORM	Communist Information Bureau
CSCE	Conference on Security and Cooperation in Europe
DD	destroyer
DDG	guided-missile destroyer
ECM	electronic countermeasures
EDC	European Defense Community
EEC	European Economic Community
EW	electronic warfare
FUG	reconnaissance amphibious vehicle
GCI	ground-controlled intercept
GDR	(East) German Democratic Republic
ICBM	intercontinental ballistic missile
IRBM	intermediate-range ballistic missile
KMM	large mechanized bridge
LCT	landing craft tank
LPD	landing platform dock

LRTNF	long-range theater nuclear force
LST	landing ship tank
MBFR	mutual balanced force reductions
MBT	main battle tank
MIRV	multiple independently targetable reentry vehicle
MRV	multiple reentry vehicles
MTU	bridge transporting mount
PCC	Political Consultative Committee
PCS	submarine chaser
PKO	Soviet antispace weapons command
PMP	bridge laying
PRO	Soviet antiballistic missile command
RAP	rocket-assisted projectile
RPG	antitank rocket launcher
SAM	surface-to-air missile
SAU	self-propelled artilery mount
SHAPE	Supreme Headquarters Allied Powers Europe
SKOT	medium-wheeled armored transporter
SLBM	submarine-launched ballistic missile
SLOC	sea lines of communication
SP	self-propelled artillery (gun)
SSB	ballistic missile submarine (conventional)
SSBN	nuclear-powered ballistic missile submarine
SSG	cruise missile submarine (conventional)
SSGN	nuclear-powered cruise missile submarine
SSM	surface-to-surface missile
SSN	nuclear-powered attack submarine
SSW	antisurface warfare
STOL	short takeoff and landing
SU	self-propelled gun mount, WW II designation
TMM	heavy mechanized bridge (scissors)
TNF	theater nuclear force
VTA	Soviet military transport aviation
ZSU	self-propelled antiaircraft mount

FIGURES AND TABLES

THE PRINCIPAL
POLITICAL
RELATIONSHIPS

The Warsaw Treaty After Twenty-five Years: An Entangling Alliance or an Empty Shell?*

ANDRZEJ KORBONSKI

On 14 May 1980 the Warsaw Treaty Organization celebrated its twenty-fifth anniversary. If the impact of this event produced little more than a ripple in the world media, it is because seldom in recent history has there been an international organization whose existence was taken so much for granted but about whose workings so little was known in the West or, for that matter, in the East itself.

To some extent this aura of secrecy was not surprising. The Warsaw Pact was initially conceived as a political and military alliance of eight European Communist countries—Albania, Bulgaria, Czechoslovakia, East Germany, Hungary, Poland, Romania, and the Soviet Union—and the military character of the organization was largely responsible for the paucity of information concerning the functions and operations of the alliance. Moreover, during the first decade of its existence, the treaty remained essentially on paper, playing a more or less symbolic role in Communist international relations. Until fairly recently, the available information about the activities of the Pact consisted mostly of official communiqués published on the occasions of the meetings and conferences of the leaders of the alliance. Only rarely did a sentence or two in a speech by a Soviet or East European leader throw some light on the inner workings of the organization.

The past few years witnessed a significant change in this respect. The criticism of the Pact, voiced regularly by Romania, has not only partially lifted the veil of secrecy surrounding the alliance but also has focused world attention on an organization that many had considered largely dormant. The events in Czechoslovakia during 1968, culminating in the invasion of that country by Pact forces in August, contributed further to the growth of interest in the alliance. United States-Soviet

---

*Research for this paper was aided by a grant from the UCLA Center for International and Strategic Affairs, the assistance of which is hereby gratefully acknowledged.

3

détente and its two offsprings—the Conference on Security and Cooperation in Europe (CSCE) and the mutual and balanced force reductions (MBFR) negotiations—reawakened western interest in the treaty.
The Soviet invasion of Afghanistan, the resulting deterioration in East-
West relations, and, most recently, the threat of a Warsaw Pact military
intervention in Poland further strengthened that concern.

Chronological and historical accounts covering the twenty-five years
of the Warsaw Pact's existence are well known, and the large collection of
literature is still growing.[1] Thus, instead of repeating familiar arguments,
the role of the Warsaw Treaty will be reexamined in terms of its initial
objectives and the degree to which these original goals have or have not
been fulfilled. Some fifteen years ago a distinguished British authority in
the field of international relations made the following observation:

> Alliances are a means to an end, whether it is primarily to increase the
> security of a group of sovereign states in the face of a common
> adversary, or to increase the diplomatic pressure which they can bring
> upon him, or to share the economic cost and the international system
> in an environment in which the fears and goals of nation states,
> whether they be allies or adversaries, do not remain constant; con-
> sequently, alliances—especially those embracing large states or a large
> group of states—have rarely lasted for a long span of time.[2]

Although Buchan's statement pertains to NATO, it could apply
equally to the Warsaw Pact. It shall serve as a basis for an investigation
and evaluation of the performance of the Warsaw Treaty in the course
of the past twenty-five years under three separate, albeit interrelated,
rubrics: as a security or military alliance, as a diplomatic actor on the
international scene, and as an instrument of political integration in Eastern
Europe.

---

[1]For details see Lawrence T. Caldwell, "The Warsaw Pact: Directions of Change,"
Problems of Communism 24, no. 5 (September–October 1975): 1–19; Dale R. Herspring,
"The Warsaw Pact at 25," ibid. 29, no. 5, pp. 1–15; A. Ross Johnson, Robert W. Dean, and
Alexander Alexiev, "East European Military Establishments: The Warsaw Pact Northern
Tier," *Rand Corporation R-2417/1-AF/FF* (December 1980); Christopher D. Jones, "The
Military-Political Mechanisms of the Warsaw Pact," *Final Report to National Council for
Soviet and East European Research*, no. 621-1 (1981); William R. Kintner and Wolfgang
Klaiber, *Eastern Europe and European Security* (New York: Dunellen, 1971); Roman
Kolkowicz, "The Warsaw Pact: Entangling Alliance," *Survey*, no. 70-71 (Winter–Spring
1969): 86-101; Andrzej Korbonski, "The Warsaw Pact," *International Conciliation*,
no. 573 (May 1969): 73; Malcolm Mackintosh, "The Evolution of the Warsaw Pact,"
Adelphi Papers, no. 58 (June 1969); Robin Remington, *The Warsaw Pact* (Cambridge,
MA: MIT Press, 1971); and Thomas W. Wolfe, *Soviet Power and Europe 1945–1970*
(Baltimore: Johns Hopkins University Press, 1970).

[2]Alistar Buchan, "The Future of NATO," *International Conciliation*, no. 565
(November 1967): 5.

THE WARSAW TREATY AS A MILITARY ALLIANCE

Was the Warsaw Treaty initially conceived primarily as a military alliance and has its creation greatly enhanced the security of its signatories? To answer these questions it is important to differentiate between the Soviet Union—both then and now the hegemonial power in the region—and its junior East European allies.

Starting with the USSR, the four major objectives that motivated Stalin in aiding and abetting the Communist takeover of Eastern Europe were: 1) denying the region to countries hostile to Moscow and potentially threatening to the latter's security, 2) ensuring that the domestic political systems in the area remained under control of elements friendly to the USSR, 3) utilizing the region's resources for the purpose of aiding Soviet postwar economic recovery and development, and 4) using Eastern Europe as a potential jumping-off place for a possible offensive against the West.[3] Since these objectives were formulated in the prenuclear age, it may be assumed that some are not as valid or relevant in the early 1980s as in the mid-1940s or 1950s, which witnessed the formal signing of the Warsaw Treaty.

While a good case can be made that the initial Soviet goals in Eastern Europe are still valid today with one possible exception, the important point is that all of them concerned Soviet security, with Eastern Europe being viewed by the Kremlin as a buffer zone or cordon sanitaire against possible western encroachment. It was also Soviet security interests, more than anything else, that were responsible for the establishment after 1948 of a Stalinist satellite system in the region, ruled by Moscow with the help of multiple networks of formal and informal controls.[4]

It is interesting to note that while the process of Stalinist *Gleichschaltung* showed considerable progress in the political, ideological, and economic spheres, its accomplishments in the military arena were much less impressive. In fact, as pointed out by Malcolm Mackintosh, "Stalin's military policy toward Eastern Europe has been both primitive and wasteful."[5] Although by the early 1950s the Soviet Union was linked by bilateral mutual defense treaties with its junior allies, there was almost a total absence of any coordinating mechanism that would attempt to integrate the East European military establishments with that of the USSR.

---

[3]Zbigniew Brzezinski, *The Soviet Bloc*, rev. and enl. ed. (Cambridge, MA: Harvard University Press, 1967), pp. 4–5.

[4]Ibid., pp. 120–23.

[5]Mackintosh, "Evolution of the Warsaw Pact," p. 2.

To be sure, the absence of a unified high command in the area was compensated for by a number of other factors. Since the end of World War II, both the Soviet Union and its East European partners had sought to eradicate "bourgeois-nationalist" influences from the armed forces. This effort took the form of large-scale purges of the officer corps, which was rapidly replaced by new, presumably more reliable, cadres. Soviet military advisers were present throughout the entire military establishment in the region, and in some countries, notably Poland, they held the top command posts. They served as eyes and ears of Moscow alongside political, economic, and secret police experts operating the complex network of Soviet controls.

In addition, as early as the Korean War the East European countries had been forced to produce Soviet-type weapons and equipment, either by expanding their existing defense industries or by creating new ones. These industries were heavily dependent on the Soviet Union for blueprints, parts, and know-how, and the output of various individual weapons was likely to be centrally coordinated, providing still another instrument of control held by Moscow.

Despite the absence of a formal multilateral defense treaty and a unified command, the Kremlin exercised a high degree of control in the coordination of the defense systems of its Eastern European partners. Since the Warsaw Treaty for quite some time did not introduce any new elements into the bloc's military arrangements, the need for a regional collective security system in Eastern Europe cannot be easily accepted as the primary reason for the timing of the treaty, unless the signing is interpreted as simply a *de jure* recognition of the existing state of affairs.

From a purely military viewpoint, even more important than the role of Soviet military advisers was the presence of Soviet troops in four of the seven Eastern European countries (East Germany, Hungary, Poland, and Romania). The only conceivable argument for linking the timing of the Warsaw Treaty to a problem of regional security is the fact that the Austrian State Treaty was signed by Austria and the Big Four on 15 May 1955, one day after the Warsaw Treaty. It terminated the agreements by virtue of which Soviet troops had been stationed in Hungary and Romania for the avowed purpose of guarding lines of communication between the USSR and the Soviet occupation zone in Austria. According to some observers, the Warsaw Pact, in giving the USSR the right to station its forces in the territories of member countries, thus offset the provisions of the Austrian Treaty.[6] In view of the fact that the treaty was only one of

---

[6] B. Meissner, ed., *Der Warschauer Pakt-Dokumentensammlung*, 1 vol. (Cologne: Verlag Wissenschaft und Politik, 1962), pp. 12–13. See also G. Strobel, *Der Warschauer Vertag und die Nationale Volksarmee* (Bonn: Studiengesellschaft fur Zeitprobleme, 1965), pp. 15–22.

several justifications for the invasion of Hungary and Czechoslovakia, it can be assumed that the Soviet Union always could come up with an excuse to maintain its garrisons in, or to send its troops to, the territories of its Eastern European allies without a formal treaty. It is difficult, therefore, to imagine that the Warsaw Pact was created largely in response to the provisions of the Austrian State Treaty.

Nevertheless, the possibility that the prospect of Soviet withdrawal from Hungary and Romania was among the Eastern European developments that motivated Soviet military leaders to exert pressure for a formal military alliance cannot be excluded. During the struggle for power that characterized the post-Stalin interregnum and that terminated in February 1955, the military establishment supported Nikita Khrushchev in his conflict with Georgi Malenkov. The Soviet military leaders appeared to be unhappy with Malenkov's emphasis on nuclear weapons and insisted on maintaining, and even strengthening, the existing conventional defense establishment.[7] It is not inconceivable that some of the leaders disapproved of the "New Course" in Eastern Europe as leading to a weakening of the bloc's defense and demanded the creation of a multilateral military alliance that would reverse the trend. As argued earlier, all these factors still have not provided a convincing security rationale for the treaty. In this light it is logical to ask whether the Warsaw Pact was established in response to a growing exogenous threat directed against the Soviet Union and/or its allies.

It is a well-known fact, however, that in November 1954, a few months before the signing of the treaty, the Conference on European Security took place in Moscow. Under the leadership of Soviet Foreign Minister Vyacheslav Molotov, the conference strongly criticized the western-sponsored remilitarization of the Federal Republic of Germany and issued a warning that the Communist states would have to take steps to ensure their security jointly should West Germany enter NATO as a full-fledged member.[8] The Moscow conference was part and parcel of the Soviet campaign against West German rearmament, which began soon after the three western foreign ministers decided in September 1950 to remove restrictions on the West German military establishment. Except in an official note issued in March 1952, in which it appeared to have become reconciled to the recreation of German armed forces, the USSR, seconded by its Eastern European allies, periodically attacked the concept of West German rearmament. This was true both during and after Stalin's

---

[7]For a discussion of this period see Herbert S. Dinerstein, *War and the Soviet Union* (New York: Praeger, 1962), chap. 4; and Wolfe, *Soviet Power and Europe*, chap. 7.

[8]*Conference of European Countries on Safeguarding European Peace and Security, November 29–December 2, 1954* (Moscow: *New Times*, 1954).

rule and remained a significant exception to the "New Course" in Soviet foreign policy initiated by Malenkov and Khrushchev.

The preamble to the treaty made it clear that the official reason for signing it at that particular time was the ratification of the Paris agreements and the entry of West Germany into NATO. As such it fitted neatly into the effort to dramatize once again the implications of German rearmament. This effort was directed both at the Eastern European countries and at the NATO members. The former had to be convinced that a close military alliance was necessary, whereas the emphasis on the danger of a rearmed Germany was calculated to create dissension among NATO member states, some of which had expressed misgivings on the subject.

In the absence of any solid evidence, it can be speculated that there were, in fact, several reasons for the creation of the Warsaw alliance at that time. It is difficult to accept the official reason that West Germany's entry into NATO alone was responsible for the treaty. It is true that both the Soviet Union and its allies in Eastern Europe had remained suspicious of West Germany since the end of World War II, and that they were strongly opposed to its remilitarization. At the same time, it should have occurred to them that a rearmed West Germany, belonging to either the European Defense Community or to NATO, represented less of a threat than a West Germany not subject to any institutional restraints. The inclusion of the Federal Republic in NATO restricted the freedom of action of the Bundeswehr, which was made subject to NATO command.

A question may be raised as to why no Soviet-sponsored military alliance was signed immediately following the creation of NATO in April 1949, or even after the initial announcement concerning West German rearmament in 1950. It may be presumed that the Soviet Union did not seriously consider NATO an aggressive alliance until West Germany was invited to join. The preamble to the Warsaw Treaty implied that a sudden transformation of NATO from a defensive to an offensive alliance took place on 9 May 1955, the day of Germany's entry. This particular reasoning, however implausible, was likely to appeal to at least some Eastern European countries obsessed with a genuine fear of West Germany, alone or as part of NATO.

If neither the outside threat nor the need for a tighter mutual security system was by itself a sufficient reason for creating a treaty, the combination of the two did provide an incentive for the establishment of a collective defense system. However, other developments in the region, to be discussed below, most likely had a more decisive influence on the timing and the form of the Warsaw Treaty.

While an argument can be made that the Kremlin has viewed the creation of the Pact as contributing to the strengthening of Soviet security, the same was only partly true for the junior members of the alliance. Of the seven smaller East European countries only two, or possibly three, probably welcomed the treaty as safeguarding their own security. In the middle of 1955 Poland still looked at West Germany as an adversary, eager to rectify the territorial arrangements reached at Yalta and Potsdam, and hence Warsaw most likely appreciated a more formal military alliance that would strengthen its own position vis-à-vis Bonn. It also may be taken for granted that East Germany strongly favored the treaty, since it would reinforce its own status as a full-fledged member of the alliance, not mentioning its fear of a rearmed West Germany. Finally, Czechoslovakia was the only other country in the region that has had a long-standing territorial quarrel with the Federal Republic and that presumably welcomed the treaty for the same reason as did Poland. It is therefore not surprising that it was these three countries that became known during the next two decades as the Northern Tier, or the Iron Triangle, and thus formed the core of the alliance.

The remaining four members were clearly much less concerned about the security aspects of the treaty. None of them viewed West Germany as a revanchist country committed to the revision of the postwar status quo in the region. Moreover, none of them was directly exposed to a threat emanating from any other member of NATO. Finally, the "New Course," proclaimed by Malenkov shortly after Stalin's death, signaled an impending thaw in East-West relations that was bound to reduce whatever insecurity and paranoia that remained in the minds of the leaders of the respective countries.

A good case, therefore, can be made that in the mid-1950s the Warsaw Treaty made some sense as a military alliance. It was perceived by at least half of its signatories as strengthening their own security vis-à-vis West Germany and NATO. Nonetheless, it also can be shown that this particular aspect of the treaty has not loomed very large in the annals of the organization. There is no evidence suggesting that much progress in the direction of strengthening military cooperation among Pact members took place until 1961, when the Berlin crisis provided the opportunity for the first display of collective action in the staging of joint military maneuvers. The periodic conferences of the Pact's defense ministers were the only major accomplishments related to the collective security of the area. Judging by the explicit and implicit criticism of the Pact by some of its members, the unified command envisaged in the treaty was never fully implemented and remains today essentially the monopoly of the Soviet Union.

It is impossible to say whether Soviet domination of the unified command of the Pact's armed forces contributed to the military strength of the alliance. All that is known is that it turned out to be the major object of dissatisfaction on the part of Romania and Czechoslovakia, which demanded a greater voice for the smaller partners. Thus, it can be argued that the Soviet role in the unified command introduced an element of disruption into the organization and weakened its cohesion.

The institutional changes in the treaty's command structure announced at the summit meeting of the alliance leaders in Budapest in March 1969 were partially intended to meet the criticism of the Soviet domination of the unified command voiced by some of the junior partners.[9] Nonetheless, judging by the continuing dissatisfaction with the treaty, most recently articulated by Romania at another summit meeting in Moscow in November 1978,[10] the changes have not resulted in a radical departure from the past, which means that for all practical purposes the unified command remains today an appendix to the Soviet *stavka*.

Insofar as joint military exercises are concerned, there have been seventy-one separate Warsaw Pact maneuvers spanning the period from 1961 to 1979.[11] Whether they have contributed significantly to the strengthening of the treaty's military prowess is anyone's guess. The armed intervention in Czechoslovakia in August 1968 provided the only example of a concerted military action undertaken by the treaty. Although western observers generally were highly impressed with the precision and efficiency of the invasion, the participation of the troops of the smaller partners was largely symbolic, and the major burden was born by the Soviet army. Consequently, the intervention in Czechoslovakia does not seem to provide convincing proof that all of the national armies of member states could participate effectively in a large-scale joint military operation.

The conventional military strength of the alliance was significantly diminished following a series of highly publicized troop reductions between 1955 and 1960, but since then it has been steadily increasing to the point where today it represents, at least on paper, a formidable fighting force.[12] Since there is little or no information concerning the allocation of nuclear weapons to members of the alliance, one can only speculate that Warsaw Pact arrangements in this respect are probably not substantially different from those operating in NATO. It is known that the smaller East European countries have some delivery vehicles such as short-range, surface-to-surface missiles, but there is no evidence that they have direct access to nuclear warheads.

There remains the problem of the commitment to the treaty by the member states, which can be viewed from two different perspectives. One aspect of it concerns the willingness of a member country to participate

---

[9]Caldwell, "The Warsaw Pact," pp. 1–19.

[10]Charles Andras, "A Summit with Consequences," Radio Free Europe Research, *RAD Background Report/271 (Eastern Europe)*, 14 December 1978.

[11]Jones, "Military-Political Mechanisms of the Warsaw Pact," p. 138.

[12]For details see *The Military Balance 1979–1980* (London, IISS, 1980), pp. 13–16, 108–13.

fully in the treaty's activities, including joint maneuvers, weapons standardization, and possibly combined military operations. Here the most visible maverick has been Romania, which for some time has shown its strong aversion to being involved in the Pact's activities. Aside from its refusal to take part in joint military exercises, Bucharest has initiated its own defense doctrine, patterned closely after the Yugoslav concept of the "People's War," and has frequently called for the dissolution of military alliances in Europe.[13] On the strength of that doctrine, it may be presumed that in the event of an East-West confrontation, Romania could not be counted upon as a reliable member of the Warsaw Pact that would be ready and willing to shed blood in defense of Soviet interests.

The other aspect of the problem concerns the reliability of the national military establishments of the treaty members. The emergence of new political and military elites, characterized by often virulent nationalism, has raised the question of whether the Pact has become a dependable fighting force that could be used in any future East-West conflict. Evaluating reliability of combat troops is a difficult task, the results of which tend to be unreliable. A recent systematic attempt at estimating the reliability of East European armies in the event of an East-West confrontation concluded that the only army that could be counted upon to participate in the treaty's military operations—both offensive and defensive—was that of East Germany. All the remaining military establishments were viewed as not being entirely reliable.[14] Admittedly, the evidence used in support of the above contention tends to be impressionistic and intuitive, yet at the same time it does correspond to a widely held popular perception of the role played by the individual countries in the overall activities of the Warsaw alliance.

One interesting aspect of the smaller members' attitude toward the treaty has been their insistence that the Warsaw Treaty apply only to Europe. Over the years there have been unconfirmed reports that the USSR attempted to persuade its junior allies to deploy units of their national armies outside of Europe, primarily on the Sino-Soviet border, in Vietnam, and, most recently, in Afghanistan. Soviet requests apparently have been consistently turned down by the East Europeans and, if true, it would testify to certain decline in Soviet domination of the alliance. In turn, this also would affect the military potential of the Pact.

---

[13]For an excellent discussion see Alexander Alexiev, "Romania and the Warsaw Pact: The Defense Policy of a Reluctant Ally," *The Rand Corporation, P-6270* (January 1979).

[14]Dale R. Herspring and Ivan Volgyes, "Political Reliability in the Eastern European Warsaw Pact Armies," *Armed Forces and Society*, 6, no. 2 (Winter 1980): 289. See also Johnson et al., "East European Military Establishments," pp. 63–67, 116–21, 163–64, 175–76. See also Thomas Cason's essay in this volume.

On the other hand, certain member states, notably Czechoslovakia and East Germany, have acted as Moscow's proxies in various parts of the Third World, most likely on Soviet orders. Their presumed goal was to spread Soviet influence in selected African, Asian, and Latin American states and thus improve the Soviet position vis-à-vis both China and the West through the shipments of arms and advisers to countries such as Angola, Ethiopia, Zimbabwe, and Afghanistan as well as Nicaragua and El Salvador. While all these activities have been conducted outside the formal framework of the treaty, they may be viewed nonetheless as fulfilling the same objectives as those of the Pact by strengthening Soviet security against western threat.

While such a threat, real or imaginary, may have existed in the minds of the Kremlin leaders in the mid-1950s, by the early 1970s it was clearly superseded by East-West détente, which was symbolized in the official western recognition of East Germany; the settlement of the Berlin issue; the 1970 treaties between Bonn, Moscow, and Warsaw; and the negotiations concerning MBFR and European security. As in the case of NATO, the decline in the intensity of the external threat was bound to affect the degree of military preparedness of the Warsaw Pact. While in the late 1970s the East-West détente began to show signs of wear and tear and its deterioration has accelerated in the wake of the Soviet intervention in Afghanistan and the events in Poland, West Germany, the villain of the 1950s, assumed the role of an intermediary and hardly could be viewed by the Kremlin and its junior allies as a serious threat to the Warsaw alliance.

In this respect, the histories of both the Warsaw Pact and NATO show striking similarities. Both alliances were established for a specific purpose. It does not matter that in both cases the reasons for their creation were more apparent than real. What mattered was that both the senior and junior partners in the respective alliances perceived the presence of an outside threat. In 1949 the United States may have anticipated Soviet pressure against the West, although a good case can be made that at that very moment Stalin already had decided to abandon any aggressive posture toward the western defense perimeter.[15] Similarly, in 1955 the Soviet Union may have persuaded itself that as a result of West Germany's joining NATO, the latter had become an aggressive organization, one that was determined to destroy the status quo in Eastern Europe without seriously reflecting on the possibility that West Germany tied to NATO might be less dangerous that it would be with no restraints on the pursuit of its own independent policy. It may be argued that once both sides began to doubt that the threats were real, the two organizations lost

---

[15]For an interesting treatment of this question see Marshall Shulman, *Stalin's Foreign Policy Reappraised* (Cambridge, MA: Harvard University Press, 1963), chapts. 1–3, 5, 6. See also Boleslaw Adam Boczek's essay in this volume.

their *raison d'être*, at least insofar as their security aspects were concerned.

This mutual loss of perceptions, in conjunction with the various difficulties discussed earlier, provides evidence that from a purely military security standpoint, the accomplishments of the Warsaw Pact in the past twenty-five years have not been very impressive, especially when contrasted with the initial goals of the Soviet Union, which were ultimately partly responsible for the creation of the alliance.

THE WARSAW TREATY AS A DIPLOMATIC ACTOR

As was suggested at the outset, another reason for the creation and timing of the Warsaw Pact was Moscow's desire to establish an organization similar to NATO that could be used as a counterbalance to NATO in the East-West negotiations on European questions scheduled to begin in Geneva in July 1955. The Soviets were known to be extremely sensitive about preserving parity in East-West relations and to attach great importance to maintaining this image. The fact that negotiating parity was relatively less important at the time of NATO's birth in 1949, when the intensity of the Cold War precluded East-West negotiations, helps to explain why the Warsaw Pact was not formed at that time. That reestablishing parity was an important motive behind the treaty may be assumed from Article 11, which in essence states that in the event of the signing of an all-European collective security treaty, the Warsaw alliance automatically would be dissolved.

Apart from the question of parity, the Pact always could be used as an important bargaining point. Its dissolution would not be a unilateral act on the part of the Soviet Union but would involve some concessions either by NATO or by the United States. The value of the Pact as a bargaining point was then most notably one of the overriding reasons for the creation of the treaty.

The treaty's role as a tool of Soviet diplomacy also proved to be limited in scope and character, although its creation, to some extent, improved the Soviet bargaining position. If there had been no Warsaw Pact, the USSR would have had to face NATO countries alone across the conference table, whereas the existence of the treaty gave the Soviet Union, at least formally, a much greater voice as an arbiter of European and world peace. In the various East-West negotiations following the Big Four conference held in Geneva in July 1955, the Soviet Union no longer represented itself alone but spoke for the entire Eastern European bloc. This new role also had certain practical consequences. For example, the Warsaw alliance began to be treated as an equal partner in the disarmament talks alongside NATO and the uncommitted countries. This gave the USSR additional votes that otherwise might have been much more difficult to obtain. This aspect of the treaty probably also enjoyed the genuine support of the smaller Eastern European countries, which not only acquired additional status and worldwide attention but also were enabled, by gaining access to East-West meetings, to establish closer contacts with some of the Western European countries. After a decade of almost total isolation from the West, this was indeed a welcome change.

The two most important areas of diplomatic activity directly or indirectly involving the Warsaw Treaty were the problem of arms control and disarmament and an all-European collective security pact. Article 2 of the Warsaw Treaty proclaimed the willingness of its members to adopt measures for the general reduction of armaments and the prohibition of atomic, hydrogen, and other weapons of mass destruction. Most of the members of the Warsaw alliance were represented in the two disarmament committees created by the United Nations. The Soviet Union, Bulgaria, Czechoslovakia, Poland, and Romania belonged to the Ten-Nation Committee on Disarmament, which met from September 1959 until June 1960, when the Warsaw Treaty members refused to participate as a result of the U-2 incident and the breakup of the Paris summit meeting. Less than two years later, however, the same five countries joined the Eighteen-Nation Committee on Disarmament, which was established at the sixteenth session of the United Nations General Assembly in December 1961. It soon became apparent that this committee was the chosen platform for Warsaw alliance disarmament ideas, and the Pact's members began to use the Geneva meetings of the committee to present their proposals. It may be suspected that the major reason for the latter was that the meetings of the Eighteen-Nation Committee often drew the attention of the entire world, and thus offered far greater possibilities for publicizing Soviet views than the meetings of the Political Consultative Committee of the Pact.

This impression is reinforced by the manner in which the Rapacki Plan, probably the best-known disarmament proposal emanating from the alliance, was presented. The plan was proposed for the first time in October 1957 at the United Nations General Assembly, rather than at a meeting of the treaty's Political Consultative Committee, and appeared to be, at least on the surface, a unilateral Polish initiative. Subsequent versions of the plan were elaborated outside the framework of the Warsaw alliance, despite the fact that the meetings of the Political Consultative Committee seemed to provide a logical platform for that purpose. The only major disarmament measures announced in connection with sessions of the committee were two reductions in the numerical strength of the Warsaw Treaty's forces (May 1958 and February 1960). Even in this case, the spotlight was stolen by previous announcements of similar reductions in 1955 and 1956 made outside the institutional framework of the treaty.

Another important series of arms control negotiations involving both the Warsaw Pact and NATO was focused on mutual and balanced force reductions. The talks, which opened formally in Vienna in October 1973 and which have continued ever since without reaching an agreement, were part and parcel of U.S.–Soviet détente that reached its peak during the signing of the SALT I agreement at Moscow in May 1972. The Warsaw Pact was represented at the Vienna negotiations by the Soviet Union, Czechoslovakia, East Germany, and Poland; the remaining three Pact members enjoyed a "special status."

Considering the fact that MBFR negotiations have been ongoing for eight years, their accomplishments have been meager.[16] By the end of the 1970s, the talks had reached a deadlock that could be removed only if either side were prepared to make major concessions. The main disagreement focused on the number of troops maintained by the Pact in the reduction area: the NATO negotiators claimed that the Warsaw Pact had deployed 150,000 troops over and above the number officially admitted.

In light of the prolonged impasse it is appropriate to ask whether Moscow has been seriously interested in force reduction in Europe. On the one hand, it may be speculated that the USSR was sincerely concerned with reducing its defense burden, and thus it was willing to discuss troop reduction. Furthermore, it also might view the MBFR talks as a way of driving a wedge between the United States and the rest of NATO. In addition, the Kremlin might have seen the Vienna negotiations as an inducement for the United States to move faster in the direction of the European Security Conference, which at that time at least enjoyed top priority in the Kremlin. On the other hand, an equally plausible argument could be made, suggesting that the Soviet leadership was not at all interested in changing the balance of conventional forces in Europe and that it was in fact committed to the maintenance of the status quo.

While the Soviet attitude toward MBFR cannot be easily fathomed, it may be taken for granted that the junior Pact partners, especially Hungary and Poland, were strongly in favor of troop reduction in Central Europe, which presumably would include the Soviet troops stationed on their territory. Moreover, such a reduction also would reinforce the

---

[16]For additional details see U.S., Congress, Senate, Committee on Foreign Relations, *Prospects for the Vienna Force Reduction Talks,* 95th Cong., 2d sess. (Washington, DC: Government Printing Office, 1978); Stockholm International Peace Research Institute, *Force Reductions in Europe* (Stockholm: Almqvist and Wiksell, 1974); and Paul E. Zinner, "A Report on the Status of MBFR Negotiations as Observed in Vienna in the Fall of 1977" (unpublished paper, February 1978).

process of East-West détente that has been strongly supported by most of the East European countries.

In any event, by 1981 it became abundantly clear that the MBFR negotiations had become hopelessly stalled and that there were few, if any, prospects of their early successful conclusion. If indeed the Kremlin had any serious interest in troop reduction and if it hoped that being a leader of a military alliance would aid in that task then its expectations were not fulfilled. Again, the Warsaw Pact in its role as an instrument of Soviet diplomacy has not proved particularly helpful.

The creation of an all-European collective security system was accorded a prominent place in the treaty. The emphasis given to the need for such a system, based on the participation of "all European states irrespective of their social and political structure," reflected continued Soviet efforts to bring about the withdrawal of U.S. forces from Europe. The importance attached by the Soviet Union to an all-European security treaty was clearly expressed in Article 11, which tied the existence of the Warsaw alliance to such a treaty by explicitly offering to disband the former in the event of the establishment of the latter. Thus, the article represented a potential Soviet concession designed to attract Western European countries to the idea of an all-European treaty.

The urgency that had characterized previous Soviet attempts in this field also was reflected in the appeals issued after meetings of the treaty's Political Consultative Committee between 1956 and 1970.[17] Almost every official communiqué called for the signing of a nonaggression treaty between the Warsaw Pact and NATO as the first step in the direction of an all-European collective security system. The preparatory talks for CSCE opened formally in November 1972 and the Final Act of the conference was signed almost three years later in Helsinki on 1 August 1975.

While Soviet intentions with regard to MBFR were ambivalent, to say the least, this was not the case vis-à-vis CSCE. There is no doubt that Moscow was most eager to reach an understanding with the West that would finally ratify the territorial status quo in Europe and reaffirm Soviet hegemony east of the Elbe. In order to achieve this goal the Kremlin was apparently willing to accept the provisions of Basket Three of CSCE and of Article 6 of the Final Act, both with their emphasis on human rights.

Was the Warsaw Treaty helpful in achieving Soviet objectives with regard to CSCE? In urging the West to come to Helsinki the USSR, speaking on behalf of the alliance, appeared more credible than if it had

---

[17]For an extensive discussion see A. Ross Johnson, "The Warsaw Pact's Campaign for 'European Security,' " *Rand Report R-565-PR* (November 1970); and Charles Andras, "European Security and the Security of Europe," Radio Free Europe Research, *East-West Relations/1* (March 1970).

represented only itself. Moreover, as in the case of MBFR, most of its junior partners strongly supported the idea of CSCE as contributing to a further reduction of international tension and a growing rapprochement between both parts of Europe. Thus, in this particular respect it may be argued that the Warsaw Pact fulfilled its role as a useful bargaining tool.

Although the signing of the Helsinki Final Act was initially viewed as a major Soviet gain, it soon became obvious that it was at best a Pyrrhic victory. With relatively little attention paid to Baskets One and Two, the world's attention soon became focused on the human rights provisions of Basket Three, to the obvious discomfort of the Kremlin which clearly had not expected such a turn of events. While the Soviet Union strongly hoped to derive some tangible benefits from CSCE, especially with regard to East-West economic transactions, the major achievement of the Final Act was instead to endow dissident movements in a number of Pact members with international legitimacy.

It is therefore not surprising that the two follow-up CSCE meetings at Belgrade (1977–78) and Madrid (1980–81) accomplished almost nothing apart from focusing again on the violation of human rights in the USSR and in some of its junior allies. By the end of the final meeting, Moscow had lost most of its interest in CSCE, but the same was not necessarily true for the smaller East European countries, among which only Czechoslovakia and East Germany continued steadfastly to toe the Soviet line.

From a perspective of the past twenty-five years, the accomplishments of the Warsaw Treaty as a bargaining tool and as an instrument of Soviet diplomacy vis-à-vis the West hardly have been impressive. On paper, the alliance appeared as a useful international actor to be manipulated by Soviet policymakers in order to obtain concessions from the West. In reality, however, its utility proved to be quite limited. Its sole achievement was the convening of the Helsinki Conference, and when that failed the Pact lost a great deal of its initial *raison d'être*. Ultimately, all the major decisions in the realms of arms control, the future of Germany, or European security were made outside the framework of the treaty, usually as a result of an agreement between the United States and the Soviet Union or between the USSR and the western Big Three of Britain, France, and the United States.[18]

It also should be noted that even in the area of East-West diplomatic negotiations, the Soviet Union has been unable to maintain total unity among Warsaw Pact members. As early as 1967 Romania broke ranks by establishing diplomatic relations with West Germany against Moscow's

---

[18]For a somewhat different perception of the treaty's role in East-West negotiations concerning Berlin and the future of Germany, see N. Edwina Moreton, *East Germany and the Warsaw Alliance: The Politics of Detente* (Boulder, CO: Westview Press, 1978).

18   THE WARSAW PACT

wishes. Two years later Poland's increasingly favorable responses to
West German overtures culminated in the signing of a treaty between
Warsaw and Bonn in December 1970. While Moscow has not openly
opposed Poland's initiative, there is some evidence that the rapid Polish-
West German rapprochement was not fully supported and appreciated by
the Kremlin.

THE WARSAW TREATY AS AN INSTRUMENT OF
POLITICAL INTEGRATION

The presence of an outside threat and the need for a Soviet-
sponsored mutual security system to deal with it, as well as Moscow's
interest in creating an organization that could be utilized by the Soviet
policymakers in East-West diplomatic negotiations, have been examined
in discussing the rationale for the signing of the Warsaw Pact in May
1955. Other developments, however, probably had more decisive influence
on the timing and the form of the Warsaw Treaty. Two interpretations of
the relation of these developments to the Pact seem especially plausible.

The first interpretation links the signing of the treaty directly to the
change in the system of controls over Eastern Europe that followed the
death of Stalin in 1953. In dealing with the bloc, Stalin had relied upon a
variety of informal control devices, and the only two formal multilateral
bodies, the Communist Information Bureau (COMINFORM) and the
Council on Mutual Economic Assistance (widely known in the West as
COMECON), existed mostly on paper. In the Soviet Union, the transfer
of power from Stalin to Malenkov to Khrushchev was accompanied by a
gradual elimination of the informal instruments of control and their
replacement by somewhat more conventional means.

The Moscow-controlled satellite empire was to be reshaped into a
new socialist commonwealth of nations. A multilateral defense treaty and
a resurrected multilateral organization for economic cooperation were
intended to institutionalize the new form of the East European Communist
bloc. Several tasks could be fulfilled by these two bodies: they could
replace the universally hated informal devices as well as legitimize and
strengthen the Soviet hold over Eastern Europe. The multilateral character of the Warsaw Pact and COMECON fit in especially well with the
new emphasis on the "conciliar" aspects of Moscow's rule, which was
based on regular consultations among the individual leaders. Furthermore, the presence of both organizations was likely to make it more
difficult for member countries to withdraw from them and from the Soviet-
controlled "commonwealth."

One immediate effect of the treaty, although probably not a major motive for its signing, was that it permitted Soviet forces to remain stationed in Hungary and Romania after the conclusion of the Austrian State Treaty. The presence of Soviet troops in East Germany and Poland required no legitimation by the Warsaw Pact, while there were no Soviet garrisons in the remaining member states—Albania, Bulgaria, and Czechoslovakia. Therefore, Hungary and Romania were the key countries with respect to this use of the Warsaw Treaty at the time of its signing. Most likely, it would not have been difficult for the Kremlin to ensure the continuing presence of its forces in both these countries through other arrangements such as bilateral treaties, but the Pact was clearly the far more convenient device. A multilateral treaty involved the entire bloc, thus endowing the continued presence of Soviet troops with a collective importance.

This particular aspect of the treaty acquired considerable significance beginning in 1956 when it was first invoked by Moscow as one of the justifications for the entry of additional Soviet forces into Hungary for the purpose of suppressing the rebellion in that country. The treaty also figured prominently in the Moscow declaration of 30 October 1956, which announced the willingness of the Kremlin to discuss the question of the stationing of Soviet forces with the countries concerned. In May 1958 a meeting of the Warsaw Pact's Political Consultative Committee provided the opportunity for proclaiming the withdrawal of Soviet troops from Romania and the reduction of their strength in Hungary.

Between 1958 and 1968 the question of Soviet garrisons in Eastern Europe was seldom mentioned. The outbursts in Hungary and Poland in 1956 were followed by Status of Forces agreements between the USSR and a number of other member countries, which seemed to take the steam out of this particular issue. There was no evidence that the presence of Soviet forces in East Germany, Hungary, and Poland was a major political problem throughout the 1960s. Thus, it would appear that the Warsaw Pact, in its capacity as the instrument legitimizing the stationing of Soviet troops in several East European countries, has generally performed a useful role. As an instrument of politico-military integration, it was clearly more acceptable than the discredited Stalinist devices and from the Kremlin's point of view it was probably more effective than the network of informal controls.

It is noteworthy that the three Pact members that began to challenge Soviet hegemony in the region during the 1960s were those that had no Soviet troops stationed within their borders. The first of the member countries to do it was Albania, which moved from the Soviet to the Chinese orbit after 1961. While Albania's departure did not greatly weaken the Pact's military potential, the psychological impact of the defection on the outside world and especially on the rest of the alliance was much more serious. The fact that a founding member of the alliance could defy the Soviet Union and the Warsaw Treaty with impunity did little to strengthen the cohesiveness and prestige of the organization. Instead, it created a precedent for the future.

Romania's resistance to certain Soviet ideas began shortly after Albania's defection from the treaty. Whether the challenge to Soviet leadership presented by Bucharest was the outcome of a "demonstration effect" created by Tirana is difficult to judge, but some linkage between the two cannot be entirely discounted.

The most serious challenge to the Soviet domination of the alliance since the 1956 Hungarian Revolt was the Prague Spring of 1968. For the first three months following the assumption of power by Alexander Dubček, the members of the Warsaw Pact had been observing Czechoslovak events with interest and apparent equanimity. This attitude changed rapidly, however, especially after violent demonstrations by Polish university students who openly expressed their admiration for Dubček. This support alarmed the Polish regime and provided the alliance with its first pretext for a strong reaction.

A series of Pact meetings took place in Dresden (March) and in Moscow (May). One of their tangible results was the ominous announcement that Warsaw Pact "staff exercises" would be staged in Czechoslovakia in June. Clearly unwilling to make a complete break with the treaty, the Dubček regime, which together with Romania was absent from the Moscow meeting, consented and detachments of Soviet troops entered the country. This conciliatory act on the part of the Prague leaders did not satisfy the other member states, which met again in Warsaw in July in a final effort to bring Czechoslovakia to heel.

The events of the remainder of the Prague Spring are well known. The two August meetings—in Cierna, between the Soviet and Czechoslovak leaders and in Bratislava, between the Czechoslovaks and the leaders of the other Warsaw Pact countries again with Romania absent— probably reflected a Soviet desire to achieve a political rather than a military solution of the conflict. When these efforts failed, forces of five members of the Pact entered Czechoslovakia, and a new chapter in the treaty's history began.[19] Official Soviet justifications of the occupation were reminiscent of similar justifications of the intervention in Hungary. However, a major difference between the two explanations was that in the Czechoslovak case emphasis was given to collective action and to the threat represented by West Germany.

The unstated reasons for the invasion most likely included pressures exerted on Moscow by the Polish and East German governments, who were worried about the effects of the developments in Czechoslovakia on

---

[19]For an excellent discussion of the invasion see Jiri Valenta, *Soviet Intervention in Czechoslovakia* (Baltimore: Johns Hopkins University Press, 1979).

their own populations; similar fears expressed by various groups in the USSR; the conviction on the part of the Soviet leaders that only drastic action could prevent a collapse of communism in Czechoslovakia; and the Soviet belief that at this stage only an armed intervention would demonstrate to the other actual or potential defectors that the Kremlin was determined to keep the Warsaw Pact intact.

Thus, faced with the real or imaginary danger of the "domino effect" in Eastern Europe, the Soviet Union decided to strike. The USSR clearly succeeded in impressing the outside world with its determination to take even the most drastic measures to safeguard its hegemony in the region and to maintain the integrity of the Warsaw alliance. After a seemingly prolonged period of indecision and procrastination, the Soviet Union finally acted decisively and managed to score significant points. It stopped the process of democratization in Czechoslovakia and calmed the fears and anxieties of its own leaders as well as those of Poland and East Germany. It forced Romania to abandon, if only for the time being, its virulent attacks and disruptive criticism. Finally, the relative efficiency and smoothness with which the treaty's forces seized Czechoslovakia underscored the military prowess of the alliance.

What remained to be done was for the Soviet leaders to take advantage of the impact of the intervention on the alliance to reaffirm Moscow's hegemony and strengthen the unity of the Pact. Less than one month after the attack, the Kremlin proclaimed the so-called "Brezhnev Doctrine," which provided an *ex post facto* ideological justification of the intervention.[20] The Soviet Union assumed the role of the guardian of the alliance and was responsible for its security and integrity. Any attacks from the outside or any changes from within that threatened the "socialist achievements" of any member of the bloc were to be considered as attacks on the treaty as a whole, triggering an automatic response by the USSR and the rest of the membership.

This new Soviet concept of the alliance was strongly reminiscent of some of the pronouncements regarding "proletarian internationalism" made in the late 1940s. It might be argued that it went even further than any comparable declaration of the Stalin era, which as suggested earlier was characterized by reliance on informal rather than formal linkages between the USSR and its East European satellites. Moreover, following concepts such as "separate roads to socialism," "polycentrism," and "socialist commonwealth," the Brezhnev Doctrine represented a significant

---

[20]S. Kovalev, "Suverenityet i internatsionalnye obyazonnosti sotsialisticheskikh stran" [Sovereignty and the internationalist obligations of socialist countries], *Pravda*, 26 September 1968. Brezhnev restated his doctrine at the 5th Congress of the Polish Communist Party in November 1968. See "Rech tovarishcha L. I. Brezhneva" [Comrade Brezhnev's speech], *Pravda*, 13 November 1968.

switch in the Soviet policy vis-à-vis Eastern Europe. It served notice to friend and foe alike that no interference with, or criticism of, the Pact would be tolerated by the Kremlin.

The message that the new doctrine was intended to convey was not lost on the Warsaw Pact membership, including Romania, the only country so far to have been able to castigate the treaty with relative impunity. For the next twelve years the alliance enjoyed considerable tranquility, even though Romania already had resumed its independent stance in the mid-1970s. It was only in the wake of the Polish events in the summer of 1980 that some of the half-forgotten Soviet pronouncements and tactics were brought into play once again.

The developments in Poland, which followed the wave of strikes in July and August 1980 and the establishment of the Solidarity trade union movement, represented probably the most serious challenge ever, not only to the integrity of the Warsaw Pact but also to Soviet hegemony in Eastern Europe and the sheer survival of Communist rule in the region. It was more threatening even than the Titoist heresy of 1948.

The reaction of the Soviet Union and the rest of the Warsaw Pact to the events in Poland showed a number of striking similarities in the attitude toward the Prague Spring. In both cases, the initial reaction was that of "more sorrow than anger" in the hope that the Polish Communist Party would be able to reestablish its authority in the country. When that failed to materialize, criticism escalated, and predictably the main critics turned out to be the Soviet Union, Czechoslovakia, and East Germany. By early December there was growing evidence that the Kremlin might intervene militarily to stop the rot. Instead, at the last minute all the Warsaw Pact leaders, this time including President Nicolae Ceauşescu of Romania, assembled in Moscow in mid-December and gave the embattled Polish party a mildly worded vote of confidence, expressing the hope that the party would be able to put its own house in order.[21]

The next three months witnessed the continuation of the tug-of-war between the unions and the Polish regime, with the latter increasingly on the defensive. It soon became clear that the Solidarity movement was not a transitory phenomenon but a new and permanent actor on the Polish political scene with momentous implications for the future of the Communist system, not only in Poland but also in the rest of the Warsaw Pact, including the Soviet Union. The unions represented a frontal attack against a fundamental principle of Marxist-Leninist politics—the hegemony of the Communist Party. Although by spring 1981 there was still no evidence of any significant spillover from Poland into the other member countries, their leaders, especially those of Czechoslovakia and East Germany, maintained a steady stream of criticism directed at the Polish

---

[21]The *New York Times*, 6 December 1980.

party, making increasingly frequent allusions to the dormant Brezhnev Doctrine.

During that time the Kremlin remained conspicuously silent, apparently letting its Czechoslovak and East German proxies maintain the pressure on Poland. At the 26th Congress of the Soviet Communist Party in late February 1981, Brezhnev himself made an unmistakable reference to his own doctrine, but even then the tone of his criticism remained relatively restrained. However, immediately after the CPSU Congress at a surprise Soviet-Polish summit meeting, the Soviet leader lashed out against the Poles for allowing the situation to get out of control.

Soon thereafter Moscow announced that joint military exercises, involving contingents from the USSR, Czechoslovakia, East Germany, and Poland would take place in northwestern Poland in the second half of March. Once again, as in December, western intelligence sources warned that the Soviet army was ready for intervention and that it could take place on a few hours' notice. The war of nerves continued for several days as Pact troops engaged in prolonged maneuvers that were not officially ended until early April. Simultaneously, Brezhnev, addressing the Czechoslovak Communist Party Congress in Prague, once again signaled the postponement of the intervention, offering the Polish party an additional breathing spell. Although the maneuvers in Poland were officially ended, there was no evidence that the Pact troops had returned to barracks, which suggested that the treaty forces could be deployed at a moment's notice.

The next critical juncture on the Polish and Warsaw Pact horizons was the extraordinary 9th Congress of the Polish Communist Party, held in July 1981. The Congress ratified various liberal reforms introduced in the past year and elected a new Central Committee and Politburo to administer them.

There are many indications that Moscow and most of its junior allies in Eastern Europe were opposed to the Congress and did their utmost to postpone it, perhaps indefinitely. If the example of Czechoslovakia in 1968 has any lessons to offer, the possibility cannot be excluded that the Kremlin even may have considered the use of force to prevent the Congress from convening. What this would have done to the Warsaw Pact is anyone's guess.

The actual Soviet invasions of Hungary and Czechoslovakia and the threat of an intervention in Poland represent the three most flagrant cases of the Pact's failure to maintain the cohesion of the alliance. However, there were also less drastic examples of the treaty's inability to ensure stability in the region. There is considerable evidence of a nationalist revival in the region, which has threatened the fabric of the alliance. As long as the treaty was faced with an outside threat in the form of West Germany or the United States, the traditional national animosities tended to be suppressed. The gradual disappearance of the threat under the guise of East-West détente signaled the reemergence of historical antagonisms. It is necessary only to mention the perennial conflict between Hungary and Romania, which clearly has weakened the Pact's southern tier. More recently, Poland's economic collapse and the emergency aid granted Warsaw by Czechoslovakia, East Germany, and the Soviet Union also have contributed to the rekindling of dormant national antagonisms. Regardless of the final solution of the Polish problem, these conflicts are not likely to disappear overnight, and their presence will do little to strengthen the cohesion of the alliance.

Nonetheless, looking back at the performance of the Warsaw Treaty as a Soviet-controlled instrument of politico-military integration of Eastern Europe, the Pact has appeared quite useful to the Kremlin leaders. While the treaty has been unable to maintain absolute unity among its members in the course of the past twenty-five years, it has proved relatively successful in minimizing defection and open discontent. Albania's defection represented a loss of face but little else. Despite recurrent expressions of unhappiness with the treaty, Romania has refused so far to leave it. Reflecting on the lessons provided by the fate of Hungary in 1956, neither Czechoslovakia nor Poland, notwithstanding internal upheavals, has voiced its disapproval of the Pact.

This fact alone must give Moscow considerable satisfaction. The presence of the treaty, perceived since 1968 as a tool for the implementation of the Brezhnev Doctrine, has proved sufficient to maintain a rather remarkable degree of cohesion within the alliance, despite Romania's maverick stance. In this respect, the treaty has turned out to be a much more valuable instrument at the disposal of Moscow than in its role as a military alliance or a tool of Soviet global diplomacy.

CONCLUSION

The overall conclusion that emerges from the examination of the Warsaw Treaty after twenty-five years is that the Pact, which had been initially envisaged as a vehicle for external military and diplomatic crisis management, essentially has failed in that task, while generally succeeding in its role as an instrument of internal control maintained by the Soviet Union over its East European allies. In light of this, can the Warsaw Treaty today still be viewed as an "entangling alliance," or should it be more appropriately termed an "empty shell," a facade shielding a basic lack of accomplishment?

The answer lies somewhere between the two extremes. At the time of the signing of the treaty there appeared to be a high degree of consensus among the member states, especially with regard to the nature of the adversary, the threat of an East-West confrontation, and the need for a politico-military alliance. As time went by, however, each of the three major points of agreement became subject to change, which in turn created differences of opinion among the signatories; each proceeded to interpret that change in a different way. Consequently, by the end of the first decade of the Pact's existence, the initial consensus was substantially weakened. It has never fully recovered. Of the original seven East European members, only Bulgaria and East Germany could be counted among the staunch supporters of the treaty throughout the entire twenty-five year period. This alone has made it difficult to view the alliance as entangling.[22] On the other hand, the Pact has succeeded over the years in institutionalizing some of the linkages inherited from the Stalinist period and, as such, it has strengthened Soviet hegemony in the region. Hence, it has amounted to more than just an empty shell.

What about the Pact's future? It may be assumed that it will be conditioned by developments in the international system, the evolution of NATO, changes in the Kremlin and in the domestic-political systems of the smaller East European states, socioeconomic trends in the area, and a host of other variables. One of the key questions that will determine the future path taken by the Warsaw alliance is whether Eastern Europe as a whole will be perceived by Moscow as a Soviet asset or liability. In the final analysis, this judgment will lie in the eyes of the beholder—the Soviet leadership. It also will continue to be a function of Soviet national interest, as interpreted by the future occupants of the Kremlin. As some of these interests change, so will the perception of the treaty as serving or undermining Moscow's goals and objectives.

On another occasion this author hypothesized that over the past quarter-century the Soviet Union has learned several lessons from the events that took place in Eastern Europe during that period, and that at some point the Kremlin began to see itself more as a leader of a conventional politico-military-economic alliance than as a *vozhd* of an ideological camp engaged in a sharp struggle with the capitalist world.[23] Whether this interpretation is valid or not remains to be seen. It may be argued that Soviet reluctance to intervene militarily in Poland is at least partly due to Moscow's new self-image. If this is true, then some interesting changes in the nature of the Warsaw Pact in the foreseeable future may indeed be expected.

---

[22]In contrast, one authority on the subject views the Pact as a "vital institution for the management of Soviet-East European political affairs" that "has become so important that its sudden disappearance would, to paraphrase Voltaire, force Pact members to invent another structure to take its place." Herspring, "The Warsaw Pact at 25." Needless to say, these conclusions disagree with Herspring's thesis.

[23]Andrzej Korbonski, "Eastern Europe: Soviet Asset or Burden? The Political Dimension," in Ronald H. Linden, ed., *The Foreign Policies of East Europe* (New York: Praeger, 1980), pp. 306–7.

The Warsaw Pact and the
Northern Member States

JÖRG K. HOENSCH

Compared with the extensive publicity with which military-political developments of NATO are studied in Eastern Europe, western analyses of political and military relations within the Warsaw Pact are rather unassuming. Western lack of interest in military cooperation among the members of the Pact can be explained partly by the traditional assumption that the East European political and military system is a monolithic bloc, in which the Soviet leadership is fundamentally dominant. In this view there exists practically no actual military cooperation relevant to East-West relations; there is just a Soviet military policy, to which the other Pact members must submit.[1]

A number of real political and military factors seems to support such a conclusion: standardization of East European armies after the Soviet model, nomination of only Soviet officers to important military assignments within the alliance, a high portion of Soviet units under unified command. Yet, do these factors account for the full range of military-political realities or are they the principal relics of Cold War mentality, when both sides refused to register differences of individual interests or of social structures within the opposite system? Even though the obvious necessity for military détente in Europe should militate against superficial answers, the occupation of Czechoslovakia by Soviet troops and the Afghanistan invasion might have posed a temptation to return to the simple and therefore perhaps more comfortable friend-enemy conception of the Cold War. Faulty evaluation of military and security-political relations within the Pact, as they were apparent in western and especially in West German efforts to isolate the German Democratic Republic (GDR) within the socialist camp, can only endanger the military détente that Europe needs so badly. Just as in the mid-1960s when western interest in economic cooperation with Eastern Europe made necessary more realistic analyses of the national economies and the nature of international economic relations within COMECON, western interest in

---

[1]The absence of detailed research on the military policies of the smaller Pact member states, except for the GDR, demonstrates this lack of interest.

military détente in Europe today should generate objective research on military and political cooperation within the Warsaw Pact.

However, such an approach has to overcome the additional disadvantage of nonexistent or unreliable reference materials. East European bureaucracies do not discuss military-political controversies in public and provide little information about the modalities of their military cooperation, and only in exceptional cases do published sources hint at disagreement.[2] This restrictive information policy demands an historical analysis of military cooperation within the Pact in order to understand current developments within the East European alliance system. Publications in the people's democracies tend more to conceal than to expose military information; a detailed study of military cooperation in Eastern Europe by East European specialists and military historians is still missing.[3]

FIRST PHASE: POLITICAL EVENTS

Following West German admission to NATO on 6 May 1955, the Soviet government invited seven East European people's democracies to Warsaw on 11 May to prepare and sign a multilateral "Pact on Friendship, Cooperation, and Mutual Aid," knowing that it could count on the unconditional support of the Polish and Czechoslovak governments. The brutality of the Nazi war administration with its countless victims was not forgotten, and the fear of possible West German remilitarization and active revanchism under cover of John Foster Dulles's rollback strategy was still so real that Nikita Khrushchev had little difficulty in persuading Warsaw and Prague to cooperate.

At first the Kremlin seemed to value the political implications of the Warsaw Pact more highly than the purely military arrangements, the latter providing for the placement of troops under joint command for the purpose of mutual defense. For Moscow, the Pact represented an additional political means of curtailing sovereignty within the socialist camp and of intervening in their internal affairs.

---

[2]V. Prchlik, a Czechoslovak general, was taken to court in 1971 for having criticized the forms of military cooperation within the Pact in a July 1968 public press conference. See R. Crusius et al, eds., *CSSR. Fünf Jahre "Normalisierung" (Dokumentation)* (Hamburg: Association Verlag, 1973), p. 235.
[3]Only one study has attempted to deal systematically with developments in the East German Army. See G. Glaser et al., *Zur Geschichte der Nationalen Volksarmee der DDR– Thesen, Beilage zu: Militärgeschichte* 4 (East Berlin: Militärverlag der DDR, 1973).

In Boleslaw Bierut's Poland that was nothing new. Soviet Army Marshal K. K. Rokosovsky had been appointed minister of defense in November 1949 and had been promoted to vice-premier and full member of the Polish politburo in May 1950. Some seventeen thousand Soviet officers had been active in the political and tactical coordination of the Polish army, streamlining it after the Soviet model.[4] Although the aftermath of World War II and the forced adoption of a Soviet-style planned economy had brought a severe economic crisis and a prolonged low standard of living, large industrial capacities had to be furnished for arms production, which resulted in even more deprivation. Thus the traditional Polish aversion to things Russian, the product of centuries, was now married to a healthy antipathy toward the unpopular Polish Communist regime, and although the Polish nation seemed united in its willingness to defend its new western border along the Oder and Neisse rivers, the Kremlin must have doubted whether the Polish army would be capable of withstanding an imperialist surprise attack in the first phase.[5]

The Czechoslovak army was considered a more reliable ally. Alexej Čepička (Klement Gottwald's son-in-law), as minister of defense since 1950, had worked hard to reform the national forces on the Soviet pattern and to replace the old officers' corps; additionally, he had devoted great efforts to Marxist-Leninist indoctrination.[6] The experienced and productive armament industries in Plzeň and Brno helped in equipping the army with modern weapons. As Czechoslovakia was initially the only Pact country to share a border with a NATO member, Soviet military hardware was supplied in abundance. It was only the suppressed yet still smoldering Slovak demand for full autonomy and the consequent national tension that raised certain doubts as to the unconditional reliability of Czechoslovak troops.[7]

However, close military cooperation between Prague and Warsaw was hampered by the border dispute in the Teschen-Klodzko region,

---

[4]*East Europe and Soviet Russia*, 13 March 1952, p. 5; R. F. Starr, *The Communist Regimes in Eastern Europe* (Stanford: Stanford University Press, 1967), p. 285.

[5]Polish defense forces number about 317,500 men: 210,000 serve in the army, 22,500 in the navy, and 85,000 in the air force. The paramilitary border guards have 18,000 men, and the security forces contain about 77,000 heavily armed specialists. The people's militia *ORMO* includes about 350,000 men. *The Military Balance 1980–1981* (London: IISS, 1980), p. 16.

[6]*Die Geschichte der kommunistischen tschechoslowakischen Volksarmee und ihr Verhältnis zu den anderen Ostblock-Armeen–Wehrpolitische Schriftenreihe*, no. 1 (Bonn: Studiengesellschaft für Zeitprobleme e.V.27, 1956).

[7]In Czechoslovakia some 195,000 soldiers serve in the armed forces: 140,000 in the army and 55,000 men in the air force. In addition, around 11,000 border guards and 60,000 security troops are available. The people's militia counts some 120,000 men. *The Military Balance 1980–1981*, p. 15.

which, although formally settled, was still an emotional issue. Domestically, traditional Pan-Slavic entente, cleverly manipulated propaganda presenting the Red Army as the sole liberator from the yoke of Nazi occupation, and the portrayal of the USSR as the only guarantor against a new Munich agreement permitted the Soviets to count on broad sympathy and support for their military orders in Czechoslovakia. Even reservations about the new socialist neighbor, Moscow's foster child, the GDR, were not as pronounced as in the Polish People's Republic.

The confused constitutional position of the GDR had caused Khrushchev to do without its participation at the initial meeting of the Warsaw Pact.[8] On 18 January 1956 it was announced that the 60,000 militarily trained and equipped troops of the People's Militia paramilitary police troops were to be transferred on 1 April to the National People's Army; the GDR was to be accorded full membership in the Warsaw Pact. The rapid expansion of the rigidly disciplined East German units emphasized the Kremlin's efforts to assign a new and higher priority to the GDR within the socialist camp and to make the fullest possible use of her personnel and material resources.[9]

Nevertheless, there were second thoughts about the reliability and the military value of East German troops not only in the USSR but also in Poland and Czechoslovakia. That might have been one of the reasons why until the mid-1960s the GDR National People's Army received newly developed military equipment only with due delay and why it was subjected to close supervision by the twenty Soviet divisions stationed in the GDR. Besides, there were psychological barriers to overcome: the East European Communist regimes after 1945 had officially preached hatred of all Germans to explain the expulsion of German minorities and in the hope of uniting and consolidating their own peoples. Although after the

---

[8]T. M. Forster, *NVA–Die Armee der Sowjetzone* (Köln: Verlag Wissenschaft und Politik, 1965); G. W. Strobel, *Der Warschauer Vertrag und die Nationale Volksarmee–Wehrpolitische Schriftenreihe*, no. 18 (Bonn: Studiengesellschaft für Zeitprobleme e.V., 1965).

[9]The GDR has forces totaling 162,000 men, among them 108,000 serving in the army, 38,000 air force personnel, and 16,000 men in the navy, in addition to 46,500 border guards, 25,000 security police, and the militarily trained People's Militia. *The Military Balance 1980–1981*, p. 16.

Also, some 500,000 men are organized and trained in the "fighting cadres of the workers class" (*Kampfgruppen der Arbeiterklasse*) within factories, farm cooperatives, and the administration; it is their task to guarantee domestic peace, the logistic support of the armed forces, and the protection of strategic positions. See H. J. Sachau, "Stellenwert und politische Einbindung der 'Kampfgruppen der Arbeiterklasse' in der DDR," *Wehrwissenschaftliche Rundschau* 26 (Herford/Bonn: Verlag E. S. Mittler & Sohn, 1977): 118–23.

Within the Gesellschaft für Sport und Technik [Society for Sport and Technique], some 1.5 million members have undergone paramilitary training. In 1978, against the protests of the churches, "Wehrkunde" [defense science] was introduced as a subject of instruction in all schools.

foundation of the GDR in October 1949, anti-German propaganda had been directed solely against West Germany, widespread aversion to, and fear of, all Germans remained. Walter Ulbricht's formal recognition of the Oder-Neisse border in the treaty at Goerlitz (6 July 1950), the normalization of diplomatic contacts between Prague and East Berlin on 23 June 1950, and the declaration of the Polish and Czechoslovak governments in February 1955, ending the state of war with that part of the former German Reich represented by the GDR, had not been able effectively to eliminate the misgivings of the Poles and Czechoslovaks.

The growing tendency, especially apparent in recent years, to cultivate the Prussian military tradition in the GDR has not furthered the popularity of the East German army.[10] The participation of East German units in the invasion of Czechoslovakia in August 1968 and the sabre rattling of the GDR against current developments in Poland have raised anew the fear and resentment of its neighbors in the east and the south. On the other hand, the East German military leadership has taken great care to reduce doubts about the operational preparedness of its army and ideological orthodoxy through the demonstration of special subservience toward, and uncomplaining acceptance of, Moscow's orders.

DeStalinization, actively pursued after the invitation for Yugoslavia to rejoin the socialist camp in June 1955 and especially after the CPSU's 20th Party Congress in 1956, in the long run had a destabilizing effect on the three Warsaw Pact members of the Northern Tier, although popular uprisings such as those in Berlin (1953) or in Hungary (1956) were avoided in Poland and Czechoslovakia. Yet, the internal developments of 1956 in Poland were serious enough, all the more so as it was only through the efforts of regular army units that the initially economically motivated strike by Poznan workers was crushed; the demonstrations had in fact gained momentum as a political conflict with strong anti-Soviet overtones.[11] The subsequent "Polish spring in October" made it clear to the Kremlin leadership that the ferment, previously limited to the intelligentsia, had now taken hold of the Polish workers as well, and only a willingness to meet the demands for changes in the national party leadership and to permit different paths to socialism could guarantee a return to long-term peace.

---

[10]In October and November 1980, when an invasion by Pact troops seemed imminent, it is reported that Polish officers threatened to renounce their oath of loyalty and to fight if East German units participated in an armed attempt to "consolidate" the situation in Poland.

[11]P. E. Zinner, ed., *National Communism and Popular Revolt in Eastern Europe: A Selection of Documents on Events in Poland and Hungary, February–November 1956* (New York: Columbia University Press, 1956), pp. 126–42; "Polen in Summer 1956," *Osteuropa* 6, 4 (August 1956): 292–302.

Although the threat to restore dependence through direct Soviet military intervention had no significant effect, the subsequent bloody suppression of the Budapest uprising, which had been followed with great sympathy by the Poles, initiated a process of accommodation in Poland that demanded great patience and tactical flexibility.[12] Wladislaw Gomulka, a "national" Communist, was installed as party chief. As long as Poland needed the fullest support of the USSR to defend its western border, Moscow could even agree on 17 December 1956 to sign a formal agreement on the further stationing of Soviet troops in Poland that conceded the right of control over movement and deployment of Soviet troops to the Polish government. However, the hard-won policy of relative internal autonomy covering the renunciation of forced collectivization, toleration of broad cultural liberties, and a *modus vivendi* with the Catholic church, was slowly reversed by Gomulka himself; thus, the situation in Poland after 1960 was no longer a substantial source of worry for the Kremlin.[13]

In Czechoslovakia a timely propaganda campaign with the cringing slogan "all the way with the Soviet Union" helped the leadership of Antonin Novotny to overcome all danger of a thaw. In the person of Minister of Defense Čepička the right man was soon found to take sole blame for the "violation of socialist legality" in the past. Brutal enforcement of repressive measures stifled students and writers. As social and economic conditions in Czechoslovakia were somewhat more favorable than in the other people's democracies, a superficial modification of the Stalinist system and a moderate improvement in the living conditions of the working class were sufficient to isolate critical intellectuals and to prevent revolutionary sparks from Poland or Hungary igniting Czechoslovakia.[14]

As long as that portion of the East German population discontented with the political or economic realities still had the opportunity to escape to the West, the GDR leadership easily could check the outbreak of new disturbances. While a small yet slowly growing number of people could identify with the Communist state, mainly for opportunistic rather than ideological reasons, the East Berlin leadership knew full well that its political future depended solely on the goodwill and active support of the Soviets.

---

[12]K. Syrop, *Spring in October: The Polish Revolution of 1956* (London: Weidenfeld and Nicholson, 1957); *Survey of International Affairs 1956–1958* (London: Royal Institute for International Affairs, 1962), p. 80.

[13]Z. K. Brzezinski, *The Soviet Bloc: Unity and Conflict* (Cambridge, MA: Harvard University Press, 1967), pp. 338–66.

[14]*Literarni Noviny*, 28, 29 April 1956; T. Szulc, *Czechoslovakia Since World War II* (New York: Viking Press, 1971), pp. 127–29.

FIRST PHASE: THE MILITARY FACTORS

Most western military experts assigned little or no military importance to the Warsaw Pact in the first phase of its existence, which seems to be confirmed by the assertion that the Pact did not play a major military role during these years. This somewhat faulty evaluation of the alliance's early history appears to have influenced western attitudes toward the importance of East European military cooperation until the present. The theses that the USSR founded the Pact solely to gain political barter leverage vis-à-vis NATO, or simply to discipline and control its allies, or to use the Pact as a transmission belt for Soviet foreign policy, neglect the critical East-West military confrontation at the time of the foundation of the Warsaw Pact. NATO's decision to build up military forces in West Germany and to integrate them into NATO really was of substantial importance in the establishment of the eastern Pact as well as for the subsequent formal enlargement and upgrading of the National People's Army in the GDR in 1956.[15]

The negligible military importance usually attributed to the early Warsaw Pact was, and still is, explained by western analysts and foreign policy spokesmen by the argument that the Soviet Union easily could have forgone a multilateral military organization, as it was secured militarily in the East European states by a system of equally effective bilateral treaties on friendship, cooperation, and mutual aid. However, at the time of the foundation of the Pact the bilateral Pact system was not complete; until 1964 the GDR took no part in it. The possible abolition of the Pact without simultaneous introduction of the GDR into this bilateral system would have been considered by the East German leadership as a serious diminution of its security status. Given its military-geographic and special political situation, it seems likely that its unique status was of some influence in the decision to establish a multilateral military organization.

If the East European governments had indeed followed a policy of alliance that would have kept open the exchange of the Warsaw Pact for a bilateral treaty system, then it might be expected that the new agreements signed after 1964 would have taken this possibility strongly into account. But this was not the case. The cessation of the regional restrictions—the old treaties were valid, like the Warsaw Treaty, in the event of conflict in Europe only—argues strongly that the bilateral treaties were meant to supplement but not replace it.[16] The degree of military integration reached

---

[15]For more detailed information about discussion in the West of the negligible role of the Pact, see St. Tiedtke, *Die Warschauer Vertragsorganisation zum Verhältnis von Militär—und Entspannungspolitik in Osteuropa* (München, Wien: Oldenbourg, 1978), pp. 15–19.

[16]P. H. Lange, *Der Warschauer Pakt im Prozess der Europäischen Entspannungspolitik* (Ebenhausen: Stiftung Wissenschaft und Politik, 1974), p. 70.

in the 1960s hardly could have been maintained on the basis of bilateral agreements; at the very least it would have caused serious organizational problems.

What are the reasons why the Warsaw Pact seems to have been so ineffective militarily during the first years? It was not due to a lack of interest by the supreme power. Rather, military and military-political factors retarded the building of a more efficient alliance. First of all, the policy governing the modernization of land forces was a result of Khrushchev's reevaluation of the strategic situation under nuclear war conditions. The new Soviet estimation of the initial phase of a world war— that it would be fought by ICBMs—led to a far-reaching reorganization of Soviet land forces and to a dramatic reduction in manpower and wide-ranging reorganization from 1955 to 1959.[17] In East Europe the failure of the Hungarian army during the national uprising confronted all of the governing bureaucracies with the task of intensive ideological education of their troops, and thus they could give less priority to technological training and to closer military cooperation.[18] The plan to build up a multilateral force was pigeonholed indefinitely.[19]

The rapid rearmament of the GDR supports the thesis that the foundation of the Warsaw Treaty initiated a new phase in East European military policy. During the years from 1956 to 1958, increased arms and technical equipment, as well as an expansion of military personnel, signaled that important changes within the East German military apparatus were taking place. Yet, the necessity to fill the rank and file with trustworthy personnel, combined with the relatively modest standard of instruction, had reduced the military efficiency of the East German army before 1960 and had prevented cooperation on a wider basis within the Northern Tier. This situation demanded a remedy; while the Soviet Union reduced its military spending by 0.7% in 1960 and announced it would save another 17.6% in 1961, the three members of the Northern Tier at the same time had to increase military expenses between 5.7% (Poland) and 11% (GDR).

To enable East Germany to contribute a relevant and continuous military share, the country had to be consolidated socially and politically.

---

[17]K. Greese and G. Glaser, "Über die Politik der SED zum Aufbau des militärischen Schutzes innerhalb der Verteidigungsgemeinschaft sozialistischer Staaten Europas (1955/56–1961)," *Beiträge zur Geschichte der Arbeiterbewegung—Sonderheft zum 25. Jahrestag der SED* (East Berlin: Institut für Marximus-Leninismus bein Zentralkomitee der SED, 1971), p. 128.

[18]This was demonstrated using the East German example by D. R. Herspring, *East German Civil-Military Relations: The Impact of Technology 1949–1972* (New York: Praeger, 1973).

[19]J. Halmai, "Die ungarische Volksarmee seit 1956," *Wehrwissenschaftliche Rundschau* 10 (1958): 584.

The building of the Berlin Wall in August 1961 was the means to that consolidation; after that the East Berlin leadership could create military-social conditions similar to those of its alliance partners without being hampered any longer by a severe loss of population through escape. A visible expression of this was the introduction of general conscription, a necessity in the management of socialist defense policy.

There is some evidence that before 1955 a more limited regional defense alliance between the GDR, Poland, Czechoslovakia, and the Soviet Union had been planned.[20] This hints at a somewhat larger task for the GDR than is usually portrayed in western analysis. The GDR played a politically vital role among the smaller member states not only at the foundation of the Pact but also during the transition to intensified military cooperation. The East German leadership supported military integration to achieve full political acceptance within the socialist camp and to reach full equality with the other Warsaw Pact member states. In this sense there are certain similarities between the courses pursued by the GDR and the German Federal Republic: in Konrad Adenauer's foreign policy West German rearmament was not mainly directed against an East European military threat, although this argument played a vital part, but rather it was to serve the recovery of full sovereignty, equality of international rights, and the integration of the Federal Republic into the western political system. The strict subordination of East Germany's military contribution to Pact interests and efforts to build up an efficient army in the shortest possible time certainly were enforced by the USSR, yet they suited the foreign political aims of the East German leadership as well. They were objectives that could not be pursued solely by economic cooperation. Western interpretation of East Germany's military development, which looked like nothing but Soviet aggressive manipulation of East Germany, tends to overlook this intra-Pact aspect.

GROWTH OF MILITARY INTEGRATION IN THE 1960s

The realization that an unchecked arms race would prevent pressing economic reforms and could create new disruptive potential, combined with the necessity to bolster cohesion within the European socialist camp against Chinese challenges, probably motivated Khrushchev on 14 January 1960 to order a continued reduction of Soviet forces and to intensify

---

[20]See O. Grotewohl's speech at the Conference of European Countries for the Maintenance of Peace and Security in Europe in December 1954, in *Dokumente zum Warschauer Vertrag (1954–1961)* (East Berlin: Deutscher Militärverlag, 1962), p. 14.

military and political cooperation within the Warsaw Pact framework.[21] A Polish refusal to participate may have been a reason why the Prague decision of January 1956 to meet twice annually for consultations had not been observed regularly before 1960. A real integration of forces, the holding of large-scale joint military exercises, or coordination of general staff duties had not taken place. Only the standardization of military hardware, the improvement of national arms production with some division of labor (whereby the USSR claimed the sole right to develop and produce major weapons), and a more precise definition of the tasks of the various national armed forces had been accomplished. Polish Minister of Foreign Affairs Adam Rapacki had given this relative freedom of action a test with his proposal for partial European disarmament and a prohibition of the production of stockpiling of nuclear warheads in Central Europe. His attempt to shift the rigid Cold War fronts was little appreciated in the West.[22]

Subsequently, as a result of the two Berlin crises of 1958–59 and 1961 and the escalating tension with Peking, Soviet military thinking was directed toward closer military cooperation in the interest of increased collective efficiency of Pact armed forces.[23] Possibly starting from a local conflict the armies of the Northern Tier were expected, in close partnership with the Soviet army, to destroy the enemy, occupy northwestern Europe, and cut off American reinforcements.[24]

The first large-scale Warsaw Pact joint maneuvers occurred at the beginning of October 1961 when Polish, East German, and Czechoslovak units cooperated with Soviet troops. It soon became clear that the Kremlin was prepared to grant the Warsaw Pact members an increasingly important role under the command of the dynamic Marshal A. A. Grechko.

---

[21]The lack of qualified workers had caused a demobilization after May 1955, when in the USSR alone 1.84 million men in sixty-three divisions were sent home. The return of the Soviet units from Romania and the regrouping of Soviet troops led to another reduction of 300,000 men to a total of 3.6 million. Against the opposition of the Soviet High Command, Nikita Khrushchev announced a further reduction by one-third to a total of 2.4 million. This demobilization was stopped after the Vienna meeting between Khrushchev and President John Kennedy in June 1961. It was followed by an increase in defense spending of 3.1 billion rubles on 8 July 1961.

[22]Z. Artymowska, *Plan Rapackiego–za i przeciw* (Warsaw: Interpress, 1958); A. Albrecht, *Der Rapacki Plan–neue Aspekte* (Poznan: Institut Zadochni, 1964).

[23]J. Tiedtke and St. Tiedtke, "Auswirkungen innerpolitischer Probleme der Sowjetunion auf die Entwicklung der Warschauer Vertragsorganisation," E. Jahn, ed., *Sozioökonomische Bedingungen der sowjetischen Aussenpolitik* (Frankfurt: Campus Verlag, 1975), p. 166.

[24]H. S. Dinerstein, *War and the Soviet Union: Nuclear Weapons and the Revolution in Soviet Military and Political Thinking* (New York: Praeger, 1959); Thomas W. Wolfe, *Soviet Strategy at the Crossroads* (Cambridge, MA: Harvard University Press, 1964); R. A. Remington, *The Warsaw Pact. Case Studies in Communist Conflict Resolution* (Cambridge, MA: Harvard University Press, 1971).

Almost simultaneously with that of the USSR the conventional artillery of the countries of the Northern Tier was augmented by tactical missiles, considerably increasing mobility and fire power. At the same time the deployment of T-54 and T-55 tanks, the introduction of antitank rockets and self-propelled projectiles, and the delivery of the first MiG-21 *Fishbed* and Su-7 *Fitter* aircraft, provided East European ground forces and tactical air support units with substantial additional striking power. In 1964 the USSR handed over nuclear-capable tactical missiles with a range of some one hundred fifty miles to the national people's armies; however, the Soviets did not allow them access to nuclear warheads. The increased military cooperation and the higher state of preparedness were justified as a means of raising fighting strength and readiness for action, improving the coordination of contacts between troops and staffs, developing common policy on the application of conventional and nuclear weapons, and becoming better acquainted with each other's territory and the training methods in Pact armies.[25]

The homogeneity of the military apparatus and military-political assumptions, visible already in the mid-1960s, is understood in the West as mainly a result of Soviet domination within the Pact. Certainly, Soviet pressure can explain in many ways the high conformity within the alliance, but it is also the consequence of a strategic cohesion of interests that is structurally different from NATO's.[26]

Relations within NATO are irritated by a persistent doubt that the United States would actually endanger its own territory over a military conflict in Europe. When NATO changed its strategy from "massive retaliation" to "flexible response," West Europeans were even more apprehensive about the reliability of the American guarantee of protection. In contrast to NATO, the Soviet Union and its allies still to this day adhere to a strategy of massive retaliation. Historical, military-geographical, and political evidence seems to defend this strategy, which grants the smaller Pact members a high measure of Soviet nuclear protection. Soviet military planning for possible war in Europe calculates no precisely limited nuclear response and does not expect that Soviet territory will be spared. As this strategy does not allow the Soviet Union any room to separate itself from a possible Central European war, the three members of the Northern Tier seem to be especially supportive of this apparent Soviet merger of its security with that of its allies.[27]

Soviet strategic thinking is strongly influenced by socioeconomic

---

[25]See Marshal Grechko's proclamation, *Novosti, Press Release,* 26 February 1964; or *Voenno-istoricheskii zhurnal,* no. 5 (May 1965): 24.

[26]See also St. Tiedtke, *Rüstungskontrolle aus sowjetischer Sicht. Die Rahmenbedingungen der sowjetischen MBFR-Politik* (Frankfurt: Hessische Stiftung für Friedens-und Konflikt forschung, 1980), pp. 20–26.

[27]St. Tiedtke, *Die Warschauer Vertragsorganisation*, pp. 15–19.

developments within the socialist camp; "worst case" analyses have to take into consideration western threats to exploit social, national, and ethnic conflicts within the bloc. The precarious balance between the governed and the governing bureaucracies in Eastern Europe has confronted the USSR with the domestic instabilities of its allies, especially of those in the Northern Tier who are of utmost importance for conventional defense. A short war fought on enemy territory could minimize these potential dangers.

However, even though such considerations would have to play a role in the "worst case" analyses of Soviet and Pact military planners, they hardly influence direct military cooperation in practice. On the governmental level of interaction a high measure of uniformity exists. The homogenous social-political organization of the various party and state apparatuses and the similar social-economic bases, unaffected by a capitalistic principle of competition, allow an extensive harmony of interests among the dominant bureaucracies, built on the Soviet model. But this harmony is disrupted frequently by the means that the national bureaucracies must adopt in formulating their alliance policies, which must take into consideration the contradictions between their ideological fraternity and their national interests. Besides, they also have to take into account the interests of each other's bureaucracies. The boundaries for the regulation of social conflicts within the alliance are reached when social and political changes in the national realm of one member seem to endanger the rule of the other bureaucracies as for example in Hungary 1956, or Czechoslovakia 1968.

DÉTENTE AND THE PRAGUE SPRING 1968

By the mid-1960s the entire political situation in Central Europe had undergone alteration. The announcement by General de Gaulle on 19 January 1966 that he was withdrawing French troops from NATO and the ever increasing military engagement of the United States in Southeast Asia had biased the prevailing distribution of forces in favor of the Warsaw Pact, although Romanian particularism, as well as a general economic stagnation accompanying domestic demands for a fundamental reform of the national economies, all had caused substantial unrest within the Pact membership.

The slow movement in the Federal Republic of Germany toward recognition of the status quo in East Central Europe and its progress toward making its contribution to a reduction in tension were generally welcomed in the socialist countries. At the same time the new West

German foreign policy disquieted the regimes in Warsaw, Prague, and East Berlin, which were uneasy about the possible loss of the propaganda enemy. Too many questions, including the full recognition of the GDR, the acceptance of all borders, and indemnities for the victims of Nazi terror, were still unsettled when Romania, eager to demonstrate its independence, opened full diplomatic relations with Bonn in January 1967. This forced the three Warsaw Pact members of the Northern Tier to draw closer together in defense of what they saw as their vital interests. Nevertheless, it was apparent that everywhere in the socialist camp groups infected by the Romanian virus were beginning to rise. The new Brezhnev-Kosygin leadership, in spite of lip service from subservient East European leaderships, had problems in enforcing the supremacy of the USSR as well as absolute solidarity within the socialist bloc.[28]

The national reform movement gained momentum especially in Czechoslovakia, where in spite of several partial purges a real deStalinization had not taken place. The run-down Novotny regime had proved incapable of diverting the pressing Slovak demand for real federalization of the republic, reversing the growing economic stagnation, or of accepting the challenge of a thorough reform of the socialist system along more democratic lines. In Poland the demands of important intellectuals and nationalistic economists for overdue reforms also were more and more frequently articulated. The nationalist "partisans," under the leadership of internal security chief General Mieczyslaw Moczar, put pressure on the Gomulka establishment with anti-Semitic slogans. And in Prague a rather fragile coalition of intellectuals, economists, students, and Slovak federalists campaigned for democratic reforms to achieve a "socialism with a human face" and to replace the existing corrupt and incapable party leadership. When Novotny failed to silence his critics with Soviet support or to rid himself of them with an armed putsch in December 1967 he was bitterly disappointed; not only Brezhnev but also his own military commanders refused him assistance.[29] Thus, he had to submit to his replacement by Alexander Dubček in January 1968.

Surprised by the rapid pace of the reform movement, the Kremlin attained at least three goals with the military occupation of 21 August 1968: the movement was cut off once and for all, the subsequent treaty of 16 October 1968 granted the right to maintain an arbitrary number of Soviet troops for an indefinite period of time on Czech soil, and finally, the socialist confederation was taught the lesson that in the future any real erosion of Soviet authority and leadership would not be passively

---

[28]J. K. Hoensch, *Sowjetische Osteuropapolitik 1945–1975* (Königstein: Droste/Athenäum, 1977), pp. 260–98.

[29]*Obrana lidu*, 24 February 1968, interview with Major General E. Pepich; Szulc, *Czechoslovakia*, pp. 253–55.

accepted.[30] The Pact command also could pride itself on the mainly satisfactory coordination of the five participant forces during the completion of the military intervention against a deviant Pact member.

On 6 May 1970, the twenty-fifth anniversary of Czechoslovakia's liberation by the Red Army, the new Husak-Strougal leadership had to sign a treaty of friendship and mutual aid into which was inserted not only the Soviet thesis of the special socialist and internationalist character of relations but also the principle of the Brezhnev Doctrine, according to which "assistance, consolidation and the defense of socialist achievements . . . " was declared to be "the common internationalist duty of Socialist countries."[31] In addition, Articles 9 and 10 settled the geographically infinite range over which the commitments of mutual aid were valid; thus, in the case of an unprovoked attack on the USSR, Czechoslovakia was obliged to assist both in the European as well as in the Asian theater. The GDR had to accept similarly extensive concessions when its bilateral friendship treaty was renewed on 7 October 1975 until the year 2000. The pressure of some seventy-five thousand Soviet troops stationed in Czechoslovakia, the growing influence of Soviet advisers controlling that country's key political positions, the consequent persecution of politicians and intellectuals suspected of reformist sympathies, and a growing disillusionment with socialist reality meant in the end that the "course of normalization" prescribed by the Soviets resulted in the calm of a churchyard spread over Czechoslovakia, to be broken only modestly a decade later by Charter 77.

In the course of the Prague Spring, military-political controversies between the Pact members received little attention in the West. Yet there is good reason to suspect that they too influenced the decision to intervene. Voices critical of military-political conditions within the Pact could have been heard in Czechoslovakia as early as 1966.[32] During the Prague Spring this criticism was intensified and included demands for wider participation of the smaller member states in military and strategic planning, equal influence in the decision-making process within the alliance command system, and intensified activity of the Warsaw Pact's Political Consultative Committee. This criticism was further intensified through

[30]Text in *Pravda* and *Rude Pravo*, 19 October 1968; T. Schweissfurth, "Der sowjetisch-tschechoslowakische Truppenstationierungsvertrag vom 16. Oktober 1968," *Berichte des Bundesinstituts für ostwissenschaftliche und internationale Studien, Köln*, no. 13 (1968).
[31]Text in *Pravda* and *Izvestia*, 7 May 1970; K. Schmid, "Das Prinzip des proletarisch-sozialistischen Internationalismus Dargestellt am sowjetisch-tschechoslowakischen Bündnisvertrag vom 6 Mai 1970, Und anderen früheren bilateralen Bündnisverträgen der Sowjetunion und der Tschechoslowakischen Republik in Osteuropa," *Berichte des Bundesinstituts für ostwissenschaftliche und internationale Studien, Köln*, no. 7 (1971).
[32]St. Tiedtke, *Die Warschauer Vertragsorganisation*, p. 83.

changes in Czechoslovak army personnel that closed many of the informal channels maintained by the Soviet security services with the Czech military command. These demands and actions nourished doubts among the other Pact members about Czechoslovakia's readiness to support unconditionally the alliance's policy. They interpreted the Czechoslovak demands as endangering military cooperation and integration as put down in principle at a Political Consultative Committee meeting in March 1968.

Further doubts arose when the new Dubček leadership refused to allow the permanent stationing of even one Soviet division on Czechoslovak territory. This Soviet demand, made before 1968, apparently was aimed at closing the tactical nuclear gap in the Pact defense system, since due to the absence of Soviet forces, there were no tactical nuclear warheads on Czechoslovak soil.[33] The Prague leadership saw in this demand a Soviet attempt to exercise military pressure on the reform movement. In response, the Czechs insisted on the retention of the strategy of massive retaliation, as if to emphasize the lack of any need for a token Soviet tactical contingent. Thus, even though the invasion of Pact troops mainly served to stamp out the social and political reform movement, the military-political background of the intervention should not be ignored.

It is widely assumed that the occupation of Czechoslovakia did not significantly retard the process of easing tensions in Europe. This generally accepted viewpoint requires careful review. The Prague Spring could have been a prelude to the disintegration of the Warsaw bloc. Since integration is a vital part of Warsaw Pact détente policy, no easing of tension between the two blocs was possible until the stability of the East European bureaucracies was assured. Military intervention was necessary to restore that condition of stability.[34] During the struggle over future development in Czechoslovakia the demand for further integration, as put forward mainly by the GDR, was generally accepted. The GDR, having reached political equality with the other members of the alliance by 1964, then began to pursue a goal of international recognition. For that it needed the support of its allies well established in the world of international political relations. This assistance in the initial process of détente apparently was no longer easily forthcoming; the GDR concentrated its efforts on preventing unilateral actions of its allies at the expense of its international reputation and security. An important means was the enforcement of closer political and military integration of the other nations of the Pact.

---

[33]This aspect is covered by L. L. Whetten, "Military Aspects of the Soviet Occupation of Czechoslovakia," *The World Today* 25, no. 2 (February 1969): 60–68.

[34]E. Jahn, "Zur Ambivalenz von Entspannungspolitik nach der KSZE," J. Delbrück et al., eds., *Grünbuch zu den Folgewirkungen der KSZE* (Köln: Verlag Wissenschaft und Politik, 1977), p. 57.

An agreement on a new set of military-political relations within the eastern defense alliance was reached with the reform of the Pact organization enacted at the Political Consultative Committee meeting in Budapest in March 1969. The results show the compromise character of the decisions taken. The USSR could not press through all of its demands, while at the same time the decision to install three new institutions, a committee for the coordination of military technology, the Military Council of the Unified Command, and the Committee of Defense Ministers, raised the possibility of the smaller Pact members gaining wider participation in military planning. However, the reform also intensifed military integration. This became clear in the effort to reform the Czechoslovak army.

In Poland the struggle for control between the centrists of Gomulka, supported by the Soviet leadership and the radical nationalists around Moczar, gained momentum in March 1969. The Kremlin took care that no second national communist experiment gained ground. Gomulka was even permitted to sound out West German willingness to reach an understanding and to test the depth of the *Ostpolitik* of the new social-liberal coalition that had taken office in October 1969.

The signing of the treaties at Moscow on 12 August 1970 and at Warsaw on 7 December 1970 was in line with the Kremlin's policy to reduce tension in East Central Europe in the face of growing Soviet-Chinese antagonism and the possibility of a military confrontation. In this connection pressure for an all-European conference on security and cooperation was intensified. Given their economic problems, the three Northern Tier members supported every Russian initiative that promised to free additional funds for technological innovation and augmentation of the standard of living.[35]

The upheaval among workers along the Polish Baltic coast in December 1970, suppressed by police and regular army units, illustrated the necessity of fundamental economic reforms once again. In subsequent purges nearly all the members of the old Polish leadership were removed. The technocrats rallied around the new first secretary Edward Gierek, who granted priority to rapid economic expansion with the help of western loans and technology.

At the same time resentment also grew among the hard-pressed populations of Poland and Czechoslovakia against the GDR, because the latter enjoyed extraordinary advantages through preferential treatment by West Germany and the European Economic Community. The GDR also claimed further favorable conditions within the COMECON due to its exposed strategic and political position. The easing of travel and buying

---

[35] Hoensch, *Sowjetische Osteuropapolitik,* pp. 373–84, 403–48.

restrictions among the peoples of the Northern Tier, cautiously implemented in 1972 and steadily reduced since, did not really stop friction and
envy.

The sudden economic boom in Poland up to 1974, to which western
loans contributed to a substantial increase in productivity and in the
standard of living as well as the relative political and ideological freedom
that prevailed in contrast to the GDR and Czechoslovakia, irritated the
more rigid and restrictive party leaderships in East Berlin and Prague.
When after the Yom Kippur War of October 1973 a substantial rise in
prices for raw materials and for energy was imposed, the Polish economic
miracle proved to be a *fata morgana*: labor unrest in Radom and Ursus in
June 1976 proved that social peace could be kept only through the
maintenance of a system of high subsidies for basic food supplies. The
rapidly growing foreign indebtedness was used mainly to plug holes
without eliminating the real problems in the system. The discrepancy
between the demands of the population for better housing and a higher
standard of living, along with less work, and the limited capacity of the
planned agrarian-industrialized national economy grew irresistably.
These problems found their expression in the labor unrest that has
dominated Polish domestic affairs since June 1980. This continuing
upheaval on the USSR's sensitive western border has been a growing
source of Kremlin discomfort.

The Soviets have had no such disagreeable development to face in
the GDR. The transfer of power from Ulbricht to Honecker took place
without any apparent problem. Every GDR leadership has been well
aware that it can survive only by absolute loyal adherence to Soviet
orders. The Berlin Treaty of 4 September 1971 and the Treaty on the
Basis of Relations between the Federal Republic of Germany (FRG) and
the GDR have strongly upgraded East Berlin's international reputation
and finally have accorded it the *de facto* status of a fully sovereign
country. Although time and again the ambitious targets of its economic
plans could not be realized and economic setbacks had to be overcome, a
slow but steady economic momentum has been achieved, bringing about
inner consolidation. Efforts to reach complete ideological and political
separation from the FRG have proved unsuccessful, as close personal
contacts and West German television and radio broadcasts have prevented the growth of a separate East German national mentality. Yet in
the Socialist Unity Party and in the National People's Army there exists a
growing cadre of orthodox Communists who are gaining control of all key
positions. The efforts of the East Berlin leadership to develop this individual state personality, harnessing the Hohenzollerns to the task and
accentuating the democratic and progressive elements and virtues within
the old Prussian army after the reforms of Scharnhorst and Gneisenau,

certainly have been guided by aspirations to raise the fighting spirit of the East German army and to eliminate any last doubts about its loyalty to the Pact and its operational preparedness. By their presence alone, the approximately twenty Soviet divisions still stationed in the GDR exercise an important function of control and intimidation and are strong enough to nip in the bud any attempt at revolt against the Communist leadership.

MILITARY DEVELOPMENTS IN THE 1970s

The military importance of the East German army can be demonstrated by the standard of its armaments and its participation in Warsaw Pact maneuvers. By the mid-1960s the East German army was being equipped with modern Soviet weapon systems as fast as were the Czechoslovak and Polish armies.[36] The GDR has a most impressive record: between 1956 and 1970 twenty-one multilateral maneuvers were conducted in the Northern Tier; the East German army participated in twenty of them and was host fourteen times. In addition, frequent mixed field training sessions have been conducted between East German and Soviet elite divisions. During these exercises East German troops gave evidence of their high standard of battle preparedness. The expanding military potential of the three northern Warsaw Pact partners in the early 1970s induced the American analyst Thomas W. Wolfe to speak of a growing military dependence by the USSR on its allies due to the rapid military integration and modernization within the eastern alliance.[37]

Although the number of troops in the Northern Tier remained about constant during the 1970s, the military effectiveness of the armed forces was considerably increased through further upgrading and standardization of armaments and equipment, the improvement of military training and instruction, the creation of more qualified and devoted cadres for military leadership, the strengthening of troop discipline, and the supply of advanced missiles to all military branches. Persistent scientific research and development, mainly in the fields of electronics, automation, and in the construction of missiles; the enlargement of shipyard and aircraft construction capacity; exploration of space for military purposes; the elaboration of new theories of military science with special regard to technical revolutions in military affairs; the decentralized and strongly supported buildup of armaments industries; the constant consolidation of

---

[36]The technical standard of equipment in the armies of the smaller Pact members is discussed by St. Tiedtke, *Die Warschauer Vertragsorganisation*, p. 72.

[37]Thomas W. Wolfe, *Soviet Power and Europe, 1945–1970* (Baltimore: Johns Hopkins University Press, 1970), p. 492.

air defense; and the intensified perfection of a well-structured civil defense system under military command also improved the effectiveness of Pact troops.[38] Thousands of modern tanks of the T-62 model, the exchange of the outdated SAM-2 and SAM-4 for the newer SAM-6 missiles, the deployment of the MiG-25 *Foxbat* fighter and Su-24 *Fencer* tactical fighter and fighter-bomber aircraft were key parts of the modernization measures of the Warsaw Pact armies during the 1970s.

Due to the general economic deterioration that took place in the second half of the 1970s, the technological gap in the state of preparedness between the Soviet army and the troops of the Northern Tier widened. To reduce the vulnerability of their units in battle, the smaller member states were forced to introduce, at least in part, some of the new Soviet weapon developments. Even so, their budgets and general economic situation prevented significant new defense spending. A new round of rearmament in the Northern Triangle is just now getting into full swing. An early manifestation of this is that the modern T-64 and T-72 tanks are being deployed with the forces of the GDR, Poland, and Czechoslovakia.[39]

At the same time the gap between the professional soldier and the civilian population becomes ever wider. The necessity for the maintenance of troops for defense is generally accepted, although the people surely have not accepted the image of a bellicose NATO that is eagerly awaiting the chance for a surprise attack on the peace-loving socialist camp, seeking to annihilate all the "splendid achievements" of socialism, and planning to restore the pre-World War II borders. Compulsory military service is generally accepted, strict discipline is observed, and the hard-drilling methods reluctantly respected. The paramilitary training of juveniles during school and apprenticeship enlarges the manpower reserves. Preferential treatment accorded long-serving professional soldiers in respect to accommodation and foodstuffs as well as the relatively attractive salaries and good professional prospects all have contributed to forming a sufficient reservoir of applicants for a military career. On the Soviet model, the maintenance of a politico-ideological system of controls through *politruks* attached to the military commanders at all levels, as well as an indoctrination with the major ideas of Marxism-Leninism during officer training courses, have helped to create a situation where 90 percent of the officers, selected from among the working class and smallholder families, are members of the Communist Party or of its youth organization.[40]

---

[38]G. Zieger, *Der Warschauer Pakt* (Hannover: Niedersachsische Landerzentrale für politische Bildung, 1974), pp. 60–108.

[39]*The Military Balance 1980–1981*, pp. 14–17.

[40]H. J. Belde, "Der Polit-Stellvertreter in der NVA—Multiplikator im Ausbildungsdienst oder Politruk?" *Wehrwissenschaftliche Rundschau* 28 (Herford/Bonn: Verlag E. S. Mittler & Sohn, 1979), pp. 178–83.

The number of high-ranking military men in the parliaments, the central committees, and even in the politburos of the national Communist parties has risen constantly over the past twenty years and in 1980 reached approximately 16 percent of the total in the GDR. Because of their influence, military requirements could be put forward with special emphasis at all levels of decision making. On the other hand, the military leadership has taken great care not to become involved in intraparty struggles for control unless the Kremlin has made up its mind which faction is to be supported. This could be one reason for the relatively long terms of office of the national ministers of defense like H. Hoffmann since 1960 in the GDR, M. Dzur since April 1968 in Czechoslovakia, and W. Jaruzelski since July 1968 in Poland, who all have weathered changes in top personnel.

Although today national traditions are observed in the cut and color of uniforms, the Soviet system of training and command is dominant. Officers are promoted to higher command positions only after successfully attending qualified courses of instruction at Soviet higher military schools and academies; the recommendation of Soviet superiors brings especially rapid promotion. This dependence on Soviet protection has repeatedly led to an isolation of professional soldiers within the population, which in turn suspects them of a lack of national loyalty. The growing ill-feeling over the preferential treatment given to the army and security troops was manifested in the Polish strike movement in 1980, when an end to the one-sided privileges for their long-serving members was demanded.

In publications appearing in Eastern Europe on the Warsaw Pact, there are always references to the mutual and equal determination of political and military policies within the socialist camp.[41] But as impressively demonstrated following the Yom Kippur War, the USSR has retained its predominance in the military field. The military equipment of Warsaw Pact armies originates only in small part from national production. Weapons are mainly placed at their disposal directly by the USSR. Heavy weapon systems are developed and produced solely by the USSR; licensed production or independent deployments are somewhat rare and often costly. Soviet armament plans and developments remain top secret even within the alliance until the new equipment is introduced for extensive field testing. The smaller Pact members bear the risk that any independently developed weapon systems will not receive Soviet approval. Due to the large capacity of its armaments industry the USSR easily can manipulate the prices of its products and thereby cut off weapon

---

[41]A. Latzo, *Der Warschauer Vertrag. Instrument zur Sicherung des Friedens* (East Berlin: Staatsverlag der DDR, 1972); S Vladimirov and L. Teplov, *Varshavskii dogovor i NATO: Dva kursa, dve politiki* [The Warsaw Pact and NATO: Two courses, two policies] (Moscow: Myezhdunarodnye otnoshenia, 1979).

sales by other Pact members, both within the alliance and to the developing countries. Thus, Poland and Czechoslovakia, the only countries with significant national armaments industries, increasingly have concentrated on the manufacture of smaller weapons and equipment closely related to civil production. The Soviets have encouraged a closer cooperation in the production of war material, in which the other alliance members have to deliver parts and technical systems to the Soviet armaments industry. The GDR has gained a substantial reputation for the production of high-quality components. In this sense the growing complexity of modern weapon systems, the narrowing of differences between civil and armaments production in certain sectors, and the growth of some specialization in COMECON to some extent have increased the dependency of the USSR on her alliance partners.

CONCLUSIONS

In recent years cooperation between the main political administrations of the forces of the Pact member states—the Communist Party military oversight agencies—has been enlarged further, as has coordination in the important military-technological sector. Joint maneuvers by ground force, naval, air force, and staff units have been given high priority. On the twenty-fifth anniversary of the Warsaw Pact, the responsible political and military leadership proclaimed with great emphasis the alliance's achievement of consolidation, arising from the coordination of basic political and ideological principles and in view of common strategic aims, tactical objectives, training, and the fullest possible standardization of military hardware. Yet only a modest diversification in the command structure and limited participation in decision making has been permitted by the Kremlin, which always has insisted that all positions of influence be reserved for Soviets. The increased Soviet demand for fullest coordination of ideological strategies and of reactions to general political events has engendered some resistance, especially in Poland. The Kremlin was disappointed over the luke-warm response to its efforts to convene a new world congress of Communist parties in order to punish dissenters such as China and Albania, as well as to expose the heresies of the self-confident Euro-Communists. As a result, Brezhnev may have decided to follow a double strategy, combining ideologically defensive measures with a political offensive in such a way that bloc politics coordination in Eastern Europe could be combined with a propaganda campaign against NATO and her "continuously aggressive aims."

Although the central pretext for the foundation of the Warsaw Pact—the threat of a rebirth of militarism in West Germany—has lost its original menace, the Kremlin has shown little inclination to loosen the eastern military pact. The Pact is used by the USSR not only to maintain the military balance vis-à-vis NATO and to control the national forces of the member states, but also it has become above all an instrument of dominance serving to tighten the manifold links of the USSR with its East European member states. All political and strategic decisions of crucial importance are solely in the hands of the Soviet leadership and its completely reliable military establishment. The Warsaw Pact's Political Consultative Committee is not so much an advisory body or a decision maker in military-political affairs as it is a forum from which to transmit the various political positions of the Soviet leadership. There is no indication of any single Warsaw Pact political or strategic position having been developed independently of Soviet tutelage or against Soviet initiative. Thus following the Soviet-Chinese confrontation and the invasion of Czechoslovakia, the Warsaw Treaty organization has been expanded from an instrument primarily to stabilize the international balance of military power between East and West in Europe to one that also acts as an important Soviet control device aimed at preserving and managing the status quo within the socialist camp.

The Three Southern Members
of the Warsaw Pact

> The Soviets' inability to acquire loyalty in Eastern Europe is an
> unfortunate historical failure, because Eastern Europe is within their
> scope and area of natural interest.
>
> Helmut Sonnenfeld
> December 1975

This study focuses on the three southern members of the Warsaw
Pact, that is, Bulgaria, Hungary, and Romania, and will include a brief
reference to Albania, which was a founding member. The mutual assistance treaty, signed on 14 May 1955 in Warsaw, Poland, formally joined
the Soviet Union and six of its East European satellite states—Albania,
Bulgaria, Czechoslovakia, Hungary, Poland, and Romania—in a military
alliance of traditional enemies. The following year in 1956 East Germany
joined the Pact.

ASSUMPTIONS

Since the formation of the Pact certain general assumptions have
arisen. Not all of them have been explicitly committed to paper, or even
spoken of too boldly, but they exist nevertheless and tend to influence
strategic thinking. These include a NATO presupposition that the Warsaw Pact has an offensive role and conversely a Warsaw Pact assumption
that NATO is a belligerent combination of aggressive nations. Another
mutual assumption is that the great decisive land battles of World War
III would be fought on the north German plain, with the three northern
Warsaw Pact members deeply involved and the three southern ones less
so. Yet another assumption, which is also held by both, is that the southern
members of the Warsaw Pact are less trustworthy and less important to
Moscow than the northern ones, and that their armed forces may be less
reliable and their expeditionary potential extremely limited. This may
have originated with the Hungarian rising in 1956 and continued with the

independent line taken by the Romanians, but illogically it does not seem to have been modified by the Czech situation in 1968, or the various manifestations of Polish discontent in 1956, 1970, and 1980–81. Geography is probably the key, even in this thermonuclear age.

The three southern members of the Warsaw Pact have several features in common. All three began World War II in the German camp and ended it in that of the Allies, and all were occupied by Soviet armed forces in 1944–45, which enabled the Soviet government eventually to install Communist regimes in power and to make favorable bilateral treaties and agreements with them. Another common feature is that all three during the past hundred years or so either have taken slices of territory from another or have had territory snatched from them by one of the others, perpetuating age-old Balkan rivalries that smoulder on even to this day. In short, the traditional enemies of the Bulgarians are the Romanians, Yugoslavs, Greeks, and Turks; those of the Hungarians are the Czechs, Romanians, and Russians; and those of the Romanians are the Bulgarians, Hungarians, Russians, and Turks. It is only the binding cement of Soviet enforced Marxist-Leninist communism that holds these uncomfortable allies together.

Another striking feature is their comparatively small populations: Bulgaria has only about 8.8 million people, Hungary only 10.6 million, and Romania approximately 21.8 million, which totals just over 40 million people inhabiting an area of about 170,000 square miles. This is of no small strategic importance since these countries comprise most of the Balkan Peninsula, the southern portion of which is in possession of two NATO members, Greece and Turkey.

ROLE OF THE SOUTHERN MEMBERS

When Greece and Turkey joined NATO in 1952, they posed a threat to the three southern members, which at that time had only bilateral defense agreements with the Soviet Union. The southern members' main role in Soviet thinking came to be the defense of the Balkan Peninsula against NATO, with the subsidiary task of providing military formations for the anticipated main battle against the Turks and to a lesser extent with the Greeks as well. Because of the mountainous terrain, the Soviets had some confidence that this part of its southern flank could be held against a NATO attack. The Balkan Peninsula would be turned into a prickly defensive hedgehog spine that would absorb invading troops, slow down or curtail their freedom of movement, and force them into a defensive posture, thus leaving the armed forces of the northern members of the Pact to concentrate upon the main potential battlefield. Had Yugoslavia, led by

Tito, not already defected from Moscow in 1948, this plan would have been much more credible.

THE WARSAW PACT

The Warsaw Pact started as a twenty-year treaty of friendship, cooperation, and mutual assistance. The latter expression refers to Soviet military assistance that only would become a unified command under rigid Soviet control in time of war, since it has never had a separate peacetime military logistic system. The main obligation of the Warsaw Pact is that in the event of an armed attack on any one member state, the others must render immediate assistance. The Pact's concept is confined entirely to Europe, which accounts for its distinct disinterest in Middle Eastern, Southwest Asian, and Soviet southern and Far Eastern strategic problems. Any East European presence in those areas is the result of agreement outside the Warsaw Pact's organizational framework.

The Warsaw Pact was a Soviet idea; it is Soviet dominated, and in time of war the armed forces of the member countries would be commanded by a Soviet commander in chief. The Warsaw Pact GHQ staff and inspectorate, based in Moscow, consists mainly of Soviet personnel, with only nominal satellite national representation. Its framework provides Moscow with one way of controlling its buffer states, enabling the Soviets to transmit political and military directives to them and to ensure that these are implemented. The commander in chief of the Warsaw Pact Joint Armed Forces is always a Russian officer with senior ministerial status. At present, it is Marshal Viktor Kulikov, who is not only the first deputy defense minister but also deputy commander in chief of the Soviet National Air Defense Forces (Voiska PVO), which is a considerable slice of power.

Soviet military missions, commanded by senior Soviet officers, are sited in the capital cities of all the East European member countries, with the exception of Romania, and have wide powers of inspection and supervision of training. Large-scale joint training exercises, involving the armed forces of several member countries, are frequently held. The main advantage that the Warsaw Pact has over NATO is that all member nations have a standardization of strategic and in most cases tactical doctrines, command and staff procedures, and of weaponry and equipment. No fundamental deviations are permitted, and there is no such thing, for example, as a separate Warsaw Pact strategic doctrine.

The member states, excluding the Soviet Union, had military manpower available, of which the Soviets always have been short. However, in the early 1950s their armed forces were equipped with old weapons, mostly of Soviet manufacture; their staff procedures, training, and tactics varied; and there previously had been little military liaison between them. In fact the various military forces were traditionally hostile to, and suspicious of, each other. In short, disparate and divided as they were then, from the Soviet point of view they were incapable of defending their own particular sectors of the so-called "Yalta Zone," or the buffer zone between the USSR and the West outlined at the Yalta summit.

When the Pact was formed, Soviet military missions assigned to member countries set to work to rectify these weaknesses, to rearm them, and to standardize military concepts, weaponry, training, and organization on the Moscow model. Officers of the regular military cadres of member states attended courses of instruction and indoctrination at Soviet military training establishments. The USSR concluded status of forces agreements with Bulgaria, Hungary, and Romania to allow the stationing of Soviet troops on their soil. The agreement with Romania lapsed in June 1958, and Soviet troops left that country. However, that withdrawal did not interrupt periodic joint Warsaw Pact military exercises in the area.

THE HUNGARIAN UPRISING, 1956

The first major spasm of dissidence within the Pact erupted in Hungary. By 1952 practically the entire Hungarian economy had been nationalized, but in 1953 Imre Nagy, who followed a more liberal policy, became the party leader. Nagy was ousted in April 1955 and replaced by Matyas Rakosi, who tightened the Communist grip again, although not sufficiently. In July he too was replaced as secretary general of the Hungarian Communist Party by Erno Gero. Meanwhile, the people of Hungary, having tasted liberalism, demanded more and called for the return to power of Nagy. On 23 October 1956 demonstrations developed into open revolt. The following day Soviet troops entered Budapest and on the 25th opened fire on assembled demonstrators, killing many of them. The previous day the Soviets had allowed Nagy to head a new government and following the initial skirmish, the situation in the capital temporarily quieted down. The last Soviet troops were withdrawn from Budapest by the 30th. Nagy began to work on his liberalization program, and on 1 November he announced the withdrawal of Hungary from the Warsaw Pact. Two days later he formed an "all party" government.

This proved to be too much for the Kremlin leaders to stand. It may be recalled that these events coincided with the Suez crisis, which then held world attention. At dawn on 4 November a large-scale Soviet invasion of Hungary was undertaken by a military force that consisted of about 150,000 troops in ten divisions, with about 2,500 tanks and armored vehicles backed by air support. There were already approximately 20,000 Soviet troops in the country. The Soviets seized the parliament buildings in Budapest, the radio station, bridges, and other key installations. Although the uprising was quickly put down in the capital, sporadic resistance lingered on elsewhere in the country for some weeks.

The Hungarians lost over 3,000 and more than 200,000 fled the country, of whom about 56,000 eventually returned under a 1963 amnesty. Estimates of casualties still vary and tend to be unreliable. Soviet losses, which were never officially published, were thought to exceed 1,000. Imre Nagy, who took refuge in the Yugoslav embassy, was eventually betrayed and captured, and in 1958 he was executed.

On 4 November, the day of the Soviet invasion, a quisling government was established under Janos Kadar, who became the first secretary of the Hungarian Communist Party and immediately annulled his country's defection from the Warsaw Pact. The Hungarian armed forces were virtually disbanded and remained inoperative until the early 1960s. The major part of the Soviet invasion force eventually withdrew from Hungary, but about 40,000 Soviet troops, some four divisions with about 3,400 tanks and 350 aircraft, remained in occupation and are still there.

The reasons for this prompt, brutal, heavy-handed Soviet invasion of Hungary included the Kremlin leaders' objections to the multiparty system of government and defection from the Warsaw Pact, which cracked the thin veneer of Soviet Communist binding cement. But if Nagy's Hungary had been able to link up with Tito's Yugoslavia, that might have shattered the newly formed Warsaw Pact. Prompt, punitive military action had to be taken, and it served as a stern warning to any other potential defectors.

Although elements of the Hungarian army fought with the insurgents against the Soviet invaders, they were a minority, as the Soviets successfully prevented many attempts by Hungarian insurgents to contact and subvert the Hungarian army by using senior Soviet officers and pro-Soviet Hungarian officers to thwart such contacts and to spread confusion. Much of the army simply melted away. It has since been suggested that had communications with the Hungarian army been better, a larger section of it would have fought with the insurgents and the insurgency would have lasted longer, although none suggest it ultimately could have been successful.

WARSAW PACT EXPANSION: THE 1960s

By the beginning of 1960 the Warsaw Pact standing forces, excluding those of the USSR, totaled about 750,000. After the Berlin crisis and the building of the Berlin Wall in 1961, a serious attempt was made to increase overall troop strength. By the end of 1961 the East European Pact forces numbered over 1 million. The following year the command and structural organization had been tightened and more modern Soviet weapons had been delivered to the armed forces of member states.

In the early 1960s the military strengths of the three southern members also had risen. Bulgaria had about 100,000 soldiers formed into ten divisions, about 15,000 in the air force, and another 5,000 in the navy, together with some 40,000 paramilitary personnel. Bulgaria was then spending about 4.5% of its national income on defense. Hungary had an army of about 75,000 men, which was beginning to revive, an air force of about 5,500, and about 35,000 paramilitary personnel. Hungary was only spending about 1.8% of its national income on defense. Romania had an army of about 200,000 soldiers in thirteen divisions, an air force of about 15,000 men, a navy of about 7,000, and approximately 60,000 paramilitary personnel. Romania was spending about 3.8% of its national income on defense. The naval forces of Bulgaria and Romania consisted of only a handful of small coastal craft in the Black Sea. All three southern members were completely equipped with Soviet weaponry and military equipment by the early 1960s.

Bulgaria

From Moscow's viewpoint, Bulgaria was its most solid and reliable ally. Its only political blemishes were those of being too friendly toward China (after the Sino-Soviet split in 1960) and for a while having too much contact with West Germany. The Bulgarian government followed the Moscow line so slavishly because of the traditional Bulgarian gratitude for Russian help in obtaining independence in 1878 from Ottoman rule. It was a weak Bulgarian leadership that depended heavily upon Soviet backing and the substantial economic aid that the Soviet Union was pouring into the country, enabling it to form an industrial base.

The attempted military coup in 1965, if that is what it really was, came as a surprise. Evidently the conspirators were led by Major General Tsevetko Anev, commander of the Sofia garrison, along with Ivan Todorov-Gorunya, a member of the central committee of the Bulgarian Communist Party, and Krustev Kamanov, a senior official in the Bulgarian foreign ministry. The plot, which was to be implemented on 14 April, was discovered prematurely; General Anev, Kamanov, and others were arrested, and Todorov-Gorunya committed suicide. On 16 July 1965, Todor Zhivkov, chairman of the council of ministers and first party secretary, stated that the accused men, eventually five military officers and four civilians, were pro-Chinese elements, but it is likely they were more nationalist than Communist and wanted to adopt an independent line.

During this period, Zhivkov was trying to increase party political influence in the armed forces and to enforce tighter political controls on them. The conspirators, who all had a common World War II partisan background, may have felt they were being unnecessarily curbed and unfairly treated. Several senior officers had been removed from their posts and others reshuffled. Since 1965, President Zhivkov has kept Bulgaria faithful to the Kremlin party line.

Albania

This tiny country with only very small armed forces possessed a stretch of strategically valuable Adriatic coastline. Albania was a founding member of the Warsaw Pact and at first a whole-hearted one. However, when the Sino-Soviet rift came out into the open in 1960, Albania took the Chinese side in the ideological dispute. The Soviet Union ceased providing aid and withdrew its submarines from the Albanian naval base at Saseno Island opposite the Albanian port of Valone. Albanian representatives ceased attending Warsaw Pact meetings or participating in Pact business in any way. In 1965 Albania was once again invited to attend a meeting of the Political Consultative Committee but declined. Instead, it submitted a long list of complaints, accusing the Soviet Union of conspiring with Yugoslavia, Greece, and the United States to overthrow the Hoxha regime by force. Albania remained a nonactive member until just after the Czech crisis of 1968, when it formally withdrew from the Warsaw Pact.

Romania

After joining the Warsaw Pact, Romania had continued to accept the Moscow political line without question, but from 1963 onward it began to follow an increasingly independent foreign policy. Romania, for example, remained strictly neutral in the Sino-Soviet dispute. The last Soviet-Romanian-Bulgarian joint ground forces exercise was held in 1964, where the emphasis was on the use of conventional artillery and infantry carried in armored personnel vehicles, as compared with the emphasis on missiles and tanks in joint exercises carried out by the northern members. In April 1964 the Romanian Communist Party plenum statement made it clear that Romania was to put its own national interests before those of the USSR and declared that nations had a right to determine their own destiny as well as rights of national sovereignty.[1] It

---

[1] *Scinteia*, 23 April 1964.

advocated a loose form of commonwealth, bound together by common ideology and interests. In November 1964 the period of national service in Romania was reduced from two years to sixteen months, and even a personal visit by the Warsaw Pact Soviet commander in chief failed to change that decision.

In 1965, Nicolae Ceauşescu came to power in Romania. He was a sincere Communist by conviction but also a dedicated nationalist. That year a strong nationalist theme was injected into the routine ideological political indoctrination of the Romanian armed forces, which brought with it the shadow of possible Soviet military intervention along the lines of that in Hungary. In May 1966, after meeting Yugoslav leaders, Ceauşescu stated that he favored abolishing military blocs, dismantling foreign bases, and withdrawing foreign troops. This statement was directed against Soviet policy as applied to the Warsaw Pact, even though no Soviet troops were permanently stationed on Romanian soil. In January 1967, Ceauşescu established links with West Germany, and in August of that year American President Richard Nixon visited Romania. Later, Ceauşescu refused to join the Soviet government in its condemnation of Israel as the aggressor in the June 1973 war in the Middle East.

THE BREZHNEV DOCTRINE, 1968

In January 1968, Alexander Dubček came to power in Czechoslovakia. His program of liberalization caused anxiety among most Warsaw Pact countries, but he was openly supported by President Ceauşescu and also by Marshal Tito. From March onward Romanians were excluded from all Warsaw Pact meetings that had the Czech problem on the agenda. On 15 July 1968 the so-called "Warsaw letter," signed by all members of the Warsaw Pact except Romania and Albania and including Bulgaria and Hungary, was sent to Dubček, urging him to accept the Soviet Communist leadership's advice and to slow down his liberalization program.

Dubček ignored this warning advice, and in August a massive Soviet military invasion of Czechoslovakia was launched, in which two understrength Hungarian divisions and a small Bulgarian contingent took ineffectual part. It is of interest that the Soviet invasion force was commanded by General Ivan Pavlovsky, commander in chief of the Soviet Ground Forces, and not by Marshal Ivan Yakubovsky, then Warsaw Pact Joint Armed Forces commander in chief.

Czech troops were not involved, as were some Hungarian soldiers in

1956; they instead stayed quietly in barracks. It was said they had not been ordered by their government to fight the Soviet invaders, and there is no evidence that they offered any resistance. This could have indicated that a strong military link and bond of loyalty had been forged between the Czech armed forces and the USSR, stronger perhaps than the civilian political one, which had shown signs of strain and fraying. The Czech episode revealed the potential unreliability to the Kremlin leaders of some of the Communist governments of the Warsaw Pact states, including the northern ones.

The Soviet action in Czechoslovakia was a demonstration of what became known as the Brezhnev Doctrine, even before it had been formally enunciated. It was not until November 1968 in Warsaw that Brezhnev actually explained that there was a limitation of sovereignty for Communist bloc countries, and that they have only the right to self-determination as long as it does not jeopardize the interests of communism in their own countries or in any other state of the socialist commonwealth. The Brezhnev Doctrine enunciated the right of the Soviet government to interfere, militarily if necessary, in the internal affairs of other Communist states, most especially those with Warsaw Pact membership.

How did the Czech crisis affect the three southern members? In faithful Bulgaria the lesson was not necessary; in Hungary, once again becoming tainted by western influence, the lesson must have been heeded; and in Romania it was noted. It probably curbed, although it did not stop, President Ceauşescu's brinkmanship.

ROMANIA IN THE 1970s

In Romania, soon after the Czech crisis of 1968, an interesting incident came to light known as the "Serb affair." The Law of State Secrets was passed in December 1971, virtually forbidding Romanians from having any substantial contact with foreigners and decreeing harsh penalties for passing on to them any state information. On 14 February 1972 western news reports indicated that General Ion Serb, who commanded the Bucharest military district, had been arrested for passing military secrets to the Soviet military attaché; some reports even alleged he had been executed. It was confirmed by the Romanian embassy in Vienna on 16 February that Serb was no longer a general. The Soviet military attaché concerned was expelled from Romania.

General Serb seems to have opposed certain parts of Ceauşescu's policy, especially when it was at variance with that of the Soviet Union.

There were strains between a group of senior Romanian military officers and the party at the time, but the Serb affair appeared to be an isolated incident and only affected a few Romanian officers. Apparently Serb could not muster sufficiently pro-Soviet and anti-Ceauşescu military support, and his protest, however it was manifested, hardly could be dignified by being referred to as an attempted military coup.

Later in 1972, President Ceauşescu passed another law on the organization of national defense, which prohibited capitulation in wartime to any invading forces and emphasized the concept of defense based on popular resistance. Ceauşescu, who again must have had the Soviet Union in mind, created a part-time paramilitary force known as the Patriotic Guards for defense against any external military threat. Most Romanians realized they could not successfully resist a combined Warsaw Pact invasion similar to that of Czechoslovakia in 1968, but all hoped that the visible popular will to put up a vigorous initial defense would act as a good deterrent. By 1972 there was neither a Soviet military mission in Romania nor any Soviet military advisers with the Romanian armed forces.

At the November 1978 meeting of the Warsaw Pact's Political Consultative Committee, President Ceauşescu refused to place his Romanian defense forces under the Supreme Military Command—the Soviet Union. In a major speech on 23 November, Ceauşescu declared there was no imminent danger of war with the West. Ceauşescu, who in 1978 and 1979 had refused to increase Romanian defense spending, decided in 1980 to cut the military budget by some 16 percent. The money was to be reallocated to economic development and welfare. Also, in September only a handful of noncombatant Romanian military staff officers attended the Warsaw Pact joint maneuver, "Comrades-in-Arms," the biggest held for ten years, involving over 40,000 men, which incidentally coincided with the massive NATO "Crusader" exercise involving over 85,000 men.

Romania's comparative economic strength, based on adequate natural resources such as oil and a healthy petrochemical industry, may have enabled them to take this bold line. President Ceauşescu's apparent fine sense of brinkmanship let him know exactly how far to go without provoking Soviet punitive military action. Soviet tolerance was perhaps tempered because Romania did not border any non-Communist state and was hemmed in from the south by Bulgaria. In 1978 a four-ship ferry service opened between the Bulgarian port of Varna and Odessa, each of the ships being able to carry about 150 tanks or railway wagons and several thousand troops. This meant that well-equipped Soviet troops in large numbers could be moved quickly to Bulgaria, thus bypassing Romania. Another mitigating factor in Soviet eyes was the fact that the Romanian Communist Party was actually in control domestically and there was no danger of the dreaded pluralism creeping in.

WARSAW PACT TRENDS IN THE 1970s

In March 1969, shortly after the Czech crisis, the Warsaw Pact structure was revised ostensibly to give member countries a greater say in policy, and a Council of Defense Ministers of member countries emerged as the highest authority. Under this council came the Joint High Command, whose purpose was to prepare contingency plans in case of war and to determine the development of its troops; it was chaired by the Soviet commander in chief of the Warsaw Pact. Within the Joint High Command, the commander in chief and his chief of staff were always senior Soviet officers, and Soviet officers occupied all other key positions. Then came the Military Council, the main channel to transmit Soviet orders in peacetime, which included the Chiefs of Staffs of all member countries and through which all military members should submit their views. There is also a Warsaw Pact Military Staff that includes non-Soviet officers, but in time of war all Warsaw Pact armed forces are to be subordinated to the Soviet High Command. The Romanians will not agree to this latter arrangement.

The command structure of the air defense system covering the entire Warsaw Pact area is situated in Moscow under the control of the Soviet commander in chief of the Soviet National Air Defense Forces—the Voiska PVO. The Soviet-controlled GHQ for the "Southern Group of Forces," that is, Bulgaria, Hungary, and Romania, is based in Budapest. Elements of Soviet tactical Frontal Aviation are stationed in Hungary, but there are none in either Bulgaria or Romania, nor are there any Soviet troops permanently stationed in those two nations.

OVERSEAS OPERATIONS

Warsaw Pact countries long have been helping the Soviet Union outside Europe by providing personnel for various Soviet military and training missions in the Middle East, Africa, and elsewhere where Soviet arms supply projects are ongoing. The Soviet Union is short of manpower for these extraneous tasks and is glad to coopt some from Warsaw Pact countries. Generally, they seem to favor East Germans and Poles, but it is interesting to note that in recent reports there are several hundred Hungarians in Iraq and 400 Bulgarians in Libya working as military advisers and technicians, and that during the fighting in the Ogaden in the Horn of Africa in late 1977 the Western Somalia Liberation Front claimed to have held prisoner "Seven Russians, three Bulgarians, and two East Germans."[2] Recently, the Bulgarian defense minister accompanied the Soviet defense minister on a visit to Angola, which must cause speculation as to whether more Bulgarians will soon be working for the Soviet government in Africa, or even perhaps becoming proxy troops such as the Cubans. Although these operations do not take place through the Warsaw Pact's framework, the high degree of integration within the Pact's senior officer staffs undoubtedly enhances cooperation in overseas projects.

ACHIEVEMENTS TO DATE

What has the Warsaw Pact achieved so far in the southern states? Apart from the defection of Albania in 1969, the alliance has remained intact as a defensive treaty upon which has been imposed the Brezhnev Doctrine. In Soviet eyes at least it has helped to deter NATO aggression. Two southern members, Bulgaria and Romania, have been able to satisfy the USSR that the Balkan road to Moscow would be a tough one for NATO. However, the Soviets probably are not convinced that this would deter either Greece or Turkey, or cause them to hesitate to invade northward into the Balkan Peninsula if the situation were opportune. Mutual military inferiority in the area is probably seen as the most obvious deterrent.

What is the political and military reliability of the armed forces of the three southern members? Will their armed forces always obey their political masters and be willing to fight outside their own national territory? Will there be military deviation from the Moscow line? And will the military ever reach out to snatch political power? The three incidents—the Hungarian uprising of 1956, the Bulgarian plot of 1965, and the Serb affair in Romania in 1972—give sparce guidance.

Communist military establishments do not clash with their own governments over the usual military issues such as better pay and conditions and more up-to-date weaponry; all these professional demands are voiced, together with any criticisms or complaints, to the Warsaw Pact's Military Council. It is true there is growing sense of military professionalism, which feels slighted when non-Warsaw Pact nations like Iraq or Libya receive more modern weapons than Pact members. Within the national armies of the three southern members, normal promotional disappointments, personal ambitions, jealousies, and clashing personalities exist, but all of the armies have a Soviet military commissar surveillance system designed to identify and weed out active discontent and

---

[2]*Washington Post*, 4 July 1977.

to enforce political loyalty. There seems to be little chance of a military coup against any party government, except perhaps in Romania where Soviet military control and influence are the least effective. In Romania military elements might gang up against Ceauşescu, possibly with organizational assistance from Moscow, if his policy became too anti-Soviet.

Generally, political leaderships might object to their armed forces fighting outside their own country, but ethnic prejudices and fears could influence such decisions. For instance, Hungary would willingly combine with the USSR to "punish" Romania. To operate the Brezhnev Doctrine, in certain cases Soviet forces might have to act alone because reluctant southern member countries, in any ostentatious show of Warsaw Pact military unity and political solidarity, simply might be a bigger handicap than asset.

VALUE IN WAR

What would be the southern members' value in a major conflict against NATO forces? It is almost certain that Bulgaria and Romania would strongly defend their own territory and if overrun would activate a form of popular guerrilla warfare. They might fight against western imperialism, but their own national defense would be paramount and the degree of cooperation in expeditionary projects, even from faithful Bulgaria, might be extremely limited. The mood of Hungary has changed since 1956, and it would probably try hard to avoid becoming involved in any military action. Hungary looks longingly to the West and only dutifully toward Moscow. Janos Kadar has matured and turned out to be a moderate leader who follows the Kremlin line in foreign policy but has brought non-Communist economists into his industries.

Although ostensibly the Warsaw Pact is a defensive alliance, the Soviet Union must have considered its offensive capabilities and uses. Looking southward, Soviet strategic aims in the Balkan area probably would be limited to reaching the Aegean Sea and controlling the Dardanelles and the Bosporus in order to secure a safe passage for its Black Sea Fleet into the eastern Mediterranean. In a war the most likely Warsaw Pact southern offensive would be through Bulgaria into Thrace to reach the Aegean Sea. This would drive a wedge between Greece and Turkey, neither of which would be overly eager to rush to the other country's aid. Old Balkan rivalries, greeds, and prejudices would be roused and Turkey then would have a "two-front" war on its hands. The southern members probably would share in a local military success

against the NATO southern flank; the real future of the region undoubtedly would rest on the results of the conflict in the north and the
strategic outcome.

THE FUTURE

Excluding World War III, there seem to be three principal possibilities for the future of the southern members: the continuation of the
status quo, the spread of an East European brand of Eurocommunism, or
the formation of a new and exclusively Balkan pact. First, as long as the
East-West strategic balance remains roughly what it is today and tensions
continue, there is the possibility that the status quo may last through the
onset of the twenty-first century, with perhaps only a gradual loosening of
the tight Moscow political control. In fact, it even could continue until the
USSR became more deeply involved in its confrontation with China.

The second possibility could be the spread of a kind of Eurocommunism into the southern Warsaw Pact countries. All three southern
members cater to tens of thousands of West European visitors each year
and West European socialism appears increasingly attractive. There
already have been frequent contacts between Spanish and Italian Communist leaders and those of Hungary and Romania. These countries
could remain under their Communist regimes but be more independent of
Moscow. The member countries, still Communist but also becoming more
nationalistic, eventually might shrug off much of Moscow's domination.
They would still need some collective military protection against being
individually gobbled up or having sections of their territory taken away
from them. Therefore, a reconstituted Warsaw Pact might survive as a
more purely military alliance.

The third possibility might be the southern members' eventual
separation from the Warsaw Pact, probably one by one, perhaps to form
an entirely new Balkan grouping that would include Yugoslavia and
maybe also Albania. This pact then might become a major neutral bloc,
with economic factors being the principal influence. For example, the
southern members obtain about 70 percent of their petroleum from the
Soviet Union at below OPEC prices and most of their other raw materials
also arrive on similar terms. These deliveries will be at far less favorable
prices from 1981 to 1985, causing them to rely more on western imports
and to look to the West for modern technology. Western contacts, and
perhaps western encouragement, inevitably will generate pressure for
more political freedoms. Such an independent neutral Balkan group could
trade with COMECON, the EEC, and indeed with any country or bloc.

The Soviet Union obviously would try to prevent this, possibly by arousing trouble between Bulgaria and Yugoslavia over the Macedonian issue, or between Romania and Bulgaria over their mutual border.

What is more likely, however, is that movement will be made on all three courses simultaneously and a compromise will be reached. In the short term, the first course—the continuation of the status quo—is most probable. But when China finally emerges as a major antagonist of the USSR, the third course of Balkan neutrality surely will gain momentum.

NATO AND THE WARSAW PACT

NATO and the Warsaw Pact: The Past*

LAWRENCE S. KAPLAN

In 1982 the Warsaw Treaty Organization looms larger on the European scene than it did when it was created in 1955. References in the press and in journals regularly equate it with the North Atlantic Treaty Organization. The Warsaw Pact symbolizes the East bloc almost as clearly as NATO stands for the West. In this sense the Soviet Union has achieved a success that it may not have anticipated or even intended in 1954 and 1955 when the Pact was germinating.

While the precise intentions of the Soviet Union still remain obscure, informed conjectures may be made about the intentions of the framers of the Warsaw Pact. An even clearer picture of NATO's perception of the treaty may be limned a generation later. What seemed common to both antagonists in 1955 was the relative unimportance of the new organization. The reasons for the low estate of the Warsaw Pact are worth examining in view of its present prominence. A history of the circumstances of its birth might yield insights into the relationship between NATO and the Soviet Union in the mid-1950s. Sketchier though it must be, judgments also can be made of the changes in the past quarter century that account for the present relationship between the two alliances.

GERMANY AND THE REASONS
FOR THE WARSAW PACT

The first impression made by the Warsaw Pact upon the West was that of a "counter-NATO," a distorted mirror image of the original. Western diplomatists were insulted by its pretensions. NATO, after all, was "a voluntary coalition of free countries," as Canadian Foreign Minister Lester Pearson expressed it, "under a treaty freely negotiated and approved, with one exception, by the democratically elected members of their legislatures." By contrast, the Warsaw Pact was a typically

---

*Research for this essay was conducted in the course of study as a NATO Research Fellow, 1980–81.

clumsy Soviet imitation imposed by fiat upon its satellites without any reference to public opinion. Soviet will prevailed at all times in its "NATO," while the United States could not, "without great difficulty," impose its way upon its allies.[1]

Nonetheless, the language of the Pact invites inspection of similarities as well as differences with the North Atlantic Treaty. On 14 May 1955 eight signatories—Albania, Bulgaria, Czechoslovakia, East Germany, Hungary, Poland, Romania, and the Soviet Union—completed a pact of friendship, cooperation, and mutual assistance, which was so similar to the Treaty of Washington that, in the words of Andrzej Korbonski, "one might venture to guess that those responsible for the final version of the Warsaw Treaty had a copy of the NATO text at their elbows."[2] Mutual consultation in the event of an outside threat, as provided for in Article 3, is reminiscent of Article 4 of the North Atlantic Treaty, while Article 4 of the Warsaw Pact is almost a replica of Article 5 of the North Atlantic Pact in its response to external attack and in its appeal to Article 51 of the United Nations Charter. A counterpart to the North Atlantic Council in Article 9 of the Atlantic Pact is the Political Consultative Committee of Article 6. The twenty-year terms specified in both treaties—Article 11 of the Warsaw Pact and Article 13 of the Atlantic Alliance—complete the identification. A spirit of equality among the signatory powers pervades the text of the Warsaw Treaty and is symbolized by the special mention in Article 11 that the texts of the treaty in Russian, Polish, Czech, and German are "equally authentic." Probably the most significant reference to NATO also was to be found in Article 11 in an apparent plea for its own dissolution: "Should a system of collective security be established in Europe, and a General European Treaty of Collective Security concluded for this purpose, . . . the present Treaty shall cease to be operative from the day the General European Treaty enters into force."[3]

The message clearly was that the Soviet Union and its allies were forced against their will to counter an aggressive NATO, and particularly the grave new threat imposed by the incorporation of the Federal Republic of Germany into NATO in May 1955. As stated in the preamble, the contracting parties were motivated by "the situation created in Europe by the ratification of the Paris agreements, which envisage the formation of a new military alignment in the shape of 'Western European Union,' with

[1]John A. Munroe and Alex I. Inglis, eds., *Mike: The Memoirs of Lester Pearson*, 3 vols. (Toronto: University of Toronto Press, 1972), 2:91.

[2]Andrzej Korbonski, "The Warsaw Pact," *International Conciliation*, no. 573 (May 1969): 13.

[3]Treaty of Friendship, Co-operation and Mutual Assistance, Warsaw, 14 May 1955, translation published in *New Times* (Moscow), no. 21, 21 May 1955. See also the pamphlet "The Atlantic Alliance and the Warsaw Pact: A Comparative Study" (Brussels: NATO Information Service, n.d.).

the participation of a remilitarized Western Germany and the integration of the latter in the North-Atlantic bloc, which increases the danger of another war and constitutes a threat to the national security of the peaceable states. . . ."[4]

There should be no doubt about the authenticity of the Soviet Union's concern over West Germany's role in NATO. It had been proclaimed repeatedly ever since the NATO allies began to pick up the pieces of the failed European Defense Community (EDC) in the fall of 1954. When the foreign ministers of the North Atlantic allies signed an agreement with the West Germans in Paris to enlarge the old Western Union, to restore formally the sovereignty of West Germany, and to call for the admission of West Germany into the Atlantic alliance, the Soviets acted.[5] On 23 October, the very day on which the Paris protocols were signed, was the occasion for the Soviet Union to propose discussion of an "all-German" election, a goal the West had worked toward for years. The purpose was obviously to prevent ratification of the changed status of West Germany. Should the western allies fail to attend a conference, the governments of East Europe would meet anyway and take their own steps to inhibit ratification of a German membership in NATO.[6]

Predictably, the allies dismissed the invitation as containing nothing more than had been suggested at a foreign ministers' conference in Berlin earlier in the year. They found the refrain of a mutual withdrawal of forces and of a new collective security system to be familiar and shopworn. The notion of "free" elections went undefined, with no mention of how that freedom would be safeguarded. Still a response had to be made; German public opinion, among others, was vulnerable to any prospect of reunification even on terms that would require neutralization. The three major foreign ministries of NATO then informally expressed their willingness to meet after the London and Paris agreements had been ratified.[7] Perhaps the strongest statement at the time came not from the officials of the Big Three of NATO but from its secretary general, Lord Ismay, who labeled the Soviet proposals an "absolute mockery" of western ideals. Speaking before the Royal United Service Institution, he denied that Stalin's death had removed the military threat from the East. The NATO Council, he observed, found "no evidence that the military danger has ended." The West must be vigilant against Soviet attempts to weaken its resolve.[8]

---

[4]Treaty of Friendship, Co-operation and Mutual Assistance, translation published in *New Times* (Moscow), no. 21, 21 May 1955.

[5]See Denise Folliot, ed., *Documents on International Affairs* (London: Oxford University Press, 1957), pp. 28–33, 102–8.

[6]Ibid., pp. 96–101.

[7]See Adam B. Ulam, *Expansion and Coexistence: Soviet Foreign Policy, 1917–73*, 2d ed. (New York: Praeger, 1974), p. 559; president's news conference, 27 October 1954, *Public Papers of the Presidents: Dwight D. Eisenhower, 1954*, p. 965.

[8]*New York Times*, 7 November 1954.

These negative reactions did not deter the Soviets from issuing to twenty-three European governments another invitation, on 13 November, to an "all-European conference." After reminding them of the German menace, which the western allies had let loose through the London and Paris agreements, the Soviet statement pointed out the end of any possibility for Austrian as well as German unification should they be ratified. To frustrate German militarism they called for a new system of European security to be established at a conference in Moscow or in Paris on 29 November 1955: "Postponement in convening this conference would be inexpedient inasmuch as consideration of ratification of the Paris agreements is beginning in December in certain European countries. Such ratification would complicate the whole European situation in a major degree and possibilities of settling the unresolved European problems, and first of all German problems."[9]

When the western allies finally issued a coordinated official reply to the Soviet Union, it was a combined response to the 23 October proposal for a meeting of foreign ministers and the 13 November proposal for a larger meeting on European collective security.[10] No acceptance of either proposal was possible until the question of ratification of the West German status had been completed and after some earnest of good faith on the Soviet part had been made, such as positive steps toward an Austrian treaty. As Secretary of State John Foster Dulles expressed it in a broadcast from Chicago on 29 November, the day of the U.S. communiqué, "we don't want to bother to talk with the Soviet representatives when their only purpose is to divide the free nations and to prevent their taking necessary measures for their own security."[11] Harrison Salisbury of the *New York Times* found:

> [that] the whole pattern of the Soviet proposal for a November 29 general European conference resembles one of Pavlov's famous conditioned reflexes. It has all been gone through before. Every time some step is taken in the West, which appears to bring a German military contribution one step closer to fulfillment, the conventional counter-response of the Soviet foreign office has been to propose a conference—just as the Russian scientist's dogs salivated automatically at the sound of the feeding bell.[12]

It was in this Pavlovian context that the West interpreted the Soviet-sponsored conference of 29 November. The meeting was held without western participation and became a forum for warnings against German

---

[9]Department of State *Bulletin* 31 (13 December 1954): 905–7.
[10]Ibid., pp. 901–3.
[11]Address by Dulles to National 4-H Club, 29 November 1954, Department of State *Bulletin* 31 (13 December 1954): 894.
[12]*New York Times*, 21 November 1954.

rearmament. The principal weapon, it seemed, would be the establishment of a joint military command comparable to NATO's to defend Eastern Europe against the increased dangers from the Atlantic Alliance. If the Paris agreements were ratified there would be "joint measures in the sphere of organization of their armed forces and their command."[13]

In clearing most of the agreements, western response was best expressed in the actions of the British House of Commons on 18 November, followed by similarly positive measures in the Norwegian Storting on 25 November and in the Italian Foreign Affairs Committee on 3 December. While the U.S. Senate would not consider the agreements until 1955, President Eisenhower had made a strong recommendation for prompt action on 16 November. The threat of an eastern military alliance, presented in the final declaration of the Moscow conference on 2 December, was judged to "consist of little more than long-winded threats."[14]

NATO's persistence in moving ahead with plans for ratification stimulated Soviet propaganda. Warnings were repeated and escalated. When Premier Georgi Malenkov resigned on 8 February 1955, Foreign Minister V. M. Molotov used the occasion to assert once again that the creation of a Western European Union would guarantee the establishment of a mutually protective society in the East.[15] On 21 March, while the French Council of the Republic pondered ratification, the Soviet Foreign Office published a communiqué, noting that eight Communist nations had agreed on the principles of a "unified command which will be created in the event of the ratification of the Paris agreements."[16] And when the Western European Union finally came into being on 5 May, the Soviets announced that the long-promised conference would convene in Warsaw on 11 May to put into effect the decision of 21 March.[17]

Special progaganda attention had been paid to the British, French, and Germans in frantic final efforts to stop the incorporation of West Germany into NATO. According to *Izvestia*, the British had forced the French to accept German militarism in order to ingratiate themselves with their American masters. They were the surrogate of the United States and as such would be rewarded with a special role in Europe.[18] To punish both

---

[13]Declaration of eight East European countries, Moscow, 2 December 1954, in Peter V. Curl, ed., *Documents in American Foreign Relations* (New York: Harper & Brothers, 1955), pp. 243–56.

[14]Richard B. Stebbins, ed., *The U.S. in World Affairs, 1954* (New York: Harper & Brothers, 1956), pp. 174–75.

[15]Hollis W. Barber, ed., *The U.S. in World Affairs, 1955* (New York: Harper & Brothers, 1957), p. 36.

[16]Ibid., p. 36; *Facts on Files* 15, no. 751 (17–23 March 1955): 91.

[17]Ibid. 15, no. 758 (5–11 May 1955): 159.

[18]TASS statement in *Izvestia*, 8 January 1955; *Current Digest of the Soviet Press* 7, no. 2 (23 February 1955): 17–18.

the British and French the Anglo-Soviet Treaty of 1942 and the French-Soviet Treaty of 1944 were placed in jeopardy. The allies had been warned in December 1954, and the following year in April the Council of Ministers duly sent the treaties to the Supreme Soviet Presidium for annulment proceedings, a unilateral action that mystified more than intimidated the French and British.[19] For German consumption the damage was less elliptical and less theoretical. By accepting membership in NATO they sacrificed all hope of a reunification of Germany. But should they reject the Paris agreements they could have both unification and a peace treaty.[20]

In hindsight the Soviet activity seemed to have been fruitless as the agreements moved inexorably toward completion. Yet there was enough softness and ambivalence in the French and German positions to keep Soviet hopes of influence alive. French fears of a German component in NATO were in continuing evidence. In December 1954 the French Assembly initially voted against rearming Germany, and if this was not the ultimate voice, it was partly because of party maneuvering and partly because of a knowledge that Britain and the United States would go ahead with Germany without France if the legislature reneged on France's commitment. The U.S. State Department had prepared alternative statements based on the decision of the French Assembly, one congratulating the Chamber of Deputies on its decision, the other intending "concerted action" excluding France.[21] But uncertainty about France remained. As James Reston expressed it, "Premier Pierre Mendes-France got his vote of confidence from the French National Assembly but France herself gets no vote of confidence here."[22] The Soviet Union had reason to believe that the French commitment to West Germany in NATO was always susceptible to change.

German concerns about the Paris agreements were equally deep but

[19]*Pravda* editorial, 10 April 1955; *Current Digest of the Soviet Press* 7, no. 15 (25 May 1955): 23. It is worth noting that the language of 1955 was not substantially different, although the recommendations were, from the Soviet charges against the North Atlantic Treaty in 1949 when Britain and France were chastised for abandoning their obligations under the 1942 and 1944 agreements "not to conclude any alliance and not to take part in any coalition directed against one of the High Contracting Parties." See memorandum of the Soviet government on the North Atlantic Treaty, 31 March 1949, as reported in *Pravda* and *Izvestia*, 1 and 2 April 1949 respectively, in *Current Digest of the Soviet Press* 1, no. 11 (3 May 1949): 31–33.

[20]Soviet government statement on German question, *Pravda* and *Izvestia*, 16 January 1955; *Current Digest of the Soviet Press* 7, no. 3 (2 March 1955): 23.

[21]Two alternative statements sent to Arthur Minnich at the White House for transmission to president, 27 December 1954, Papers of John Foster Dulles, Box 85, Princeton University, Princeton, New Jersey (hereafter cited as Dulles Papers). Photocopies from John Foster Dulles Files, Eisenhower Library, Abilene, Kansas (hereafter cited as Dulles Files).

[22]*New York Times*, 31 December 1954.

more variegated. On the one hand, there was resentment over French demands for a subordinate German role in Europe; on the other, there was apprehension that the acceptance of membership would make division permanent. Social Democrats appeared to weigh favorably the prospect of neutralization as the price for unification. Nationalists wondered if Germany would lose its bargaining power by throwing its lot in with the West. To these criticisms Chancellor Konrad Adenauer, supported by most of the Christian Democrats, countered by proclaiming in January 1955 that only a strong West could force the Soviet Union to concede free choice to Germans in the East: "I believe that the only concrete possibility of bringing about a relaxation of the conflict in Europe, and thus of achieving German unification, lies in an attempt by the Western European Union and the Atlantic Community, acting jointly, to seek a solution of the pending problems with the Soviet Union sooner or later."[23]

No matter how confident he sounded Adenauer had his own doubts about the West's commitment to Germany, and they included American and British as well as French resolve. Détente with the Soviet Union in the Four-Power summit that would follow in the summer of 1955 might be achieved at German expense. British Prime Minister Anthony Eden was too optimistic over prospects for disarmament within a new security pact, which could include, as the *Times* of London suggested in June, a recognition that there was no alternative to the division of Germany.[24] Memories of Nazi Germany and of Soviet suffering remained to be tapped. William Matthews, publisher of the *Arizona Star*, urged Americans in a letter to the *New York Times* to understand Russian obsessions about German military power and skepticism about NATO's ability to restrain it: "Unless we moderate our stand on recognition of the Oder-Neisse boundaries, we can scarcely expect the Russians to give up their valuable outpost of East Germany."[25] Small wonder that Adenauer could join the Social Democratic leaders in worrying about the possible sacrifice of German vital interests in the deliberations of the superpowers at Geneva. Less than three months after the Federal Republic had joined NATO, Adenauer wrote Secretary of State Dulles that "with the conclusion of the Geneva Conference we have entered into a new phase of East-West relations, which are no less dangerous than they have been in the past."[26] Given the volatility of the German mood, the Soviets not

---

[23]Konrad Adenauer, "Germany: The New Partner," *Foreign Affairs* 33, no. 2 (January 1955): 82.
[24]Terrence Prittie, *Konrad Adenauer, 1876–1967* (London: Tom Stacey, 1972), p. 246; *Times of London*, 16 June 1955.
[25]Letter to editor, *New York Times*, 19 June 1955.
[26]Konrad Adenauer, *Erinnerungen, 1953–1955*, 2 vols. (Stuttgart: Deutsche Verlags-Anstalt, 1966), p. 472.

unreasonably regarded the West German decision of May as an open question.

Whether or not the USSR was motivated by fear of the potential German contribution to NATO or by hope that the NATO action of May 1955 opened new opportunities to divide the West, its Warsaw Pact played a role in exacerbating fissures within the Atlantic Alliance. East Germany's membership in the Pact signified permanent separation of the East from the West. At the same time the Warsaw Pact from its inception held aloft a standing offer to the European allies to abandon NATO. In the preamble as well as in Article 11 of the treaty there was the promise of dissolution of the Pact, and with it the solution not only of German unification but also of European collective security. The means of achieving this desirable goal was the dismantling of the Atlantic Alliance and the removal of the United States from Europe. This interpretation of the Warsaw Pact does not exhaust the possibilities; in addition, the Pact legitimized Soviet military presence in Eastern Europe, offered a rampart behind which Communist forces could gather, and served to tighten Soviet control over its eastern neighbors.[27] These functions take on a special potency when considered in the context of East European history over the past twenty-five years. They were employed to justify Soviet troops in Hungary and Romania after the signing of the Austrian State Treaty in 1955, providing legal excuse for putting down Hungary's attempt to leave the bloc in 1956, and supplying the infrastructure for the invasion of Czechoslovakia in 1968. Valid as these judgments may be they apply to a growth of the organization after its inception. Germany and NATO still loom as the most significant focuses of the Warsaw Pact in 1955, whether its purposes were offensive or defensive.

NATO AND THE EMERGENCE OF THE WARSAW PACT

The West took into account the stated purposes of the new alliance and immediately discounted and trivialized them. NATO could not take the treaty seriously. The idea of a "counter-NATO" was a travesty of the western alliance; it would change in no way a relationship between the Soviet Union and its "satellites," a term that never characterized the relationship between the Soviet Union and its "allies." The Soviet forces

[27]For example, see Ulam, *Expansion and Coexistence*, p. 561; Korbonski, "The Warsaw Pact"; Z. Brzezinski, *Soviet Bloc: Unity and Conflict* (Cambridge, MA: Harvard University Press, 1960), p. 171; and Robin Remington, *The Warsaw Pact: Case Studies in Communist Conflict and Resolution* (Cambridge, MA: MIT Press), p. 6.

already controlled the East, and a cosmetic title would neither increase nor decrease that danger. As for the charges about German rearmament, the NATO countries found them difficult to accept. The question of German membership in the alliance had been a staple of NATO thinking from the time of the Korean War. If anything, the London and Paris agreements reduced the danger of German militarism by carefully circumscribing the specific contributions West Germany might make to NATO. Nuclear weapons, long-range missiles, and bombers were excluded from German manufacture.[28] The only rational explanation for Soviet distress would be their disappointment over the reinvigoration of the Alliance in October 1954 after the apparently mortal wounds inflicted on NATO from the collapse of the EDC two months before.

Consequently, when U.S. policymakers looked at the prospect of an anti-NATO bloc in the nine months before the signing of the treaty, they found it to be just another maneuver in the continuing Soviet effort to block the integration of the Federal Republic into NATO. It summoned memories of Soviet behavior in 1949. When the Federal Republic was established on 21 September 1949, within "a matter of days," as Deputy Undersecretary of State Robert Murphy pointed out, ". . . October 7 to be exact, the Soviet authorities created a puppet German government by military fiat in the East Zone and announced that this so-called 'German Democratic Republic,' set up without benefit of elections, was the legitimate spokesman of the German people."[29] The signing of the Warsaw Pact was an updating of the action of 1949. There should be no excuse for Germans to be beguiled by the empty promises that accompanied empty threats. Furthermore, Murphy believed that NATO should reject the Soviet accusation that the Paris agreements were provocative or indicative of a hardening of lines or of a repudiation of proposals for a relaxation of tensions. According to Cecil Lyon, director of the U.S. State Department's Office of German Affairs, "the truth is that the world situation is now kept in a deep freeze, because Soviet, not Western, policy is rigid; it is so because Soviet strategy has not changed one iota, in spite of what the spokesmen of the Kremlin may say a hundred times a day."[30]

These reactions in the State Department suggest that the perceived danger of the Warsaw Pact would not originate from concerns about new military strength in the Eastern bloc but from propaganda for a détente that accompanied the negotiations for the treaty. After Stalin's death in 1953, the new leaders of the Soviet Union appeared to be using the

---

[28]Stanley Hoffmann, *Gulliver's Troubles: Or, the Settling of American Foreign Policy* (New York: McGraw Hill, 1968), p. 413.

[29]Robert Murphy, "Germany in the Free World," Department of State *Bulletin* 32 (July 1955): 47.

[30]Cecil Lyon, "The New Germany," Department of State *Bulletin* 32 (31 January 1955): 187.

Warsaw Treaty as part of their campaign to rid Europe of all treaties,
especially the North Atlantic Treaty. The foreign ministers' meeting at the
NATO Council in December 1954 made no specific reference to the
military character of the potential treaty.[31] Instead of raising the issue of a
new Soviet-dominated military command as a reason for asking for more
monies or manpower from its members, the council communiqué warned
its members against being diverted by "some outward signs of flexibility"
on the part of the Soviet Union and only went through the motions of
observing that Soviet power was "backed by ever-increasing military
power."[32]

In his testimony before the Senate Foreign Relations Committee in
March 1955, General Alfred A. Gruenther, Supreme Allied Commander
Europe, underscored the absence of any new military threat from the East.
NATO was strong, compared with the situation of 1950. He reminded
his listeners of the familiar story that when General Eisenhower first came
to SHAPE all the Russians needed to march to the English Channel was a
sufficient supply of shoes. "They need more than shoes now." It is
noteworthy that Gruenther gave no consideration to the prospect that an
Eastern European alliance would change the balance of forces. The "80
satellite divisions" only created a problem of political reliability.[33] It is
equally worth noting that the prospective Soviet alliance aroused little
concern among senators. When Senator Alexander Wiley asked Secretary
Dulles in the course of the Senate's consideration of the London and Paris
agreements what significance such a pact would have for the West, he
replied confidently:

> ... the answer is zero, because of the fact that they have already
> completely dominated and completely run all the military force of
> their satellite countries, and to say now, that they are going to create
> unity between them and their satellites is somewhat absurd in view of
> the fact that they have already absorbed the satellites to such an
> extent, for most practical purposes including armament, they do not
> today and have not had for a long time any real independent
> existence.[34]

The most that was granted to the Warsaw Treaty when it came into
being in mid-May was its value as a political ploy just as it had been

---

[31]Verbatim record of the fiftieth meeting of the council, held in Paris on 17 December
1954, Box 85, Dulles Papers.

[32]Text of communiqué issued in Paris on 18 December 1954 by North Atlantic
Council, Department of State *Bulletin* 32 (3 January 1955): 3.

[33]U.S., Congress, Senate, Committee on Senate Foreign Relations, *NATO and Paris
Accords Relations with West Germany*, 84th Cong., 1st sess., 1955, pp. 2–3.

[34]U.S., Congress, Senate, Committee on Senate Foreign Relations, *Protocol on
Termination of Occupation Regime in the Federal Republic of Germany and a Protocol to
the North Atlantic Treaty*, 84th Cong., 1st sess., 1955, p. 16.

portrayed when the notion was raised in the fall of 1954. True, the *New York Times* cautioned that "it would be a mistake to discount the Warsaw pact too much, since it did open up possibilities for enlarging the Eastern bloc forces in the future and subjecting them to even greater Soviet control than in the past," but the editorial pays lip service to this future problem. Essentially, by using terms such as "Eastern NATO" or "Eastern 'anti-NATO' " as did the *New York Times*, or "Ost-Block NATO" in the *Frankfurter Allgemeine Zeitung*, the press was belittling the new organization. The fact that the treaty could be dissolved in a general accord, and that its announcement was timed to preparations for a Four-Power accord over Austria, made it an obvious bargaining move, as *Le Monde* observed. Similarly, the *Times* of London brushed aside any military significance and emphasized its political function. The "sudden flowering" of the principle of coexistence rather than the interbloc hostility caught the attention of the Moscow correspondent of the paper.[35]

The press commentary reflected the sentiment of western statesmen. Despite Soviet objections to West Germany's position in NATO, Prime Minister Eden claimed that he "did not set much store by this. I was sure that, once ratified, they would pass into history and be accepted with realism which is part of Communist practice."[36] Dulles said almost the same thing at a background conference he gave the press on 7 May 1955, when he recalled that at the NATO Council meeting in December the Soviets were "hurling threats about in the most violent way [saying] that if the Paris accords were ratified that would practically mean war." Dulles "prophesied" then that the West actually would be stronger as a consequence of the ratification, and he claimed that events proved him to be right.[37] There is little importance attached to the Warsaw Pact in this kind of reflection. Jean Chauvel, the shrewd French diplomatist, shared Dulles's and Eden's confidence when he made only passing reference to the Warsaw Pact in his memoirs, noting that the reason given for its conclusion was the western decision to ratify the Paris accords. Instead, Chauvel's brief reference mostly emphasized the Soviet Union's disposition for compromise, moderation, and détente, as evidenced by its actions in Vienna and Belgrade in May 1955 and in Geneva in July.[38] In short, the Warsaw Pact appeared to be evidence of Communist defeat. They had failed to stop the new Western European Union, and they attempted to mask their failure by accepting the Austrian State Treaty the day after they made their alliance and by accepting western proposals for a

---

[35]*New York Times*, 15 May 1955; *Frankfurter Allgemeine Zeitung*, 13 May 1955; *Le Monde*, 15 May 1955; *Times of London*, 10, 16 May 1955.

[36]Anthony Eden, *Full Circle* (Boston: Houghton Mifflin, 1960), p. 319.

[37]Press conference—background, 7 May 1955, Box 96, Dulles Papers.

[38]Jean Chauvel, *Commentaire: de Berne à Paris* (Paris: Fayard, 1973), p. 157.

conference on the reunification of Germany despite all their threats of the past year.

The Pact itself barely surfaced as even an issue amid the sense of triumph felt in Washington in May 1955. On the occasion of the secretary of state's report to the president on the events of "an historic week," the emphasis was on the Austrian State Treaty of 15 May and not the Warsaw Treaty of the previous day.[39] And on 17 May, in response to reporters' questions, the president touched on the Austrian treaty, the construction of B-52 planes, and the planned Big-Four summit meeting.[40] No one thought to ask about the significance of the "counter-NATO" established four days before, and Eisenhower never introduced the subject on his own. It is not surprising then to find in his memoirs an extensive commentary on both the Austrian treaty and the Geneva conference but only a single aside on the Warsaw Pact. The reference was to Premier Nikolai Bulganin's proposal for its dissolution, along with NATO's.[41] Dulles, as he recounted the exciting events of that month—the seating of West Germany in the NATO Council, the expected withdrawal of Soviet troops from Austria ("the first such withdrawal to have occurred in Europe since they took their forward position ten years ago"), and the Soviets' "planning a humble pilgrimage" to Yugoslavia—had nothing to say about the Warsaw Treaty.[42]

Behind the near disappearance of the Warsaw Pact from NATO's view lay a mosaic of events that helps to account for it. The images of London and Paris, Vienna and Belgrade, and then Geneva are parts of this pattern. The sequence began with the almost concurrent inauguration of Eisenhower and death of Stalin in 1953. It is not that the changing of the guard in either of the superpowers ushered in a new era of peace or even an immediate reduction of tension. The militance of Dulles alone would have precluded such a course, and the brutal Soviet repression of the East Berlin disturbance in June 1953 confirmed western belief in the consistence of a malignant Communist enemy in Moscow. Yet, in the words of Edmond Stillman and William Pfaff there was "a quality of indecision, a loss of spirit among the Communist parties of Eastern Europe which boded ill for Soviet ambitions."[43] Bound by its own ideological rigidity and

[39]"An Historic Week," report of the secretary of state to the president, 17 May 1955, Department of State *Bulletin* 32 (30 May 1955): 871.

[40]President's news conference, 18 May 1955, *Public Papers of the President: Dwight D. Eisenhower, 1955*, pp. 505–18.

[41]Dwight D. Eisenhower, *The White House Years: Mandate for Change* (Garden City, NY: Doubleday & Company, 1963), p. 517.

[42]News conference statement, press release, 24 May 1955, Department of State *Bulletin* 32 (6 June 1955): 914.

[43]Edmund Stillman and William Pfaff, *The New Politics: America and the Postwar World* (New York: Howard McCann, 1961), p. 63.

bemused by the contest in the Soviet Union over the succession to Stalin, the Eisenhower administration had difficulty in finding, let alone exploiting, the cracks in the Soviet empire.

Still, the disarray in the Soviet world after Stalin's death was a fact, and it was manifested over the next years in the successful rise to power of Malenkov, Bulganin, and Khrushchev as well as the concomitant decline in Molotov's influence, despite his nominal presence at most diplomatic functions in 1955. Even if they articulated the same goals as in the past, the new leaders adopted a style of "sweet reasonableness" in making familiar proposals. Was it possible, speculated Salisbury in November 1954, that George Kennan's idea on firm containment was indeed producing the mellowing he had predicted almost a decade before?[44]

This was not the signal that Dulles read into Soviet behavior in the Austrian treaty or in proposals for a collective security agreement. If the Soviet Union had retreated, it was only a tactical withdrawal before the West's firmness. The neutralization of Germany and the destruction of NATO were to be pursued by other more guileful but equally dangerous means. NATO complacency, as a consequence of a milder Soviet manner, could be disastrous. Instead, Dulles heard the soothing notes and not the strident ones of the Warsaw Treaty, the latter being muffled by the Soviets' nullification of their threats. Four days before the treaty was signed in Moscow, Jacob Malik revived disarmament proposals at the UN Disarmament Subcommittee in London. It would involve immediate evacuation of troops of the major powers from German territory, including presumably the territory of East Germany, a major ally in the Warsaw Pact. Three days before the treaty's completion Bulganin announced from Warsaw "a favorable attitude toward the idea" of a summit meeting. And just one day after the treaty was in effect the Soviet Union signed an agreement, accepting for the most part western terms for the removal of their troops from Austria. Whatever dangers Dulles foresaw in the future, it is understandable that he did not see them emerging from the new military character of the eastern alliance.

THE GENEVA FALLOUT

Geneva and not Warsaw symbolized to the secretary of state the hurdles ahead for American leadership within the alliance. It was the putative peaceful objectives of the summit meeting in July that preoccupied him and not the military mobilization of the new Warsaw Pact.

---

[44]*New York Times*, 21 November 1954.

Dulles feared that his allies would be lured into Soviet traps. The British were particularly susceptible as Prime Minister Eden floated his "zone of equalized armaments" in Germany, which would stretch sixty miles on either side of the internal frontier.[45] British softness was a matter of concern. In speaking with Congressman John Vorys shortly before leaving for Geneva, Dulles observed that there was a belief in Europe that, if there were no meeting, "left-wingers" in Britain might carry elections there.[46] Even Chancellor Adenauer, normally a model of rectitude and consistency from the American perspective, seemed temporarily carried away by the prospect of Soviet willingness to unite Germany. One month before the Geneva meeting Adenauer informed British Foreign Minister Harold Macmillan at the Waldorf-Astoria in New York that the Soviets probably wanted détente and might even abandon East Germany to achieve it.[47]

However, there was no alternative to risking entrapment. The president had committed himself and his secretary of state. As early as 10 May he told the Republican Women's National Conference that he and Dulles "stand ready to do anything, to meet with anyone, anywhere, as long as . . . there is any slightest idea or chance of furthering this great cause of peace." Still, he claimed to have no illusions about spectacular results. He felt that "Foster and I should be able to detect whether the Soviets really intend to introduce a tactical change that could mean, for the next few years at least, some real easing of tensions." For Eisenhower, the primary pitfall was in raising the public's hopes too high.[48]

Dulles was much less sanguine in his expectations. For one thing the history of summit meetings gave no reason for satisfaction. From Versailles to Yalta the record was dismal. Both the president and the secretary of state were conscious of how President Woodrow Wilson had fared at the first great summit meeting in 1919 and were determined to avoid his fate. Careful attention was paid to protocol, as Dulles recalled the loss of status Wilson had suffered by associating as an equal with chiefs of governments. The president's status was diminished by his consorting with prime ministers. Would Eisenhower's prestige also be tarnished? Would he even recognize slights to his office if they were inflicted on him? Dulles was uncertain and agonized over accepting an invitation for the president to dine with the French premier at Geneva.[49] The more substantive question of Europeans taking advantage of Americans surfaced as well; the aura of excessive concessions through executive agreements had been

        [45]Prittie, *Adenauer*, p. 247; Eden, *Full Circle*, p. 324.
        [46]Telephone conversation with John Vorys, 7 July 1955, Box 1, Dulles Papers. Photocopies from Dulles Files.
        [47]Harold Macmillan, *Tides of Fortune, 1947–1955* (New York: Harper & Brothers, 1969), p. 607.
        [48]*Public Papers of the Presidents: Dwight D. Eisenhower, 1955*, p. 484; Eisenhower, *Mandate for Change*, p. 506.
        [49]*New York Times*, 17 July 1955.

only recently exorcised by the publication of the Yalta papers in the spring of 1955 after a decade of political mischief. Eisenhower rejected the charge that his participation at the meeting of the Big Four powers was an act of appeasement: "There is no appeasement in my heart that I know about."[50] Yet, Livingston Merchant, assistant secretary of state and friend of Dulles, remembered the secretary's concern "over the respectability that would be given to the Russians by being photographed in social gatherings, or group photographs with the president and with the French and British heads of government."[51]

Dulles's apprehensions were clear: he was convinced that the Soviets would use Geneva to continue their policy of splitting the allies and driving the United States out of Europe. Three weeks before the meetings the secretary of state outlined his estimation of Soviet expectations from the summit meeting. Generally, they wanted the "appearance of moral and social acceptance on a basis of equality of what will help to maintain satellite rule, by disheartening potential resistance, and help increase neutralism by spreading the impression that only 'proper blocs,' and not moral issues, are involved." Specifically, they wanted an "acceptance in principle of a European security system, which will tend to eliminate U.S. 'bases' and U.S. troop organization in Europe and involve acceptance of its Soviet dominated 'Warsaw' system...."[52] This was one of the few occasions in which the Pact figured at all into the American projection of East-West relations, and its consideration was hedged and ultimately nullified by the quotation marks set around it.

What followed at Geneva seemed to confirm Dulles's worst expectations. The Soviets took full advantage of the "spirit of Geneva" to pursue their divisive program. Their smiles were more unnerving than their scowls. They refused to allow on the agenda any discussion of the subjugation of East Europe; they proposed a security pact that would have destroyed NATO; and they would consider German unification only after the military organizations—NATO and the Warsaw Pact—had been dismantled. If mutual dissolution of blocs were not immediately possible, they would accept a treaty between the two blocs whereby the "member states of the North Atlantic Treaty Organization and of the Paris agreement on the one hand, and the parties to the Warsaw Treaty, on the other hand, undertake to refrain from the use of armed force against one another."[53] The Pact was fully employed as a Soviet weapon in the assault

[50]President's news conference, 10 May 1955, p. 516, *Public Papers of the Presidents: Dwight D. Eisenhower, 1955,* p. 516.

[51]Livingston Merchant in John Foster Dulles Oral Histories, Dulles Papers.

[52]Handwritten estimation of what Soviets seek from summit, 1 July 1955, Box 92, Dulles Papers.

[53]Soviet proposals for treaty between blocs, 5th Plenary Meeting of Geneva, 21 July 1955, Box 92, Dulles Papers. The idea of a nonaggression pact was a continuing concern of Khrushchev, as Spaak noted in his conversation in 1956. See Paul-Henri Spaak,

against NATO. Dulles claimed that the Soviet leaders exhibited an "unconcealed anxiety . . . to obtain a 'relaxing' of tension with the Western world, . . . not because of any change in their basic purpose but because of their own need, external, for new policies."[54]

Yet, for all the gloomy predictions the Soviet gains at Geneva were limited and predictable. If they showed a peaceful temper to the world in urging the end of alliances and advocating a new system of collective security, their propaganda was less successful in projecting a wish for accommodation than was Eisenhower's "Open Skies" proposal, wherein both nations would exchange blueprints of their installations and provide each other with facilities for aerial photoinspection. The president was as effective as Nikita Khrushchev in promoting a spirit of goodwill, and very likely more sincere when he recorded his "great satisfaction in telling him [Khrushchev] that the entire western world would cheerfully abide by the decision of the German electorate, regardless of the outcome."[55] And while the Soviets followed up the summit conference with an invitation to Adenauer to visit Moscow and then capped the visit with the Soviet recognition of the Federal Republic of Germany, this was not necessarily a Soviet coup. As a result, West Germany neither withdrew from NATO nor recognized East Germany.

In the summer of 1955 the Geneva summit meeting wound down, ending, as did the subsequent meeting of foreign ministers in Geneva three months later, in a renewed stalemate. Nevertheless, the summit meeting entered into history as a symbol of a temporary softening of the mood of the Cold War. It gave a human face to communism and opened the world to the closed men of the Kremlin, who even had spoken of the horrors of nuclear warfare as the ultimate imperative for peace.

The uprisings and suppressions in Hungary and Poland and the threats of war over Berlin in the next few years helped to deflate "the spirit of Geneva." These events also may have obscured what Dulles fitfully recognized, namely, the outcome of the West's contest with the East in Geneva was more successful than unsuccessful. The Geneva summit may have been a testament to the limits of Communist power in the post-Stalin era. It is not beyond the realm of possibility that the Kremlin would rather have had West Germany, if it had to be armed, constrained within NATO. For all the talk about dismantling NATO, the organization was a known entity, and an immediate prospect of West German aggression was no greater than that of NATO aggression. If the Soviets could not remove

The Continuing Battle: Memoirs of a European, 1936–1966 (Boston: Little Brown & Company, 1971), p. 409.

[54]U.S. post-Geneva policy—Dulles comments, 15 August 1955, Box 92, Dulles Papers.

[55]Eisenhower, Mandate for Change, p. 523.

the Americans from Europe at the moment and could not prevent the militarization of West Germany, they would settle for a divided Europe, the status quo of 1945.[56] Geneva then symbolized the success of the United States and its NATO allies in constraining Soviet power, even if this success could not include the freeing of Eastern Europe from Soviet control. In this light the invitation to Adenauer to visit Moscow, offered in June before Geneva and implemented in September after Geneva, with considerable ceremony, was a confession that the Soviet Union had failed to prevent the integration of Western Europe in the Atlantic Alliance.[57]

The Warsaw pact assumed another function for Soviet diplomacy when the initial plan for dismantling was abandoned. It was no less a pawn, but it became one that served to legitimize the division of Europe between the two blocs. The recognition of West Germany implied that the Soviets accepted for the time being a divided Germany even if the western half would be completely western in orientation. Rather than being scuttled, the Warsaw Pact wished to coexist with NATO on terms of equality. But such an equation of the two blocs was not palatable to the West in 1955. When Dulles reviewed the international situation in December of that year at the opening session of the North Atlantic Council in Paris, the only reference he would make to the existence of the Warsaw Pact was that Soviet rigidity over Germany showed that they were "nervous about the status of their whole satellite structure."[58]

NATO, THE WARSAW PACT,
AND DISENGAGEMENT

The minimal role of the Pact in Soviet and American diplomacy in 1955 changed radically over the next twenty-five years. The rise of the organization as a factor in East-West relations came about partly because of the position it occupied in the crises in Budapest in 1956 and in Prague in 1968. The Warsaw Pact first came into prominence in world headlines as Soviet tanks rolled into Budapest to prevent Hungary from detaching itself

---

[56]Hoffmann, *Gulliver's Troubles*, p. 413; See also Pierre Melandri, "Les Etats-Unis face à l'unification de l'Europe, 1945–1954," 3 vols. (Ph.D. dissertation, Université de Paris, 1977), 3:979; and Walter C. Clemens, Jr., "The Future of the Warsaw Pact," *Orbis* 11, no. 4 (Winter 1968): 1013.

[57]Acting Secretary of State Herbert Hoover reported for Dulles "that the one new thing from the Russian side is their apparent acceptance of West German participation in NATO." Minutes and Documents of the Cabinet Meetings of President Eisenhower, 22 July 1955, Reel 3, Eisenhower Library, Abilene, Kansas.

[58]Dulles's review of the international situation at the opening session of the ministerial meeting of the North Atlantic Council, Paris, 15 December 1955, Box 96, Dulles Papers.

from the organization. The Prague Spring ended when five members of the
Pact invaded Czechoslovakia in August 1968 to force that state to respect
the obligations of membership. These momentous events alone would have
increased the visibility and importance of the Pact in the eyes of the West
as well as in the policy of the Soviet Union. But equally important was the
ongoing activity of the organization in pressing over the years for an all-
European collective security pact and for the neutralization of Germany. In
the long run the discomfiture in NATO over the persistence of these efforts
accorded the Pact a legitimacy among NATO members, which its military
activities by themselves would not have achieved.

Almost every communiqué issued after meetings of the Warsaw
Pact's Political Consultative Committee from 1956 to 1965 called for a
nonaggression treaty with NATO as a first step toward a European
settlement.[59] Since NATO ignored this litany for the most part, a case can
be made that the organization was a minor actor in the Soviet drive; the
United Nations was its major platform. The Rapacki Plan, the major
vehicle for neutralization in the 1950s, was launched in October 1957 at
the 12th session of the General Assembly of the United Nations rather
than at a meeting of the Pact's Political Consultative Committee. Yet, the
Rapacki proposal for an atom-free zone in Central Europe, embracing both
Germanies,was at the heart of Warsaw Pact plans.[60] And the standing
invitation to mutual termination extended to NATO was a constant encouragement to those in the West who looked for a break in the Cold War.

The last years of Dulles's life were filled with worries over one or
another ally succumbing to temptations from the East. These were not
simply a function of paranoia. Canadian Foreign Minister Pearson, writing
in the fall of 1955, warned the West against excessive relaxation. He
admitted that the Geneva summit was "a more comfortable and relaxing
place for a meeting than 'summits' often are," but coupled this admission
with the admonition that if there is "approaching peaceful coexistence, it
will be competitive coexistence." In the "sunshine of Geneva there was the
danger of giving away too much; NATO must resist, for example, any
limitations on armaments which would create an imbalance in Europe."[61]
Britain's Labour opposition leader in NATO affairs, Denis Healey,
pointed out the consequences of intoxication from the spirit of Geneva, and
cited as a case in point Foreign Minister Macmillan's attribution of a
genuine change in the Soviet outlook on the world in a speech he had made
before the Foreign Press Association on 22 September 1955. This was

---

[59]Note proposals made at meetings on 24 May 1958, 4 February 1960, 28–29 March
1961, and 19–20 January 1965, listed in Francis A. Beer, *Alliances: Latent War Com-
munities in the Contemporary World* (New York: Holt, Rinehart & Winston, 1970), p. 167.

[60]Korbonski, "The Warsaw Pact."

[61]Lester Pearson, "After Geneva: A Greater Task for NATO," *Foreign Affairs* 34,
no. 1 (October 1955): 14–22.

wishful thinking according to Healey; the Russians will change, in the words of Khrushchev, "when shrimps learn to whistle."[62]

Caveats notwithstanding, the lure of "disengagement" was a primary by-product of the summit conference, and the Warsaw Pact was a useful instrument for its dissemination throughout the decade. The impact on Germany inevitably was powerful, given the inherent ambiguities in Adenauer's position on unification. He had promised that West Germany's ties with NATO would produce a weakening of Soviet opposition to unification. Instead, German membership in NATO had produced a hardening of lines, as East Germany became a full member of the Pact. A possible route open to him was withdrawal from NATO and a subsequent freeing of East Germany to join a new neutralized nation. Left and Right wings were tempted. Nationalists had long urged abandonment of Adenauer's western orientation and adoption of a policy of playing West against the East. Left-wing pacifists were equally critical and even more tempted, since neutralization was a desirable objective to many of them and NATO a standing assault on their sensibilities. Erich Ollenhauer, leader of the Social Democratic party, had argued that the ties to NATO would result in the permanent division of Germany.[63] Again, the disposability of the Pact was an earnest to them of Soviet openness for unification on reasonable terms.

Adenauer's position was not helped by the spectacular implications of a major NATO field exercise immediately after Germany's accession to NATO—"Operation Carte Blanche." At the very moment that the Big Four powers were meeting in Berlin, the value of the alliance became suspect to many Germans in the West. Operation Carte Blanche, an air maneuver demonstrating the capabilities of tactical atomic weapons against enemy bases theoretically would take a toll of 1,700,000 civilian lives before the enemy had been repulsed. Such a projected disaster not only stimulated a neutralist spirit but also gave support to proponents of an independent German deterrent in the new German defense ministry.[64] It is not surprising that the idea of an atom-free area in Central Europe would find advocates in sectors of the population outside the Social Democratic Party. Only the enormous prestige of the inflexible chancellor, abetted by visceral distrust in Soviet promises, stemmed the tide of disengagement in Germany.

---

[62]Denis Healey, "When Shrimps Learn to Whistle: Thoughts after Geneva," *International Affairs* 32, no. 1 (January 1956): 1–3.

[63]Ollenhauer speech of 15 December 1954, *Das Parlement*, 24 December 1954. See Lawrence S. Kaplan, "NATO and Adenauer's Germany: Uneasy Partnership," *International Organization* 15, no. 4 (November 1961): 621–22.

[64]Gordon A. Craig, "Germany and NATO: the Rearmament Debate, 1950–1958," in Klaus Knorr, ed., *NATO and American Security* (Princeton, NJ: Princeton University Press, 1959), pp. 240–41.

Other members of the alliance lacked the intensity of feelings over the unification of Germany; in fact, some of them, notably France, believed that the continuing division was not an unreasonable tradeoff for the rearmament of the western portion of the country. Yet, the attractions of détente and of ending the inherently unstable confrontation in Central Europe affected all Europeans. As Michael Howard stated in 1958, "the negotiation of a Russian military withdrawal in return for an equivalent military withdrawal by the West, will remain a standing challenge to the statesmen of Western Europe and the United States."[65] Their appeal was reflected in the many variations of Prime Minister Eden's plans for phased disarmament and particularly in the specific plan for limited disengagement put forth by Hugh Gaitskell and Denis Healey of the Labour Party, both of whom were fully sensitive to Soviet wiles. It involved a "disengaged area" in Central Europe that would include a reunited Germany and all the Warsaw Pact countries except Albania. The United States and the Soviet Union would jointly guarantee neutralization of this territory and the removal of all foreign troops. The plan's chances for realization rested on the assumption of a willingness on the part of the Soviet Union to dissolve the Warsaw Treaty Organization. NATO would remain in place after the Federal Republic had withdrawn.[66]

Even more influential in the late 1950s were ideas on total disengagement, which were advocated by retired American diplomat George Kennan in his Reith radio lectures for the BBC delivered in London in 1957 on six successive Sundays beginning on 10 November and published as a book in the following year. If the Gaitskell plan would eliminate the Warsaw Pact, the Kennan plan would cut the heart out of NATO as well. Drastic though Kennan's position was, it would be more welcome to the Soviet Union than Gaitskell's, since a Soviet withdrawal from Central Europe would be matched by "a compensatory withdrawal on the Western side," perhaps even the withdrawal of American forces from all of Europe. The end product, according to Kennan, would be the nullification of all nuclear weapons for all parties and possibly the end of conventional standing armies. Once the Soviet Union was freed of its fears over NATO and Germany, presumably liberalization of controls would follow in the East. While NATO as such was not to be dismantled, its new minimal functions would soon cause atrophy. NATO countries would still require, he admitted, "in addition to the guarantees embodied in the NATO Pact, some sort of continuing local arrangements for their own defense." But this was not the real issue. "We must get over this obsession that the Russians

---

[65]Michael Howard, "Disengagement and Western Security," *International Affairs* 34, no. 4 (October 1958): 469.

[66]Ibid., p. 470.

are yearning to attack and occupy Western Europe, and that this is the principal danger."[67]

Mostly because of their timing the shock waves from the Reith lectures were seismic in their effects. The major charges were made just a few weeks in advance of the NATO heads of government meeting at Paris in December 1957, and followed the announcement of the successful Soviet launching of the first earth satellite, the *Sputnik*, with its intimations of Russian superiority in intercontinental ballistic missiles. Kennan was not daunted by this conjunction of events any more than he had been by the terrible price paid by the Hungarians for their revolt in the previous year. He urged his listeners to heed not only the threats of the Soviet Union but also the promises that emanated from Khrushchev's petitions for "an agreed gradual withdrawal of troops from Germany." The present dangers in Europe would continue for only as long as the Soviets felt the need to dominate.[68]

As for the Communist response to Kennan's propositions, none was more eloquent than that which Polish Foreign Minister Adam Rapacki already had offered before the United Nations on 2 October 1957 and renewed after the Reith lectures in a formal note to the United States on 14 February 1958. Kennan recognized these symbiotic connections in his memoirs, but he never came to grips with the substance of the U.S. response to Rapacki's communication. Without nuclear weaponry, American Ambassador to Poland Jacob Beam responded, the West would be exposed to the superior forces of the Soviet Union.[69]

The reaction within NATO was less diplomatic than Beam's note. Abuse poured in from all sides. "My punishment was not long in coming," as Kennan noted. "I had, after all, offended all the leading NATO statesmen now in power and some who were not."[70] While former Secretary of State Dean Acheson led the pack with a scathing *ad hominem* attack on ideas that "are almost as vague as the style is seductive,"[71] Dulles, Adenauer, and Selwyn Lloyd were not far behind. They all translated his views into a general American abandonment of Europe. The Soviet forces would be sitting next to the neutralized area, whereas American troops would be an ocean away from Europe.

---

[67]George F. Kennan, *Russia, the Atom, and the West* (New York: Harper & Brothers, 1958), p. 62.

[68]George F. Kennan, *Memoirs: 1950–1963* (Boston: Little Brown & Company, 1972), pp. 240–41.

[69]Jacob D. Beam (U.S. ambassador to Poland) to Polish Deputy Foreign Minister Jozef Winiewicz, 3 May 1958, Department of State *Bulletin* 38 (19 May 1958): 821–22.

[70]Kennan, *Memoirs*, p. 249.

[71]Dean Acheson, "The Illusion of Disengagement," *Foreign Affairs* 36, no. 3 (April 1958): 374.

Disengagement never materialized in the 1950s, but it was not because the objectives were not worthwhile. It was simply unrealizable given the geopolitical bases of the two superpowers. The judgment of NATO statesmen was that its implementation would undo the sense of security that had permitted the renascence of Europe over the past decade. The real danger, as Michael Howard argued, was "not military but political and moral."[72] Would Europe defend itself without an American presence on the front line or without a nuclear deterrent as a vital source of psychic support? NATO's answer was negative. Kennan sensed another reason for failure, namely, that neither side genuinely wanted change. Quoting the perceptive French observer Raymond Aron, he concluded that "a clear partition of Europe is considered, rightly or wrongly, to be less dangerous than any other arrangement."[73]

Whichever the direction disengagement would take, the Warsaw Pact had its place in the Soviet scheme. If it had succeeded, the Warsaw Pact would have been dismantled but not before it also had served as a valuable aid in dismantling NATO. When disengagement as an issue faded at the end of the Eisenhower administration, the Pact remained as a rampart of an organized eastern bloc as well as a symbol of a permanent division of Germany.

NATO AND THE WARSAW PACT AS EQUALS: 1968–81

The U-2 incident froze relations between Eisenhower and Khrushchev in 1960, and the next few years brought new issues to the fore. In all the agonizing over the problems of the disengagement of forces in Europe, the Warsaw Pact had been on the periphery of NATO's vision of the problem. Its eye was always on the Soviet Union and not the Soviet Union in association with its allies. NATO leaders had paid attention to the Pact only when the Kremlin presented it as a pawn in its diplomatic games with the West. It figured in the mutual dissolution of both alliances as well as in the nonaggression pacts that Khrushchev periodically presented, and it was a part of the package linking it with NATO under a new European security organization. But when none of the above found their mark, the Soviets showed a harsher visage to the West in the U-2 issue of 1960, in the Berlin Wall of 1961, and in the Cuban missile crisis of 1962. It was in this period that the refashioning of the Warsaw Pact as a significant

---

[72]Howard, "Disengagement and Western Security," p. 475.
[73]Kennan, *Memoirs*, p. 253.

military entity began, which in turn moved from the periphery to the center of NATO's vision.

The acting out of the Brezhnev Doctrine by the Pact in order to suppress the putative defection of Czechoslovakia in 1968 proved to be a watershed in NATO's perception of the eastern bloc. Prior to that time the minor attention that it had received in the West placed it in the context of Soviet problems with its neighbors; for example, troubles with Albania which eventually left the organization, or discontent with Romania that limited its participation. In 1955 the Pact did not even rate a separate entry in the *New York Times* index, and for the next twelve years only a handful of its listings concerned the organization. Rarely would a statement about the Pact evoke a response in the West. Just such a rare occasion was a speech delivered in March 1966 at the height of NATO's crisis in France, which asserted that "should NATO lose some of its aggressive character, this would be correspondingly reflected in the Warsaw Pact. It is logical that should NATO be liquidated, there would no longer be any need for the Warsaw Pact which would disappear."[74] These were the words spoken by Valerian Zorin, Soviet ambassador to France, at the time of NATO's crisis over its position in France and in anticipation of President Charles de Gaulle's visit to Moscow. Although no answer was immediately forthcoming, Harlan Cleveland, U.S. ambassador to NATO, retorted eighteen months later, after NATO's headquarters had been moved from Paris to Brussels, that the Atlantic Alliance would remain in effect no matter what may be the fate of the Warsaw Pact.[75]

After 1968 consciousness of the Pact's existence permeated every area of NATO. The trauma over Czechoslovakia slowed but did not derail a powerful movement toward mutual and balanced force reductions (MBFR) that was fueled by the European members of NATO and expressed in the Harmel Report of 1967.[76] The impetus for MBFR, coinciding with American absorption in the Vietnam War, brought in the Pact as a partner in the enterprise. The Warsaw bloc and not the United Nations was the forum for the eastern response and for the planning that led to the Helsinki conference on security and cooperation in Europe and to the Vienna talks on MBFR.[77] At Helsinki the Soviet Union won both the long-sought western acceptance of the status quo in the East and a new and equal status for its Warsaw Pact. These gains were more than symbolic. After years of studiously snubbing the Warsaw alliance, in

[74]Statement of Valerian Zorin, Soviet ambassador to France, 17 March 1966, *Facts on File* 26, no. 1329 (31 March–6 April 1966): 115.

[75]*New York Times*, 13 October 1967.

[76]Thomas W. Wolfe, *Soviet Power and Europe, 1945–1974* (Baltimore: Johns Hopkins University Press, 1970), pp. 276–77.

[77]Dale R. Herspring, "The Warsaw Pact at 25," *Problems of Communism* 29, no. 2 (September–October 1980): 4.

December 1970 NATO communiqués began to mention routinely the Pact as a negotiator in the talks that would lead to the Helsinki agreements. By 1972 the phrase "bloc to bloc" implied full equality.[78]

The Warsaw Pact in the 1970s took on more than an appearance of equality. In its strengthened military form it raised alarm within NATO that the organization was superior to NATO's and that it was a dangerous antagonist growing stronger as NATO grew weaker. Alarms like this were not new in NATO's history. What was different in the reports of the past decade was the attribution of power to the bloc and not just to the Soviet Union and its manipulated satellites. Western commentators underscored the qualitative and quantitative superiority they now saw in the East by counting the differences in manpower and weaponry between NATO and all the member countries of the eastern alliance. In its annual reports the London-based International Institute for Strategic Studies tracked the growing imbalance in all varieties of conventional weaponry by listing figures that were inflated by the inclusion of allies of the Soviet Union. Not that the commentators saw the Warsaw Pact as a monolith; the *de facto* exclusion of Albania and the widely known qualifications that Romania had placed upon its membership were duly noted. Still, such knowledge did not diminish the Pact's new stature, since the Romanian stance could be likened to France's captious behavior within the Atlantic Alliance.

Even when a ray of sunshine was visible, which was not often in the mid-1970s, the Pact was the focus of observation. For example, NATO's Economic Committee noted a well-documented report on the falling birthrate of the Pact nations, which will widen a population gap in favor of NATO. But even this small satisfaction would have to be deferred for a decade, as there would be no serious shortage of eastern manpower in the 1970s and early 1980s.[79]

When NATO ultimately mobilized at the end of the 1970s to seek a reversal of the imbalance between East and West, there was no counterpart effort to reduce the status of the Pact no matter how many doubts the Soviet Union may have had about the military effectiveness of its allies. Articles in prominent journals continued to use titles such as "NATO and the Warsaw Pact," as if there were no doubt that one was the counterpart of the other.[80] The equality was official as well. In 1979 the Department of State *Bulletin* issued a special "NATO-Warsaw Pact Balance Sheet,"

---

[78]See final communiqué of NATO ministerial meeting, Brussels, 4 December 1970, *Atlantic Community Quarterly* 9, no. 1 (Spring 1971): 103. Secretary General Joseph Luns spoke at Bonn about "bloc to bloc" talks on 22 November 1972. *Atlantic Community Quarterly* 11, no. 1 (Spring 1973): 55.

[79]*New York Times*, 5 March 1972.

[80]For example, see "NATO and the Warsaw Pact: Good-Small vs Good-Big," *The Economist* 27, no. 7145 (9 August 1980): 35–38.

drawn from the International Institute for Strategic Studies, in which the Soviet Union was not identified in the head note. "Soviet allies" was as close as the analysis comes to mentioning the USSR.[81]

Twenty-five years after its inauspicious birth the quotations should be removed from the "counter-NATO" skepticism of 1955. The Pact occupies a place in the consciousness of the western alliance that had not been foreseen a generation ago, doubtlessly not even by the Soviet Union. This does not mean that the Warsaw Pact is as powerful an entity as NATO rhetoric has suggested in recent years, or that it has fulfilled all of the expectations of the Soviet Union. The internal divisions within the Pact are probably as deep or deeper than those of NATO in 1981; the Polish crisis of 1980–81 was a symptom of its malaise. Nor does it mean that the "satellites" of the Soviet Union have become the equivalents of the "allies" of the United States in NATO. It does mean, however, that the Warsaw Pact has succeeded in impressing upon NATO its status as an equal a generation after its inception as an artificial "counter-NATO." This is no small achievement in view of its stature in 1955.

---

[81]"NATO-Warsaw Pact Balance Sheet," Department of State *Bulletin* 79 (April 1979): 3.

NATO and the Warsaw Pact:
The Present and Future

BOLESLAW ADAM BOCZEK

Lawrence S. Kaplan's historical review of the NATO-Warsaw Pact relationship, included in this volume, shows how NATO's perception of the Pact has changed in the past twenty-five years from discounting the Soviet-led alliance as a travesty of NATO to gradually recognizing the Pact, first as a militarily equal organization, then as a dangerous antagonist rapidly increasing its capabilities, and now, to all appearances, searching through its hegemonic leader for military superiority over the western alliance. This ominous development is perceived by NATO as posing a grave threat to the balance of power in the European theater. Such a perception of the Pact has been explicit in all recent statements of the North Atlantic Council and other enunciations of the western alliance.[1] Yet this perception is not necessarily shared by all layers of public opinion in the European members of NATO. A growing perception gap seems to exist between the official pronouncements of NATO governments on defense needs, especially in the area of the long-range theater nuclear forces (LRTNF), and some sections of European society opposed to NATO's plans to counter the Soviet threat to Western Europe.

It is the Soviet Union itself that represents the major component of the military equation between the East and the West in that it provides, in addition to its military and ideological leadership, the bulk of the conventional forces of the Pact and controls all nuclear weapons and their means of delivery available to the alliance. However, setting aside the fact that the USSR is a military superpower in its own right, the Warsaw Pact has become a vital and helpful element of Soviet military and political strategy. In reviewing the Pact after twenty-five years, another contributor to this volume, Andrzej Korbonski, analyzes the role played by it as a tool of Soviet diplomacy and military strategy and an instrument designed to

---

[1]Typical is the following statement in the Final Communiqué of the North Atlantic Council of 12 December 1980: "The enormous growth over a number of years of Warsaw Pact and in particular Soviet military power gives rise to legitimate concern in Europe and throughout the world. This build-up contradicts the frequent assurances by the Warsaw Pact countries that their aim is not military superiority." *NATO Review* 29, no. 1 (February 1981): 25–26.

maintain the political cohesion of the Soviet bloc. While adding further to this train of thought, this essay also will focus on what has emerged as the salient theme of NATO's perception of the Warsaw Pact today; namely, concern about the threat to the balance of forces in Europe inherent in the Pact's growing military superiority in the Central European theater, both in conventional forces and in LRTNF. Briefly summarized will be the military balance between NATO and the Pact and subsequently NATO's response to its perception of this balance, including plans to strengthen the military capabilities of the West and determination to engage in meaningful arms control talks with the East.

After more than twenty-five years of the Warsaw Pact's existence, the military and political advantages as well as the problems that the alliance provides to its leader should be appreciated by the North Atlantic Alliance. Militarily, the Pact secures for the Soviet Union a wide buffer zone of allied territory in Central Europe for both defensive and offensive purposes. These advantages could be secured on the basis of the otherwise existing bilateral arrangements, but there is no doubt that the coordinating machinery and the common institutions of the Pact make it much easier for the Soviet Union to implement its military strategy in Europe. Apart from the questions of the combat role, efficiency, and political reliability of the East European allies of the Soviet Union, the sheer size and utility of the satellite armed forces cannot be entirely discounted.[2] However, more than the Pact's role as a military alliance it is its usefulness as an instrument of political and ideological orthodoxy and of control maintained by the Soviet Union over its Eastern European allies that is emphasized in most western analyses. As a major signal in the rules of the game between the East and the West, the Pact formalizes in Europe the territorial range of what the Soviet Union considers its vital core interests, both militarily and ideologically, in the defense of which it is ready to use military force and even risk a general conflagration.

Yet despite the dominant position of the Soviet Union in its alliance with the East European countries, it is noted by some perceptive observers of the Pact that Soviet hegemony must not be exaggerated. The western alliance has been undergoing a continual series of crises, but the Warsaw Pact is not without its strains. The recalcitrance of Romania and the Polish

---

[2]Out of the total of forty-six divisions of Warsaw Pact ground forces available without mobilization in Northern and Central Europe, twenty are satellite. Of the total 19,500 tanks 7,000 belong to Soviet allies. In Southern Europe (Hungary, Romania, Bulgaria), out of twenty-one Warsaw Pact divisions only four are Soviet (in Hungary). And out of the 6,700 tanks 2,500 are Soviet. The Soviet allies' contribution of reinforcing formations of land forces is much lower than that of forces available without mobilization. The satellite armed forces contribute 1,720 tactical aircraft out of the total of 3,950 in Northern and Central Europe and 930 out of the total of 1,525 in Southern Europe. *The Military Balance 1980–1981* (London: IISS, 1980), pp. 110–12.

crisis are well known. Other problems that have arisen within the Pact are related to the difficulties of elaborating monolithic positions on such foreign policy issues as China, Afghanistan, Vietnam, and the Middle East. In view of the strained economic situation in the East, the problem of the satellites' contribution to the Warsaw Pact defense budget has emerged as a major controversial item within the Pact, with such members as Romania and Poland opposing any increase in military spending.[3] These and other symptoms of strain within the alliance will make it increasingly difficult for its leader to maintain cohesion and secure from its allies total obedience in the councils of the Pact.

THE MILITARY BALANCE: NATO AND THE WARSAW PACT

As noted above and in other contributions to this volume, the military balance in Europe generally is perceived by western experts to be shifting in favor of the Warsaw Pact forces. The difficulties inherent in any balance of power assessment are well known, and an assessment of the NATO-Warsaw Pact balance would require a comparison of many, often incomparable, quantitative and qualitative components and factors and, as a rule, unquantifiable intangible variables.[4] Also, depending on what particular assumptions underlie the comparison, it is possible to arrive at either an optimistic or pessimistic view of the balance. For example, an optimistic western assessment of the Pact would view the hierarchical structure of the Soviet alliance not as a source of efficiency but as an element of rigidity, inhibiting initiative and leading to distrust. An optimist would also stress the unreliability of the satellite armies. For a pessimist, the integrated hierarchical nature of the Pact would be viewed as contributing an element of strength to the Pact's decision-making ability and to its military efficiency. The optimist would not give the Pact forces benefit of the doubt in absence of concrete data, whereas the pessimist would rather err on the side of overestimating their strength. An optimistic assessment would consider quantitative one-to-one comparison of like items as probably misleading, whereas a pessimistic view would tend toward comparing totals of like things while excluding elements of strength that are not easy to compare. An optimist would also assume, for example,

---

[3]For a discussion of strains and areas of disagreement within the Pact, see Dale R. Herspring, "The Warsaw Pact at 25," *Problems of Communism* 29, no. 5 (September–October 1980): 1–15.

[4]The complexities of comparing elements of military power for purposes of arriving at a balance are discussed in *The Military Balance 1977–1978*, pp. 102–10.

that all of the NATO territorial and reserve units as well as the French forces would be involved in the conflict and that Soviet reinforcements would be delayed, compared to a pessimist who would include only active NATO divisions and would assume rapid reinforcement of the central front by the Warsaw Pact forces.[5] Subject to all these reservations and without entering into detailed comparisons, the emerging trends in the military balance between NATO and the Warsaw Pact in the areas of defense expenditures and armed forces, including both nuclear weapons and conventional forces, in the Central European theater will be summarized.[6]

As far as the comparison of NATO and Warsaw Pact defense spending is concerned, the most alarming feature has been a sustained growth of Soviet defense outlays, at least over the past fifteen years. There are various methods of analyzing Soviet military spending and only rough estimates are possible in this area, but all analysts agree that the Soviet Union has been spending substantially more on defense than the United States.[7] Since the 1970s Soviet expenditures have been growing at about 4.5% a year in real terms, while those of the United States have declined. It is estimated that the defense expenditures of the Soviet Union take about 11% to 15% of its gross national product (GNP), as compared to 5.2% of the United States.[8] What is important is the fact that over 50% of the Soviet outlays is spent not on personnel, as in the United States and other NATO countries, but on defensive investment.[9] It is significant that the Soviet allies devote much less of their respective GNP to defense spending than their leader, and with the exception of the German Democratic Republic their expenditures, relative to GNP, have declined since 1975.[10] The Soviet Union accounts for about 85% of the Pact's defense costs, whereas the U.S. defense expenditures are about 50% of the total

---

[5]For the difference that various pessimistic or optimistic assumptions can make in portraying the military balance between NATO and Warsaw Pact, see Wolfram F. Hanrieder, ed., *Arms Control and Security: Current Issues* (Boulder, CO: Westview Press, 1979), esp. App. C: "NATO-Warsaw Pact Military Balance: How to Make the Balance Look Good/Bad."

[6]For details see *The Military Balance 1980–1981*.

[7]Problems related to estimating Soviet defense expenditures are analyzed in *The Military Balance 1973–1974*, pp. 8–9; *1975–1977*, pp. 109–10; *1980–1981*, pp. 12–13. See also W. T. Lee, *The Estimation of Soviet Expenditures, 1955–75: An Unconventional Approach* (New York: Frederick A. Praeger, 1977).

[8]*The Military Balance 1980–1981*, pp. 13, 96.

[9]It is estimated that since 1970 the Soviet Union has out invested the United States in military capital by at least $200 billion. See "NATO and the Warsaw Pact," *The Economist* 276, no. 7145 (9 August 1980): 36. Soviet research and development spending amounts to 20% of the Soviet defense budget, whereas the United States is only about 10%. Robert Komer, "Looking Ahead," *International Security* 4, no. 1 (Summer 1979): 108, 110.

[10]In 1979 the defense expenditures of the Soviet allies represented between 6.3% (the exceptionally high case of East Germany) and 1.4% (Romania). The European NATO members spent between 4.9% (Great Britain) and 1% (Luxembourg) of their respective GNPs. *The Military Balance 1980–1981*, p. 96.

NATO figure. As far as the NATO-Warsaw Pact relationship as a whole is concerned, NATO still seems to be ahead of the Warsaw Pact in monetary terms, but its outlays have fallen much behind the Pact's spending on the procurement of weapons and equipment.[11]

The problem of the balance of long-range strategic ("central") nuclear weapons goes far beyond the scope of this review. It is common knowledge that the Soviet Union over the past decade rapidly has increased and modernized its strategic forces, thus achieving at least parity with the United States. It has overtaken the United States in most measures of strength: total megatonnage, number of missiles, and weight lift. Only in the number of warheads has the United States not fallen behind, but even this advantage is disappearing with the introduction of Soviet MIRVed strategic missiles. Also, in view of the fact that a higher proportion of the American deterrent is carried by bombers and submarine-launched missiles than in the case of the Soviet Union, the latter is ahead of the United States in the number of reliable and accurate warheads and will remain so even after the United States has deployed its new generation of highly accurate air-launched cruise missiles.[12]

Whereas an approximate parity is still believed, perhaps too optimistically, to exist in the strategic systems, the Warsaw Pact, or strictly speaking the Soviet Union, has gained a large and growing advantage in the long-range theater nuclear forces, that is, intermediate range missiles able to hit targets in Western Europe. Calculating the actual LRTNF balance in Europe depends on the criteria adopted for defining an LRTNF system, including the boundary lines vis-à-vis battlefield tactical nuclear forces on the one hand and strategic systems on the other; the nature of the mission (counterland or countermaritime, for example); the point of mobilization at which the balance is calculated; the value of the systems (indices of survivability, reliability, and ability to penetrate defenses); and, finally, their range.[13] Without the inclusion of the Poseidon missile, which in principle is a strategic system whose use in the LRTNF role would escalate the conflict to the strategic level, the Soviet Union has an advantage in arriving warheads of about 3.1:1.[14] In any case, it has superiority both in the inventory total and in warhead counts.

Of particular concern for NATO is the fact that while retaining the older LRTNF systems, the Soviets since 1977 have been rapidly deploying the new SS-20 and perhaps even more modern intermediate range

---

[11]Ibid.

[12]For data on the strategic forces of the superpowers, Great Britain, and France, see *The Military Balance 1980–1981*, pp. 5–6, 9–10, 21, 25.

[13]Ibid., pp. 116–17. See also Lawrence Freedman, "The Dilemma of the Nuclear Arms Control," *Survival* 23, no. 1 (January–February 1981): 2, 5–6. The 160km. range is a rough separation of short-range battlefield from long-range theater nuclear weapons.

[14]*The Military Balance 1980–1981*, p. 117.

missiles, most of which are targeted against Western Europe. The SS-20 is a mobile missile of 5,000km. range (2,700 nautical miles), carrying three independently targetable warheads with far greater accuracy—300 meters circular error probable (CEP)—than the older Soviet missiles. The deployment of these systems has been proceeding at about 60 to 100 per year, reaching at least 250 in mid-1981, with an estimated number of up to 460 missiles in 1983. The deployment of these relatively invulnerable sophisticated missiles, more modern than any at NATO's disposal at the present time, has upset the LRTNF balance in Europe. Moreover, it largely has reduced the impact of NATO's 2:1 superiority in battlefield tactical nuclear weapons.

The disparity is being widened by annual deployment of about 30 *Backfire* supersonic bombers that can fly at low altitudes, have a range of 4,025km., and carry a three or four warhead load. In 1980 there were seventy-five *Backfires* deployed in addition to about 4,000 other less advanced aircraft.[15] Currently NATO can counter this Soviet superiority in LRTNF only with fifty-seven aging British *Vulcan* B-2 and 156 F-111 E/F. Because of their unrefueled range (*Vulcan*: 2,800km.; F-111: 1,900km.), these two aircraft are not easily able to reach a significant number of Soviet military targets. The implications of the Warsaw Pact advantage in LRTNF for the strategic options of NATO will be discussed below.

In land and air forces the Warsaw Pact, which already had an overall conventional superiority in the 1960s, has increased its advantage, both numerically and through a surprisingly rapid modernization of its conventional forces. For example, in Northern and Central Europe, Warsaw Pact tank superiority has increased in the last decade from 2:1 to 3:1 and that of artillery from 1.5:1 to almost 4:1. Traditional NATO air power supremacy in sophisticated equipment is also being eroded as more modern Soviet aircraft are introduced not only for interception missions but also for battlefield attack.[16] In sum, even though the overall balance of conventional forces would still involve incalculable risk for the aggressor, NATO's qualitative advantages are being matched by technological advances in the Warsaw Pact forces, and "in general the pattern is one of a military balance moving steadily against the West."[17] To complete this rather discouraging balance sheet, it is essential to consider the Soviet navy whose buildup in the past two decades, especially in submarines, means that the United States no longer has the assured control over supply lines across the North Atlantic that is so vital in the case of a conflict in Europe.[18]

---

[15]Ibid., p. 118.

[16]See details in the essays by Bill Sweetman and Robert W. Clawson in this volume.

[17]*The Military Balance 1980–1981*, p. 114.

[18]See details in Steve F. Kime, "Warsaw Pact Naval Power," in this volume. In the Baltic the Warsaw Pact has a 3-to-1 advantage. In the Mediterranean NATO still enjoys an

THE IMPLICATIONS OF THE
WARSAW PACT BUILDUP

What has been NATO's response to the changing security balance brought about by the quantitative and qualitative expansion of the Warsaw Pact's offensively oriented conventional capabilities and the LRTNF? NATO's reaction is to pursue two parallel and complementary goals: strengthening its defense capabilities on the one hand and continuing to promote negotiations on arms control and disarmament on the other. This two-track approach has been repeatedly emphasized by NATO in statements and communiqués.

In restoring a satisfactory military balance, NATO's first priority was to increase the defense outlays of the alliance. Inititated by the Carter administration, the 1977 pledge of an annual increase in defense expenditures of about 3 percent in real terms was endorsed at the Washington summit in 1978.[19] This "three percent solution" was to provide guidance for the allies' defense spending in the coming years. However, primarily because of the perception gap that exists between the United States and its European allies in the matter of the Warsaw buildup and also because of ostensible budgetary difficulties, the 3-percent target of the formula guidance has not been entirely met even though it has been repeatedly reaffirmed by NATO, most recently at the defense ministers meeting in May 1981.[20]

The rather modest increase in NATO's defense spending has had to be complemented by a much stronger effort at an alliance-wide coordination of national planning in order to strengthen NATO's defense capabilities by achieving a greater degree of cooperation and rationalization. The Long-Term Defense Program adopted by NATO in May 1978 was designed to meet these challenges. The program recommended a series of detailed actions to improve NATO's capabilities and cooperation in ten priority areas: readiness, reinforcement, reserve mobilization, maritime posture, air defense, communications, command and control, electronic warfare, logistics, and theater nuclear modernization.[21]

Action on the modernization of LRTNF was taken in December 1979 when NATO's foreign and defense ministers decided to modernize these forces by the deployment, starting in 1983 in selected European

---

advantage but can no longer be assured of exercising necessary overall sea control. Bernard W. Rogers, "Increasing Threats to NATO's Security Call for Sustained Response," *NATO Review* 29, no. 3 (June 1981): 1.

[19]North Atlantic Council, Final Communiqué, *NATO Review* 26, no. 4 (August 1978): 28, 29.

[20]See Elizabeth Pond, "US Gets NATO Allies' Commitment on Defense Spending," *Christian Science Monitor*, 14 May 1981.

[21]See North Atlantic Council, Final Communiqué, "The Long-Term Defence Programme: A Summary," *NATO Review* 26, no. 4 (August 1978): 29–31.

NATO countries, of U.S. ground-launched systems comprised of 108 Pershing II launchers (to replace the existing Pershing I) and 464 cruise missiles, all with single warheads. As an integral part of the LRTNF modernization plan it was decided to withdraw 1,000 American tactical nuclear warheads as soon as possible.[22] Although the deployment of the new systems is not to start until 1983, the withdrawal of the 1,000 older warheads was completed in 1980.[23] All of the 108 Pershing II launchers are to be deployed in the Federal Republic of Germany. The location of the 464 cruise missiles is projected as follows: Great Britain 160, Federal Republic of Germany 96, Italy 112, and the Netherlands and Belgium 48 each.

Even if the NATO LRTNF were deployed by the mid-1980s, the Soviet Union is expected to be further ahead in such forces than it was when NATO's modernization plan was adopted. Moreover, the new NATO systems, although very accurate (20m.–40m. CEP for Pershing II and less than 80m. for the cruise missile), would have a shorter range than that of the Soviet SS-20; 1,000km. for the Pershing II and 2,000km. for the cruise missile. Also, the relatively slow speed of the cruise missiles would preclude any first strike by this particular weapon. Despite all these considerations, the Soviet Union, while in actual fact enjoying superiority in "Eurostrategic" missiles, has reacted strongly against the NATO plan, charging the United States with attempts to upset what they allege is an approximate LRTNF parity and start another spiral of nuclear arms race and increased military confrontation.[24] The sharp Soviet reaction is prompted by a number of motivations: desire to prevent deployment of new nuclear systems targeted against the Soviet homeland from the territory of Russia's historical enemy; fear of an LRTNF arms race; renewed anxiety about U.S. forward-based systems; and, last but not least, a continuing desire to weaken NATO militarily and politically, split the western allies, and maintain Soviet LRTNF superiority in Europe.[25] A diplomatic and propaganda offensive against the NATO's LRTNF modernization plan, unprecedented in its scope and intensity, has been launched by Moscow, and the issue has assumed a central place in the NATO-Warsaw Pact confrontation, involving the two superpowers and especially America's European allies, which naturally are the main targets of Moscow's campaign.

[22]Communiqué of the Special Meeting of NATO Foreign and Defense Ministers, *NATO Review* 28, no. 1 (February 1980): 25.
[23]North Atlantic Council, Final Communiqué, meeting of 11–12 December 1980, *NATO Review* 29, no. 1 (February 1981): 25–27.
[24]For a typical Soviet perception of the NATO plan see Boris Ponomarev, "A Pact for Peace and a Pact for Aggression," *World Marxist Review* 23, no. 8 (August 1980): 3, 6.
[25]See the discussion in Stephen M. Millett, "Soviet Perceptions of the Theater Nuclear Balance in Europe and Reactions to American LRTNFs," *Naval War College Review* 34, no. 2 (1981): 3–17.

The LRTNF confrontation shows how the Soviet perception of the nuclear balance in Europe, and military security in general, differs from the way in which the same issues are perceived by the western alliance. The Soviet Union claims that the projected deployment of the new western LRTNF represents a dangerous escalation of the nuclear arms race that would upset the existing balance of such forces in Europe. In the Soviet view the SS-20s and the *Backfires* represent only a modernization of the Soviet forces necessary to counteract NATO's nuclear advantages in Europe, including American tactical battlefield nuclear weapons, the three NATO-assigned Poseidon submarines with 400 MIRV warheads, and the British and French nuclear arsenals. The Soviet Union sees in the projected American weapons a new and most dangerous threat to its homeland, since such weapons would be able to hit targets located there, including the Soviet strategic arsenal itself, with serious implications of a shift in the U.S. strategic doctrine toward a counterforce strike against the Soviet Union. Moscow also alleges that the NATO plan would be a violation of the Carter-Brezhnev agreements and, in general, seriously would endanger détente, especially the Soviet interpretation of this vague concept.[26]

The western perception of the European LRTNF issue must be placed within the context of the changes in the overall strategic relationship between the United States and the Soviet Union that have occurred in the last two decades or so.[27] When the Soviet Union lagged behind the United States in its strategic intercontinental nuclear arsenal, the Soviet superiority in the otherwise less sophisticated LRTNF and its conventional strength could still be interpreted as a defensive rather than offensive posture, since any Soviet action against Western Europe would trigger an all-out response from U.S. strategic nuclear forces under the doctrines of "extended deterrence" and "massive retaliation." With the emergence by 1977 of strategic parity and the looming threat to the invulnerability of U.S. land-based strategic missiles, there appeared, according to western observers, to be no further need for the Soviet Union to develop sophisticated nuclear weapons targeted specifically against Western Europe. Yet, they were developed and are being rapidly deployed with the result that, under the concept of its flexible response strategy, NATO no longer has the viable option of escalating any conventional conflict to the more favorable tactical nuclear level because it would be

---

[26]Ibid.

[27]For example, see, Stephen Hammer, Jr., "NATO's Long-Range Theatre Nuclear Forces: Modernization in Parallel with Arms Control," *NATO Review* 28, no. 1 (February 1980): 1–6; and Paul Buteux, "Theatre Nuclear Forces: Modernisation Plan and Arms Control Initiative," *NATO Review* 28, no. 6 (December 1980): 1–6. See also the analysis in Stanley Hoffmann, "New Variations on Old Themes," *International Security* 4, no. 1 (Summer 1979): 88–107. For a popular overall review see Elizabeth Pond, "The State of the Alliance: the Missile Watch," *Christian Science Monitor*, 19 June 1981.

deterred from resorting to tactical battlefield nuclear weapons by the unique capability of the Soviet Union to use its SS-20 and other modern LRTNF for strategic uses limited to Europe. The 1979 NATO decision to deploy new countervailing LRTNF is designed to close this gap in the continuum of its military options between the conventional and battlefield nuclear forces in Europe on the one hand and the strategic nuclear weapons of the United States and its allies on the other.[28]

It soon became obvious that the Soviet deployment of new LRTNF, while securing for the USSR a bargaining advantage in the escalation process of an actual armed conflict against NATO (something that NATO had hoped to achieve under its flexible response strategy), also could serve as an instrument of political pressure against the Western European allies of the United States within the range of the Soviet weapons.

THE PERCEPTION GAP WITHIN NATO

In its campaign against the western plan to deploy LRTNF, the Soviet Union is exploiting the growing perception gap that exists between the way the problem is seen by the NATO decision makers, especially the American representatives, and the way it is viewed by large segments of Western European public opinion, articulated by the various antinuclear and peace movements. These groups and many individual Western Europeans do not seem to share NATO's anxiety over the threat posed by the Soviet LRTNF and are opposed to the deployment by NATO of missiles to counter that threat.[29] For West Germany, the key NATO country in Europe where all the 108 Pershing II and 96 out of 145 cruise missiles are to be located, the LRTNF issue is extremely sensitive because such deployment means that for the first time missiles capable of reaching Soviet territory will be placed on German soil even though they will remain under American control. Caught between conflicting American and Soviet pressures, the West German government, while agreeing to

---

[28]This gap was emphasized by West German Chancellor Schmidt in his now famous address at the International Institute for Strategic Studies in London in the fall of 1977, in which he called upon the United States to counter the Soviet deployment of the LRTNF systems. Initially, President Carter (but not the Pentagon) was reluctant to do so in adherence to the concept of mutual assured destruction and the principle of joining Europe with America for defense purposes. See Pond, "The State of the Alliance."

[29]On the same day that the Warsaw Pact Conference was held at Kent State University a conference on nuclear war reflecting this opposition was taking place in Groningen, the Netherlands. See Elizabeth Pond, "US, European Antinuclear Groups Join in Peace Quest," *Christian Science Monitor*, 28 April 1981.

deployment on its territory, insisted on the precondition of concurrent acceptance of the missiles on the territory of at least one other NATO member on the continent (the "no-singularity provision").[30] It also consistently has emphasized the need to engage in LRTNF arms control negotiations with the Soviet Union as provided by NATO's 1979 dual decision: modernization plus negotiations.[31]

The West German government is the main target of the Soviet anti-NATO campaign, which at the same time faces a growing opposition from the left wing of its own Social Democratic Party and from the spreading antinuclear protests. In the Netherlands, according to public opinion polls, two-thirds of the population oppose the deployment of the 48 cruise missiles there. The parliamentary election of May 1981 failed to produce the majority necessary for the approval of deployment on Dutch soil and the government, which originally had accepted NATO's modernization plan, postponed its final decision until December 1981. The position of the Belgian government also is ambiguous. Denmark and Norway long ago refused to accept nuclear weapons on their soil. The Italian government is committed to accept 112 missiles, but domestic political instability in Italy must be of some concern to NATO planners. In Great Britain, where 160 cruise missiles are to be deployed, Prime Minister Margaret Thatcher is strongly committed to the NATO plan against Labour Party opposition and a growing antinuclear movement. There is also concern in NATO that as a result of the worsening economic situation a Labour government may come to power before the implementation of the modernization plan.[32]

---

[30]During the discussions leading to the two-track decision to proceed with the deployment of LRTNF and engage in arms control negotiations with the Soviet Union, West Germany urged that the NATO LRTNF missiles be based on ships at sea. See interview with Chancellor Schmidt in *Frankfurter Rundschau*, 30 June 1981, trans. by the German Information Center, New York, *Release from Bonn—Statements and Speeches* 4, no. 11 (6 July 1981).

[31]For example, see the statement by Chancellor Schmidt, ibid. See also his statement before the *Bundestag* on 9 April 1981, trans. by the German Information Center, New York, *Release from Bonn—Statements and Speeches* 4, no. 6 (10 April 1981); and his statement before the *Bundestag* on 26 May 1981, trans. in ibid., no. 10 (27 May 1981). See also the statement by the West German minister for Foreign Affairs in a *Deutschlandfunk* interview, 13 April 1981, trans. in ibid., no. 7 (13 April 1981).

[32]For a review of the position of the European NATO members on the issue of deploying LRTNF, see Gary Yerkey, "Europe's Antiwar Movement of '60s Turns to Antinuclear Protest for '80s," *Christian Science Monitor*, 28 April 1981; Elizabeth Pond, "Dutch Election Results Reflect Antinuclear Mood," ibid., 28 May 1981; and David K. Willis, "Europe Blows Hot and Cold over New NATO Missiles," ibid., 29 June 1981. It is perhaps ironic that the new socialist government of France under President Mitterrand is among one of the strongest opponents of the Soviet missile build-up and staunchly supports NATO's LRTNF modernization plan with concurrent pursuance of arms control talks with the Soviet Union. See Mitterrand's interview with the *New York Times*, 3 June 1981, reprinted in excerpts in French embassy, *Statements from . . . FRANCE*, no. 81 60.

ARMS LIMITATION NEGOTIATIONS
FOR THE EUROPEAN THEATER

From the very beginning the modernization decision of 1979 has been linked to a parallel NATO call for arms control negotiations with the Soviet Union to limit the deployment of LRTNF systems to mutually acceptable levels. Such talks would represent only one forum in the ongoing process of arms control negotiations between East and West. At the strategic level the SALT I agreement on limiting offensive missiles expired in 1977 and SALT II, although signed, is unacceptable to the U.S. administration and has no chance of being ratified. Any new negotiations on the strategic arms control that are likely to be resumed in the coming year will have to be thoroughly prepared in consultation with America's European allies and coordinated with talks on limiting LRTNF systems.

Since 1973, as far as forces in Central Europe are concerned, NATO and the Warsaw Pact have been engaged in negotiations in Vienna on mutual and balanced force reductions (MBFR) and in Central Europe, specifically in Belgium, the Netherlands, Luxembourg, the Federal Republic of Germany, the German Democratic Republic, Poland, and Czechoslovakia, involving the armed forces of these seven countries and those of the United States, Canada, Great Britain, and the Soviet Union. Although consensus has been reached on a number of points, these relatively forgotten negotiations so far have failed to produce any concrete agreement.[33] Perceiving the Warsaw Pact's superiority, NATO's basic objective in the MBFR talks has been to establish a more stable conventional balance in Central Europe, whereas for the Warsaw Pact the main motivation has been to limit the growth of NATO's forces, especially those of West Germany.

In the course of protracted negotiations the positions of the two sides softened substantially from the original extreme stands. Thus, in 1978 the Warsaw Pact countries made a major concession on the issue of the method of calculating reductions by agreeing that the forces should be reduced to a combined ceiling of ground and air forces totaling 900,000. A compromise also was reached on the scheduling of reductions, under

---

[33]For a detailed study of MBFR talks see John G. Keliher, *The Negotiations on Mutual and Balanced Force Reductions: The Search for Arms Control in Central Europe* (New York: Pergamon Press, 1980). See also *Third German-American Roundtable on NATO: The MBFR Negotiations* (1980; Cosponsored by the Konrad Adenauer Stiftung and the Institute for Foreign Policy Analysis Inc.); and Ernst Jung, "The Vienna MBFR Negotiations after Seven Years," *NATO Review* 29, no. 3 (June 1981): 6–9. For a study of the relationship between détente and MBFR, see "Detente and the European Force Reduction Negotiations" (Unpublished paper by P. Terrence Hopmann, prepared for delivery at the 22d annual Convention of the International Studies Association, Philadelphia, Pennsylvania, 18–21 March 1981).

which they would proceed in two phases; the first was to include only the Soviet and American forces and the second to concentrate on reductions by all parties. There was also consensus on the need for so-called "associated measures," that is, measures to enhance confidence and facilitate verification of compliance that were to legalize the "confidence-building measures" envisaged by the Final Act of the Helsinki Conference on Security and Cooperation in Europe of 1975. However, it so far has not been possible to agree on what concrete verification procedures should be adopted.

The most divisive issue of the MBFR negotiations concerns the number of troops to be taken as the starting point for reductions. Whereas NATO claims that the existing disparity of ground forces between the two alliances amounts to 150,000, the Warsaw Pact admits to only 14,000. To accept the Soviet data would mean codifying the sizable Warsaw pact advantage for purposes of calculating reductions. Hence, the issue remains unresolved. It reemerged again as the fundamental impediment to agreement at the latest rounds of MBFR talks in the winter and summer of 1981. No progress was made in the worsened international climate.

The protracted debates in Madrid at the 1980–81 second follow-up meeting of the 1975 Helsinki conference considered plans for a conference on security and disarmament in Europe, submitted by, among other participants, France on behalf of the West and Poland on behalf of the Warsaw Pact. These proposals appear to be doomed to failure primarily because of a lack of consensus on the specific nature of mandatory and verifiable confidence building measures and on the territorial scope of their applicability on the European continent.

Despite all these failures at arms control in relations between NATO and the Warsaw Pact, NATO's decision on the modernization of its LRTNF was balanced by a willingness to negotiate with the Soviet Union on arms control measures concerning these weapons systems. The first round of talks opened under the Carter administration in October 1980 and quickly ended at an impasse, having been undertaken simply to reassure domestic pro-arms control concerns without any coherent strategy or adequate preparation for the complex problems involved.

In view of rising popular pressures in Europe against nuclear armaments and for disarmament talks, it was a foregone conclusion that the Reagan administration would have to resume negotiations on LRTNF with the USSR.[34] However, Soviet pressure for a mutual East-West moratorium on the deployment of LRTNF was dismissed by NATO as a

---

[34]In June 1981 the United States and the Soviet Union agreed to resume talks on the limitation of LRTNF. See the *New York Times*, 6 June 1981. The talks are to begin in November 1981. See ibid., 24 September 1981. For an exposition of the current U.S. policy on arms control, see the address by Secretary of State Alexander Haig before the Foreign Policy Association in New York on 14 July 1981, reprinted in U.S., Department of State, Bureau of Public Affairs—Current Policy, No. 292.

ploy to camouflage and stabilize Soviet superiority in LRTNF as well as to allow their continued buildup of the SS-20s force and perhaps more advanced intermediate-range missiles.

In the current tense climate of international politics, chances for a successful outcome of LRTNF talks appear to be even less promising than in the past. Moreover, the task of arriving at a mutually acceptable scheme of LRTNF reduction is challenging indeed when the two sides are divided by seemingly intractable differences. There is no agreement on what weapons are actually to be included in the negotiations as LRTNF, how they are to be counted (in missiles, the Soviet position, or warheads, NATO's preference), or what should be the geographical scope of the limitations.[35] Finally, there remains the problem of the link between the LRTNF talks and the SALT agreements. In this regard integrating the LRTNF missiles into the overall ceiling on strategic weapons would be advisable. It is imperative, however, that should the LRTNF talks produce an agreement, they should be complemented by equal progress in the area of the limitation of the strategic systems of the two superpowers.[36]

CONCLUSIONS

Today in the rather delicate and critical period prior to the mid-1980s' deployment of NATO's new LRTNF the question remains: How can the security system of the western alliance adapt to the present strategic and political reality? Strategically, the NATO-Warsaw Pact relationship is characterized by a military balance shifting toward the Pact, especially in view of the Soviet deployment of new LRTNF. NATO's long-term defense program and LRTNF modernization only partially can reduce its inferiority. Politically, the relationship between the two alliances must be viewed in the foreseeable future as one dimension of an intensifying confrontation that has spread beyond the traditional confines of NATO's geographical area and was precipitated by Soviet activities in Africa and Indochina, its military intervention in Afghanistan, the crisis in Poland, and the turmoil in the Middle East. NATO needs a more determined and coherent strategy in order to deal with these realities of the 1980s.

[35]For the difficulties inherent in LRTNF arms control negotiations, see Freedman, "The Dilemma of the Nuclear Arms Control." See also James A. Schaer, "European Arms Control: Right but Risky," *Christian Science Monitor*, 23 June 1981. For a more detailed analysis see Robert Metzger and Paul Doty, "Arms Control Enters the Gray Area," *International Security* 3, no. 3 (Winter 1978/79): 17–52.
[36]This is emphasized by Freedman, "The Dilemma of the Nuclear Arms Control."

As shown by the debate on the deployment of LRTNF, it is of crucial importance for NATO to narrow the gap that exists between public opinion in Europe and the NATO governments concerning their respective perception of the Soviet threat. The development of a shared perception regarding the LRTNF problem is a necessary condition for a successful implementation of the modernization decision of 1979. Parallel to this political task must be the effort to proceed to improve the military balance not only by NATO as a whole but also by the individual, especially the key European members of the alliance: West Germany, France, and Great Britain.[37] It appears that because of decline in the credibility of the American nuclear umbrella and the growing LRTNF disparity, the French and British nuclear forces will have to complement the U.S. systems that are to be deployed in the 1980s. Perhaps the time has come for France to rejoin the military arm of the Atlantic Alliance in Europe. Despite disappointing results so far, NATO must supplement its defense programs by negotiations with the Soviet Union and its alliance for realistic, security-enhancing, and verifiable arms control agreements in order to achieve a balance at preferably the lowest level of armaments and to reduce as much as possible any incentive to use force by the potential adversaries.

The challenges faced by NATO are enormous, but to counterbalance this rather pessimistic portrayal of NATO-Warsaw Pact relations, it is important to recall that the Warsaw Pact and its leaders are not without their own problems and even serious dilemmas. Seen in future perspective, the Polish situation is of particular interest since it may prove to be not only a turning point in the history of Soviet-style communism in Europe but also of its institutionalization in the form of military alliance. If the Soviet Union acquiesces in the changes that have occurred in its major ally, despite intimidation and threats to use force, it will have to undertake a general reassessment of the Pact's role as an instrument of ideological cohesion of the Soviet bloc. Will such reappraisal lead to a gradual transformation of the Pact into a traditional military alliance? Even if such an optimistically hypothesized deideologization of the Warsaw Pact actually occurred, it would not necessarily mean the end of confrontation in Europe. Another and more likely prospect is that the Soviet reassessment of the Polish question will lead to the strengthening by the Warsaw Pact leader of the ideological and military cohesion of the Pact, tightly insulating its allies from the Polish example; to economic strangulation of Poland; and possibly, as a final resort, to military intervention. This last solution, however, would pose a grave dilemma for the Soviet Union, since it would create a wide breach in the defenses of the

---

[37]For some thoughts on this theme see Pierre Lellouche, "Europe and Her Defense," *Foreign Affairs* 59, no. 4 (Spring 1981): 813–34.

Pact and might even mean the virtual end of the Pact as it is known today. These speculations aside, the western alliance must apply itself to rectifying the unfavorable balance in the European theater as it stands today, concurrently pursuing the course of arms control negotiations at the conventional and nuclear levels. Such negotiations can be successful only if NATO secures for itself a stronger bargaining position than the one in which it finds itself at the present time.

THE FORCES

The Soviet Armed Forces:
Perceptions Over Twenty Years

JAMES T. REITZ

Any attempt to summarize the state of the Soviet armed forces runs multiple risks, not the least of which is the obvious fact of Soviet military secrecy; it remains formidable and, in most ways, effective. It is also easy to ignore historical trends, thus undervaluing the nature and scale of the Soviet armed forces buildup and modernization that has been underway for more than two decades.

This study is designed to illustrate, with the best information available, just how far the Soviet armed forces have come in the last twenty years. Such a purpose requires a substantial dose of numerical data; yet, it is important not to lose sight of the general impressions that the cumulative process produces. During the 1960s and 70s the Soviets, with no possible doubt, have made both quantitative and qualitative gains that only can be described as astonishing. Most remarkable, even to the seasoned observer, is the grinding, steady, seemingly inexorable progress that the Soviets have been making across the board in every major category of armed forces equipment and even in most of the subordinate parts of major components. In a few instances the numbers have been reduced, but in almost every such case numerical reduction has been accompanied by a major technological advance, thus substituting increased quality for quantity.

Considering the total spectrum of Soviet military forces, the USSR's apparently unbounded drive and determination to build raw military power is nothing less than awesome. This is a particularly noteworthy point coming as it does on the twentieth anniversary of the abortive Bay of Pigs invasion and not long before the same anniversary of the Cuban missile crisis, when the Soviets last felt it prudent to back down.

This essay will not include net assessments or systematic comparisons of East versus West. The present effort is directed at analyzing Soviet achievements: where they were twenty years ago and where they are as of 1980, by branch of service. The first to be considered will be the Strategic Rocket Forces, still regarded by the Soviet leadership as the first among equals. Figure 1 provides a simplified overview of the Soviet armed forces and special purpose troops as of 1980.

Figure 1. Soviet Armed Forces—1980

MINISTRY OF DEFENSE

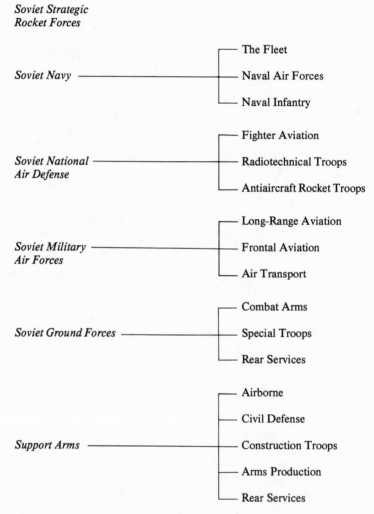

*Soviet Strategic
Rocket Forces*

Soviet Navy ——————————————
— The Fleet
— Naval Air Forces
— Naval Infantry

*Soviet National
Air Defense* ——————————————
— Fighter Aviation
— Radiotechnical Troops
— Antiaircraft Rocket Troops

*Soviet Military
Air Forces* ——————————————
— Long-Range Aviation
— Frontal Aviation
— Air Transport

Soviet Ground Forces ——————————————
— Combat Arms
— Special Troops
— Rear Services

Support Arms ——————————————
— Airborne
— Civil Defense
— Construction Troops
— Arms Production
— Rear Services

MINISTRY OF INTERNAL AFFAIRS (MVD)
Internal Security Troops

COMMITTEE FOR STATE SECURITY (KGB)
Border Guards

STRATEGIC ROCKET FORCES

ICBMs

In ten short years from 1960 to 1970, the Soviets moved from an almost negligible ICBM force of thirty-five missiles to a position of virtual numerical parity with the United States with five models in a 1,300-missile inventory that was entirely less than ten years old. Technologically, in 1970 they were just beginning to perfect multiple reentry vehicles (MRV). Ten years later in 1980 the Strategic Rocket Forces had not increased their ICBM force by much, mainly because they have adhered to the restrictions of the bilateral SALT I agreement. However, in that period they introduced three new models: SS-17, SS-18, and SS-19. Half of their inventory in 1980 was less than five years old and they successfully had mastered the necessary technology to equip their missiles with complex multiple independently targetable reentry vehicles (MIRVs). They appear in 1980 to have had four more new intercontinental missiles in testing and, with deployment, that would make the fifth generation of Soviet ICBMs in slightly over twenty years (see Table 1).

Table 1. Soviet Land-Based ICBM Forces, 1960–80

Period	Manpower	Type	Number	Year Intro.	Range (miles)	Fuel	Warhead
1960	200,000	T-3	35	1958	5–8,000	Liquid (L)	Single (SGL)
1970	350,000	SS-7	220	1961	6,900 }	Storable	SGL
		SS-8		1963	6,900 }	Liquid (SL)	SGL
		SS-9	240	1965	7,500	L	SGL
		SS-11	800	1966	6,500	SL	SGL/MRV
		SS-13	40	1968	5,500	Solid (S)	SGL
			1,300				
1980	385,000	SS-11	580	1966	6,500	SL	SGL/MRV
		SS-13	60	1968	6,200	S	SGL
		SS-17	150	1975	6,200	L	MIRV
		SS-18	310	1975	6,600	L	SGL/MIRV
		SS-19	300	1975	6,900	L	SGL/MIRV
			1,400				

IRBMs

The intermediate- and medium-range missile inventory has shown a somewhat different trend. Ten years of quantitative expansion was fol-

lowed subsequently by little change in numbers or quality until the
introduction of the SS-20 in 1977, for which they produced a reloadable
mobile launcher as well as the MIRVed warhead. At the end of the 1970s
it was learned that a new vehicle, the SS-22, was in the development stage
(see Table 2).

Table 2. Soviet Land-Based Intermediate- and Medium-Range
Ballistic Missile Forces, 1960–80

Period	Type		Number	Year Intro.	Range (miles)	Fuel	Warhead
1960	SS-4	MRBM }	200	1959	1,200	L	SGL
	SS-5	IRBM }		1960	2,500	SL	SGL
1970	SS-4	MRBM }	700	1959	1,200	L	SGL
	SS-5	IRBM }		1960	2,500	SL	SGL
1980	SS-4	MRBM	380	1959	1,200	L	SGL
	SS-5	IRBM	60	1960	2,500	SL	SGL
	SS-20	IRBM	160	1977	3,100	S	MIRV

Manpower

An important corollary point relates to the number of personnel
estimated to be associated with these missiles. It is just possible that
Nikita Khrushchev and his rocket marshals beefed up the new 1960 elite
branch to 200,000 (a number far beyond that necessary to service the
weapons on hand—35 ICBMs, 200 IRBM/MRBMs), through transfers
from branches being reduced and in preparation for what they knew would
be a later rapid expansion. The western force estimate was revised to
about 110,000 in the mid-1960s, which also could have reflected a slow
partial demobilization. By 1970, however, the force once again was
deemed a formidable one, reaching about 350,000 men. It is also possible
that earlier western manpower estimates were a good deal less reliable
than major technical equipment estimates.

THE SOVIET NAVY

Submarines

The Soviet navy, although for protocol purposes always listed last
among the five major force components of the Soviet ministry of defense,
is also a participant in the strategic ballistic missile mission through its

fleet of ICBM submarines. Between 1960 and 1980 the USSR's seaborne missile capability has grown at a rapid rate from none in 1960 to nearly 300 missiles in 1970 and more than 1,000 in 1980. With quantitative progress now slowing down by international agreement, the Soviets have embarked on an intensive qualitative development of submarine-launched multiple reentry vehicles, both MRVs and MIRVs (see Table 3).

Table 3. Ballistic Missiles of the Submarine Component
of the Soviet Navy, 1960–80

Period	Type	Number	Year Intro.	Range (miles)	Fuel	Warhead
1960	none	0				
1970	SS-N-4 ⎫	120	1961	250–350	SL?	SGL
	SS-N-5 ⎭		1963	700	SL?	SGL
	SS-N-6	160	1968	1,800	SL	SGL
		280				
1980	SS-N-4	9	1961	250–350	SL?	SGL
	SS-N-5	60	1964	700	SL?	SGL
	SS-N-6	469	1968	1,800	SL	SGL/MIRV or MRV
	SS-N-8	302	1973	4,800	SL	SGL
	SS-NX-17	12	1977	3,100	S	SGL/MIRV or MRV
	SS-N-18	160	1978	4,500–	?	MIRV
		1,012		5,200		

Additionally, tests of a new missile have been observed, evidently destined for the recently identified giant *Typhoon* class of submarine. The vast majority of Soviet ICBM-capable subs are nuclear powered; a significant number of diesel-powered boats remain available in reserve.

The Soviet submarine-launched cruise missile force has gone from none, or testing only, in 1960 to about 300 short-range missiles in 1970 and approximately 450 in 1980. Slow but steady progress has resulted in the surface-launched SS-N-12, representing not much change in range (300 miles) but probably a much improved warhead and guidance system. This missile was not yet fully operational by 1980.

The Soviet submarine fleet includes not only the various missile boats but also the attack versions. By 1960 the Soviet submarine force of almost 450 boats was exceptionally large, the majority of which were short-range coastal defense craft. Any nuclear-propelled vessels were still in the preoperational phase. Ten years later the total number of submarines actually had been reduced by approximately 15%. By 1970, however, most of the short-range craft had been retired and the force stood at above 20% nuclear propelled. By 1980 the submarine fleet was almost half nuclear with construction under way of two new nuclear classes, the *Typhoon* ballistic missile sub and the *Oscar* attack vessel, as well as the continuing production of other recent classes. Over the two decades both the ballistic missile and attack missions showed a dramatic increase in displacement. The largest vessels in 1960 were 2,400 tons, then 10,000 tons in 1970, and finally 11,000 tons in 1980, with at least one of the two far larger new classes up to about twice the 1980 figure.

Major Surface Vessels

With regard to the major surface combat element of the Soviet fleet in 1960, the cruiser force consisted of twenty-five vessels, all conventionally armed. However, 80% of them were less than fifteen years old. In 1970 the figure was still twenty-five, but the oldest class—the prewar *Kirov*—had been retired and 40% of the cruiser fleet was armed with at least first generation naval surface-to-air (SAM) and cruise missiles. By 1980 the number had increased to thirty-seven cruisers, nearly 70% of which were armed with both SAMs and cruise missiles. The trend during the period had been toward smaller ships (6,000–9,000 tons). At the beginning of the 1980s the startlingly larger (32,000 tons), more heavily armed, and reportedly nuclear powered *Kirov* class cruiser was undergoing trials.

By 1970 the Soviet navy had made a belated entry into the field of aircraft carriers with two small helicopter carriers of the *Moskva* class. This type, terminated after only two ships were launched, was followed by two larger aircraft carriers of the *Kiev* class. By 1980 it was reported that at least two additional examples of this class were being built. Less substantiated rumors also persist, indicating that construction of a larger nuclear-powered carrier may be under way.

Destroyers

The destroyers of the Soviet postwar navy by 1960 reportedly numbered almost 250 vessels, displacing up to 2,700 tons. Most were fairly new but fewer than ten mounted SAMs or cruise missiles. In 1970 the number had dropped by about 60% to around 100 vessels, possibly as a long-term result of Khrushchev's open preference for the nuclear submarine force. However, a new destroyer element had been built in which about 20% were SAM or cruise missile armed and were larger, more capable ships. By 1980 the destroyer count had dropped to 75, but more than half were missile armed with either SAMs or cruise missiles; some, such as the *Kashins*, had both.

Naval Aviation

Soviet naval aviation in 1960 had a bomber component of some 750, all of fairly recent vintage and all more or less conventional and committed to anticarrier and antisubmarine missions. By 1970 the force had been reduced to about 350 aircraft. Many of them, however, were much more powerfully armed with nuclear antinaval missiles. By 1980 there had been an increase of some 10% over 1970; almost 20% were the new supersonic *Backfire* bombers.

The naval fighter contingent, a broad mixture of more than 2,200 in 1960, was wiped out by the Khrushchev-inspired defense reforms of the early 1960s. By 1970 it still had not made any kind of recovery and in 1980 it stood at less than 100 aircraft, primarily of the ground attack variety. About half of the 1980 component were the carrier borne and less impressive vertical takeoff Yak-36 *Forgers*; the other half were the more potent land-based Su-17/20 types that evidently are nuclear capable.

With reference to other specialized aircraft, there were probably very few in 1960. In 1970 there were more than 150 dedicated antisubmarine warfare (ASW) aircraft serving, two-thirds of which were helicopters. Some 100 long-range reconnaissance and airborne tanker planes also had been identified along with a group of 200 miscellaneous transports. By 1980 the ASW force had been tripled by adding some older long-range bombers, possibly from air force resources. The reconnaissance and tanker element had grown slightly and the addition of an electronic warfare (EW) and electronic countermeasures (ECM) capability had been noted.

Vessels and Manpower

Over the twenty-year period the Soviet navy made steady and continuous qualitative improvement while reducing its inventory of major ships and aircraft (see Table 4).

Submarines were down from 430 all-diesel boats to about 350, with nearly half nuclear-propelled; they also were far larger and vastly better armed than their predecessors. Cruisers were up from 25 to 37, and many were now armed with SAMs and cruise missiles instead of naval guns. Destroyers were down two-thirds, from 230 to 75, but many were larger and more lethal combat ships. Other vessels were down by almost half, but the Soviet navy still had swarms of modern frigates, corvettes, smaller missile and torpedo boats, many of which are hydrofoil craft, as well as smaller patrol boats; many of these vessels have substantial combat capabilities. It not only had better than 300 minesweepers and 100 to 150 amphibious ships and landing craft but also a reported assortment of more than 400 logistics support craft, including some capable of filling multiple support roles. In addition, in 1980 the Soviets had a small naval infantry contingent, some coastal missiles and artillery, and naval base shore support personnel. It had eleven officer candidate schools and a naval (war college) academy. Naval strength in 1980, including naval air force, naval infantry, coastal artillery, and rocket troops, was estimated to be approximately 433,000 in four major fleets (Northern, Baltic, Black Sea, and Pacific) and one flotilla (Caspian), and sizable *ad hoc* forces also are maintained in the Mediterranean Sea and Indian Ocean.

Table 4. Soviet Naval Strengths, 1960–80

Period	Ship Type	Number		Manpower
1960	Submarines (all attack)	430	(nuclear: 0)	500,000
	Major surface combat ships	255		
	Cruisers		(25)	
	Destroyers		(230)	
	Other vessels	2,000+		
	Aircraft	3,000		
1970	Submarines	370	(nuclear: 90)	475,000
	Attack		(271)	
	Ballistic missile		(50)	
	Cruise missile		(49)	
	Major surface combat ships	126		
	Carriers		(2)	
	Cruisers		(25)	
	Destroyers		(99)	
	Other vessels	1,150+		
	Aircraft	860		
1980	Submarines	344	(nuclear: 162)	433,000
	Attack		(189)	
	Ballistic missile		(87)	
	Cruise missile		(68)	
	Major surface combat ships	115		
	Carriers		(4)	
	Cruisers		(36)	
	Destroyers		(75)	
	Other vessels	1,325+		
	Aircraft	1,300		

NATIONAL AIR DEFENSE FORCES

The major component of the Soviet armed forces dedicated to strategic air defense until recently was known to them and to the West as PVO Strany. This separate and distinct command, standing outside direct air force and artillery control since 1948, is charged with defending against threats to Soviet air space with fighter interceptors, SAMs, and ABMs. It also maintains a wide complex of air warning and operations direction centers and includes the radar troops to man various forms of electronic defense.

In a move early in 1981 that surprised many western experts, the Soviets quietly dropped from their open military literature the term "PVO Strany" (national strategic air defense) in favor of the term "Voiska PVO" (air defense forces). Most of the main staff of PVO Strany already have been identified as members of the staff of Voiska PVO. Many western analysts believe that Ground Forces air defense troops, PVO Strany/ Fighter Aviation, and even Air Forces Frontal Aviation either have been or soon will be affected by this reorganization to a degree not yet clear. However, the main focus of this work is on the period between 1960 and 1980, when PVO Strany accurately designated the strategic air defense forces.

Fighter-Interceptor Aviation

In 1960 PVO Strany employed six fighter-interceptor types; most of the same aircraft were also in use with the Soviet tactical air force known as Frontal Aviation. Only the Su-9 *Fishpot B* and MiG-21 *Fishbed* were operationally supersonic while only one, the Yak-25 *Flashlight*, was a truly all-weather aircraft (see Table 5).

Western estimates of 10,000 PVO Strany fighters in 1960 may have been considerably exaggerated. However, the drop to 3,300 planes by 1970—a reduction of two-thirds—also could have been the result of Khrushchev's surgery on Soviet conventional armed forces in the early 1960s. It is perhaps most likely that the radical change in the number of PVO Strany aircraft serving between 1960 and 1970 resulted both from cutting and original exaggeration in western estimates.

By 1970 four new aircraft had been added to assume the roles of two that had been retired; the additions included the Tu-28P *Fiddler*, Yak-28P *Firebar*, Su-11 *Fishpot C*, and Su-15 *Flagon*. In 1970 four were all-weather, while one—the Tu-28P *Fiddler*, a giant forty-ton aircraft—was a very long-range, all-weather fighter-interceptor. Five models were flying near to or above Mach 2. Also, by 1970 the Soviets were operationally flying the Tu-126 *Moss* Airborne Early Warning and Control System

Table 5. Soviet Strategic Air Defense Forces
Fighter Aviation Aircraft Strengths, 1960–80

Year	Type	Number	Speed (mph)	Range (miles)
1960	Day fighters (MiGs 15, 17, 19, 21)		730–1,400	425–700
	All-weather (Yak-25)	10,000	680	2,000
	Limited all-weather (Su-9)		1,200	700
	Other			
1970	Day fighters (MiGs 17, 19, 21)		730–1,400	600–850
	All-weather Yak-28P, Su-15)		740–1,650	1,500–1,600
	Long-range, all-weather (Tu-28P)	3,300+	1,200	3,100
	Limited all-weather (Su-9, 11)		1,200–1,400	700
	AWACS (Tu-126)		460	5,500
1980	All-weather (Yak-28P, Su-15, MiGs 23, 25)	2,050	740–2,100	900–1,800
	Long-range, all-weather (Tu-28P)	135	1,200	3,100
	Limited all-weather (Su-9, 11)	430	1,200–1,400	700
	AWACS (Tu-126, 11-86)	20	460–590	2,200–5,500
		2,635		

(AWACS). Although technically somewhat primitive, the Soviet system was reportedly deployed before the U.S. AWACS.

The total number of PVO Strany interceptors again had fallen by 1980, this time by 25%, but substantial qualitative improvement had been achieved with the addition of the MiG-23 *Flogger* and MiG-25 *Foxbat*. The latter approached Mach 3 and all others were above Mach 2. The MiG-23 *Flogger*, also employed in Frontal Aviation for air cover, has been credited with a look-down, shoot-down capability.

SAMS

The surface-to-air component of PVO Strany in 1960 was equipped with two SAM systems, both of which had limited tactical mobility. The SA-1 *Guild* was installed only around Moscow, and the other was the better known SA-2 *Guideline*. At that time antiaircraft guns and automatic weapons were still deployed at numerous sites.

By 1970 there had been a proliferation of Soviet strategic air defense SAM systems. An antiballistic missile (ABM) force of sixty-four missiles and launchers had appeared around Moscow. The missile—the ABM-1 *Galosh*—could reach outside the atmosphere and explode a warhead in the megaton range, although its effectiveness against an ICBM attack has been in question among certain western analysts. As before, the SA-1 *Guild* remained only in the Moscow area. Some 8,000 SA-2 *Guideline* missiles were thought to be deployed throughout various parts of the USSR. Two new systems—the SA-3 *Goa*, a low-altitude missile, and the SA-5 *Gammon*, a long-range, high-altitude missile—were being deployed. The SA-3 *Goa* was given fairly wide distribution to meet U.S. low-altitude strategic penetration tactics then being publicized, and possibly also in anticipation of the next generation of U.S. strategic supersonic bombers that never really materialized except for the F-111 conversion. Antiaircraft guns, particularly the then newly introduced twin and radar controlled quad 23mm. units, were probably in local storage but readily available.

Technologically, the PVO Strany SAM picture changed little between 1970 and 1980. The SA-2 *Guideline*, whose deployment was decreasing, may have picked up a nuclear capability, while numbers of SA-3 *Goa* and SA-5 *Gammon* missiles continued to be added. In 1980 it was estimated that some 12,000 surface-to-air missiles were deployed throughout the strategic air defense complex. Of particular interest for the future is the system designated as the SA-10, which reportedly is undergoing tests as an anticruise missile weapon to be widely deployed in the 1980s.

Radar

PVO Strany radar and associated operations direction capabilities, which long have been the weaker links in Soviet air defense, by 1980 were widely deployed, widely variegated, and ever improving. Western estimates indicated some 7,000 items in place and operational, including satellites as well as early warning ground control intercept, anti-ICBM, anti-SLBM, over-the-horizon, and fire control units. The broad qualitative improvements were real and observable.

Manpower

Troops assigned to the PVO Strany in 1980 were estimated to consist of 550,000 men. Until 1980 there were two major Soviet Air Defense Districts with headquarters in Moscow and Baku. Both were routinely identified by the Soviets.

THE MILITARY AIR FORCES

In addition to the aviation resources of the naval air arm and strategic air defense, the multicomponent Military Air Forces branch incorporates strategic, tactical, and transport aviation in an independent air service. Though a separate service, the Military Air Forces maintain close links with the Ground Forces, particularly where tactical and transport air capabilities are concerned. While there recently has been evidence of some modification of strategic aviation's organizational situation, during the period between 1960 and 1980 it controlled all major intercontinental aircraft able to deliver nuclear weapons in a semi-autonomous service attached to the Military Air Forces. The Military Air Forces normally rank fourth in Soviet service protocol lists.

Strategic Aviation

In 1960 Long-Range Aviation—the strategic bomber component—was comprised of about 200 intercontinental aircraft, approximately 1,000 smaller medium bombers, and a modest inventory of airborne tankers, all of which were fairly new aircraft types (see Table 6).

In 1970 the same long-range bombers still appeared, but they were fewer by one-quarter and had aged a decade in service. Medium bombers also were reduced by about one-quarter, with the addition of only one new model—the Tu-22 *Blinder*. Some variants of these bombers also could carry nuclear air-to-surface missiles (ASM). The tanker force, although also aging, remained essentially the same.

By 1980 western estimates indicated a slight increase in the long-range force made up mainly of the same old basic types. The medium-bomber force continued to diminish to just over 500 aircraft, or half what estimates had included in 1960. However, the new Mach 2.5 Tupolev Tu-26 *Backfire* bomber was being added at a respectable rate. A considerable contingent of nearly 150 ECMs and reconnaissance aircraft had been identified with Long-Range Aviation during the 1970s. The older tankers were like the long-range bombers and were long overdue for replacement

**Table 6. Strategic Bomber and Support Strengths
of Long-Range Aviation, 1960–80**

Year	Type	Number	Speed (mph)	Range (miles)
1960	Long-range bombers (Tu-95,* M-4)	190	500–600	6,900–7,900
	Medium bombers (Tu-16, M-50)	1,000+	600–Mach 2	1,600–4,000
	Tankers (Tu-16, M-50)	"some"	600–Mach 2	1,600–4,000
		1,190+		
1970	Long-range bombers (Tu-95, M-4)	140	500–660	6,900–7,900
	Medium bombers (Tu-16, Tu-22)	725	600–920	2,000–4,000
	Tankers (Tu-16, M-4)	50	500–660	6,900–7,900
		915		
1980	Long-range bombers (Tu-95, M-4)	156	500–660	6,900–7,900
	Medium bombers (Tu-16, Tu-22, Tu-26)	518	600–Mach 2.5	2,000–5,000
	Reconnaissance (Tu-95, Tu-16, Tu-22)	34	500–920	2,000–7,900
	ECM (Tu-22)	100	920	2,000
	Tankers (Tu-16, M-4)	45	600–660	4,000–6,900
		853		

*Tu-95 is the design bureau designation commonly used in western literature. The service designation is Tu-20.

by newer types. Despite the addition of a modest number of impressive *Backfires* and ECM planes, Long-Range Aviation apparently has remained a second-priority service.

Frontal Aviation

Frontal Aviation—the Soviet tactical air arm–forms a very powerful element of Soviet military aviation. Linked closely as it is to the battlefield of tanks and infantry fighting vehicles, this ground support component seems to occupy a particularly favored position in Soviet military planning. Thus, it quite naturally controls a substantial and modern selection of aircraft (see Table 7).

Table 7. Tactical Air Strengths of Frontal Aviation, 1960–80

Year	Type	Number	Speed (mph)	Range (miles)
1960	Light bombers (I1-28, others)		520	1,500
	Reconnaissance (Yak-27, others)	4,000	570	2,000
	Fighters and fighter-bombers (MiGs 15, 17, 19, 21, Yak-25, others)		680–1,400	425–2,000
1970	Light bombers (I1-28, Yak-28)		520–740	1,500–1,600
	Reconnaissance (Yak-27, MiG-21)	4,000+	570–1,400	700–2,000
	Fighters, fighter-bombers (MiGs 17, 19, 21, Su-7, Yak-28P, others)		730–1,400	600–1,600
1980	Reconnaissance (Yak-28, MiG-21RF, MiG-25R, Su-17)	635	740–2,100	700–1,600
	ECM (An-12, Mi-4, Yak-28R)	55	130–740	150–3,500
	Fighters (MiGs-21, 23S)	1,750	1,400–1,520	700–1,800
	Fighters, ground attack (MiG-21, Su-7, Yak-28P, Su-17, 24, MiG-27)	2,635 5,075	740–1,650	800–2,500

In 1960 western open-source estimates perceived some 4,000 Frontal Aviation planes, including a mixture of light bombers, fighter-bombers, fighters, and reconnaissance aircraft. The principal light bomber was the Ilyushin I1-28 *Beagle*, which was already ten years old. The main fighters and fighter-bombers were a mixed group made up of the older MiG-15 *Fagot* and MiG-17 *Fresco*, the newer MiG-19 *Farmer* and Yak-25 *Flashlight*, and the brand new MiG-21 *Fishbed*. Most were day fighters or at best had limited all-weather capabilities. Only one, the Yak-25 *Flashlight*, also in the inventory of the PVO Strany, was an authentically all-weather fighter and only the MiG-19 *Farmer* and MiG-21 *Fishbed* were supersonic. The principal tactical reconnaissance aircraft was the newly introduced Yak-27R *Mangrove*, although there was also a MiG-21 *Fishbed* variant.

Ten years later Frontal Aviation's strength was estimated still to be at about 4,000. Approximately 1,200 were light bombers with a newer and somewhat faster aircraft—the Yak-28 *Brewer*—sharing the task with the old *Beagles*. In the fighter and fighter-bomber category, the MiG-15 *Fagot* had been retired along with the Yak-25 *Flashlight*. Two new aircraft—the Sukhoi Su-7 *Fitter A* and Yak-28P *Firebar*—had been integrated into the force. The latter, also deployed with the PVO Strany, added a high-performance, all-weather fighter to replace the *Flashlight*. The new Su-7 *Fitter A*, although not as fast as the *Fishbed*, had a maximum speed of nearly Mach 2.

By 1980 Frontal Aviation had added two new reconnaissance aircraft—the Su-17 *Fitter H* and MiG-25 *Foxbat*. These two, along with the constantly upgraded MiG-21 *Fishbed*, gave Frontal Aviation battlefield reconnaissance a substantial increase in technological sophistication. A variety of ECM planes and helicopters had been added as well. In the fighter and fighter-bomber classes, the aged Il-28 *Beagle* had been withdrawn from front-line service, along with the MiG-17 *Fresco* and MiG-19 *Farmer*. Four new aircraft were added during the 1970s: the Su-17 *Fitter C*, MiG-27 *Flogger D*, Su-24 *Fencer* ground attack aircraft, and MiG-23 *Flogger* dedicated air combat fighter.

Frontal Aviation had shown dramatic growth in the quality and quantity of its assets during the 1970s, reflecting decisions made in the previous decade. Six of the aircraft serving in 1980 had speeds of near or above Mach 2; combat ranges had been markedly increased; four of the ground attack aircraft were nuclear capable; several were variable-geometry and all-weather aircraft; and the MiG-23 *Flogger* evidently possessed some form of look-down, shoot-down capability. In short, Frontal Aviation achieved spectacular improvements in the twenty-year period, seemingly keeping pace with the modernization and increased mobility of the Soviet Ground Forces. In addition to the modernization of its aircraft, Frontal Aviation also apparently grew some 20% over 1970 to include over 5,000 fixed-wing aircraft.

VTA

Military Transport Aviation, known in both East and West by its Russian initials VTA, until recently had been a relatively neglected service, one that was not easily counted by western estimators. In 1960 it had a murkily perceived strength of some 2,000 aircraft, including some basically civilian models such as the Tupolev Tu-104 *Camel*, Il-18 *Coot*, and Antonov An-12 *Cub*. However, most of the fleet was made of older, smaller, and shorter range types.

By 1970 the larger passenger service Tupolevs, apparently found unsuitable, had been removed. Some newer Antonovs had been added, including the giant An-22 *Cock*, and VTA had two short takeoff and landing (STOL) planes in its fixed-wing inventory. Whether by actual count or closer estimating, total numbers were perceived to have dropped to 1,700. Ten years later the total strength had dropped to 1,550 aircraft, a 25% decrease since 1960.

However, even VTA had benefited from the general building programs of the late 1960s and 1970s, enabling it better to meet the needs of the Ground Forces and the airborne branch. Several new types had been deployed by 1980, again including some adapted from earlier civilian models. About sixty huge An-22 *Cocks* had been added, along with other newer heavy duty aircraft such as the jet passenger Il-62 *Classic* and jet cargo Il-76 *Candid*. At least five of the nine models in the VTA inventory were credited with rough-field STOL capability. Also by 1980 the average range of VTA aircraft had been greatly extended, and the service had achieved true intercontinental capabilities.

When estimating Soviet air transport strength, it is important to note that the resources of *Aeroflot*, the Soviet national airline, have been put to military use in the past. The management structure of the enterprise is integrated closely with the armed forces, in fact, the civil air minister is an active air force marshal, and a number of his staff have been identified as senior air force generals.

Helicopters

Where to include the rapidly expanded Soviet military helicopter strength is not entirely clear. Some western sources list them, with the exception of naval helicopters, along with the Ground Forces; others carry them under VTA or Frontal Aviation. The answer well may be that they are split all three ways, which is a typical Soviet solution, or that many VTA helicopters come under Ground Forces operational control. In any event, they are becoming an increasingly important component. In 1960 there were probably a few hundred light helicopters serving with the Military Air Forces and none of them were armed.

By 1970 the estimated helicopter contingent had grown to 1,500 with five models carrying more than ten passengers, three able to lift more than twenty-five, and one—the Mi-6 *Hook*—capable of transporting sixty-five passengers or equivalent freight for fairly long distances. Variants of these models were armed with an assortment of machine guns, missiles, and rockets or bombs. Four of the models were less than ten years old. And by 1980 the perceived inventory had doubled to more than 3,000. The addition of the new Mi-24 *Hind* gave the Soviets a heavily armed assault helicopter as well as a heavily armed and armored gunship variant that has both an antihelicopter and antitank role.

Manpower

As of 1980 Soviet Military Air Forces had an estimated personnel strength of about 520,000 men. Some analysts contend that at least until the recent turmoil in the air defense forces the Military Air Forces were organized into three long-range air armies, all in the USSR, and sixteen tactical air armies of greatly varying sizes. Four of the latter evidently were located along with the four groups of Soviet forces in East Europe and one each in twelve of sixteen military districts in the USSR. Others merely identify Frontal Aviation elements in each of the military districts. The VTA is reportedly organized into separate air regiments.

GROUND FORCES

The Soviet Ground Forces comprise by far the largest of the five major armed services of the Ministry of Defense. They are always listed second in armed forces protocol lists. Within the Ground Forces the tank remains the principal combat system and has been the focus of both intensive and extensive development over the last twenty years.

Tanks

In 1960 Soviet Ground Forces already were equipped with an enormous number of about 35,000 tanks of which some 20,000 were considered first line. One model of main battle tank (MBT), the T-54, was of postwar vintage and the heavy T-10 tank was brand new; they also had introduced a postwar light amphibious tank, the PT-76. Some of the T-54s had a vertical stabilizing mechanism and the T-10 may have been fully stabilized for horizontal as well as vertical fire adjustment. Some of the T-54s and all of the T-10s had infrared driving and fighting capabilities, while the T-10 also may have had nuclear, biological, and chemical (NBC) warfare protection. Even at that time some of the T-54s and T-10s had deepwater snorkeling equipment (see Table 8).

Table 8. Soviet Tank Strengths, 1960–80

Year	Type	Number	Main Armament	Secondary Armament
1960	T-34 MBT		85mm. gun	2 machine guns (MGs)
	T-54 MBT		100mm. gun	2 MGs, some have AAMGs
	JS-3 heavy	35,000	122mm. gun	MG, AAMG
	T-10M heavy		122mm. gun	MG
	PT-76 amphib.		76mm. gun	MG
1970	T-54 MBT		100mm. gun	2 MGs, some have AAMGs
	T-55 MBT		100mm. gun	1–2 MGs, some have AAMGs
	T-62 MBT	42,000	115mm. (smooth)	MG, some have AAMGs
	JS-3 heavy		122mm. gun	MG, AAMG
	T-10M heavy		122mm. gun	MG, AAMG
	PT-76 amphib.		76mm. gun	MG
1980	T-54 MBT		100mm. gun	2 MGs, some have AAMGs
	T-55 MBT		100mm. gun	1–2 MGs, some have AAMGs
	T-62 MBT		115mm. (smooth)	MG, some have AAMGs
	T-64 MBT	50,000	125mm. (smooth)	MG, AAMG
	T-72 MBT		125mm. (smooth)	MG, AAMG
	JS-3 heavy		122mm. gun	MG, AAMG
	T-10M heavy		122mm. gun	MG, AAMG
	PT-76 amphib.		76mm. gun	MG

In 1970 the total tank stock was estimated to be up about 20% to 42,000. The T-34 (85mm.) tank of Great Patriotic War fame was thought finally to be retired from Soviet front-line service and two new main battle tanks had been deployed—the T-55 and T-62. Both the T-54 and T-55 had 100mm. guns and the T-62 was armed with a 115mm. smoothbore cannon that can fire, among other rounds, a fin-stabilized projectile. Several types had NBC protection, some or full stabilization, infrared fighting capability, and snorkeling equipment. No change in the heavy tank situation was observed since 1960, except that there seemed to be fewer heavy tank units in evidence and probably more of the heavy tanks were going into storage.

By 1980 still another main battle tank had been added—the T-72 and a variation, the T-64. The new tanks had a bigger (125mm.) version of the T-62's smoothbore cannon, NBC protection, infrared equipment, stabilized sights, snorkeling capability, and a new automatic loading device that eliminated the need for one crewman. The Soviets also were reported to be testing a new T-80, similarly equipped but carrying a stronger laminated armor. Estimates of deployed Soviet tank strength in 1980 reached the astonishing figure of 50,000.

APCs

In the twenty-year period under consideration the Soviets have placed progressively more emphasis on ground combat as a war of movement. One logical outcome of that focus has been the development of an extensive force of armored personnel carriers (APCs) and related infantry combat vehicles (see Table 9).

**Table 9. Soviet Armored Personnel Carriers and
Infantry Combat Vehicle Strengths, 1960–80**

Year	Type	Number	Capacity (persons)	Armament
1960	BTR152		19	MG
	BTR40		10	MG
	BTR50p	10,000	22	MG
	BRDM		5	AAMG
	Others			
1970	BTR152		19	MG, twin AAMGs, or mortar
	BTR40		10	MG or twin AAMGs
	BTR50p		22	MG or up to 85mm. antitank gun
	BRDM	unknown	5	MG or 3–6 ATGMs
	BTR60p		18	1–3 MGs
	OT64		20	1–2 MGs
	BRDM2		4	2 MGs, 6 ATGMs, or 4 SA-7s
	BMP-1		11	73mm. gun (smoothbore, autoload), MG, ATGM rail, SA-7
1980	BTR152		19	MG, twin AAMGs, or mortar
	BTR40		10	MG or twin AAMGs
	BTR50p		22	MG or up to 85mm. AT gun
	BRDM		5	MG or 3–6 ATGMs
	BTR60p	62,000	18	1–3 MGs
	OT64		20	1–2 MGs
	BRDM2		4	2 MGs, 6 ATGMs, or 4 SA-7s
	BMP-1		11	73mm. gun, ATGM rail, MG, or SA-7
	M1970		13	MG
	BMD		9	73mm. gun (smoothbore, autoload), ATGM rail, 3MGs, SA-7

In 1960 they were thought to have had less than 10,000 APCs; trucks were used for personnel transport. There were four APC types and all were less than ten years old; two were wheeled, one was wheeled and amphibious, and one was tracked and amphibious. Most of them mounted heavy machine guns, some more than one.

By 1970 a substantial proliferation of APC types had occurred. All the old models remained in service, apparently on the assumption that they were better than trucks without armor. Many of the earlier models were sporting new overhead cover or carrying mortars or antitank guns internally mounted; others had been converted to antitank or SAM guided-missile mounts. Four new types had been added, including three wheeled APCs, one of which was a Czech-made vehicle. The most impressive innovation made during the 1960s, however, was the addition of an infantry combat vehicle, as distinguished from the armored personnel carrier. The first Soviet example, the tracked amphibious BMP-1, mounted substantial offensive firepower, a 73mm.-smoothbore autoloaded gun, a machine gun, SA-7 SAMS, and even antitank guided missiles (ATGM). By this time variants of several of the vehicles, including the BMP-1, were equipped with NBC protection.

By 1980 two more tracked amphibious carriers were introduced. One was the M-70, which was essentially a prime mover or cargo hauler; the other, the BMD, is the airborne troop version of the BMP with additional machine guns. The armament in particular makes the Soviet infantry fighting vehicles superior to any other personnel carriers in the world. However, in the Yom Kippur War of 1973 Soviet tacticians learned that these vehicles were vulnerable unless continuously supported by heavier units. In 1980 western analysts estimated the Soviet Ground Force inventory of APC/fighting vehicles at the astronomical figure of 62,000.

ATGMs

Antitank missiles form a significant portion of the firepower available to the Soviet Ground Forces, although they have not received the same high development priority as tanks and armored vehicles. After their own armor, the Soviets apparently see the ATGM as a preferred second line of defense against enemy tanks.

In 1960 no ATGMs were thought to be deployed with Soviet Ground Forces, although they were undoubtedly testing prototypes. By 1970 there were three types in service—two wire-guided (AT-1 *Snapper*, AT-3 *Sagger*) and one radio-controlled (AT-2 *Swatter*)—on an assortment of vehicular, ground, and helicopter mounts. Armor penetration of these three types was reported to be from fourteen to twenty inches. By 1980 two new radio-guided models (AT-4 *Spiggot*, AT-5 *Spandrel*) were available. NATO has identified a new IR or laser-guided missile (AT-6 *Spiral*) deployed on the Mi-24 *Hind* helicopter gunship as well as on various other mounts.

Air Defense

The air defense of the Ground Forces also has been the focus of a good deal of weapons development. The Soviet Ground Forces are now protected by probably the most comprehensive system of forward combat air defense in the world. In 1960 the SA-2 *Guideline*, which also was assigned to the PVO Strany, was the only missile in Ground Forces service along with two postwar 57mm.-antiaircraft guns systems. One, the S-60, was a towed single-barrel weapon. Also deployed was the ZSU-57-2, a self-propelled, dual-mounted, antiaircraft gun system on a heavy-tracked chassis. These were backed by a diverse spread of older World War II and even pre-World War II guns and light automatic weapons.

By 1970 four more SAM missile systems had been added. One of these—the SA-3 *Goa*—was also deployed with PVO Strany as a low-altitude weapon. The other three included the SA-4 *Ganef*, SA-6 *Gainful*, and SA-7 *Grail*. The *Ganef* and *Gainful* were mounted on tracked launchers while the SA-7 *Grail* could be shoulder-fired. Principal mobile antiaircraft gun systems available were the two 57mm. variants and two newer 23mm. variants—a towed twin ZU-23-2 and the tracked four-gun version, the ZSU-23/4. Many older AA guns and lesser automatic weapons were still in the inventory.

By 1980 two additional systems were operational, the SA-8 *Gecko* and SA-9 *Gaskin*, both of which were on wheeled amphibious launchers. The SA-4 *Ganef* and SA-8 *Gecko* were air transportable due to the availability of new heavy cargo aircraft. The SA-9 *Gaskin* was assumed to be a scaled-up and improved version of the *Grail*. The not yet deployed SA-11 was thought to be a laser-guided version of the SA-6 *Gainful*. Up to 8,000 of the twin and quad 23mm. and 57mm. automatic weapons were still thought to be in use, as were several other obsolescent types of antiaircraft guns and automatic weapons.

Artillery

Conventional tube artillery traditionally has provided a very major portion of the tsarist and then Soviet offensive punch. Though somewhat overshadowed by battlefield missiles, especially since 1960, conventional artillery support is still assumed to be a critical element in Soviet combat doctrine. The following data is for tube artillery upward from 100mm.

In 1960 two 100mm. gun types of World War II origin, including a self-propelled (SP) model, were in the artillery inventory, supplemented by a towed gun first deployed in 1955. In the 122mm.–130mm. category there were five weapons: one pre-World War howitzer, a World War II SP gun, and three postwar guns, one of which had a 360-degree traverse. In the 152mm. or larger class, there were one pre-World War II howitzer, two World War II weapons—a howitzer and a SP gun-howitzer—and two postwar towed guns. Incidentally, as an indication of how wrong western estimates can be, one of the latter two was a 180mm. gun that, until the Israelis captured one and measured it, had been identified for nearly twenty years as a 203mm. piece. By 1970 a revolutionary 100mm.-smoothbore gun had been added that fired, among other rounds, a fin-stabilized projectile. In addition, a new 122mm. all-round traverse divisional howitzer had entered service. In the larger caliber category, the same five pieces remained through 1970.

In 1980 the 100mm. class remained essentially the same, while a revolutionary SP howitzer—the 122mm. M-1974—had entered service. It was amphibious, had all-round traverse, and probably carried NBC protection. In the largest bore category, another new SP howitzer—the 152mm. M-1973—had been deployed. Like the new 122mm. piece, it was mounted on a *Ganef* chassis and, among other things, fired rocket-assisted rounds. The two SP howitzers were being produced and deployed at a rapid rate. A new 203mm. SP gun, which is also able to fire rocket-assisted rounds, is reported to be in service with the Soviet Group of Forces in Germany. Nuclear capability is claimed for both the 152mm. and the newer 203mm.

SSMs

In 1960 Soviet Ground Forces had deployed one mobile-tracked guided surface-to-surface missile (SSM)—the *Scud A*—and three unguided rockets known as *Frogs* 1, 2, and 3. These latter were also track-mounted and all four were thought capable of firing high explosive (HE), chemical, or nuclear rounds. By 1970 an additional guided missile, the *Scud B*, and three more *Frog* types—4, 5, and 7—were added, giving a greater variety of ranges and mobility. Several of the *Frogs* were on amphibious chassis, while another was on a wheeled vehicle. By 1980 some of the early *Frogs* had dropped out and an improved *Scud* and another longer range missile, the *Scaleboard*, had been added and two or perhaps three more guided-missile models were reported in testing.

Also throughout the entire twenty-year period, Soviet Ground Forces have been supplied with increasingly sophisticated multiple rocket launchers mounted on trucks, which were generated from the system so widely used in the Second World War under the nickname of "Katyusha."

In addition, a whole panoply of smaller-wheeled and shoulder-fired rocket launchers, recoilless rifles, and light, medium, and heavy mortars have been available in vast numbers.

Manpower

In assessing Soviet military manpower numbers, the Ground Forces present perhaps the greatest trouble for the western analyst. In 1960 they were estimated to be about 2 million strong; in 1980 they were supposed to be 1,875,000. Equipment figures, which are more easily checked than manpower, are probably close to the mark. If so, given the equipment figures already noted—50,000 tanks, 62,000 APC/fighting vehicles, 20,000 conventional artillery tubes between 100mm.–180mm., not to mention the *Frogs*, *Scuds*, ATGMs, and SAMs, etc., and even counting a portion of the approximately 180-line divisions at cadre or reduced strength—it is difficult to see how the Soviet Ground Forces could number fewer than 2 million men.

SECURITY TROOPS

The Soviets count the Internal Troops of the Ministry of Internal Affairs (MVD) and the Border Troops of the Committee for State Security (KGB) as part of their armed forces whether western analysts do or not. These are not simply police units but highly trained and well-equipped elite military organizations performing specialized tasks. In peacetime the Border Troops mainly perform an antipenetration and exit function and the Internal Troops are deployed to suppress civil disorder, particularly in urban areas. In wartime the Border Troops are to be the first line of defense against invasion, and the Internal Troops are to play a rear area security role. Both would have special security roles in occupied territory.

Although not armed with heavy equipment, the Border Troops in particular have a wide selection of helicopters, light aircraft, small armed cutters, electronic detection, surveillance, and control systems as well as the best communications equipment available. Both they and the Internal Troops have light artillery and armor. They both had impressive records as defense and assault units during World War II. The West did not even include them in its manpower estimates in 1960; in 1970 a figure of about 250,000 was estimated. By 1980 the figure had been nearly doubled to about 460,000 men, a figure almost two-thirds the size of the U.S. Army.

In fact, there is fair evidence to suggest that their combined manpower of as many as 750,000 men may match their World War II strength.

CONCLUDING REFLECTIONS

Over the years questions have arisen as to the capabilities of the military manpower of the Warsaw Pact nations to operate the great masses of equipment that make up the material half of the Soviet war machine. This is a complex issue worthy of a special study in itself. However, the case of the Soviet career officer is probably the simplest to handle. Knowledgeable western experts conclude that there may be from 750,000 to almost 1,000,000 of these officers, who are products of a system comprising approximately 140 officer commissioning schools, almost all of which have four- and five-year curricula.

Above these schools are superimposed more than twenty branch academies and higher officers' courses, most of which are three to five years long. Thus, the Soviet officer is as well schooled as any in the world. Additionally, as many as 90% or more of the Soviet officer corps are members of the Communist Party or Young Communist League (Komsomol) and have a vested personal interest in regime preservation. Perhaps 5% to 10% of the Soviet forces are made up of a combination of the new warrant officer class and the old extended service or career enlisted men. These individuals are also trained and, for the most part, are dedicated, professional soldiers with probably a lesser percentage of party members and Komsomols among them.

What about the other 75% of the Soviet forces that are made up of the conscript whose average term of service is two years? He is better educated than the Soviet G.I. of World War II or of even twenty years ago. He has had, as a rule, a long period of both political indoctrination and premilitary training in the public school system, in the numerous junior auxiliaries of the Communist Party, and in various other pre-induction training organizations. At worst, he is passively reconciled to military service and, in the case of possibly one out of three, an enthusiastic Komsomol or other nonparty type of activist. He is probably more of a patriot than an enthusiast for the current political regime and is more urbanized than his predecessor. By tradition, he is dogged, enduring, physically strong, and long suffering. His training is harsh, repetitive, and designed to instill automatic, instinctive response. Neither junior officer nor enlisted conscript training appears to be based on much originality and initiative. Rather it seems designed to combat the traditional streak of indolence and lack of self-discipline characteristically associated with Russian and later Soviet conscripts.

In two world conflicts the Soviet soldier and his tsarist predecessor surrendered in unprecedented millions when the tide of battle was
against them. Yet, in other phases of the same conflicts, he fought hard
and tenaciously under incredibly harsh conditions. Depending on external
circumstances, he could follow either or both patterns again.

BIBLIOGRAPHY

Aircraft

Green, William, and Swanborough, Gordon, comp. *The Observer's
    Soviet Aircraft Directory.* New York: Frederick Warne & Company,
    1975.
Gunston, Bill, cons. ed. *Encyclopedia of World Air Power.* New York:
    Crescent Books, 1980.
Soviet Aerospace Handbook (AF PAM 200-21). Washington, DC:
    Government Printing Office, 1978.
Sweetman, Bill, and Gunston, Bill. *Soviet Air Power.* New York: Sala-
    mander Books, 1978.
Taylor, John W., ed. *Jane's All the World's Aircraft.* 1971–81.
Taylor, John W., and Swanborough, Gordon. *Military Aircraft of the
    World.* New York: Charles Scribner's Sons, 1973, 1975.
———. *Military Aircraft of the World.* Shepperton, Surrey, England: Ian
    Allen, 1979.

Armies

439th Military Intelligence Detachment (strategic). *USSR - Deployment
    of the Soviet Ground Forces' Divisions by Military District* (un-
    classified). Washington, DC: Government Printing Office, 1975.
Reitz, James T. *Security Troops: The Kremlin's Other Armies.* McLean,
    VA: BDM, 1980.
Wiener, Friedrich. *The Armies of the Warsaw Pact Nations.* Vienna:
    Carl Ueberreuter Verlag, 1976.
Wiener, Friedrich, and Lewis, William J. *The Warsaw Pact Armies.*
    Vienna: Carl Ueberreuter Verlag, 1977.

Missiles

Pretty, Ronald, ed. *Jane's Pocket Book of Missiles.* New York: Collier
    Books, 1975.
Taylor, John W. R., and Taylor, Michael J. H. *Missiles of the World.*
    New York: Charles Scribner's Sons, 1976.

Navies

Blackman, R. B., ed. *Jane's Fighting Ships*. New York: Jane's Publishing Inc., 1967–68, 1971–72.

Couhat, J. L., ed. *Combat Fleets of the World, 1980/81*. Published in the United States under the auspices of the U.S. Naval Institute.

Moore, John E., ed. *Jane's Fighting Ships*. New York: Jane's Publishing Inc., 1976–81.

Tanks and Artillery

Bidwell, Shelford, ed. *Brassey's Artillery of the World*. New York: Bonanza Books, 1979.

Bradford, George, and Morgan, Len. *50 Famous Tanks*. New York: ARCO Publishing Company, 1967.

Foss, Christopher. *Artillery of the World*. New York: Charles Scribner's Sons, 1974.

———, ed. *Jane's Armor and Artillery*. 1979–80.

———, ed. *Jane's Pocket Book of Modern Tanks and Armored Fighting Vehicles*. New York: Collier Books, 1974.

Von Senger, F. M., and Etterlin, J. F. *Das Kleine Panzerbuch*. München: Lehmanns Verlag, 1966.

———. *Die Panzer Grenadiere*. München: Lehmanns Verlag, 1961.

———. *Kampfpanzer 1916–1966*. München: Lehmanns Verlag, 1966.

Additionally, the following provided important articles and information in most of the foregoing categories:

International Defense Review (undated special series).
　　　Air Defense Systems
　　　Battle Tanks (1976)
　　　Combat Aircraft
　　　Warships and Naval Systems
Jane's Defense Review 2, no. 3 (1981).

Jones, David R., ed. *Soviet Armed Forces Review Annual* 1 (1977), 3 (1979), and 4 (1980). Gulf Breeze, FL: Academic International Press.

The Warsaw Pact Today:
The East European Military Forces*

THOMAS O. CASON

The term "Warsaw Pact" inevitably produces a tendency in both the specialist and the casual observer to think primarily of Soviet military forces or of a monolithic amalgam of Soviet and East European military forces. Certainly no one would seriously argue that the real strength of the Warsaw Pact, as a military force, is not based on the Soviet military forces that are stationed in East Europe as well as those in the western military districts of the Soviet Union. It is not the purpose of this essay to minimize in any way the Soviet military component of the Warsaw Pact but, to the extent possible, the Soviet military forces will not be discussed. Instead, the focus will be on the military forces of the six East European members of the Warsaw Treaty Organization or Warsaw Pact. Each of the six armed forces will be analyzed and assessed individually because they in no sense represent a monolithic force either in terms of military capability or in overall utility to the Warsaw Pact and the Soviet Union.

In order to analyze the individual East European armed forces within the framework of the Warsaw Pact, it is necessary first to examine the Pact itself both in terms of organizational structure and of its operational modes. It is in the context of the Warsaw Pact that the East European military forces are most often cited—correctly or incorrectly—as contributing to the overall Soviet military strength in Europe opposite NATO. The value of the Warsaw Pact as an instrument of warfare in Europe also deserves to be analyzed, perhaps more closely than it has in the past. Only when the military role of the Pact itself is clearly seen and the real military capability of the six East Europe military forces are correctly assessed can one begin to understand the importance of these East European forces in any conflict in East Europe or between the Soviet Union (and Eastern Europe) and NATO.

---

*The views expressed herein are those of the author. They should not be taken to represent those of the U.S. Air Force or the Department of Defense.

THE WARSAW PACT

The basic organizational structures of the Warsaw Treaty Organization are provided for by the agreement that founded the Warsaw Pact in May 1955. The primary institutions described in the treaty are the Joint Command and the Political Consultative Committee (PCC).[1] The PCC was empowered to create auxiliary organs as they were needed. What has evolved, however, is an organizational structure that is complex and one that has expanded, like other bureaucratic organizations, its functions and increased the division of labor within the organization. Several key changes in the organizational framework were made at the 1969 Budapest meeting of the PCC and these are reflected in the current organizational arrangements (see Figure 1). For purposes of analysis the organizational structure will be viewed from two perspectives: the political and the military.

The focal point of the political organization of the Warsaw Treaty Organization is the PCC. The treaty called for the formation of a committee (Article 6) that would be composed of representatives from each government and would hold consultations to consider problems arising in connection with the terms of the treaty. The PCC is comprised of top party and government officials of the member states and has been specifically empowered to create other organizational elements as deemed appropriate.[2] When the committee met for the first time in Prague in January 1956, it approved the statute that created the Joint Command. At the same meeting a Standing Commission and a Joint Secretariat also were created, with the Joint Secretariat to be a permanent body of representatives from the member states headed by the chief of staff of the Joint Command, who initially was and always has been a Soviet general officer.[3] Another significant action taken at that initial meeting was the acceptance of the newly created army of the German Democratic Republic (GDR) into the Unified Armed Forces under the Joint Command; the German minister of defense became a deputy commander in chief of the Joint Command.[4] It is interesting to observe that the PCC has never really operated in the manner prescribed by the treaty or even by the terms laid

---

[1]See "The Warsaw Treaty of Friendship, Cooperation and Mutual Assistance" cited in Robin Alison Remington, *The Warsaw Pact: Case Studies in Communist Conflict Resolution* (Cambridge: MIT Press, 1971), Doc. 1, pp. 201–5.

[2]Malcolm Mackintosh, "The Evolution of the Warsaw Pact," *Adelphi Papers*, no. 58 (London: International Institute for Strategic Studies, 1969), p. 21.

[3]John Erickson, *Soviet-Warsaw Pact Force Levels* (Washington: U.S. Strategic Institute, 1976), p. 65.

[4]"Communique on the Session of the Political Consultative Committee of the Warsaw Treaty Powers, 28 January 1956," *For a Lasting Peace, For a People's Democracy* (Bucharest), 3 February 1956. Cited in J. P. Jain, *Documentary Study of the Warsaw Pact* (London: Asia Publishing House, 1973), pp. 149–50.

Figure 1. The Warsaw Treaty Organization

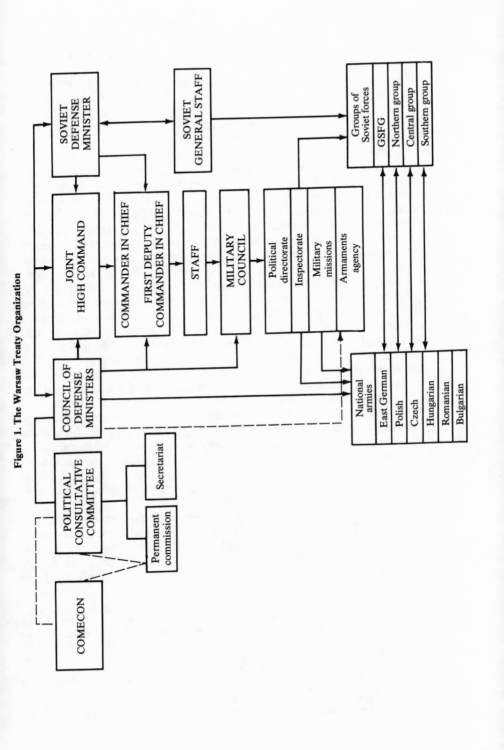

out in the first meeting; for example, it met only seven times during the
first ten years (1955–65), and there is little to indicate that it made
substantive decisions concerning the treaty organization.[5] It is particularly
clear that the critical military decisions for the Warsaw Treaty Organization had to have been made outside of the PCC.

In Article 5 the Warsaw Treaty called for the creation of a single
military structure—the Joint Command. The agreement establishing the
Joint Command, signed the same day as the treaty on 14 May 1955,
provided for the ministers of defense of the signatory states to serve as
deputy commanders in chief, with Marshal of Soviet Union Ivan S.
Konev as the first commander in chief. The newly created Joint Staff
was to be located in Moscow along with the permanent representatives of
the signatory states. From the beginning the Joint Command has been
structurally dominated by the Soviet Union; all of the top military positions in the Warsaw Pact always have been held by Soviet officers.

At the PCC session in Budapest in March 1969—the first meeting
after the invasion of Czechoslovakia in August 1968—several structural
changes were made in Pact organization. One change, and the only one
that directly involved the PCC, was the removal of the ministers of
defense from the committee and the formation of a separate Council of
Defense Ministers.[6] The ministers of defense of the East European states
ceased to be deputy commanders in chief of the Joint Command, an
arrangement that had placed the ministers of defense of East Europe as
subordinates to the commander in chief, who was only the first deputy
minister of defense of the Soviet Union. Deputy ministers of defense of the
East European states became the deputy commanders in chief of the Joint
Command. This change corrected the prestige problem and potentially
increased the power of the national governments vis-à-vis the Pact's Joint
Command by adding one additional bureaucratic layer between the Joint
Command and the national governments.[7]

A second change made at the 1969 Budapest meeting was the
creation of the Military Council (see Figure 1), which appears to operate
under the direction of the commander in chief and includes the chief of
staff.[8] The membership of the Military Council includes the deputy
ministers of defense of the East European countries, and its principal role
appears to be an advisory one.[9]

        [5]The PCC was supposed to meet twice a year and handle all substantive issues
concerning the Warsaw Treaty Organization. See Richard F. Staar, *The Communist
Regimes of Eastern Europe: An Introduction* (Menlo Park, CA: Hoover Institute on War,
Revolution, and Peace, 1967), pp. 215–16.
        [6]Erickson, *Soviet-Warsaw Pact*, pp. 65–67.
        [7]Lawrence T. Caldwell, "The Warsaw Pact: Directions of Change," *Problems of
Communism* 24, no. 5 (September–October 1975): 3–4.
        [8]Erickson, *Soviet-Warsaw Pact*, p. 65.
        [9]A. Ross Johnson, *Soviet-East European Military Relations: An Overview* (Santa
Monica, CA: Rand Corporation, 1975), pp. 15–16.

A third change made by the PCC at Budapest was to establish a permanent Joint Staff, consisting of the chief of staff of the Joint Command and the first deputy chief of staff from each of the East European countries. All of these deputy chiefs of staff have the rank of major general or its equivalent and are permanently assigned to Warsaw Pact headquarters in Moscow.[10] The original organizational structure of the Warsaw Pact, along with the changes that have been made over the past twenty-five years, provides a basic framework that can be used to understand the individual East European military establishments and their military forces as well as the potential military utility that each of them has to the overall Soviet military position in East Europe.

THE EAST EUROPEAN MILITARY FORCES

The military establishments in East Europe today have been organized mostly along the lines of the Soviet armed forces, and only in recent years have there been deviations from this model.[11] In 1944 and 1945, as the Red Army took East Europe from the control of Nazi Germany or indigenous Fascist regimes, the Soviets established new governments in which Communist parties were either in control or put in a position to gain control.[12] The present-day military establishments were born during the turbulent years from 1945 to 1949, and were formed, equipped, and trained by Soviet army establishments that had remained in each country, except Czechoslovakia, after the end of the war. Thus, the development of the East European military forces was heavily influenced by the Soviet Union. In the case of Poland, the core of the new Polish People's Army had been created in the Soviet Union in 1944 and had fought alongside the Soviet army in Poland and Germany. However, in 1945 the existing military leadership in most of East Europe was non-Communist and often was associated with the former pro-German regimes. For the first few years after the war, the Soviet army was the principal military organization present in East Europe and only gradually were the national armies transformed into competent Soviet-style military organizations.[13]

---

[10]Ibid.

[11]Examples can be seen in the reestablishment of the Polish general staff and the integration, within the Romanian army, of a large paramilitary defense organization similar to the Yugoslavian model. The deviations from the basic Soviet model in these two cases partially reflect the traditions and/or interests of the two countries concerned without regard to Soviet preferences.

[12]Poland and Czechoslovakia were occupied by German forces; the Antonescu government in Romania and the Szalasi regime in Hungary were pro-Nazi Fascist regimes. Bulgaria had a pro-Nazi regime until September 1944.

[13]Peter Gosztony, *Zur Geschichte der Europaischen Volksarmeen* (Bonn: Hohwacht Verlag, 1976).

The East European armed forces have developed in quite different patterns since the late 1940s. Today, in spite of the fact that the organizational structures of each of the armies are similar, that all of them more or less adhere to Soviet training and doctrine, and that all of the armies are mainly equipped with Soviet weapons, there are important differences in the capabilities of the East European military forces. The six East European military establishments will be examined individually in terms of their quantitative and qualitative capabilities. It is the combination of these, as well as other geostrategic and historical factors, that represents the military potential of these East European forces to the Warsaw Pact and to the Soviet Union.

If the only measure of merit relevant to the calculation of potential military capability of the armed forces of a nation were the number of men, tanks, artillery pieces, airplanes, etc., then the potential military capability of a single nation or of an alliance of nations could be determined rather quickly. But numbers alone are not an adequate measure of the potential military capability of a single nation and are perhaps significantly less relevant in the calculation of the potential military capability of an alliance.[14] Numbers are usually an important component in the calculation of potential military capability but must be considered in the light of other objective and subjective qualitative measures of merit. Some of the objective measures of merit include the age and effectiveness of the military equipment, the training and state of the equipment and its maintainability in any movement to a combat area and in combat, and the relevance of the equipment arsenal to the type and locale of combat to be undertaken. In addition to these objective and more or less calculable measures of merit, there are several subjective factors that are very important but cannot be measured in any precise way. Included in these subjective measures of merit are the military experience and military traditions of the national military forces, the fighting quality of the men of the military forces, the fighting agility and adaptability of the troops, the combat competence and resilience of the fighting force, and the commitment of the force to the purposes of the combat. This list could be expanded considerably and each of the measures listed above could be subdivided into more specific factors. In the calculation of the potential military capability of the military forces of a nation, it is necessary at the outset not only to assess the quantitative and objective qualitative factors

---

[14]The problems with using the raw numbers in computing the potential military capability of a military alliance are particularly difficult. Compatibility and interoperability are limited by military equipment; languages of the various alliance members; different emphases and stresses on training and execution; differences of perceptions of the military leadership of the alliance members; differences in military cultures, traditions, and history of the various alliance members; and, although difficult to operationalize, differences in the will to engage in military combat.

but also to consider a number of unique and highly subjective qualitative characteristics.[15]

In addition, calculation of potential military capability requires some definition of the particular conflict in which the military forces will be called upon to participate. For purposes of analysis, a four-level framework will be used to evaluate the East European military forces. The first level will be that of a defensive war in which NATO or, in some limited cases, another nation attacks the Warsaw Pact or a member of the Warsaw Pact. Potential military capability of the East European military forces is relatively higher at this level of conflict: a bona fide defensive war. The second level of conflict is that of an interbloc intervention in which the East European military forces are used against one of the other bloc members as was the case in Czechoslovakia in 1968. The third and fourth levels of conflict result from a Soviet-led offensive war against NATO. These levels are the most demanding for the East European military forces and must be examined under two very different types of circumstances in which such a war might begin: one kind of offensive war against NATO could be a surprise attack; the other might be an offensive war after full mobilization. The Soviet doctrinal preference for first strike must be weighed against the East European military forces' requirement for mobilization to be able to place the bulk of their forces on the line. The individual East European military forces will be examined at each of the four levels of conflict.

Bulgaria

Bulgarian military forces have a total strength of some 149,000 men, of which about 94,000 are conscripts. The military forces are divided among army, navy, and air force units, with the bulk of the troops (105,000) assigned to ground units. Figure 2 details the general composition and equipment of the Bulgarian military and includes the paramilitary forces.[16] One of the unique features of the Bulgarian army is the absence of tank divisions; instead, there are five tank brigades that more or less equate to two tank divisions.[17] Bulgarian military forces represent the highest percentage of the population of any of the East European nations: 1.67% of a population of 8,980,000. On the other hand, Bulgaria has the

---

[15]Most of the subjective evaluations are based on an extensive review of the literature on the Warsaw Pact and the East European military forces and on interviews with experts like John Erickson, Malcolm Mackintosh, Christopher Donnelly, and others who have studied the military forces of Eastern Europe for many years.

[16]Data for the Bulgarian military is taken from *The Military Balance 1980–1981* (London: International Institute for Strategic Studies, 1980), p. 15.

[17]Friedrich Wiener, *The Armies of the Warsaw Pact Nations* (Vienna: Carl Ueber-reuter Verlag, 1976), pp. 22–23.

Figure 2. Bulgarian Military Forces

TOTAL MILITARY FORCES
149,000 (94,000 conscripts)

ARMY
105,000 (70,000 conscripts)

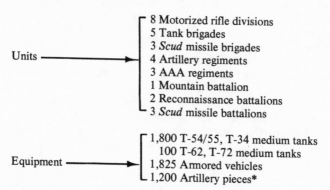

Units
- 8 Motorized rifle divisions
- 5 Tank brigades
- 3 *Scud* missile brigades
- 4 Artillery regiments
- 3 AAA regiments
- 1 Mountain battalion
- 2 Reconnaissance battalions
- 3 *Scud* missile battalions

Equipment
- 1,800 T-54/55, T-34 medium tanks
- 100 T-62, T-72 medium tanks
- 1,825 Armored vehicles
- 1,200 Artillery pieces*

NAVY
10,000 (6,000 conscripts)

AIR FORCE
34,000 (18,000 conscripts)

Combat aircraft	204
Ground attack fighters	Some MiG-23**
	64 MiG-17
Interceptors	80 MiG-21
	36 MiG-17
Reconnaissance	24 MiG-17

PARAMILITARY
FORCES

Border guards	15,000
Construction troops	12,000
Security forces	12,000
Workers' militia	150,000
	189,000

---

*Artillery in this and subsequent figures includes 76mm., 100mm., 122mm., 130mm., and 152mm. guns/HOW; 120mm. mortars; and 122mm., 140mm., and 240mm. rocket launchers. Calculations are based on 1980–81 data.
**Not included in total of 204 combat aircraft.

lowest ratio of armor to troops, with only 121 tanks per 10,000 men in the ground forces.

In spite of the fact that Bulgaria traditionally has been the most pro-Soviet ally in the Warsaw Pact, its military forces have not been modernized with the newer Soviet equipment, nor have the Soviets maintained a military presence in Bulgaria other than a large advisory group. However, there has been an increased rate of military modernization in the past few years, with the Bulgarian air force being among the first East European air forces to obtain the MiG-23 *Flogger*, and the army now is receiving the T-62 and the most modern T-72 tanks.[18] In addition, there are reports of increased structural modernization including, for instance, the hardening of existing defense facilities and the construction of new runways, buildings, and fortifications.[19] Yet, despite the recent trend, most Bulgarian military equipment is relatively old. Military expenditures are the lowest of the Pact members, except for Romania, and persistent overall economic difficulties would not support a massive military modernization program in the near future. To the extent that Bulgarian military forces can be evaluated by these objective measures of merit, they do not have a strong capability to wage an offensive war against NATO. In a defensive war they should give a good account of themselves, but in an interbloc intervention Bulgaria is geostrategically limited. Only against Romania, or perhaps in a Warsaw Pact action against Yugoslavia, does the Bulgarian military have the effective capability to intervene.

In examining the subjective aspects of Bulgarian military capability, it is immediately clear that their prospects are doubtful. Like other military forces of East Europe, most notably the Hungarian, Romanian, and Czechoslovak, the Bulgarian military does not have a positive twentieth-century military tradition, nor does it have positive military experience in recent years on which to build the psychological competence of its military forces. Bulgarian military action in World War II was particularly inappropriate as a foundation on which to build a first-rate military. It has no experienced (combat) military leaders and, like most of the other East European military establishments, has tended to draw its commanders not from the traditional elites that had provided the military leaders until 1945–48 but from the peasant and, in small part, the working classes. The present senior officers appear to be reliable members of the pro-Soviet Communist Party, but because they lack both a military tradition and significant experience and have a leadership of questionable quality, the Bulgarians' military capability must be doubted from the outset. Today the armed forces are heavily involved in public works projects.

There are, however, a number of other subjective factors about the Bulgarian military, and indeed about the military forces of most of the

[18]*The Military Balance, 1980–1981*, p. 15.
[19]Interview with John Erickson in Edinburgh, Scotland, 17 January 1977.

other East European members of the Warsaw Pact, that only can be posed as questions. First, what is the overall fighting quality of the Bulgarian military forces, particularly the ground forces? Second, how adaptable and how agile will these troops be in changing combat situations? That is, is the overall training of a high enough quality to prepare this inexperienced military force to meet the demands of a dynamic and rigorous combat environment? Related to this is a third question: How competent are they in performing combat activities and how resilient will they be if they are brought under intense pressure and suffer one or more major setbacks? And finally, what level of commitment will they have in pursuing a military goal that Bulgaria did not choose and in which Bulgarian interests may be only marginally engaged? The answers to these subjective questions are the critical substance of any complete evaluation of Bulgarian military capability and will vary with the particular military action that these forces are pursuing. In a purely defensive war to protect the Bulgarian homeland, the doubtful subjective indicators, and even some of the deficient objective characteristics, undoubtedly would be less apt negatively to affect the Bulgarian military capability. For example, in a local or regional war with Yugoslavia over Macedonia, the subjective and objective weaknesses may not seriously detract from their military capability. However, in an offensive war against NATO where Bulgarian troops could be brought under intense pressure and engaged against superior weaponry and a determined opponent, the combat potential of the Bulgarian armed forces is questionable at best.

Czechoslovakia

The military forces of Czechoslovakia number about 195,000, of which 118,000 are conscripts. Figure 3 contains the general composition and force levels.[20] Prior to the events of 1968, Czechoslovakia was considered to have had one of the best military forces in Eastern Europe, particularly its air force. However, the Prague Spring and the subsequent Soviet-led intervention did much to disrupt the Czechoslovak military. They still do have a fairly large military force, considering that they have no navy, and they do have an adequate quantity of modern military equipment—T-62 and T-72 medium tanks, MiG-23 *Flogger B* aircraft, and BMP armored fighting vehicles. The ratio of tanks to the ground forces is substantially high, with 250 tanks per 10,000 men.

The Czech military forces are second in size to Poland's among the East European members of the Warsaw Pact. With a total population of 15,400,000, Czechoslovak military strength represents about 1.27% of the population, a ratio second only to Bulgaria. Although Czechoslovakia's

[20]*The Military Balance, 1980–1981*, p. 15.

military equipment has undergone substantial modernization during the
past five years, it is difficult to discuss the objective or subjective measures
of merit without discussing briefly the impact of the Prague Spring and

Figure 3. Czechoslovak Military Forces

TOTAL MILITARY FORCES
    195,000 (118,000 conscripts)

ARMY
    140,000 (100,000 conscripts)

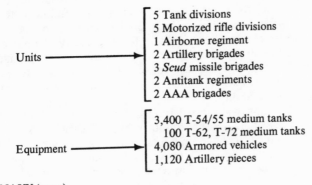

Units →

    5 Tank divisions
    5 Motorized rifle divisions
    1 Airborne regiment
    2 Artillery brigades
    3 *Scud* missile brigades
    2 Antitank regiments
    2 AAA brigades

Equipment →

    3,400 T-54/55 medium tanks
      100 T-62, T-72 medium tanks
    4,080 Armored vehicles
    1,120 Artillery pieces

NAVY (none)

AIR FORCE
    55,000 (18,000 conscripts)

Combat aircraft   471

Ground attack
    fighters   12 MiG-23
                           80 Su-7B
                           30 MiG-17
                           42 MiG-21

Interceptors   252 MiG-21

Reconnaissance   25 MiG-21
                           30 L-29/L-39

PARAMILITARY   Border guards   11,000
FORCES →   Workers' militia 120,000   (periodic drills)
                      Civil defense   2,500
                                        _____
                                        133,500

Warsaw Pact intervention of 1968. Czech military forces under the Antonin Novotny regime were considered to have been very competent and well equipped. However, the armed forces, particularly the conscripts and young officers, were in disarray after 1968. A large number of younger officers had supported the Alexander Dubček government and its reforms, and many of these officers resigned after August 1968.[21] But the effects of the Prague Spring and the Warsaw Pact intervention were not limited to the younger officers and have tended to permeate the whole military, as they have the whole society. The Soviet Union had been cast in a liberator's role in Czechoslovakia at the end of World War II, and the USSR actively had opposed the Munich agreement in 1938. That ally became the aggressor in Czechoslovakia in 1968. As a result of the naturally strong anti-Soviet sentiments in the armed forces following the intervention, there were inevitably serious Soviet reservations raised about the future loyalty of any Czech military force to the Warsaw Pact and to the Soviet Union.[22] To the degree that the anti-Soviet attitude remains or that the Soviet Union has reservations about the Czechoslovak military forces, the events of 1968 must still affect any assessment of Czechoslovak military capability.

How do the Czechoslovak armed forces rate qualitatively against the objective measures of merit? The military has relatively good and modern equipment. The Czech ground forces have large numbers of T-54/55 tanks, 100 T-62 and T-72 tanks, and a variety of armored vehicles. The ground forces are formed into ten divisions, five of which are outfitted as tank divisions. Overall, the quality of Czech small arms is very high; the economy is one of the most industrially advanced in Eastern Europe, and the Czech armaments industry is noted for the high quality of its weapons. As to the training provided to the Czechoslovak military forces, John Erickson has stated that their overall readiness is not too high, with probably only five or six of the ten divisions maintained at near full strength.[23] The training of the Czech military is thought to be adequate; a major factor in training is the overall attitude of those being trained. Czech equipment is probably well maintained and will continue to be, at least during peacetime.

[21]H. Gordon Skilling, *Czechoslovakia's Interrupted Revolution* (Princeton, NJ: Princeton University Press, 1976), pp. 713–58.

[22]Remington, *The Warsaw Pact*, pp. 101–3. Remington discusses the role of Lieutenant General Prchlik in criticizing the dominance of the Soviet Union within the Warsaw Treaty Organization as well as discussing other cases where Czechoslovak military were critical of the Soviet Union and its military policy.

[23]*The Military Balance, 1980–1981*, pp. 110–12. Also Erickson interview, 17 January 1977. Erickson has contended for many years that the East European military forces are not at full strength and that only certain "earmarked" divisions are kept at Category I status, or the Warsaw Pact equivalent. Erickson, *Soviet-Warsaw Pact*, pp. 67, 85.

Although many of the subjective factors that affect the potential military capability of Czech troops already have been discussed, the key to their significance rests first on the degree of anti-Soviet feeling remaining in the Czechoslovak forces and second on the degree to which the Soviets trust them. Together, these can critically affect their potential military utility, particularly in any Soviet offensive against NATO. There is at least some reason to doubt that Czech military forces would vigorously defend themselves against a NATO attack or counterattack where the potential battle was to be on Czech soil, unless they were effectively bound into Soviet formations in carefully calculated supplementary roles.[24]

The Czech military forces must be rated both quantitatively and qualitatively as good. Serious doubts about military value arise in relation to the subjective factors. Again, a distinction must be drawn between the use of Czech troops in a defensive or perhaps interbloc intervention role and that of an offensive role against NATO.[25] In the former, Czech forces should perform effectively; in the latter, there may be no opportunity for them to succeed or fail because of Soviet uncertainties about them and the consequent military role they would be assigned.

German Democratic Republic

The military forces of the GDR are among the smallest of the East European members of the Warsaw Pact, with only 162,000 despite its having the third largest population at 16,800,000.[26] They comprise only .96% of the population, but this figure is somewhat deceptive since the GDR does have a 71,500-man exceptionally well-armed paramilitary force in the form of 46,500 border guards and 25,000 security troops (see Figure 4). The East Germans have only six combat divisions (two tank and four motorized rifle), representing, as is also true with Hungary, the lowest number within the Warsaw Pact. This modest size is surely in no small way the result of the nineteen Soviet divisions that are permanently stationed in the GDR and the fact that the Soviet Union has shown no desire to increase GDR military forces to the point where they might become as much of a problem as a potential asset to the Soviet Union. The

---

[24]The Czechoslovak military was not used to defend the country against outside intervention, either in 1938 or in 1968. Perhaps conclusions cannot be justifiably drawn from these unique historical episodes and applied to the present. However, the potential negative psychological impact that this historical record can have on the existing military establishment should not be ignored.

[25]It is interesting to note the role played by Czechoslovakia and its party leader, Gustav Husak, in the labor troubles in Poland in 1980–81. Husak took a very hardline position against Poland and at an early date intimated that Czechoslovakia and the Warsaw Pact were ready to intervene.

[26]*The Military Balance, 1980–1981*, p. 16.

small number of GDR ground forces are very well equipped with more
than 3,200 tanks and over 2,300 armored vehicles. The GDR ground
forces have ratios of 285 tanks and 250 armored vehicles per 10,000 men.
This figure presents a significant contrast to the Polish ground forces, with
176 tanks and 250 armored vehicles and Czech ground forces of 250
tanks and 291 armored vehicles per 10,000 men. The military forces of

Figure 4. German Democratic Republic Military Forces

TOTAL MILITARY FORCES
162,000 (92,000 conscripts)

ARMY
108,000 (67,000 conscripts)

Units →
- 2 Tank divisions
- 4 Motorized rifle divisions
- 2 *Scud* missile brigades
- 2 AAA regiments
- 4 Artillery brigades
- 2 Antitank battalions
- 2 Airborne battalions

Equipment →
- 2,600 T-54/55, T-72 medium tanks
- 600 T-34 medium tanks (in storage)
- 60 PT-76 light tanks
- 2,380 Armored vehicles
- 1,033 Artillery pieces

NAVY
16,000 (10,000 conscripts)

AIR FORCE
38,000 (15,000 conscripts)

Combat aircraft   347

Ground attack
fighters   35 MiG-17
                    12 MiG-23

PARAMILITARY
FORCES →
- Border guards   46,500
- Security forces   25,000
- Workers' militia   500,000
                     571,500

the GDR are considered to be very well trained and in a high state of combat readiness. The highest degree of integration in the Warsaw Pact is between the Soviet and East German military forces.[27]

In applying the objective measures of merit to the GDR, it is apparent that the East German forces are a competent and efficient military force that is well equipped, at least in ground forces. GDR military training is considered to be very good and overall combat readiness is high.[28] Maintenance of combat equipment appears to be good and no unusual problems are anticipated. Hence, by any objective standards the military forces of the GDR appear to have a positive military utility to the Warsaw Pact. The major limiting objective factor is its small size, particularly given the strong industrial economy of the GDR. It is obvious, however, that this objective limitation is a reflection of several subjective factors that can limit the military usefulness of the East German military forces.

It is not necessary to detail the origin of the East German military forces and what these origins mean to the Soviet military leaders. The present-day GDR incorporates much of the area of prewar Prussia. It was the Prussian military system that enabled Germany to engage in two world wars and come close to success despite overwhelming numerical inferiority. Soviet hatred and fear of all things German, as a result of the Nazi invasion, were reflected in the Soviet invasion of what is now the GDR and its administration of the occupied territory. This mutual animosity and suspicion, to the degree that they still continue to exist, may lead the Soviet Union to question the utility of the East German military forces.

In spite of the positive objective measures of merit, subjective questions about the potential utility of these forces remain. First, would the Soviet Union depend on the GDR forces in a crisis? Second, would the Soviet military leaders be willing to use the GDR military forces against the West Germans? Third, would East German military forces fight effectively against the West Germans? Recognizing that these questions cannot be answered, additional questions perhaps might help give some clues to the answers. First, why are the military forces of the GDR, particularly the ground forces, kept at relatively small numbers in spite of the fact that the GDR economy and population size would support a significantly larger force? Second, why have the GDR forces not replaced Soviet troops in the defense of the GDR? Third, why are the military forces of the GDR, except for the border guards, not put in frontline

---

[27]Erickson interview, 17 January 1977.

[28]John M. Collins, *U.S.-Soviet Military Balance: Concepts and Capabilities 1960–1980* (New York: McGraw-Hill, 1980), pp. 546–57. Collins details the Category I, II, and III units for all of the Warsaw Pact military forces. All six of East Germany's divisions are considered Category I.

positions to defend the GDR against a NATO attack? In a 1977 seminar on surprise attack, Christopher Donnelly of the Centre for Soviet Studies, Royal Military Academy Sandhurst, summarized the position of the GDR military forces: "They are the most trustworthy and least trusted of the military forces in East Europe."[29] Because of the small size of the GDR military forces and their relative position vis-à-vis the Soviet forces within the GDR, the potential military utility of these East German forces must be at least questioned despite the positive potential military capability that they represent.[30]

Hungary

Numbering 93,000 the military forces of Hungary are the smallest within the bloc.[31] Hungary has only six combat divisions within its armed forces and only one is a tank division (see Figure 5).[32] The Hungarian military has the fewest tanks and the least artillery of any of the East European forces. The Hungarian air force has only 170 combat aircraft, of which just 20 are included among the most modern Soviet fighters. In addition, the Hungarians have only 60 of the most modern tanks and a few armored vehicles, and the overall quality of the older military equipment is considered to be very poor. The Hungarian military forces are not well trained nor are they efficiently organized or managed. Except for some specialized units, such as engineer and bridging battalions, the overall quality of the Hungarian military forces is not good.[33]

Considering the subjective factors that may affect the utility and reliability of the Hungarian military forces, the outlook is even less promising, at least from a Soviet perspective. The Hungarian military represents a cross section of a nation whose people have been traditionally anti-Russian and anti-Soviet. Not only were the Hungarians the enemy of Russia during World War I and the Soviet Union during World War II, but also were the people who sought most vigorously to stay out of the Soviet bloc and fought to break out of the Warsaw Pact when the opportunity arose. In 1956 the Soviet army had to put down a popular rebellion in Hungary in which top Communist political officials as well as

---

[29]Statement at the seminar sponsored by the U.S. Air Force at the Pentagon on 19 March 1977, at which Donnelly and Erickson were the guest speakers.

[30]In this volume in his article entitled "Military Management and Modernization Within the Warsaw Pact," Erickson argues that it would be easy to overstate the problems of using East German military forces, even against West Germany.

[31]It is interesting to note that this figure of 93,000 represents a decline of almost 10% from the 103,000, which was given in *The Military Balance, 1977–1978* only three years earlier, *The Military Balance, 1980–1981,* p. 16.

[32]Ibid., pp. 16, 110–12.

[33]Erickson interview, 17 January 1977.

Figure 5. Hungarian Military Forces

TOTAL MILITARY FORCES
   93,000 (58,000 conscripts)

ARMY
   72,000 (50,000 conscripts)

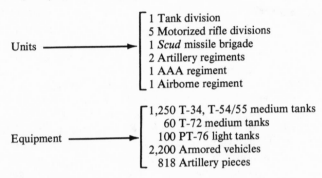

Units ────────▶
   1 Tank division
   5 Motorized rifle divisions
   1 *Scud* missile brigade
   2 Artillery regiments
   1 AAA regiment
   1 Airborne regiment

Equipment ────────▶
   1,250 T-34, T-54/55 medium tanks
     60 T-72 medium tanks
    100 PT-76 light tanks
   2,200 Armored vehicles
    818 Artillery pieces

NAVY
   None (Danube flotilla)

AIR FORCE
   21,000 (8,000 conscripts)

   Combat aircraft   170

   Fighters   20 MiG-23

   Interceptors   150 MiG-21

PARAMILITARY
FORCES ────────▶
   Border guards   15,000   (11,000 conscripts)
   Workers' militia   60,000   (part-time)
                      75,000

many military leaders tried to remove their nation from direct Soviet domination and make Hungary a neutral state.[34] The Soviet army won out and a new cast of political and military leaders emerged headed by present Hungarian Communist Party Chief Janos Kadar. But the disloyalty of the Hungarians in 1956 and the subsequent (non-Soviet model) economic reform programs of the Kadar-led Hungarian Communist Party do not seem to have helped the Hungarian image in Soviet eyes. In very simple

[34]Bela Kiraly, "Hungary's Army: Its Part in the Revolt," *East Europe* 6, no. 6 (June 1958): 3–15.

terms the Hungarian military forces have not kept pace quantitatively or qualitatively with the other military establishments of East Europe, and they do not represent a significant military capability at all because most likely the Soviets have assumed that they could not be trusted.

If the Hungarian military forces—and here it is really legitimate only to include the ground forces—have any utility to the Soviet Union, that utility can be seen in only very limited and specific situations. It is very difficult to postulate seriously the use of Hungarian military forces in a surprise attack against NATO. It is just slightly less difficult to envision these Hungarian forces being employed in an offensive war against NATO. In a regional or interbloc war or intervention, Hungarian forces, in limited numbers, could be potentially employed in certain specific conflicts. For example, in Soviet-led intervention into Czechoslovakia in 1968, the Hungarian army did participate.[35] One could argue that the Hungarians might enthusiastically take part in a Soviet-led intervention into Romania, especially if territorial rewards were offered as an inducement. Their claim to Transylvania is well known and might motivate the Hungarians to act. The probability of success against determined resistance raises another question entirely. A Soviet attack on Yugoslavia also might find support, especially if Hungarian participation were to be linked to the return of the Banat area of Yugoslavia, another part of pre-1919 Hungary. But even Hungarian military participation in these hypothetical regional wars for nationalist and irredentist motives is questionable. While the effectiveness of the Hungarian military forces in a purely defensive war must be questioned, it is also reasonable to postulate that the forces would fight to defend Hungary if it were attacked. Perhaps the decision to fight or not to fight in a defensive war would be based primarily on which nation attacked Hungary and for what reason. However, the overall evaluation that the ability of the Hungarian military forces is not high remains the same.

Poland

If the Hungarian armed forces represent the least potentially effective of the East European members of the Warsaw Pact, then Poland's represents the most capable (see Figure 6). Poland has by far the largest population with 35,700,000 people; the next largest is Romania with 22,300,000. It has the largest overall military force with 317,500 men; Czechoslovakia is second with 195,000. Poland also has the greatest number of critical military elements, in fact, in some categories significantly more than the next highest: 701 combat aircraft (Czechoslovakia

---

[35]There is some question as to how many Hungarian troops actually went into Czechoslovakia. Those that did go only occupied the areas of southern Slovakia, which had been Hungarian territory until the Treaty of Trianon in 1919. The Hungarian troops were apparently the first Warsaw Pact troops to withdraw from Czechoslovakia.

Figure 6. Polish Military Forces

TOTAL MILITARY FORCES
    317,500 (185,000 conscripts)

ARMY
    210,000 (154,000 conscripts)

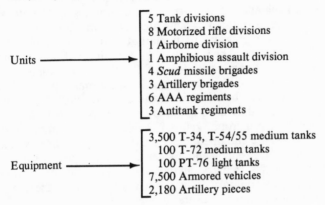

Units
- 5 Tank divisions
- 8 Motorized rifle divisions
- 1 Airborne division
- 1 Amphibious assault division
- 4 *Scud* missile brigades
- 3 Artillery brigades
- 6 AAA regiments
- 3 Antitank regiments

Equipment
- 3,500 T-34, T-54/55 medium tanks
- 100 T-72 medium tanks
- 100 PT-76 light tanks
- 7,500 Armored vehicles
- 2,180 Artillery pieces

NAVY
    22,500 (6,000 conscripts)
        1 Naval aviation regiment
        42 MiG-17
        10 IL-28

AIR FORCE
    85,000 (25,000 conscripts)

Combat aircraft   701

Ground attack
    fighters   150 MiG-17
                            35 Su-7
                            35 Su-20

Interceptors   100 MiG-17
                           300 MiG-21

Reconnaissance   72 MiG-15/21
                             5 IL-28
                             4 IL-14

PARAMILITARY
FORCES

Border guards	18,000	(minister of interior)
Security forces	56,000	
Construction troops	21,000	
Workers' militia	350,000	
	445,000	

has 471), 3,700 tanks (Czechoslovakia has 3,500), and 7,500 armored
vehicles (Czechoslovakia has 4,080).[36] But quantitative superiorities do
not stand alone. Poland has the newest and best overall equipment base,
with the possible exception of some East German ground forces' equipment, and has the best, although aging, inventory of tactical aircraft.

By most objective measures of merit, Poland has a very strong and
capable military force. Polish military equipment tends not only to be
good but also well maintained. The standard of training of the Polish
ground and air forces is also rated as quite high, and combat readiness for
selected Polish units is impressive, particularly the airborne, amphibious
assault, and armored forces. The remaining Polish military forces are not
kept at advanced states of combat readiness.[37] Polish vehicle maintenance
is apparently good, and Polish units should have no major problems in
maintaining vehicles in combat. However, the units in Silesia may have
maintenance problems if they have to deploy rapidly to the northwestern
border to form a northern front against NATO.[38] Military formations,
including the air units, are equipped to perform a variety of offensive and
defensive Warsaw Pact missions and appear to have the proper support,
such as airlift and logistics, to carry out those tasks if they are called upon
to do so. Thus, the Polish military deserves high ratings in both the quantitative and objective qualitative measures of merit.

An analysis of the Polish armed forces, in terms of some of the
subjective factors, reveals an interesting mixture of trends and characteristics. Polish nationalism and military experience and traditions are the
most obvious starting points. Polish nationalism has made the entire
population aware of Poland's long history of successes and failures,
triumphs and defeats, independence and occupation. The fact that the
Polish nation did not exist as a territorial entity between 1797 and 1919
and then reemerged as an independent state, with little loss of its cultural
or ethnic continuity, seems to confirm the validity and viability of the
people as a national entity. The Polish leadership and Polish society
are sensitive to those factors that tend to diminish anything Polish in favor
of external forces, either national (Soviet or German) or international
(communism, proletarian internationalism). The Polish armed forces are
drawn from that society and are no doubt a reflection of it. In addition,
Polish military history and its past role within the state are positive factors
in the calculation of the overall Polish military capability. In particular,
military experiences in World War II are positive factors in these calculations. Not only did the Polish military attempt heroically to defend
Poland in 1939 against the Germans but also forces fought alongside the

[36]*The Military Balance, 1980–1981*, pp. 16–17.
[37]Collins, *U.S.-Soviet Military Balance.*
[38]Erickson interview, 17 January 1977.

Soviet Red Army to liberate Poland and ultimately defeat Nazi Germany. Their resistance units carried on offensive action throughout the war. Thus, robust nationalism, along with strong military traditions and experience, are positive contributions to Polish military capabilities.

However, Polish nationalism and Poland's positive military traditions and experience are not necessarily assets to the Soviet Union and the Warsaw Pact. Poland's traditional enemies have been Germany and Russia (and the Soviet Union), and modern Polish history is a record of aggression from both countries. The Soviet Union joined Germany in the attack, defeat, and subsequent dismemberment of Poland in 1939. The controversy over the fate of the Polish military personnel in the Katyn Forest is still an important Polish memory. Soviet failure to come to the relief of the 1944 Warsaw uprising is viewed by most Poles as another blow against the Polish nation. Not less than one-third of pre-World War II Poland was annexed into the Soviet Union following the war. In spite of the establishment of the Soviet-sponsored Communist government in the immediate postwar period, there has not developed any significantly strong pro-Soviet consensus, either in the general society or within the military; instead, Polish nationalism has continued to expand. The problems that have arisen in the 1980–81 Polish labor crisis are a reminder of the unique and persistent nationalism of the Polish people and the inability of the Soviet Union or the Polish Communist Party to suppress it. The ambivalence of the Polish army in the 1956 crisis and its reluctance to become involved in recent events must raise questions in the minds of the Soviet leaders as to the overall utility of the Polish military forces.[39] The key question is what degree of reliability can the Soviet leadership assume within the Polish military forces? From a quantitative and objective qualitative point of view, the Polish armed forces represent an enormous asset to the Soviet Union and the Warsaw Pact. From a subjective qualitative viewpoint, the Soviet Union can only calculate the utility and reliability of the Polish forces with a substantial degree of caution.

The Polish military forces are fully capable, and the Polish political leadership is certainly willing to commit Polish forces to defend Poland. In any future interbloc struggle, the Poles might make a significant contribution; Polish participation in the Czechoslovak intervention was both prompt and effective. But in considering the Soviet Union's ability to use Polish armed forces in either a first-strike or mobilized attack against NATO, Polish national interest in the conflict would have to be substantially engaged before the Soviets could rely on their firm assistance.

---

[39]See Barton Repport, *Philadelphia Inquirer,* 27 November 1980; and George C. Wilson, *Washington Post,* 9 December 1980. Martial law, established at the end of 1981, has been maintained largely by the security forces.

Romania

The military forces of Romania are not particularly large (184,500) for a country its size (22,200,000) and are not particularly well equipped (see Figure 7).[40] Romania's dissident position within the Warsaw Pact and its rather cool relations with the Soviet Union in no small measure account for the status of the Romanian military forces. One of the principal points to note about their military forces is that they are geared and structured more convincingly for defense than offense. In addition, the Workers' Militia in Romania is a paramilitary defense organization, along the model of Yugoslavia's Territorial Defense Force, and it is the largest of its kind among the East European members of the Warsaw Pact. Romania's regular military force of 184,500 represents the lowest percentage (.83%) of the population of the East European Pact countries.

The military forces of Romania may not appear on the surface to be noticeably different from those of other East European Warsaw Pact members; that is, they are organized in similar kinds of units and operate with the same kinds of equipment. The present-day Romanian military forces have similar origins to the other East European military forces and overall similarities are more obvious than differences. But the similarities are superficial. Although Romania is still a member of the Warsaw Pact and does participate in a limited fashion in Warsaw Pact activities, the Romanian military forces have been given, as their primary task, the protection of the sovereignty and independence of Romania against any outside aggressor. The Romanian military capability is viewed by the Romanian political leadership as an important factor in the independent Romanian foreign policy that is aimed at serving the national interests of the Romanian state. The Romanian Communist Party leader, Nikolae Ceauşescu, has stated repeatedly that Romanian military forces are designed only to defend the Romanian state and will not be used as part of the Warsaw Pact collective actions against any nation within or outside the bloc.[41] In the Czechoslovak intervention in 1968, Romanian military forces were not used and Ceauşescu strongly criticized the Soviet-led intervention. In fact, Romanian forces were reported to have been placed on alert to repel an anticipated subsequent Soviet-led intervention into Romania.[42] In sum, there is a fundamental contradiction in the Romanian military forces from the outset; they are part of the Warsaw Pact but are not available to it and only partially participate in its activities.

---

[40]*The Military Balance, 1980–1981*, p. 17.

[41]Speech by Ceauşescu to the cadets of the General Military Academy, Bucharest, 14 August 1968. Reported and trans. in *FBIS, Eastern Europe, Daily Report*, 20 August 1968, pp. H3–H13.

[42]Ibid., 26 August 1968, pp. H1–H4. See also E. J. Czerwinski and J. Piekalkiewicz, eds., *The Soviet Invasion of Czechoslovakia: Its Effects on Eastern Europe* (New York: Praeger, 1973), pp. 164–66.

Figure 7. Romanian Military Forces

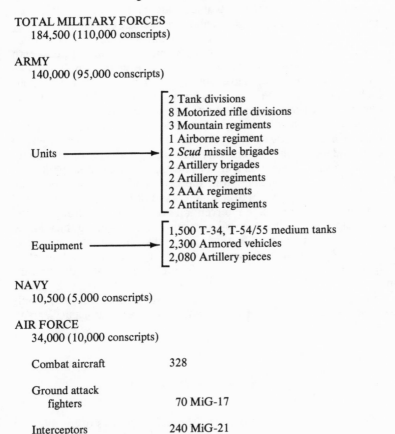

TOTAL MILITARY FORCES
184,500 (110,000 conscripts)

ARMY
140,000 (95,000 conscripts)

Units →
- 2 Tank divisions
- 8 Motorized rifle divisions
- 3 Mountain regiments
- 1 Airborne regiment
- 2 *Scud* missile brigades
- 2 Artillery brigades
- 2 Artillery regiments
- 2 AAA regiments
- 2 Antitank regiments

Equipment →
- 1,500 T-34, T-54/55 medium tanks
- 2,300 Armored vehicles
- 2,080 Artillery pieces

NAVY
10,500 (5,000 conscripts)

AIR FORCE
34,000 (10,000 conscripts)

Combat aircraft	328
Ground attack fighters	70 MiG-17
Interceptors	240 MiG-21
Reconnaissance	18 IL-28

PARAMILITARY FORCES →
Border guards	17,000	
Security forces	20,000	
Workers' militia	700,000	(patriotic guard)
	737,000	

The independent Romanian course has not been taken without cost to the military. Romania has the oldest and poorest equipment of any East European state, and it is not maintained at high standards or at high levels of combat readiness.[43] The Soviet Union has done little and in the future

---

[43]*The Military Balance, 1980–1981*, pp. 110–12.

can be expected to do nothing to alleviate the problem. But apparently Romanian military forces have been able to adapt fairly effectively to their single mission—the defense of Romania. The existing equipment is better suited to defense than offense, and the Romanians have created a large Yugoslav-type paramilitary force to augment the regular forces with partisan guerrilla action. As a defense force, the Romanian military, like the Yugoslav, may well be able to exact a toll from any attacker. However, as in the Bulgarian case, the Romanian army spends a good deal of its time on public works projects rather than on combat training.

In subjective terms there is little more to be added. The Romanians are almost as nationalistic as the Poles, and the armed forces are regarded as the defenders of the sovereignty and independence of the state. Romanians are anti-Soviet and antibloc and are becoming more politically and economically independent from the Soviet Union. The Romanian armed forces are a key link between the pursuit of this independence and its achievement. Only outside intervention could alter the situation, and the Romanian political leadership has tried to develop its military forces into an instrument that can effectively deter any outside intervention. In addition, the Romanians have very close military ties with the Yugoslavs and share similar security problems.[44] Therefore, in practical terms the Romanian military forces are unavailable in any form to the Soviet Union or Warsaw Pact and must be considered as a defensive force whose only likely attackers are the Soviet Union and other East European Warsaw Pact members.

CONCLUSIONS

The military forces of the East European members of the Warsaw Pact represent varied contributions to the overall military strength of the alliance, as summarized in Table 1. However, unless the qualitative factors that characterize the individual military forces are adequately taken into consideration, the result will be a miscalculation of the actual strengths of these forces and the likely Soviet perceptions of those strengths. The East European armed forces, particularly those of Poland, Czechoslovakia, and East Germany, certainly represent a military asset to the Warsaw Pact and to the Soviet Union, but the utility of those forces will vary significantly with the different kinds of potential conflict in which

---

[44]The joint development of the ground attack fighter between Romania and Yugoslavia is one example of the joint effort to solve a security problem. Also, Erickson has pointed out that the Romanians and Yugoslavs have an integrated air defense warning system.

Table 1. Summary of East European Military Forces

	Bulgaria	Czechoslovakia	German Democratic Republic	Hungary	Poland	Romania	Total
Total military forces (no. of conscripts in total)	149,000 (94,000)	195,000 (118,000)	162,000 (92,000)	93,000 (58,000)	317,500 (185,000)	184,500 (110,000)	1,101,000 (657,000)
Total army forces (no. of conscripts in total)	105,000 (70,000)	140,000 (100,000)	108,000 (67,000)	72,000 (50,000)	210,000 (154,000)	140,000 (95,000)	775,000 (536,000)
Tank divisions/Motorized rifle divisions	0/8*	5/5	2/4	1/5	5/8	2/8	15/38
Other divisions	—	—	—	—	2	—	2
Total tanks	1,900	3,500	3,260	1,410	3,700	1,500	15,270
Total armored vehicles	1,825	4,080	2,380	2,200	7,500	2,300	20,285
Total artillery	1,200	1,120	1,033	818	2,180	2,080	8,431
Total navy forces (no. of conscripts in total)	10,000 (6,000)	—	16,000 (10,000)	—	22,500** (6,000)	10,500 (5,000)	59,000 (27,000)
Total air forces (no. of conscripts in total)	34,000 (18,000)	55,000 (18,000)	38,000 (15,000)	21,000 (8,000)	85,000 (25,000)	34,000 (10,000)	267,000 (94,000)
Total combat aircraft	204	471	347	170	701	328	2,221
Border guards/Security forces	15,000/12,000	11,000/none	46,500/25,000	15,000/none	18,000/56,000	17,000/20,000	122,500/113,000
Workers' militia forces	150,000	120,000	500,000	60,000	350,000	700,000	1,880,000

*Bulgarian tanks are organized into five tank brigades.
**Poland has one naval aviation regiment with fifty-two aircraft.

they might be used. It is through differentiating among the possible types of conflict, whether a bona fide defense, an interbloc intervention, a surprise first-strike offensive, or a mobilized offensive, that the utility of these East European military forces and the real threats that they might pose to NATO and the West can be properly assessed. No matter what form of involvement the Soviets might devise to assure participation by the key bloc countries, they too must carefully calculate these highly uncertain variables or face the possibility of going into battle with allies that could turn out to be as dangerous as their enemies.

THE WEAPONS

Soviet and Warsaw Pact Major Battlefield Weapons

JAMES R. CARLTON

Success in military conflict depends heavily upon the ability of an army to match its weapons and systems to appropriate tactical employment doctrines. That premise has been confirmed repeatedly throughout history. The pike, lance, crossbow, musket and cannon, machine gun, airplane, and tank all represent technological innovations that, when combined with suitable tactics, supplied clear military and political advantages. To Soviet military historians it seems certain that nations that have held this edge usually have secured their foreign policy goals. That firmly held thesis has not been lost on Pact military planners. The focus here will be to examine and evaluate how the Soviets have matched tactical doctrine with weapons and other military firepower systems.

Soviet Ground Forces operations are mainly based on the use of mechanized armor units. These usually are comprised of main battle tanks, tracked and wheeled infantry combat vehicles, tracked artillery, and tracked air defense weapons. To understand fully the potential of any Soviet land operation, it is essential to have a basic understanding of each major set of weapons systems.

MAIN BATTLE TANKS

The primary weapon of any Soviet ground combat operation is the tank. It provides the mobility, flexibility, and firepower that Soviet commanders feel constitutes the necessary basis for the conduct of a successful engagement. Since Soviet offensive doctrine envisions fighting short, intense conficts rather than long, drawn-out engagements, the tank is a vital ingredient. Because speed and mobility are critical elements in modern armored warfare, all contemporary Soviet armor has been designed to maximize those deployment characteristics. This is not to say that Soviet armor and tactical doctrine always have been as complementary as they seem to be today. Only after costly experimentation during World War II and the emergence of the tank as the critical element in their victory over the Nazis, did the Soviets finally settle on a suitable doctrine matched to tank design and production. Their success in World War II ensured a continuing emphasis on armored warfare.

Even though during the first months of the German invasion Soviet frontline troops were supplied with adequate armor and in some cases had received the T-34 tank, their failure to understand the technical capabilities of those systems contributed to early German victories. Only after a number of years of combat and the achievement of significantly increased efficiency and effectiveness in the Soviet tank industry, were Soviet planners able to devise a tactical doctrine that took advantage of both technical achievement and numbers of tanks available. As one source expresses it,

> Soviet military leaders have not underestimated the serious short-comings of the wartime Red Army and did make strenuous efforts to close the gap with the formerly more sophisticated armies of Western Europe. Wartime production priorities forced Soviet heavy industries to concentrate solely on tanks and self-propelled guns. . . .[1]

What resulted from these single-minded efforts was a tactical concept based on massive frontal attack by an overwhelming force of tanks and tank-carried infantry supported by assault guns and massed artillery. As this doctrine emerged, it in turn was reflected in the design concepts of most Soviet armor produced during that period.

The T-34 is recognized in most military circles as the most successful mass-produced armored vehicle of World War II. Structured around the revolutionary concepts of American tank designer J. Walter Christie, the T-34 incorporated a number of basic elements that still could be found in all Soviet tanks up to the mid-1960s.[2] The most striking and successful technological characteristics of the T-34 was its unique suspension and track system. Christie had provided a major technological advance that resulted in significantly higher tank speeds. In the broad expanses and harsh climate of the Soviet Union and northeastern Europe, that extra speed and mobility were to prove crucial to Soviet success in battle. Christie's systems allowed the Soviets to take advantage of opportunities that were denied to the Germans. Most importantly, low ground pressure (pounds per square foot laid by the track) allowed the T-34 to move in all but the most trying weather, thus assuring tactical advantage in most cases.

Another technological characteristic of the T-34 that has persisted is

[1]Steven J. Zaloga, *Modern Soviet Armor, Combat Vehicles of the Soviet Union and Warsaw Pact* (Englewood Cliffs, NJ: Prentice-Hall, 1979), p. 6.

[2]Douglas Orgill, *T-34 Russian Armor* (New York: Ballantine Books, 1971), pp. 1–21. See also John Milsom, *Russian Tanks 1900–1970* (New York: Galahad Books, 1970), pp. 74–79.

concern for crew survivability in combat. Of all the major tank designs of World War II, the T-34, with its angled frontal slope, low turret, and combat silhouette, proved to be remarkably successful in protecting its crew. New Soviet tank designs offer the lowest combat signature of any of today's major main battle tanks (MBT).

The Soviets also have continued to assure that their tanks are supplied with sufficient firepower. Unlike most tanks used in World War II, the T-34 was not undergunned. Initially fitted with a 76.2mm. and later with an 85mm. gun, the T-34 was a match for all but the last examples of German armor. Even then the T-34's superior speed, mobility, and adequate firepower could often defeat German *Panther* and *Tiger* tanks. Each successive generation since the T-34 has been upgunned to meet changing technological and tactical requirements.

The continued emphasis given to these three characteristics in Soviet armor design—suspension, survivability, and firepower—has produced a family of technically reliable and tactically suitable tanks appropriate for any battlefield mission envisioned by the Soviet Union and the Warsaw Pact.

Postwar Soviet Tanks

Today medium tank inventories in Eastern Europe include the T-34, T-54/55, T-62, T-64, T-72, and probably some examples of the latest Soviet tank, the T-80. Also included in the reserve forces of the Pact are heavy tanks: the JS III and T-10. All the above models are of Soviet design and are produced either in the Soviet Union or under license in various bloc countries.

In the immediate years following the war, the T-34 represented the state of the art in Soviet tank design. The Soviets were able to equip all of their allies with these battle-tested machines, which were produced in vast numbers. They remained the primary MBT until the introduction of the T-54 in 1949. In fact, the T-34 served with front-line Warsaw Pact troops until the late 1950s, and many are held today in reserve storage in most Pact nations.[3]

The T-54, and later its derivative, the T-55, continued the basic Soviet design tradition. Equipped with the familiar Christie track-laying system, these tanks had an improved cruising range, while retaining almost the same maximum speed as the T-34.[4] Probably the greatest

[3]International Institute for Strategic Studies, *The Military Balance 1980–1981* (New York: Facts on File, 1980), pp. 13–19. See also Friedrich Wiener, *The Armies of the Warsaw Pact Nations* (Vienna: Carl Ueberreuter Verlag, 1976), p. 248.

[4]Pierangelo Caiti, *Modern Armor: A Comprehensive Guide* (Warren, MI: Squadron Signal Publications, 1978), p. 69. See also Ray Bonds, ed., *Modern Tanks and Fighting Vehicles* (New York: Arco Publishing, 1980), p. 122; and Armin Halle, *Tanks, an Illustrated History of Fighting Vehicles* (New York: Crescent Books, 1971), pp. 147–49.

improvement, however, was in the main gun and fire control system. Adhering to Soviet tradition, the T-54/55 was up-gunned from 85mm. to 100mm.; the new tanks also had stabilized gun tubes, improved optics, and modest night fighting capabilities. In addition, they were equipped with special NBC (nuclear, biological, and chemical) protection in the form of a filtration system in all models after the T-54B and with an antiradiation lining in all T-55s.[5]

The T-54/55 has seen combat in such diverse locations as Egypt, Vietnam, Angola, and India. In each case it has proven to be a reliable fighting machine. Within the Warsaw Pact it remained the principal MBT until the introduction of the T-62, when the T-54/55 was transferred to the motorized rifle divisions to increase their tank strength.[6] Today the T-54/55 remains in active service in Bulgaria, Hungary, and Romania.[7]

The T-62 retains many of the characteristics of the T-54/55, although there is a slight increase in overall weight and dimensions. Again, Soviet design traditions prevailed. The tank has the usual Christie suspension system, increased cruising range, and increased firepower in the main gun. The new 115mm. gun required a larger turret ring and thus contributed to the tank's marginally increased size and weight. To offset this increased weight, the Soviets developed a new 12-cylinder, water-cooled diesel engine that could develop 700hp. The new engine gave the T-62 the same maximum speed as the T-54/55, while increasing its operational performance.

The T-62, however, does have a number of drawbacks. Its relatively small size restricts crew comfort and increases the likelihood of fatigue; the T-62 is not an easy machine to maintain and operate within a combat environment. Size has restricted the type of crew (height and weight) that may operate the tank. Another possible liability results from the internal configuration and systems inside the tank; it has many exposed and pointed edges within the small turret and constricted driver's compartment. These projections pose severe restrictions on crew mobility and in time of combat could be turned into deadly missiles by near misses or nonlethal hits. In addition, the size and type of tracks (steel without rubber pads and jointed by dry pins) increases the likelihood of crew fatigue because of the strength-sapping rough ride. Also, the steel tracks present a substantial handling problem for a smaller person, and probably would restrict battlefield maintenance.

Still, the T-62 is a first-rate tank. In engagements in both the Sinai and the Golan Heights during the 1973 Yom Kippur War, the T-62

[5]Caiti, *Modern Armor*, p. 69.
[6]Phillip A. Karber, "The Growing Armor/Anti-Armor Imbalance in Central Europe," *Armed Forces Journal* 118, no. 11 (July 1981): 38.
[7]*The Military Balance 1980–1981*, pp. 13–19.

proved to be an equal match for the Israeli *Centurion* and the M60A1.[8] Today the T-62 is still deployed in many first-line Warsaw Pact tank units, although it is being replaced by newer tanks in much the same manner that it replaced the T-54/55; it is now showing up in motorized rifle divisions. The T-62 represents the last Soviet tank to employ the Christie suspension system. The combination of rough handling and ride, with the introduction of a faster combat infantry fighting vehicle, spelled the end of an era.

The T-64 and T-72

What has replaced the T-62? Western specialists agree that the T-64 and T-72 have become the new MBTs of the Pact. However, there is much confusion about the new MBTs' capabilities, deployment, and even their precise appearance. Most western journals and texts, as well as some U.S. Army training aids, appear to have an extremely difficult time correctly differentiating the two tanks.[9] Initially, western analysts thought that the T-64 was an experimental model from which the T-72 was derived, and to some extent they were right. The T-64 did represent the first completely new Soviet tank since the T-34 and, in a sense, was experimental. However, the T-64 entered series production and was deployed with all Soviet tank divisions serving in East Germany; it did not remain experimental.

The T-64 was especially revolutionary by Soviet standards. It was the first Soviet tank to abandon the flat-track Christie system in favor of a suspended track. The Christie system, which was dropped because of its inferior shock-absorbing capabilities, had hampered its tanks' ability to fire on the move. On the T-64 the five large road wheels were replaced with six smaller ones and four return rollers. The new system increased the gun platform stability while providing for increased crew comfort and improved mechanical reliability. Other performance improvements include a new top speed of 80km./hr. (50mph) according to probably overoptimistic Soviet statistics. The T-64's range is 310 miles, compared to 280 miles in the T-62. These automotive advances were mandatory if the Soviet MBTs were to keep pace with their new infantry fighting vehicle, the BMP.

Besides improved automotive characteristics, the T-64 also has a

---

[8]Edgar O'Ballance, *No Victor, No Vanquished: The Yom Kippur War* (San Rafael, CA: Presidio Press, 1978), p. 219.

[9]Probably the most interesting case of confusion on the part of western intelligence is the U.S. Army's mistake and mislabeling of the T-64 and the T-72 on its training aid, AE GTA 30-004, revised 1979. It also should be noted that most western publications have a difficult time differentiating between the two tanks. See Wolfgang Flume, "Main Battle Tank for the '90s—Problems of Cooperation," *NATO's Fifteen Nations* 26 (1981): 44.

completely new turret and fire control system. It mounts a laser range finder and computer, an automatic loader, and the usual incremental improvement in its main armament. Initially, western analysts thought that the T-64 was equipped with a 120mm. gun. That estimate was later upgraded to 125mm., making it the largest caliber MBT gun in all of Europe. The T-64 fires a high-velocity, long-rod, armor-penetrating, fin-stabilized, discarding sabot [APFDS] projectile that will penetrate any current or future NATO tank at ranges greater than 2,000 meters.[10] The new automatic loader represented a breakthrough in firepower, manpower management, overall weight, and combat silhouette. The Soviets claim that the loader significantly increases the rate of fire, although it is evidently slower than some of its western counterparts.[11] Because of the autoloader, the size of a tank crew has been reduced from four to three members. Additionally, smaller turret size reduces the weight and area needed to provide protection for the crew. In fact, this tank weighs about forty tons, approximately one-quarter less than any of its western counterparts. Its small size will make it extremely difficult to identify and hit.

Only high priority Soviet troops have been issued the T-64; recipients include, for example, Soviet Ground Forces in Germany and some Category I troops in the Soviet Union. The T-64 has never been issued to a Pact ally. Speculation varies on the rationale behind this deployment pattern. While most analysts initially believed that the T-64 was an experimental or, at best, a stopgap system, its seemingly permanent deployment in front line Soviet formations, along with the subsequent introduction of the T-72, has added to the confusion in the West. According to one source,

> It is unclear why it [T-64] would have been introduced in large numbers with the Group of Soviet Forces Germany if it had short-comings serious enough to warrant the development of a replacement design in the form of the T-72. Other speculation maintains that the two types are parallel designs and that one or another will be standardized. It is equally possible that this decision has already been reached and the runnerup is being widely displayed to confuse Western Intelligence. Some NATO analysts became very suspicious after the Soviets allowed the visiting French Minister of Defense to inspect closely a new T-72 at a Moscow area base in October of 1977. Secrecy in the Soviet Army has been so great in the past that it was only recently that the Soviets acknowledged that the designation of the T-62 was in fact T-62.[12]

---

[10]*Armed Forces Journal* (July 1981): 39.
[11]Zaloga, *Modern Soviet Armor*, p. 23.
[12]Ibid., p. 31.

Although the T-64 and T-72 may at first appear to be almost identical fighting machines, a closer examination reveals a number of major differences. First, the suspension is different. On the T-64 there are six small road wheels with four return rollers; the T-72 is equipped with six larger road wheels and three return rollers. The T-72's configuration should improve automotive performance and gun-tube stability. The turrets are also different. Although each uses the same 125mm. gun and the automatic loader, there is a variance in overall shape. Some experts attribute this to different fire control systems.

The smaller size of both designs does increase crew protection, which also has been augmented by the introduction of four springloaded skirt plates. These plates are attached in such a way that when they are engaged they will spring out at an angle of 60° from the side of the vehicle. That configuration will provide protection against an increasing abundance of antitank guided missiles (ATGM). The 1973 Arab-Israeli conflict dramatically illustrated the vulnerability of modern armor to infantry borne antitank wire-guided missiles. The shaped charge round was able to defeat any tank present on the battlefield at ranges beyond its main gun armament. Because of certain impact characteristics of these missiles, the new skirts were designed to detonate and dissipate the energy of incoming missiles before they reach the crew compartment. In addition, the latest models of the T-72 are said to be equipped with composite, or Chobham-style, armor. It apparently consists of several layers of nylon micromesh or ceramic that is bonded on either side of a titanium alloy armor plate. Although considered inferior to its western counterpart, the new armor no doubt increases battlefield survivability.

Today the primary MBT force of the Warsaw Pact is made up of the T-64 and T-72. Production of the T-64 is carried out only at Soviet state arsenals. However, the T-72 is also now being manufactured under license in Czechoslovakia and Poland. In these two models the USSR has succeeded in increasing the long-range performance of its tanks despite the higher overall vehicle weight. Both basic designs have proved their ability to work with the BMP in most battlefield situations. They have the standard Soviet NBC and fording capabilities and display the necessary speed and mobility required by Soviet planners. Evidently, they have a marked superiority over all but the latest *Leopard II* and M-1 tanks.

Still, there are several shortcomings inherent in the basic designs. Each has a relatively small internal basic load of main gun ammunition. In what is envisioned by Soviet planners to be a highly fluid combat situation with ammunition rapidly being expended, a basic load capacity of only forty rounds would mean the tanks would soon be in need of resupply. Ammunition expenditures during the Yom Kippur War were astonishingly high, which is now assumed to be characteristic of future tank battles. Additionally, the small basic design proportions of the T-64 and T-72, especially in the turret, probably will prohibit much future improvement or adaptation of the main gun and the fire control system. However, in spite of these modest drawbacks the new Soviet tanks appear to be quite suitable for their perceived role. The T-80 is expected to display additional innovations based on proven technology, particularly in armor protection.

ARMORED PERSONNEL CARRIERS AND INFANTRY FIGHTING VEHICLES

During World War II Soviet infantrymen usually were transported into battle on the backs of advancing T-34s. Close to the front they dismounted and moved forward on foot as the advancing armor made for enemy lines. The casualties inflicted on the infantry were often devastating, and this practice also placed maneuver limitations on the advancing tanks. These two factors, along with the topside carrying capacity limitations of any tank, produced new equipment needs. The introduction of authentic Soviet troop carrier vehicles would enable the infantrymen to survive in an extremely mobile environment, while at the same time freeing them to retain their traditional role of consolidation and defense; the German army had perfected this system early in the war. Yet, because Soviet industrial priorities had been focused so completely on the tank and the self-propelled gun, Soviet attention to infantry vehicles was deferred until late in the war.[13]

The first attempt by the Soviets at producing an armored infantry carrier came in 1945 when they issued the BTR-152. This wheeled vehicle was based in part on the German Sd Kfz 247 and the American M-3. It had armored sides but no overhead protection. The usual personnel complement consisted of two crewmen and nineteen fully equipped infantrymen. While most nations were concentrating on tracked infantry carriers, the Soviets chose the wheeled configuration to fit the strained economic and technical capabilities of their heavy industry. The BTR-152 sufficed until better equipment could be secured.[14] The Soviets also introduced a smaller reconnaissance vehicle, the BTR-40, which complemented the BTR-152. Each remained on duty well into the 1960s when they were replaced by a new generation.

---

[13]Ibid.
    [14]*Armed Forces Journal* (July 1981): 40. See also Richard E. Simpkin, *Mechanized Infantry* (New York: Pergamon Press, 1980), pp. 34–36.

In 1961 the BTR-60P first appeared with frontline troops. This wheeled vehicle was fully amphibious, but early models had the same armor and the same open tops as their predecessor. These shortcomings have been corrected in later models; the BTR-60PB is now fully armored and enclosed. This has been a very successful design and today remains the chief armored troop carrier within Warsaw Pact motorized rifle divisions. Complementing this vehicle is the interesting Czech-designed and produced wheeled vehicle, the SKOT (OT-64). After 1964 the original Czech project became a joint Czech-Polish undertaking. Basic configuration is similar to the BTR-40PB; it is fully enclosed with amphibious capabilities. The SKOT has become the standard armored troop carrier within the Czech and Polish armies. This vehicle is one of the few major Warsaw Pact system designs to originate outside the Soviet Union.

The first Soviet tracked carrier vehicle, the BTR-50, was introduced at about the same time as the BTR-60. It was evidently intended that the BTR-60 would be issued to the mechanized infantry, while the BTR-50 would equip the infantry serving within armored divisions. The BTR-50 is a fully armored and amphibious vehicle, featuring bench seats to hold twenty combat troops. Its running gear is based on the highly successful PT-76 amphibious tank. The BTR-50 served in all Warsaw Pact armies; in the Czech and Polish forces it was soon replaced by a Czech-manufactured version known as the OT-62. Each was deployed with frontline troops until the introduction of the revolutionary BMP-1. After that they were kept in a reserve or secondary status, mainly in storage.

The BMP

Many commentators in the West consider the BMP-1 to be the finest infantry fighting vehicle in the world. With its introduction a new era of ground forces mobility, protection, and firepower was born and long-standing concepts concerning the battlefield role of an infantryman no longer prevailed. The BMP-1 enabled a team of riflemen to engage in mechanized warfare as never before. Now they could engage hostile targets while on the move and, more importantly, they could even challenge and defeat tanks because of the introduction of ATGMs on the vehicle. With a 73mm. gun able to fire low-velocity, rocket-assisted rounds to engage hard and soft targets, the BMP-1 appears to be a dauntingly formidable fighting machine. When it was first introduced there was no system of equal capability in the West. Since then only one, the German *Marder*, has been put into production.

The armament and performance statistics of the BMP-1 are most impressive. The 13.9-ton vehicle has a crew of three: a driver, vehicle commander, and gunner. In addition, it is able to transport eight combat-equipped infantrymen. The BMP-1 has a range of 310 miles and a top speed of 80km./hr. (50mph). When it was introduced in 1967 it was faster than any tank that the Soviets possessed. As noted above, it was the BMP-1 that triggered the development of an entirely new Soviet MBT. This fast troop carrier is equipped with the standard Soviet NBC protection found on its tanks and other combat vehicles, and it is authentically amphibious. The NBC system has a fully automatic sensor that activates an alarm and a filtration system. All hatches are sealed and the inside pressure is raised to prevent seepage.

What distinguishes it from other "battlefield taxis" is its ability to engage other major targets. The main gun, situated in a small turret amidships, is a 73mm. rocket-assisted, low-pressure antitank weapon. It is automatically loaded and has a rate of fire of eight rounds per minute. The round is almost identical to the one used wth the RPG-7 antitank infantry weapon. The BMP-1 gun is capable of penetrating all but Chobham-equipped tanks. The most obvious restriction in this gun system is its range; it is ineffective beyond 1,400 meters. To engage targets beyond that the BMP-1 is equipped with the 9M14M *Sagger* missile. During the 1973 war the *Sagger* proved to be effective up to 3,000 meters. At those ranges Egyptian infantrymen were able to defeat Israeli tanks before they could get into main gun range. Since the *Sagger* is a wire-guided missile, its flight attitude may be changed en route or it may be directed against another target.

The combination of these two weapons enables an infantry team to offer effective fire on target at up to 3,000 meters. This must be considered revolutionary because prior to the BMP-1 the maximum combat range of a team was no more than 1,000 meters. In addition, outward facing seats allow the infantry passengers to fire their personal weapons and to provide the vehicle with 360° protection. Other bonuses realized in this new machine are that it is cheap, light, highly mobile, and offensively oriented. When cost effectiveness comparisons are made with other armored vehicles (for example, tanks), it seems to compare favorably.

This is not to say that the BMP-1 is without limitations. Probably its most serious liability is its relatively thin skin. BMP armor does not exceed 14mm. (½ in.). It is therefore vulnerable to a wide assortment of light antitank weapons. In fact, it can be penetrated by a .50 cal. machine gun round if fired at less than 200 meters. It is probable that if the BMP is hit with any weapon above a .50 cal., it will at least be disabled and likely destroyed if any of the onboard ammunition is detonated. Another area of concern is in crew and passenger comfort. The cramped interior suggests that passenger fatigue may prove troublesome. It appears very unlikely that a BMP would be at its most effective posture with a full complement of ten or eleven men. A more suitable configuration would be to carry seven to nine men including the crew to reduce stress and fatigue as much as possible.

Today the BMP-1 has become the standard infantry fighting vehicle within the Warsaw Pact. It has been issued to every Pact member and is produced under license in Czechoslovakia and Poland. It has been introduced in such numbers that Soviet BMPs now outnumber NATO's troop carriers by at least three to one.[15]

MECHANIZED AND SELF-PROPELLED ARTILLERY

Traditionally, artillery has been an area in which the Soviets have excelled. The massive towed artillery formations of World War II, used in conjunction with close-support, self-propelled assault guns, reaffirmed the prior Russian and Soviet preoccupation. These systems were used in their traditional roles and as mobile antitank guns. The self-propelled SU-85, SU-100, ISU-122, and ISU-152 were especially successful designs. Yet, self-propelled guns were neglected after the war. In fact, postwar Soviet concern for mobile artillery did not manifest itself again until the late 1960s; new organic Soviet artillery was unarmored and towed. The attention of Soviet designers had been on the MBT, and they appeared to be interested in self-propelled heavy weapons only for their possible limited antitank role. Even this modest concern was abandoned when the T-54/55 and T-62 designs proved successful.[16] But increased speed and mobility of armored combat teams made conventionally towed artillery obsolete. What was clearly needed was an artillery section that could advance and fight almost alongside the advancing T-64, T-72, and BMPs.

The Soviets seem to have modeled their two new self-propelled artillery pieces to some extent on standard NATO models. The SAU-122 is a fully tracked, amphibious, twenty-two-ton fighting vehicle. It has a 122mm. howitzer with a rate of fire of eight rounds per minute and a range of between nine and fifteen miles.[17] It has a top speed of 60km./hr. (37mph) with a cruising range of 310 miles. These capabilities enable it to operate in the T-64/72-BMP mechanized formation. This system also has full NBC protection.[18]

The SAU-152 is the other new addition to the Soviet artillery arsenal and is very similar to the SAU-122. It has a 152mm. howitzer that has a rate of fire of four rounds per minute and a range of ten miles. In

---

[15]Zaloga, *Modern Soviet Armor*, p. 67.

[16]U.S., Department of Defense, Department of the Army, *Handbook on the Soviet Ground Forces, FM 30–40* (30 June 1975), p. 5/11.

[17]Shelford Bidwell, ed., *Brassey's Artillery of the World* (New York: Bonanza Books, 1979), p. 76.

[18]Bonds, *Modern Tanks*, pp. 8–9.

addition, it can fire a rocket-assisted round that increases its range to about eighteen miles. It is a little slower than the SAU-122, having a maximum speed of 55km./hr. (34mph), but the range is identical. It has the full complement of night-driving equipment and has standard Soviet NBC protection. Evidently, this machine, unlike the SAU-122, is not amphibious.[19]

Deployment of the SAU-152 has been restricted to Soviet Ground Forces. The SAU-122 has been issued to Polish, East German, and Czech troops, along with Category I Soviet forces.[20] These weapons have increased significantly the fighting capacity of Warsaw Pact northern forces.

BRIDGING

At this time the Soviets maintain probably the finest bridging and fording capabilities of any major army; this augments the already formidable mission capacity of the USSR and Warsaw Pact ground forces. Engineer formations are assigned to each regiment within every line infantry division of the Soviet army. In addition, engineer platoons are sometimes placed with special operations battalions. These formations have undergone considerable improvement in both equipment and training in recent years; naturally, emphasis has been on assault river crossings. Because the bridging equipment must keep up with advancing tanks and infantry fighting vehicles, each design has emphasized mobility. The Soviets have four major vehicle-launched bridges. The T-54 MTU and the T-55 MTU-20 are the two basic tank-capable spans. The running gears are those of a T-54 and T-55, respectively. Each provides protection in a combat environment while offering an assembly time of around three minutes. Also, the Soviets have towed truck-transported, bridge-laying systems; the KMM and the TMM are designed for rapid deployment.[21] Soviet concern with river assault techniques and with proper equipment is yet another example of the extent to which they have succeeded in assuring that equipment design fits tactics.

AIR DEFENSE

In any potential conflict with the West, Warsaw Pact armies must expect to be engaged by a large number of antitank helicopters and

---

[19]*The Military Balance 1980–1981*, pp. 14–15.

[20]Richard E. Simpkin, *Tank Warfare: An Analysis of Soviet and NATO Tank Philosophy* (New York: Crane Russak and Company, 1979), pp. 104–7, 188.

[21]*FM 30–40*, pp. 6/72–80.

aircraft. In recent years NATO has made a concerted effort to offset Pact armor superiority with the introduction of a number of new weapons systems. The American A-10 aircraft and new *Cobra* helicopter gunship represent significant new antitank weapons in NATO's arsenal. To counter such airborne systems, over the years the Soviets have developed extensive and impressive mobile antiaircraft capabilities.

There are two fully armored and tracked Soviet-designed antiaircraft systems deployed with Pact forces: the ZSU-57-2 and ZSU-23-4. The former was the first such system devised by the Soviets and is now being withdrawn from frontline troops in favor of the ZSU-23-4, which has proven quite successful. Built around four ZU-23 automatic cannons with an accompanying radar system, it has a rate of fire of 3,400 rounds per minute. It fires both high-explosive fragmentation and armor-piercing incendiary ammunition that have shown to be effective in bringing down opposing aircraft. Israeli experience confirms this. It is estimated that to remain more than thirty-five seconds within the sights of a ZSU-23-4 would mean certain disaster.[22]

The Soviets also have a number of mechanized SAM systems to complete their antiaircraft capabilities. The first fully mobile SAM unit was the SA-4 *Ganef*. This system has low-altitude performance characteristics with two large missiles per vehicle and an effective vertical range of fifteen miles and horizontal range of forty-three miles. It was issued to Soviet and East German forces and is now used by most Pact armies.[23]

The next mobile Soviet system to be deployed was the SA-6 *Gainful*. There are three rockets per vehicle, with the running gear provided by the versatile PT-76 amphibious tank chassis. This design proved dramatically effective during the Yom Kippur War. Its internal guidance system is governed initially by the accompanying *Straight Flush* radar system and features terminal semiactive homing. The *Gainful*, used in conjunction with the ZSU-23-4 and the low-altitude, hand-held, heat-seeking SA-7 *Grail* antiaircraft missile, provides an effective defense.[24]

The Soviets also have two newer systems, about which less is known. The first, the SA-9 *Gaskin*, is mounted on a modified BRDM-2 scout car. The other, the SA-8 *Gecko*, is an all-weather, all-terrain electronic countermeasures (ECM) resistant system. It is the direct counterpart to the Franco-German *Roland* missile. The SA-8 is mounted on a completely new six-wheeled amphibious vehicle. The unit is large enough to house both the missiles and their accompanying radar and is the first Soviet system to have such compact capabilities. This new weapon, added to all the others, makes the entire Pact's air defense program more imposing than ever. To quote one analyst,

[22]O'Ballance, *No Victor, No Vanquished*, pp. 277–307.
[23]B. T. White, *Tanks and Other Tracked Vehicles in Service* (Dorset, United Kingdom: Blandford Press, 1978), pp. 104–5.
[24]Ibid., pp. 103–4.

The air defense complement of a typical Warsaw Pact Combined Arms Army is formidable. It provides a tightly interwoven defense of considerable mobility and firepower, that, due to the wide variety of equipment and supporting radar, is reasonably resistant to ECM jamming.[25]

CONCLUSIONS

In the event of a war with the West, Soviet and Warsaw Pact military planning calls for a short, intense, mobile conflict that would have as a minimum objective the establishment of Pact forces on the banks of the Rhine and a maximum goal of reaching the English Channel. To be successful the Soviets and their allies require a hard-hitting, flexible force that could engage any potential enemy from off the line of the march as well as have the capacity to cross the rivers of Central Europe. That force also should have the capacity to fight in any conventional, nuclear, biological, or chemical environment.

Special concern over automotive performance is well illustrated in all their latest battlefield systems. A consensus seems to have emerged within Soviet planning agencies that has emphasized road march capabilities over mobiquity on the battlefield. All of the present systems display road march characteristics that are markedly superior to their western counterparts. A true melding of both equipment characteristics and envisioned combat roles has developed. Equipment whose design emphasizes deployment speed is the logical result of this battlefield doctrine. Presently, the Soviet main tank force has an average automotive performance of over 30mph with a range of about 300 miles. These capabilities will greatly enhance the advancing Pact forces' ability to meet their proposed goals on the central front.

Taken in the aggregate, air defense capabilities, river-crossing techniques and equipment, and overall automotive and gun performance of Soviet and East European battlefield systems confront NATO defense planners with a difficult task. Still, this is not to say that NATO should concede defeat before the actual engagements, although on paper the Pact appears to have an overwhelming advantage in numbers, variety of systems, and compatibility of doctrine; only actual combat can settle the question. There are important human factors that must be considered in any analysis of equipment potential or limitation within the Pact. Even if Soviet forces appear to have the technical capabilities to fight the war they

---

[25]Zaloga, *Modern Soviet Armor*, p. 88.

envision, human error and fatigue can limit the possible advantages provided by technology.

Whether or not the Pact could successfully engage NATO positions off the line of march is questionable, particularly if NATO forces were given the tactical advantage of surprise. Because the Soviet radio network only extends down to the company and platoon commanders, quick and decisive action against an implaced enemy might be difficult. And even though new models of both the MBTs and BMPs do address the problem of crew comfort, when compared with their western counterparts they appear quite inadequate. Fatigue and its effect on overall fighting posture is a major factor, and cramped spaces and long bone-jarring rides can induce severe exhaustion. The Soviet practice of maintaining formation on the battlefield until the unit ceases to be effective could compound the fatigue factor. In actual combat it is not clear that Warsaw Pact formations would be able to maintain their fighting posture while adhering to tactical schedules.

In conclusion, today's Soviet-produced systems represent a substantial integration of technical requirements with doctrine and industrial capacities. Though not as sophisticated as their western counterparts, Soviet and East European battlefield weapons and equipment are clearly qualitatively adequate to meet most tactical goals. Weapons alone do not win wars, but when large numbers of first-class weapons are joined to appropriate doctrine and manned by well-trained and disciplined troops, the potential for battlefield success cannot be easily dismissed.

Warsaw Pact Air Power: Present and Next Generations

BILL SWEETMAN

Over the past twenty years the military planners of the Soviet Union consistently have frustrated the efforts of western analysts to forecast trends and developments in the Warsaw Pact's tactical and strategic air power. Within six years of the great 1967 display of new aircraft near Moscow, the querulous voices of western experts were heard, reminding the Soviet Union that it was time for another major air display. But none has taken place; the experts' predictions of Soviet A-10 and F-16 equivalents have not come to pass, and Frontal Aviation has surprised the West completely with a massive shift to the armed helicopter.

Particularly in the field of shorter-range combat aircraft, the current predictions emanating from U.S. scientific intelligence sources are more disturbing than ever and would appear to constitute a strong case for a reenergized western development effort. Some observers now fear "a technological surprise that could alter the tactical air power equation for the remainder of this century,"[1] as a result of an aircraft approaching operational status, while other reports have suggested that two other significant tactical aircraft, three types of air-to-air missile, and a new airborne warning and control system (AWACS) will be operational by the middle of the decade, only four years or so from now.[2]

The implications of new developments on this scale are substantial and suggest that the Soviet Union is continuing to accelerate the improvement of its tactical air forces to the point where NATO's traditional qualitative advantage will be reduced or even eliminated or reversed. The objective here will be to assess these new possibilities in the light of the recent development of Soviet air power in general and that of air power in East Europe in particular.

---

[1]Edgar Ulsamer, "The Politburo's Grand Design: Total Military Superiority," *Air Force Magazine* 64, no. 3 (March 1981): 41–49.
[2]"Soviets Press Production, New Fighter Development," *Aviation Week and Space Technology* 114, no. 11 (16 March 1981): 56–61.

181

AIR POWER IN THE EAST

There is an inherent danger in thinking in specifically western terms when considering air power in the Communist world. Air power on the eastern side of the border never has been responsible for the sort of victories that have won steadily increasing independence and priority for the western air forces since their creation. Put more simply, nobody has ever won a war using Soviet-built aircraft as his primary weapon. The Soviets' own much-vaunted strategic bomber force, the largest in the world in the early 1930s, proved a complete failure in 1941–45 and emerged in total disgrace to be rescued only by the advent of nuclear weapons. Nor did the tactical air force match up to western achievements; overwhelmingly, it was the T-34 tank that was the decisive weapon.

In the postwar period the Soviet Union's allies and clients, with few exceptions, have been outclassed by comparable western-equipped forces. The extensive use of Soviet antiaircraft and surface-to-air missiles briefly reversed this position over North Vietnam in late 1972 and over Sinai in autumn 1973, but none of this success could be attributed to the Soviet Union's combat aircraft. The heavily armed Iraqi air force was unable to attain air supremacy over Iran, even when its opponent has been hamstrung by the withdrawal of spares support.

What independence the Soviet and Warsaw Pact frontal air arms now possess has been gained in the face of an understandably cold-blooded attitude toward promises of technology-based miracles. Troops and armor on the ground are still the way to win wars, and costly developments in tactical air power have to be proven cost effective before they are approved for production.

THE DESIGN AND DEVELOPMENT PROCESS

The system by which Soviet combat aircraft are developed and procured takes about the same time as most western methods, but it may sometimes seem faster because developments are only perceptible from the time a prototype appears until the time quantity production starts, rather than from the true inception of a project to a genuine initial operational capability. The phases involved are quite different from those generally used in the West. The Soviet Union consistently has expected its design bureaus to demonstrate technology thoroughly and in full scale before any commitment to production is made. So far this commitment to technology demonstration can be seen in both major generations of supersonic combat aircraft produced. In the case of the MiG-23/27

Flogger family, for example, at least two completely different configurations were built and flight tested by the Mikoyan-Gurevich bureau—the variable-geometry E-231 demonstrator and the *Faithless* prototype with auxiliary lift jets. Simultaneously, the Sukhoi bureau developed a variable-geometry version of the Su-7 *Fitter A* in parallel.[3] The Su-24 *Fencer* superficially may seem to be an exception to this rule, but a close comparison of this aircraft with the E-231 *Flogger A* prototype reveals that *Fencer* very closely corresponds to a 1.2:1 linear scaling-up of the E-231 configuration. The smaller aircraft therefore could act as a technology demonstrator for *Fencer*.[4]

The Soviet technology demonstrator is basically equipped and may well not use the engine destined for the production aircraft. Substantial

---

[3]The MiG-23 (*Flogger B*) is a single-seat, single-engine, variable-geometry Frontal Aviation air defense fighter with secondary strike capabilities. Developed in the 1960s, it entered service in the early 1970s. The MiG-23 has a maximum speed with missiles at altitude of about Mach 2. Its service ceiling is about 55,000 feet with a combat radius of around 400 miles using a lo-high-lo flight profile. Its armament consists of a short twin-barrel 23mm. cannon and mix of air-to-air missiles. It carries fire control radar and has a limited look-down capability. The MiG-23 also was deployed with the Voiska PVO air defense forces. The aircraft has been put into service with other Warsaw Pact air forces.

The MiG-27 (*Flogger D*) is a dedicated ground attack version of the MiG-23, which entered service in the mid-1970s. It is similar to the *Flogger B* in many ways yet is completely different from the wing glove forward, resulting in an excellent downward view. The pilot is protected by side armor, upgraded in later versions. It has special radar and laser-ranging as well as terrain-following radar and radio altimeter. Fully loaded with bombs, rockets, and a large center-line fuel tank, top speed is probably no more than Mach 1.5 with a combat radius of about 550 miles using a hi-lo-hi flight profile. The MiG-27 is armed with a six barrel 23mm. Gatling type cannon. Other special features include large low-pressure tires for rough fields and extensive ECM capability. See Bill Sweetman and Bill Gunston, *Soviet Air Power* (New York: Cresent Books, 1978), pp. 126–29, 133–35. See also Ray Braybook, "Soviet Swing Wings," *Air International* 15, no. 6 (December 1978): 266–72; "Na vooruzhyonii Sovietskoi aviatsii–In Soviet Service-10: Mikoyan Flogger," *Air International* 19, no. 2 (August 1980): 70–87; and *Royal Air Force Yearbook, 1979* (London: Ducimus Books, 1979), pp. 38–39.

[4]The Sukhoi Su-24 *Fencer*, identified earlier as Su-19, is a variable-geometry, two-seat, side-by-side, dedicated interdiction aircraft. It has a maximum speed of about Mach 2 at altitude with a 55,000 feet service ceiling and hi-lo-hi combat radius of about 500 miles. It is armed with one 23mm. multibarrel cannon similar to that of the MiG-27 *Flogger D* and can carry an assortment of sophisticated air-to-air and air-to-ground ordnance on nine external weapons stations.

Delivery to Frontal Aviation units apparently began in the mid-1970s. It has wide potential capabilities but so far mainly has been committed to the deep interdiction role. The nearest western equivalent is the *Tornado*. The Su-24 is equipped with first-rate avionics, including multimode attack radar, Doppler, laser ranger, and marked target seeker as well as a complete set of EW/ECM equipment. Up until the end of 1980 the Su-24 *Fencer* has not been permanently based outside the USSR and none has been made available to other Warsaw Pact air forces. Possessing short/rough field capabilities it could fly a lo-lo-lo profile with a very heavy warload, albeit with reduced range. See Sweetman and Gunston, *Soviet Air Power*, pp. 158–60. See also "Sukhoi's Pivotal Interdictor," *Air International* 20, no. 1 (January 1981): 6–10.

changes to aerodynamics and propulsion systems are acceptable and may be included during the development of the initial production subtype, which may not attain operational status for six or seven years after the appearance of the technology demonstration prototype.

The final phase of aircraft development in the Soviet Union is the continued improvement of the basic design. A substantially upgraded aircraft such as the *Flogger G* fighter can be expected to emerge some five years after the initial production version, while the Soviet Union appears to have a propensity for infinitely extending production lives through continuous modification and updating.[5] The MiG-21 *Fishbed* and Sukhoi Su-7 *Fitter A* have been in continual production since the 1950s, far longer than any western type still being built.[6]

ACQUISITION: EAST AND WEST

The present generation of modern Soviet combat aircraft began to be produced in quantity five to six years after the enhanced versions of

---

[5]The MiG-23 derivative, known as *Flogger G*, is an air defense aircraft slightly modified over the latest production versions of the MiG-23 *Flogger B* described in fn. 3. The dorsal fin forward section has been shortened, perhaps to upgrade air combat manueverability. Some other externally visible changes include minor equipment relations or modifications. See "Mikoyan Flogger," pp. 70–87.

[6]The MiG *Fishbed* was the most widely used combat aircraft of the 1970s and has been produced in greater numbers than any comparable type. It has been exported and produced abroad in very large quantities. Designed immediately following the Korean War as a day interceptor with exceptional dogfight capabilities, it was fully supersonic (in fact able to achieve Mach 2.1 at altitude) with a service ceiling of about 60,000 feet. Its combat radius was about 680 miles; it was armed with two 30mm. cannon and carried air-to-air missiles and basic avionics. Over the more than two decades of its production (by 1977 it was estimated that about 10,000 had been built) numerous modifications to its capabilities were made, keeping it at least marginally competitive with most of its potential opponents. It has found its way into the air forces of numerous Third World states. See Sweetman and Gunston, *Soviet Air Power*, pp. 122–26.

The Sukhoi Su-7 *Fitter A* was developed in the late 1950s as a heavy swept-wing fighter in the same class as the U.S. F-100 *Super Sabre*. It seems to have been designed largely with ground attack in mind and in that mold found its way into a substantial overseas market despite serious drawbacks. It had a maximum speed at altitude of about Mach 1.6 and a service ceiling of approximately 50,000 feet. Carrying twin drop tanks it had a range of about 900 miles. Armed with two 30mm. cannons, its four wing pylons were designed primarily for air-to-ground ordnance. The *Fitter* had gone through an astonishing pattern of incremental development in which the *Fitter C* (known as the Su-17) represented a long step away from the original design by adding variable geometry and other important changes. The result is a much more formidable aircraft which, like *Fitter A*, has been widely exported. See Sweetman and Gunston, *Soviet Air Power*, pp. 149–51, 161–63. See also "Survival of the Fitter: The 25 Year Saga of a Sukhoi Tactical Fighter Family," *Air International* 20, no. 4 (April 1981): 169–72, 205.

the previous generation became fully operational. The MiG-23, for example, appeared to be operational in 1972–73, following upon the deployment of the MiG-21MF *Fishbed J* in 1966–67. In other words, the development process involved the selection of a new generation design for production as the previous program matured. This implies the availability of a new type of tactical combat aircraft to follow the MiG-23 at some point around the mid-1980s, and indeed production decisions already may have been taken.

This Soviet effort does not seem surprising if the current output of the Soviet Union's military production facilities is compared with production in the West. However, these statistics should be treated with caution, as it is clearly in the interests of the western military to quote high-side estimates. A recent and relatively hawkish source quotes total tactical aircraft production in the Soviet Union as 1,150 units a year, rather lower than the figures of 1,300 to 1,400 aircraft widely quoted in the mid-1970s.[7] The Soviet total is often and misleadingly compared with the total production of combat aircraft for U.S. forces, which amounts to about 500 a year according to most U.S. budget figures. It should be remembered that the Soviet figure must be compared with the entire fighter output of NATO and aligned countries, both for NATO's own forces and for exports; neither the East European nor any of the USSR's other allies now build combat aircraft. Thus, to the 500 U.S. Air Force and U.S. Navy aircraft should be added the increasing deliveries of F-16 and *Tornado* aircraft to NATO, the French *Mirage* program, F-5 production for export, the entire output of the Israeli *Kfir* production line, and small but significant numbers of aircraft such as *Jaguars* and *Harriers*. All of these aircraft pose threats to which the Soviet aviation industry must respond, indirectly; they have to be added to the western side of the scale, bringing NATO and aligned fighter production somewhere near the 900 mark. With increasing export deliveries of F-16s and F-18s, this figure is likely to be sustained.

Another interesting comparative statistic seldom quoted is the relative modernity of western aircraft. Of the total Soviet fighter production, only the Su-24 *Fencer* and Yak-36 *Forger* VTOL are types that made their first flights in the 1970s.[8] All the others are older in basic concept

_____

[7]"Soviets Press Production," pp. 56–61.

[8]The Yakovlev Yak-36 *Forger* is still something of a mystery despite its debut on the deck of the *Kiev* as long ago as June 1976. It evidently was designed as an air combat fighter but without sufficient speed or maneuverability to engage anything other than unarmed multiengined reconnaissance aircraft. It may have a ground attack mission but if so its warload capability is too small to have any significant impact on, for instance, a defended beach. Its VTOL mode is achieved by a large jet engine with rear nozzles and two smaller lift jets fixed in front just aft of the cockpit with its exhausts downward. It also has tail and wing tip reaction control jets. Its maximum speed at altitude is about Mach 1.8 with a service ceiling of approximately 50,000 feet. Using a hi-lo-hi profile it could perhaps have a combat

and design. Of the West's aircraft, all the U.S. teen-series fighters and the *Tornado* are types that did not attain operational status until the latter 1970s or have not yet done so. Not surprisingly, these more modern western aircraft incorporate advances in agility, survivability, all-weather operation, and firepower, which the bulk of Soviet types being built today do not possess in the same degree.

A unique feature of Soviet aircraft procurement has been the concentration of production effort on a single type. While most Soviet aircraft are produced at rates not substantially different from those at which western aircraft leave the factories (the Soviets build fewer types and slightly faster than the West), the MiG-21 and MiG-23/27 *Flogger* series have been successively produced at very high rates. The *Flogger* series is now in production at a rate of 550 to 600 aircraft a year, accounting for roughly half of the Soviet fighter production. This effort certainly should allow the MiG-23/27 family to be produced at a comparatively low unit cost.[9]

Nevertheless, in view of the age of the present generation of Soviet fighters it would be surprising if decisions on follow-on types were not imminent, even if they already have not been taken. An examination of the way the present generation has influenced and been influenced by Soviet thinking on tactical air power may be informative in an attempt to predict the likely nature of such follow-on aircraft.

THE PRESENT GENERATION

Oddly enough the Soviet aircraft of the present generation, which comes nearest to a direct replacement of 1950-type aircraft is the *Backfire* bomber, widely regarded as a completely new factor in strategic equations. Using conservative aerodynamic and constructional design and engines already under development, *Backfire* is doing the identical job as the older Tu-16 *Badger* and *Blinder* and even carries many of the weapons such as the AS-4 missile and tail cannon installation.[10] Filling

___

radius of 200 miles. In general, the Yak-36 *Forger* is considerably inferior to its only western competitor, the *Sea Harrier*. The *Forger* well may be a transition aircraft. Sweetman and Gunston, *Soviet Air Power*, pp. 186–88. See also Hans Redeman, "Jak-36 Forger," *Flug Revue*, no. 4 (1977): 28–30.

[9]Production rates on individual types can be derived from the expansion of Soviet and non-Soviet fleets averaged over the years of production. Approximate figures for the 1977–79 period, in units per year, are as follows: *Flogger*, 550–600; *Fencer*, 100–130; *Fitter G/H*, 150–170; *Fishbed*, 130–150; *Foxbat, Flagon*, and *Forger*, 50–70.

[10]The Tupolev *Backfire*, surely the most controversial aircraft of the postwar period because of its role in the SALT II debate, is a variable-geometry, supersonic-capable, medium bomber developed in the late 1960s. Its maximum speed at altitude is estimated to

the roles of maritime strike, land strike, and electronic countermeasures (ECM) and intelligence platform, *Backfire* offers far better performance than its fixed-wing predecessors, together with other substantial advantages. The ECM suite of a standard *Backfire*, for example, is comparable to that of a completely dedicated ECM variant of the Tu-16.

In the field of short-range combat aircraft, the present generation has made more dramatic advances and, in some cases, has helped to bring about qualitative improvements. The most important changes have been the massive increases in warload and operational radius made possible by the new types, and the West has been particularly shocked by the speed with which the new aircraft have replaced older types, particularly as noted above the MiG-23/27 family. Nor has the Warsaw Pact shown any signs of being ready to reduce its numerical strength as the range, survivability, and lethality of its combat aircraft have increased.

For tactical air defense the changes introduced by the present generation of combat aircraft, primarily the MiG-23M *Flogger B* and *G* interceptor, have been mainly evolutionary, and although they imply a significant advance for Frontal Aviation air defense units, they do not change the basic Soviet concept of air defense in the battle area. This still consists of giving the armor or motorized infantry a range of highly effective antiaircraft weapons and leaving them to do the job, presumably on the assumption that the troops on the ground have a direct and personal interest in ensuring that tactical air defense is effective. The *Flogger* has added weapons with beyond visual range to the armory, but there is little sign that the traditionally inflexible Soviet air-to-air tactics have been relaxed to western levels. Meanwhile, in the time that it has taken the Frontal Aviation to move from the MiG-21 fighter to the *Flogger G*—one generation of development—Warsaw Pact ground forces have moved through two generations of medium-range SAMs and are reported to be on the verge of introducing another. In the tactics manual of the 1970s there is little difficulty in working out where the priorities lie.

---

be Mach 2 with a service ceiling of over 55,000 feet. Its combat radius on internally carried fuel is thought to be about 3,500 miles; the use of in-flight refueling could greatly increase *Backfire*'s range. Its primary weapons include the somewhat aged AS-4 *Kitchen* standoff missile and probably the newer AS-6 *Kingfish* as well as a new cruise missile in the development stage. *Backfire* deployment seems to be about half to the Long Range Aviation forces and half to the naval air arm. Sweetman and Gunston, *Soviet Air Power*, pp. 171–73. See also "Backfire Proliferates," *Air International* 19, no. 4 (October 1980): 186–88.

The Tupolev Tu-16 *Badger* is an ancient, long-range, subsonic, multiengine jet strategic bomber that also has been adapted to the maritime strike/reconnaissance roles. Its extreme reconnaissance range is about 4,500 miles. *Jane's All the World's Aircraft* (London: Jane's Yearbooks, 1974), pp. 488–89.

The *Blinder* originally was designed as a supersonic twin-jet bomber in the late 1950s. Its Mach 1.4 speed and 60,000 feet service ceiling were offset by its very limited range and its vulnerability to western defenses. Its maritime strike/reconnaissance versions seem to have been the most broadly used. *Jane's*, p. 481.

It has been among the offensive ground support aircraft of the Warsaw Pact that the main advances have been concentrated. It first should be remembered that the base from which reequipment started in 1973–74 was abysmally low; Frontal Aviation's primary strike aircraft at that time was the Sukhoi Su-7 *Fitter A,* which had a zero night/adverse weather performance and a warload/radius diagram comparable with the average modern western advanced trainer. The only other strike aircraft in service was the obsolete Yak-28 *Brewer,* optimized almost entirely for the delivery of nuclear weapons.[11]

From 1973 to 1974 it became clear that these aircraft were being replaced by new generation types designed mainly for the air-to-ground missions. The first two types to appear, the MiG-27 *Flogger D* and Sukhoi Su-17 *Fitter C,* were highly interesting in that they were both developments of existing types. In particular, the Sukhoi was derived from an aircraft that had been converted as a test-bed in the *Backfire* development program. In 1976, they were followed into service by the brand new Sukhoi Su-24 *Fencer.*

The timing of the entry into service of the new types, combined with reasonable conjecture as to the speed of the processes involved in the selection and development of Soviet aircraft, suggest that go-ahead decisions were taken some time in the late 1960s. It is also most unusual for the Soviet Union to launch three new types aimed at the same basic requirement within such a short period. That decision most likely was influenced by the virtual destruction of the Soviet Union's best armed ally in the 1967 Arab-Israeli War. Air operations in that conflict were not only a dramatic demonstration of the potential of the tactical support aircraft but also were remarkable for the high degree of attrition on both sides.

In the past ten years offensive frontal power available to Soviet forces in East Europe has been vastly increased. Greater warload has been allied to a major effort to close the technical quality gap with the West. The Soviet Union was ten years behind the West in the introduction of a night/all-weather strike aircraft, fifteen years behind with air-to-surface guided weapons, and lagged several years behind in the development of internal ECM fits. However, the rapid reequipment of Frontal Aviation units with the latest types has gone a long way toward closing the quality gap. In the next step forward—the extension of night/all-weather capability from specialized two-seat interdiction/strike aircraft to other smaller types—the Soviet Union may be following the West even more closely.

---

[11]The Yakovlev Yak-28 *Brewer* was originally part of a large family of twin-jet attack and interceptor aircraft first developed from the Yak-25 in the late 1950s. At altitude it evidently could reach Mach 1.13 with a service ceiling of about 55,000 feet; its extreme range was between 1,200 to 1,600 miles. The attack version carried two 30mm. cannon with a fuselage bay for free-fall bombs. It also could mount wing pylons for externally mounted ordnance. *Jane's,* pp. 497–98.

Perhaps the most remarkable single development, however, has been the introduction of the Mil Mi-24 *Hind* armed helicopter.[12] Since initiating development of the basic aircraft in the late 1960s, the Soviet Union has created a new force in tactical aviation and probably has a new command to operate it. The operational use of *Hind* is becoming clearer now than when the type was first seen. It is a multirole night and all-weather escort for armored fighting vehicle formations intended to combat enemy AFVs and antitank helicopters while using area munitions and its own squad of combat troops against NATO's infantry antitank squads. The Soviet Union definitely has stolen a march on the West in developing *Hind*. By using a large, conservatively designed helicopter and constantly upgrading the aircraft by the addition of new weapons and sensors, it has been able to deploy a large force very quickly. In fact, the *Hind* is closely comparable to the Sikorsky S-67 *Blackhawk* armed helicopter developed from the H-3 family, which was rejected by the U.S. Army in favor of the Lockheed AH-56A and the succeeding Hughes AH-64. The *Hind* also has been a notable exception to the general rule that non-Soviet Warsaw Pact forces lag behind Soviet units in the technical standard of their equipment. While fixed-wing units in East European forces are still largely equipped with Su-7s and MiG-21s, with a minority of early type *Flogger Bs* or *Flogger Fs*, they have been issued with the latest type of *Hind*.

The development of *Hind* is a model of the sort of technical surprise that the West should learn to expect from the Soviet Union. In its initial version, it relied almost entirely on known technologies in the airframe and armament but in an innovative combination that posed new problems for its opponents. It was also a weapon without any direct equivalent in western service; in fact, the *Hind D* attack version appears to have been committed to production after the U.S. Army had become convinced that helicopter design should be biased toward protection from ground fire—armor and nap-of-the-earth flying—rather than speed.

The Soviet weapon that truly surprises western observers is one based on known technology and thus can be deployed quickly while the

---

[12]The Mil Mi-24 *Hind* helicopter was introduced in 1971. The newest version (*Hind D*) evidently has a radar-directed, four-barrel gun, a forward looking infrared scanner for target acquisition, and low-light level television. *Hind* mounts a dazzling assortment of antiarmor ordnance on its short downward sloping wings, including the wire-guided AT-2 *Swatter*, AT-6 *Spiral*, S-5 rockets in pods, and even gravity bombs. Its rear compartment fuel tank is armored, and the *Hind D* has titanium crew compartment armor forward. The front canopy is bulletproof. It is also equipped with comprehensive fire-fighting foam dispensers. The *Hind* has a top speed of approximately 180mph and a combat radius with maximum payload of only 50 to 60 miles. Sweetman and Gunston, *Soviet Air Power*, pp. 145–47. See also Thomas J. McNamara, "An Analysis of the Soviet Helicopter Threat," first published in *Military Intelligence* and reprinted in the *U.S. Army Aviation Digest* 17, no. 5 (January 1981): 45–48.

West is still anticipating Soviet development of a system equivalent to a western type. The Soviets are aided in this effort by the effective secrecy in which their procurement decisions are shrouded, which is in contrast to the considerable publicity given to western procurement decisions. The Soviets are able to achieve a fairly accurate projection of western air power for at least six years ahead and probably work with a fair degree of confidence for ten years ahead, while the West frequently has no idea what the Soviets are doing until the production equipment drifts within telephotographic range of some dollar-susceptible East German.

THE NEXT GENERATION

Given these recent developments, the question of what is likely to emerge in the next decade can be addressed as the present designs of the 1960s lose ground in comparison with new western types. As in the West, the experiences of the 1973 Yom Kippur War will have had some influence on planning. The later stages of that conflict contained many pointers to ways in which the West can reduce the vulnerability of its strike aircraft to SAM and antiaircraft artillery defenses: night/all-weather capability, provided by both internal and podded equipment; advanced ECM with basic internal suites augmented by pods and dedicated jammer- and defense-suppression aircraft; and better precision-guided weapons. This could incline the Soviets toward changing some of the ideas on air defense over land hostilities that have influenced their behavior since the early 1960s.

The two types that were most widely predicted around the mid-1970s are both close parallels to western development. The emergence of a Soviet air superiority fighter in the class of the F-16 or F-18 has been assumed almost as a matter of course, and a Soviet equivalent of the A-10 also has been reported. However, there has been a marked change in the western perception of the timing of these programs. The A-10 equivalent—referred to also as RAM-J, T-58, or Sukhoi Su-25—was reported as ready for imminent deployment more than two years ago, but it has failed to appear in service.[13] In a rather similar pattern of events the RAM-L air superiority fighter, which was first observed at Ramenskoye about 1977–78, is not expected now to lead to the introduction of a specialized air-to-air fighter until the mid-1980s. Such a development had been widely expected by the turn of the decade. Belief that Soviet aircraft programs are further advanced in time than is actually the case appears to

---

[13]Designations used by *Aviation Week and Space Technology* and *International Defense Review*.

be a besetting vice of western analysts. For instance, the 1979 U.S. defense posture statement predicted the physical appearance of a heavy bomber prototype in that year, while the 1980 U.S. annual budget report predicted the deployment of the *Super Foxbat* last year.

There are signs that western analysts may have been led astray by a tendency to assume the "worst case" in all developments, combined with the Soviet predilection for prototyping a large number of potential configurations. In the case of RAM-J assault aircraft, this has been compounded by the assumption that the Soviets automatically will counter a western system by producing an equivalent. By the middle of last year some sources were beginning to be puzzled by the nonappearance of RAM-J among the ranks of the 16th Air Army in East Germany, and there is a possibility that the success of the Mi-24 helicopter has overtaken it.[14] Also noteworthy is the continued, energetic, and in the West, quite unpredicted development of the twenty-five-year-old Sukhoi Su-7 line. The latest variable-sweep developments of this aircraft may have replaced RAM-J in forward planning, thus fulfilling the same basic role as cheap, low-level ordnance trucks. It can be assumed that with human factors remaining roughly constant that Soviet production lines are subject to the same learning-curve effects as those in the West; therefore, the Su-17 and its derivatives probably would be cheaper than an all-new aircraft.

The development of more modern fighter designs is not in the least unexpected. Work on successors to the MiG-21 and Su-7, for example, had reached the stage of flying prototypes some six years after the types became operational. It is also not surprising that the new designs that have been reported appear to lay greater emphasis on flight performance than the MiG-23 or Su-17. In the development of its current aircraft, the Soviet Union's design bureaus held the main parameters associated with air-to-air maneuvering combat to the levels established by the MiG-21. All-round visibility, short-range armament, combat thrust/weight ratio, and combat wing loading of the MiG-23 are similar to those of the MiG-21 because the design bureau concentrated instead on improving the warload/radius and offensive and defensive avionics capability. In complete contrast, the West's new generation of fighters was designed with the emphasis on maneuvering ability and air-to-air combat, with any increases in warload radius over the F-4 generation being a by-product of the primary aim.

Unofficial reports suggest that the Soviet Union is evaluating fixed-wing and variable-geometry prototypes of high thrust/weight ratio other than the MiG-23 and, like the West, is conducting early tests with new radar and missile combinations.[15] The pattern of previous developments

---

[14]Information supplied to author.
[15]"Soviets Press Production."

suggests that initial production aircraft could appear by 1984 or 1985, but that the new radar/missile combinations would not be necessarily ready at the same time. Whether one or two types will be chosen for production is a questionable point. It is most likely that only one type will be adopted, eventually replacing the MiG-23 in the fighter role.

However, Frontal Aviation is expected to deploy a new fighter within the next year; its existence has been known for nearly five years but only now are some western analysts beginning to include it in the tactical equation. Currently referred to as the *Super Foxbat*, it has caused considerable anxiety in some circles as the potential source of the technical surprise mentioned above.[16] The development of a more advanced and versatile version of the MiG-25 *Foxbat* was revealed as long ago as late 1976 by the defector Viktor Belenko.[17] Increased speed at low altitude and a more effective missile system were mentioned at that time. Tests of this missile, known as the AA-9, and its radar were observed in 1978.

As first reported, the *Super Foxbat* development was thought to be intended for service with the national air defense forces as a counter to the Rockwell B-1 bomber.[18] This view, however, contained some logical anomalies that were not generally discussed. If the new system were intended for area defense against low-flying targets, the Mach 3 speed and 80,000-foot altitude capabilities of the *Super Foxbat* would not be generally exploited. In strategic defense roles, the Su-24 *Fencer* would appear to be a more logical and suitable carrier for the AA-9 system, which from published accounts seems to be the closest Soviet equivalent to the *Phoenix*/AWG-9 system installed on the F-14.

The development of the *Super Foxbat* MiG-25/AA-9 combination did not appear to slacken in pace after the cancellation of the B-1 and remained the Soviet Union's most costly and advanced current aircraft

---

[16]Ulsamer, "The Politburo's Grand Design," pp. 41–49.

[17]The MiG-25 *Foxbat* was first flown in 1970 and a production model was made available to the West when Lt. Viktor Belenko brought his aircraft to Hokkaido in September 1976. Subsequently, much contradictory information has been leaked by various western intelligence organizations, claiming both low and high performance characteristics for the aircraft. The MiG-25 *Foxbat* was designed primarily as a very high (80,000 feet) altitude interceptor, using conventional materials and equipment to fly at a top speed of about Mach 3. Its missions radius is believed to be about 600 miles, while its dash-only intercept range is likely to be no more than 250 miles. It is armed with four large AAMs that feature semiactive radar or infrared guidance. Its skin is primarily stainless steel with titanium leading edges on wings and tails. Highly effective and virtually untouchable reconnaissance versions also were evolved. Major improvements have been added to the aircraft since the first models were produced, and it is estimated that some 300 to 400 examples of the *Foxbat* interceptor are deployed with Soviet forces. The F-15 *Eagle* was produced to counter the MiG-25. Sweetman and Gunston, *Soviet Air Power*, pp. 130–32. See also "Na vooruzhyonii Sovietskoi aviatsii–In Soviet Service-7: Mikoyan Foxbat," *Air International* 17, no. 5 (November 1979): 245–52.

[18]This recalls the earlier rationale for the development of the MiG-25 *Foxbat*—the anticipated U.S. production of the B-70 *Valkyrie*.

program. Its potential in the tactical theater, though based deep inside the USSR, is now being recognized somewhat belatedly. A parallel can be found in western perception of the *Backfire*, which was only recognized as a significant change in the balance of theater and maritime power when the myth that it was a primarily strategic system was dispelled.

The *Super Foxbat* MiG-25 also recalls the *Hind* in its combination of mature and evolutionary technology. In addition to the space program and the SA-6 missile, the original MiG-25 *Foxbat* represents one of the Soviet Union's most notable design successes. It has been and remains the only nonexotic aircraft capable of sustained flight well beyond the Mach 2.5 limit of conventional airframes. The more potent and efficient Lockheed A-11 and its derivative, the SR-71, are far more complex and expensive aircraft.

Development of the original *Foxbat* MiG-25 by the Soviet Union is analogous to the design of the *Harrier* V/STOL fighter in the United Kingdom. Both are unique aircraft, which in the form they entered service in the early 1970s suffered from payload-range penalties due to their unique performance attributes. Both concepts now have reached the point where many of those penalties have been eliminated and are as much of a threat to their opponents as they generate new options for their users.

The exact capabilities of the *Super Foxbat* MiG-25 depend on the extent of the modifications carried out from the original design; however, it is likely that it has been reengined for greater efficiency in the subsonic regime and that the warload and radius have been improved. In any event, the deployment of such a system by Frontal Aviation will create problems for the West. Because the *Super Foxbat* will be able to cruise at medium height to the border zone and recover to bases in East Germany, like the Su-24 *Fencer* its operational radius will allow it to operate from bases as far back as the western Soviet Union with scarcely diminished penetration into western airspace.

Its introduction also coincides with a growing shift by NATO to the use of airborne command, control, communications, and intelligence platforms such as the AWACS and the TR-1 reconnaissance aircraft. At the same time NATO's resources of aircraft, which have been designed with the MiG *Foxbat* as a potential target, notably the F-14, F-15, and *Tornado* F-2, are being diluted by large numbers of F-16s that have no capability whatsoever against a MiG-25 target. Even the more potent of western fighters do not approach the speed and altitude of the MiG-25. In combat a *Super Foxbat* MiG-25 probably could be destroyed only if it were lured into a disadvantageous position similar to the way piston-engined fighters of World War II caught and killed the Messerschmitt Me-262 jet. The new MiG-25 *Super Foxbat* nevertheless will threaten NATO air resources, including the vital AWACS and medium-altitude, high-energy fighters, while staying out of the range of many defensive systems and possessing sufficiently high performance to give or refuse combat at will. It follows that the two-man crew of the *Super Foxbat* MiG-25 will enjoy more independence from ground control than do the pilots of current Soviet fighters, and this may read across to the deployment of other new types later in the decade.

CONCLUDING COMMENTARY

The deployment of the new MiG-25 *Super Foxbat* variant is a reminder to the West that the Soviet Union is capable of producing high-quality aircraft when it needs to and that proposed western developments should be analyzed carefully for opportunities that they may afford the Soviet Union. Overwhelmingly, the dominant theme in Soviet air power over the past twenty years has been conservatism, but in its best possible sense. In the Soviet military lexicon, conservatism is not an euphemism for paralysis or excessive hesitation, but stands for an appreciation of the value of proven success and the need to reinforce it.

Warsaw Pact Sea Power Assets

LOUIS J. ANDOLINO*

THE USSR AND THE WARSAW PACT NAVIES

Of the six non-Soviet Warsaw Pact countries, four have navies with varying degrees of capabilities: Poland, the German Democratic Republic, Bulgaria, and Romania. These naval forces are regularly deployed in the Baltic and Black seas and are mainly comprised of vessels designed primarily to operate in their respective coastal waters. In both quantitative and qualitative terms, the Polish and GDR navies in the Baltic are clearly superior to their Bulgarian and Romanian counterparts in the Black Sea.[1]

The Soviet navy is made up of four fleets (Baltic, Black Sea, Northern, and Pacific) and one flotilla in the Caspian Sea. However, it is in the Baltic and Black Sea regions where, in concert with its Warsaw Pact allies, the USSR enjoys an overwhelming superiority over non-Warsaw Pact forces. Indeed, the motto *"mare nostrum"* is no meaningless hyperbole but is directly applicable to Soviet naval power in those seaways contiguous to the territory of the USSR. For example, it recently has been reported that Warsaw Pact superiority in all Baltic ships is about four to one over NATO.[2]

From the Soviet military perspective, the naval capability of the junior partners in the Pact is designed to bolster regional defense requirements in Eastern Europe as well as to meet the specific security imperatives of the USSR. While it is doubtful that the navies of Poland, the GDR, Bulgaria, and Romania are considered an indispensable element in

---

*The author gratefully acknowledges the kind assistance of Louis R. Eltscher in the preparation of this article.

[1]With the exception of the USSR, "only East Germany and Poland of the Warsaw Pact nations have naval forces capable of operations other than coastal defense. However, both of these navies are intended for employment only in the Baltic and thus cannot be considered potential opponents of NATO naval forces beyond those important but restricted waters." Siegfried Breyer and Norman Polmar, *Guide to the Soviet Navy*, 2d. ed. (Annapolis: Naval Institute Press, 1977), p. 553.

[2]"Soviet Buildup in North Exceeds Protection Levels," *Aviation Week and Space Technology* 114, no. 24 (15 June 1981): 104.

195

overall Soviet strategic planning, they must be viewed as playing, at the
very least, an important role supportive to Soviet naval and military
objectives in East Europe. This is especially the case in the Baltic where
the Polish and East German navies seem to be well integrated with the
Soviet navy within the context of Warsaw Pact planning and operations.
Both navies are part of a fleet commanded from the USSR, and it recently
has been reported that:

> Ships of these navies cooperate on almost a daily basis with the Soviet
> Navy by protecting the three countries' coasts and gathering intel-
> ligence. . . . The joint exercises of three Warsaw Pact navies in the
> Baltic have been held regularly since 1957. But this cooperation has
> increased significantly in the last ten years.[3]

Poland

The largest non-Soviet navy in the Warsaw Pact belongs to Poland;
it has a well-balanced fleet capable of supporting Soviet defensive and
offensive requirements in the Baltic.[4] As is the case in other Warsaw Pact
navies, a number of Poland's major naval combatant vessels were acquired over the years from the USSR. Soviet transfers to the Polish navy,
which are currently operational, include one SAM *Kotlin* class destroyer,
six *P-6* class torpedo patrol boats, and twelve *T-43* class ocean
minesweepers.[5]

It is also appropriate to consider Poland's indigenous shipbuilding
industry because it contributes significantly to Poland's naval requirements. Notable among those ships designed, constructed, and employed
by Poland are the *Obluze* PCS class and the Polish version of the Soviet
Polnochny LCT class. The diesel-powered *Obluze* is a large patrol craft
capable of twenty knots with weaponry that includes four 30mm. (two
twin) guns and two internal depth charge racks for antisubmarine
warfare (ASW). Poland currently has five *Obluze* and eight *Modified*

[3]Milan N. Vego, "East European Navies," *Proceedings of the U.S. Naval Institute*
107, no. 3 (March 1981): 34–39 (hereafter cited as *Proceedings*).
[4]"The Polish Navy's principal peacetime tasks are the surveillance of the country's
coastline, participation in Warsaw Pact exercises, and intelligence gathering missions in the
Baltic and its approaches. Its chief wartime missions would be to conduct joint operations
with the Soviet Baltic Fleet and East German Navy, to augment the amphibious lift
capability of the other Warsaw Pact forces, to support the army's maritime flank, and to
defend the country's coast." Ibid.
[5]For a listing of the transfer of Soviet warships to other countries see Breyer and
Polmar, *Guide to the Soviet Navy*, pp. 571–83. See also Paul H. Nitze, Leonard Sullivan,
Jr., and the Atlantic Council Working Group on Securing the Seas, *Securing the Seas: The
Soviet Naval Challenge and Western Alliance Options* (Boulder: Westview Press, 1979),
p. 105.

Obluze; the latter are slightly smaller than the original design.[6] The Polish amphibious force capability is heightened by the presence of twenty-three *Polnochny* class ships each armed with four 30mm. (twin) guns and two 18-barreled 140mm. rocket launchers.[7] Built in Gdansk, this ship can carry up to six tanks.

Poland's shipbuilding capacity also contributes to Warsaw Pact sea power through its ability to produce a number of amphibious ships and commercial vessels for the USSR. Foremost among these are the thirteen amphibious ships of the *Ropucha* class built in Gdansk since 1975. General purpose repair ships (*Amur* and *Oskol* classes), survey ships (*Nikolai Zubov*, *Samara*, and *Kamenka* classes), as well as several other ship types, have been transferred to the USSR in significant numbers.[8]

East Germany

Like Poland, the GDR has a better than adequate, and improving, naval force consisting of older ships transferred from the USSR, in addition to those constructed in East German shipyards. Among the major Soviet transfers to the GDR navy are: one *Koni* class and one *Riga* class frigate, twelve *Osa I* and three *Osa II* class fast attack craft (missile), and eighteen *Shershen* class fast attack craft (torpedo).[9] Examples of indigenous East German ship design and construction include approximately ten *Frosh* LST class, which is similar to the Polish *Ropucha*. This amphibious landing craft carries four 57mm. (twin) and four 30mm. (twin) guns and space provided for a rocket launcher. The *Libelle* class fast attack craft (torpedo) constitutes another major design which first appeared in 1975. In addition to two 23mm. (twin) guns and two 21-inch (stern-launched) torpedo tubes, it reportedly can be used for minelaying and commando operations.[10]

It is significant that both the Polish and GDR navies have the capacity to contribute several important types of ships to the Pact's fleet.

---

[6]Both the *Obluze* and *Modified Obluze* classes were built throughout the 1960s at the Oksywie Shipyard. See John Moore, ed., *Jane's Fighting Ships: 1979–80* (New York: Franklin Watts, 1979), p. 406.

[7]Ibid., p. 408.

[8]Ibid., pp. 549–80 details specific data relating to Polish ships transferred to the Soviet navy.

[9]Ibid., pp. 193–94.

[10]Ibid., pp. 194–95. According to Milan Vego, in peacetime the East German navy has similar tasks as that of the Polish navy. However, in wartime "the East German Navy is expected to neutralize West German naval forces deployed in the Baltic, provide amphibious lift for Warsaw Pact forces, support the maritime flank of the Warsaw Pact forces, defend the country's sea lines of communication, and provide bases and logistical support for Warsaw Pact forces in East German waters." Vego, "East European Navies." For a brief overview of the GDR navy see also "A Look at East Germany," *Aviation and Marine International* 12, no. 79 (December 1980): 34.

Moreover, their navies continue to improve in those areas that enhance Soviet and Warsaw Pact naval superiority in the Baltic: amphibious craft and minesweepers. It is hardly surprising that the combined Warsaw Pact amphibious troop force stationed in the Baltic currently consists of as many as 10,000 men, a large force for that location.[11]

The Balkans

The non-Soviet Warsaw Pact navies in the Black Sea are also designed to play a supportive role to the Soviet navy. Yet, unlike their counterparts in the Baltic, their overall contribution is very modest. First of all Romania has shown a reluctance to collaborate with the USSR on military matters. Morever, at present, the Romanian navy is restricted to coastal defense and inland patrol; it consists mainly of three *Poti* class patrol escorts, about sixty-six coastal patrol craft, including some *Osas*, and a mine warfare force of about thirty-two.[12] In terms of surface vessels, the Bulgarian navy does not fare much better, having acquired virtually its entire aging fleet as a result of Soviet transfers. The Bulgarian surface fleet currently consists of two *Riga* class frigates, three *Poti* class patrol escorts, a mine warfare force of twenty-six, and twenty-four coastal combatants, including a number of *Osa* missile boats.[13] Furthermore, in contrast to Poland and the GDR, both Bulgaria and Romania have no major shipbuilding facilities.

The Soviet Navy

While the non-Soviet navies of the Warsaw Pact have been restricted to coastal waters to support the fundamental objectives of the alliance and its dominant member, the USSR, there has been an evolutionary transformation of the policies, roles, and the very ships that make up the Soviet navy. Over the years the progression of Soviet naval forces can be best characterized as a series of policy decision and implementation stages that has produced a significant ocean-going fleet out of what was primarily a coast defense navy. Whereas the Soviet navy has achieved large-scale success in extending the USSR's maritime frontiers in the Baltic and Black seas, it also has initiated programs designed to

---

[11]This includes "a Soviet naval infantry regiment, a Polish sea landing division and elements of an East German motorized rifle division trained in amphibious warfare. Landing craft capacity makes it possible to carry 5,000 infantry troops simultaneously." "Soviet Buildup in North Exceeds Protection Levels."

[12]*Understanding Soviet Naval Developments*, 4th ed. (Washington: Government Printing Office, 1981), p. 47. Prepared at the direction of the chief of Naval Operations by the director of Naval Intelligence (OP-009) and the chief of Information (OP-007).

[13]Ibid.

create an increasingly credible "blue-water" navy that enhances its ability to project influence on a global scale. Likewise, it is clear that reaching this point cannot be attributed to consistent planning but more to fairly erratic and even contradictory policies that have resulted in shipbuilding programs marked by startling shifts and reversals as well as impressive continuities. On this point Michael MccGwire has noted:

> Soviet naval procurement since the war provides a fascinating story of their efforts, in the face of runaway technological advances, to develop a counter to the maritime capability of the West—a capability which increased at least in measure with their own efforts, and which rendered obsolescent programme after programme, before the units concerned had even entered operational service. It is a story of brave words, but frustrating results—and, anyway until recently, a persistently deteriorating balance of advantage.[14]

Soviet naval planning in the years immediately following World War II serves as a prime example of such stunning reversals in policy and programs. As a result of the rather ineffective showing of the Soviet navy when compared to the successful naval operations conducted by the other major powers (including Germany) during the war, Stalin sought to produce a more credible ocean-going naval force for the USSR. Among other things, his plans called for the construction of 1,200 submarines with an additional boost in the production of more advanced surface ships, including aircraft carriers.

However, soon after his death in 1953 Stalin's successors reversed his plans for the navy and began a series of comprehensive cutbacks and cancellations in major shipbuilding programs. Consequently, plans to construct aircraft carriers never materialized; none of the *Soviet Union* class battleships or *Stalingrad* class cruisers were completed; only fourteen of the projected twenty-four *Sverdlov* class light cruisers were finished; and the medium type submarine program was sharply curtailed. The net result over a three-year period was a dramatic 50 percent reduction in the naval budget.[15]

---

[14]Michael MccGwire, "Soviet Naval Procurement," *The Soviet Union in Europe and the Middle East: Her Capabilities and Intentions* (London: Royal United Service Institution, 1970), p. 87.

[15]Speculation as to the reasons for this policy reversal by the Soviet leadership focuses on such factors as cost, an altered perception of how best to deal with the threat of an increasingly powerful U.S. naval force, and the necessity of building a merchant fleet to help project Soviet influence throughout the world. For example, MccGwire believes that the "new" Soviet policy required merchant ships, "but with one exception, all of the major shipyards were fully occupied in naval construction, and at the same time, the mass building programmes were placing a very heavy strain on many of the key sectors of the economy." MccGwire, "Soviet Naval Capabilities," *The Soviet Union in Europe and the Middle East*, p. 36. Similar concerns are illustrated by writings attributed to Nikita Khrushchev some years after these decisions were made: "I'll admit I felt a nagging desire to have some

By all indications the promotion in January 1956 of then forty-five-year-old S. G. Gorshkov to deputy defense minister and commander in chief of the navy was linked to the dismantling of the old program. Under Gorshkov's direction, emphasis shifted from the large-vessel navy envisioned by Stalin to a missile-armed navy of smaller surface ships and submarines operating from coastal waters and protected by land-based aircraft. Growing concern for the threat posed by U.S. aircraft carriers resulted in the production of such ships as the *Komar* class guided-missile patrol boats and the *Osa* classes of fast attack missile craft, both armed with *Styx* (SS-N-2) antiship missiles. Construction of larger missile firing ships then commenced: four *Kynda* class cruisers armed with eight SS-N-3 missiles and having a range of 250 miles were commissioned between 1962 and 1964, followed in the mid-1960s by the production of *Kresta I* class cruisers armed with both SS-N-3 and SA-N-1 missiles.

The addition of the *Polaris* and *Poseidon* (currently *Trident*) submarine-launched missile systems to the U.S. nuclear strike capability drastically affected the Soviet leadership's naval policy and subsequent shipbuilding and weapons systems production. Given the specific nature of this threat, much emphasis has been focused on ASW. This was reflected in the production of two innovative ASW surface ships—the *Moskva* and *Leningrad*—launched in 1965 and 1966, respectively. These uniquely designed half-deck missile cruiser/helicopter carriers were both armed with two twin SA-N-3 missiles and were capable of carrying eighteen *Hormone* AASW helicopters fitted with bombs or torpedoes and submarine detection systems.[16] Additional reliance for ASW would be placed on submarines, while existing surface ships would be redesigned and modified. According to MccGwire, the *Kashin* class destroyers were fitted for SAM missiles, yet they were being produced at a rate of just two a year; therefore

> To ameliorate the situation, they undertook the major conversion of eight of the older *Kotlin* class destroyers, and six of the *Krupnyi* class missile units, into SAM-armed Anti-submarine ships. This gave these ships a weapons performance comparable to the *Kashin*, for delivery during the latter half of the sixties.[17]

Despite the often uneven development of Soviet naval forces throughout the years, the last two decades clearly have been a period

---

(aircraft carriers) in my own navy, but we couldn't afford to build them. They were simply beyond our means. Besides, with a strong submarine force, we felt able to sink the American carriers if it came to war. In other words, submarines represented an effective defense capability as well as reliable means of launching a missile counterattack." Quote cited in Norman Polmar, "Soviet Nuclear Submarines," *Proceedings* 107, no. 7 (July 1981): 32.

[16]Additional weaponry on both ships included "4-57mm (2 twin mountings) guns, 1 twin SUWN-1 A/S missile launcher, 2-12 tube MBU 2500A on forecastle." Moore, *Jane's Fighting Ships*, p. 250.

[17]MccGwire, "Soviet Naval Procurement," p. 38.

characterized by a massive naval buildup designed to accomplish fundamental national goals of the USSR. Doubtless, Thomas Brooks is correct when he observes:

> .... it is apparent that the Soviet Navy of the past two decades has gone through several evolutionary stages: in the 1950s and the early 1960s emphasis—both doctrinal and shipbuilding—was on anticarrier warfare (ACW); in the late 1960s through the current time, the emphasis has been on antisubmarine warfare (ASW), either to protect one's nuclear-powered ballistic submarines (SSBNs) or to destroy enemy SSBNs.[18]

The Soviet navy should now be able to deal effectively with both ACW and ASW wartime contingencies. Certainly a survey of the Soviet naval inventory, along with an analysis of the statements of its leadership, would suggest an expanding role for the fleet both during war and peacetime.[19] Foremost among the projected current objectives of the Soviet navy are: 1) a strategic nuclear strike capability, 2) maritime security that includes the ability to destroy enemy naval forces, especially those that pose a direct threat—aircraft carriers and strategic missile submarines—and to counter the considerable ASW forces of the West, 3) the interdiction of western sea lines of communication (SLOC), 4) support of ground troops, and 5) the support of state policy through a balanced global naval force.[20]

SUBMARINES

With more than 370 vessels the USSR maintains the largest submarine fleet in the world today.[21] In Warsaw Pact coastal waters the Soviet navy maintains an average of thirty-five submarines in the Baltic

---

[18]Thomas A. Brooks, "Whither the Soviet Navy?," *Proceedings* 106, no 2 (February 1980): 103–4.

[19]For example see S. G. Gorshkov, *The Sea Power of the State*, 2d. ed. (Annapolis: Naval Institute Press, 1979). For an analysis of the expansion of Soviet naval power and the important role played by Admiral Gorshkov, see also Michael MccGwire, "The Rationale for the Development of Soviet Seapower," *Proceedings/Naval Review 1980* 105, no. 5 (May 1980): 155–83.

[20]*Understanding Soviet Naval Developments*, pp. 7–13. For an assessment of Soviet naval capabilities and intentions see also Julian J. LeBourgeois, "What is the Soviet Navy Up To?" *NATO Review* 25, no. 2 (April 1977): 14–19.

[21]It is noteworthy that submarine construction is nonexistent and deployment very limited in the non-Soviet Warsaw Pact navies. For example, Poland has a submarine force of four *Whiskey* class boats acquired from the USSR between 1962 and 1969. Bulgaria also has four submarines gained through Soviet transfers: two *Whiskey* class units acquired in 1958 are in service but considered obsolete, plus two *Romeo* class submarines attained in 1972.

and thirty in the Black Sea.[22] Soviet submarines usually employed in Warsaw Pact waters include the ballistic missile (SSB) *Golf* class, the cruise missile (SSG) *Juliet* class, and torpedo attack submarines such as the *Tango, Foxtrot,* and *Zulu* classes.[23]

Though the submarine long has been considered the essential core of the Soviet navy, its importance was substantially enhanced by the advent of naval nuclear power and missile technology. With the introduction of the *Yankee* nuclear-powered ballistic missile (SSBN) class submarine in 1968, the USSR deployed a sea-launched nuclear attack capability for use against the continental United States. This new capacity, along with the traditional emphasis placed on submarines as a vital source of naval power, prompted the USSR to modernize and enlarge its submarine force. For example, while three nuclear submarines were constructed between 1954 and 1960, seventy-seven were completed from 1961 to 1970 and ninety-five between 1971 and 1980.[24] During these same periods the USSR continued production of existing types while also developing new classes of diesel submarines.

Unquestionably, the efficacy of using naval power against land targets has become increasingly obvious to Soviet defense planners in recent years. Not unexpectedly, then, the role of the submarine in the nuclear age has been promoted by Admiral Gorshkov in many different forums. In his major work, *The Sea Power of the State,* he emphasized that "scientific and technical progress has produced submarines as the most perfect carrier of nuclear weapons, the launching site of which is in effect the whole World Ocean."[25] Doubtless, this sentiment has been shared by top Soviet decision makers and has been reflected in the priority given to the design and construction of entire new generations of nuclear-powered SSBN classes such as the *Delta III* and the massive *Typhoon.*[26]

Since the completion of production of the *Hotel* and *Yankee* SSBNs, the Soviet navy has added to its strategic missile submarine fleet by extending the *Delta* class series (currently numbering about thirty-two units) to include the *Delta III.* Having joined the fleet in 1979, the *Delta III* is in production at Komsomolsk, with projected completion of thirty-four units in 1981.[27] Similar in most aspects to the *Delta II,* this modified

---

[22]Deployment figures vary over time and specific circumstances and thus only can be approximated in any given year.

[23]Nitze, et al., *Securing the Seas,* p. 97.

[24]Polmar, "Soviet Nuclear Submarines," p. 35.

[25]Gorshkov, *Sea Power of the State,* p. 278.

[26]It is instructive to note that all submarine construction is conducted at five major shipyards in the USSR: the Admiralty Yard and Sudomekh at Leningrad (Baltic), Severodvinsk (Arctic), Komsomolsk (Pacific), and Gorky (inland). Breyer and Polmar, *Guide to the Soviet Navy,* pp. 536–37. U.S. analysts believe that these yards are currently being used at less than 50 percent of their estimated capacity.

[27]Polmar, "Soviet Nuclear Submarines," p. 38.

submarine will be enhanced by its weapons system, which includes sixteen tubes for a more advanced SS-N-18 missile (with MIRV capabilities) that has an approximate range of over 4,000 nautical miles.

At twice the size of the *Delta III*, the world's largest ballistic missile submarine class, the *Typhoon*, is currently under series construction at Severodvinsk. While the initial unit was launched in 1980, it probably will be several years before it becomes fully operational. Nevertheless, the construction of this submarine class adds significantly to the Soviet strategic nuclear offensive. For example, it is believed that the *Typhoon* will be armed with twenty-four SS-N-18 missiles and have a capability of delivering independently targetable warheads. Certainly, the inclusion of the *Delta III* and *Typhoon* adds qualitatively to the strike potential of the Soviet navy. As Donald Daniel observes:

> With missile ranges of over 4,000 nautical miles, they can be within striking distance of their targets while remaining in protected waters near the Soviet homeland. They thus have an excellent potential to serve as a survivable wartime strategic reserve. This is a major mission of the SSBN fleet, which has responsibility for 39 percent of Soviet strategic missiles and somewhat less than one-fourth of missile warheads.[28]

In the last three years there has been a slight decline in the total number of units in the SSBN force. This probably is due to the fact that some older submarines are being deactivated while at the same time current policy now seems to favor qualitative advantages over quantitative considerations, as is the case with both *Delta III* and *Typhoon*. Moreover, while the SSBNs remain an integral part of the submarine force, it also seems clear that the USSR wishes to maintain a balanced fleet. For example, construction of both attack and cruise missile submarines continues at a steady pace; even more significant, perhaps, is the continued introduction of new designs to each of those types.

With regard to torpedo-attack submarines, the diesel electric-powered *Tango*, which is most likely armed with ASW missiles, is being produced at an average of one per year from the Gorky Shipyard. This submarine represents the best in Soviet diesel technology and illustrates the continued interest that the Soviet navy has in diesel subs. At the same time the nuclear-powered *Victor II* class remains in series production at the Admiralty Yard in Leningrad. The *Victor II*, which has been referred to as the "backbone" of the Soviets' nuclear attack submarine force,[29] most likely is armed with tube-launched SS-N-15 missiles and a SUBROC type

[28]Donald C. Daniel, "Navy (VMF)," in David R. Jones, ed., *Soviet Armed Forces Review Annual* 4 (Gulf Breeze, FL: Academic International Press, 1980), p. 198.
[29]*Understanding Soviet Naval Developments*, p. 97.

submerged launched antisubmarine missile system, of which this class probably can carry ten.[30]

Perhaps the most interesting development in Soviet attack submarines in recent years was the introduction of the *Alfa* class in 1979. Though in series production at the Sudomekh Yard, only a few units are currently operational. According to Daniel, the relatively small number of *Alfa* submarines being completed "is probably due to the extensive efforts required to construct a craft with a diving capability of 2,000 feet and an underwater speed of forty knots. These values far exceed those for any submarine in the world."[31]

To accent speed and stealth, the streamlined *Alfa* hull is made of light-weight, nonmagnetic titanium. Armaments probably include wire-guided torpedoes and SS-N-15 missiles. All weapon systems, radar, and sensor devices are assumed to be the most advanced in the Soviet navy. Current speculation concerning this high technology submarine rests on the assumption that it is an experimental craft designed to advance the SSN fleet beyond the currently reliable *Victor* classes. As such, it was used for experimenting on a whole series of construction techniques and innovations derived from proven technology and experience gained with earlier classes.[32]

Another major innovation in design and capability came in 1980 with the launching of an extremely large nuclear-powered cruise missile submarine. The *Oscar* class is thought to be capable of launching up to thirty SS-NX-19 antiship cruise missiles with an estimated range of 250 nautical miles. Also noteworthy is the fact that this addition to the SSGN submarine force has the capability of firing cruise missiles while submerged and can attain a running speed of over thirty knots. In essence, the *Oscar* provides the Soviet navy with the largest general purpose submarine in the world, which greatly enhances its capacity to deal with NATO naval forces on the high seas. Currently being constructed (quantity unknown) at the Severodvinsk Yard, the *Oscar* class is expected to join the fleet some time in 1981.

In the meantime, production of the nuclear-powered cruise missile ship, *Charlie II* class, continues at the Gorky Yard. The basic improvement over the original *Charlie* design includes a larger size that makes it possible to accommodate increased weaponry and sensor capabilities. Like other cruise missile submarines, the *Charlie II* will have eight

---

[30]Moore, *Jane's Fighting Ships*, p. 511.

[31]Daniel, "Navy (VMF)," p. 199.

[32]"SSN Class Alfa," *Aviation and Marine International*, no. 79 (December 1980): 37. This conclusion is also reached by Norman Polmar: "[I]t appears likely that a new SSN design will emerge during the 1980s, an improvement of the *Alfa* or at least incorporating some of its techniques." Polmar, "Soviet Nuclear Submarines," p. 38. See also MccGwire, "The Rationale for the Development of Soviet Seapower," esp. p. 180.

standard torpedo tubes, however, while designed to carry SS-N-7 missiles, there is the possibility of using SS-N-9 missiles that would improve its missile capability, including an extension of range to probably twice that of the thirty miles of the SS-N-7.[33] The *Charlie II*'s formidable ASW proficiency is further enhanced by an underwater launch capability.

Given the apparent trends in Soviet submarine construction, it seems likely that the USSR will continue to produce an average of ten to twelve units per year for the foreseeable future. Most of these submarines undoubtedly will be nuclear powered; yet, by all indications, diesel submarines like the *Tango* will continue to remain in production for many years. While diesel boats will be added at lower rates, the Soviet navy continues to place great importance on them.[34]

It also would seem that the overall numbers of submarines in the fleet will not increase significantly in the 1980s. This assessment is based on the assumption that older designs either will be deactivated or transferred to Pact navies or client states. Moreover, the Soviet navy is currently designing submarines with greatly enhanced capabilities, so that fewer units are required to pursue fundamental national objectives on a global scale. This is especially true considering that Soviet submarine force levels in regional waters of the Warsaw Pact are more than adequate for all conceivable purposes there.

SOVIET SURFACE SHIPS

A review of the USSR's current ship construction programs clearly demonstrates a Soviet preoccupation with developing a massive armada that combines a potent regional defense with a formidable presence in seas distant from its territory. In developing this potential, the USSR may have reached a watershed in naval policy that is best illustrated by the numbers and kinds of ships being produced, and especially by the innovative designs currently being introduced into the fleet. In addition to the Soviet submarine forces, the priority for providing for a balanced fleet centers around Soviet surface ships.

Numerically, the Soviet navy possesses the largest fleet of major surface ships in the world, both patrol and combatant craft. It is a navy

---

[33] *Understanding Soviet Naval Developments*, p. 88.

[34] The value of diesel-powered submarines to the Soviet navy includes such factors as the ability to maintain a large-scale submarine force at a relatively low cost, a proven reliability over some nuclear-powered submarines, the capability to fulfill certain objectives (i.e., coastal patrol), and their appropriateness as a craft for export to client states. For an informative update on Soviet diesel submarines see Thomas A. Brooks, "(Soviet) Diesel Boats Forever," *Proceedings* 106, no. 12 (December 1980): 105–7.

characterized by an increasing emphasis on creating multipurpose, long-endurance vessels more heavily armed with a broad range of antisubmarine, antiair, and antiship weapons than are most comparable ships in other navies.[35] Moreover, the inclusion of certain new and innovative surface vessels in recent years suggests an apparent willingness on the part of Soviet leaders to rectify various limitations that previously have characterized the navy. This amounts to an immense Soviet commitment of capital investment and additional resources to the expansion and modernization of its surface fleet.

The recent attention given to what they call "aviation ships" may yield an important clue to understanding current trends in Soviet naval surface ship policy. Having been ignored for many years by naval planners, ships with aircraft carrying capabilities have now found their way into the Soviet navy. The first generation *Moskva* class maintains a ASW potential as a guided-missile cruiser that also has the capacity to carry a large squadron of ASW helicopters. It is probable that production of these ships ended at two because of a combination of technical deficiencies and a decision to divert resources to the larger and more versatile *Kiev* class guided-missile V/STOL aircraft carrier.

The *Kiev* class is the largest combatant class ship ever built by the Soviet Union. Considered the first authentic Soviet aircraft carrier, this angle-decked ship is capable of deploying a mix of thirty-five to forty rotary and fixed-wing aircraft such as KA-25 *Hormone* helicopters and VTOL *Forgers*. The ship's main armament includes eight surface-to-surface cruise missile tubes, two twin SA-N-3 and two SA-N-4 SAM launchers, two 76mm. twin gun mounts, and eight Gatling guns. For ASW the ship has a twin antisubmarine missile launcher, two antisubmarine rocket launchers, and torpedo tubes as well as hull-mounted and variable-depth sonar.[36]

The first *Kiev* class ship was launched in 1972 but did not become operational until 1976. Presently, two are fully deployed while a third, which underwent sea trials in 1979, is being fitted out and a fourth is under construction in Nikolayev. Given this relatively new Soviet commitment to aircraft carriers, it is interesting to note that many U.S. analysts believe that the *Kiev* is essentially a forerunner in the development of a much larger, more conventionally designed, full-deck aircraft carrier. In a presentation before Congress in March 1981, the director of U.S. Naval Intelligence, Rear Admiral Sumner Shapiro, observed:

> We continue to estimate that the *Kiev* class carriers are but a stepping stone, and that the Soviets are well along in the planning for a larger,

[35]*Understanding Soviet Naval Developments*, p. 31.
[36]Ibid., p. 100.

nuclear-powered aircraft carrier capable of handling high performance aircraft much like our own. . . . The evidence continues to
accumulate that they are working in this direction, and that the first
such carrier with its embarked airwing will be put to sea by the end of
the decade.[37]

It seems safe to assume that if the navy is currently committed to
effective aircraft carrier deployment it would hardly wish to conclude its
program with the limitations inherent in the *Kiev* class. Unlike the *Kiev*,
which is limited to VTOL fighters, a new large-deck carrier fitted with
appropriate catapults and arresting gears would be capable of handling a
greater range and number of fighter aircraft. Therefore, while it is believed
that the *Kiev* class will remain in series production until perhaps several
more units are completed, analysts continue to believe that it will be joined
by a more conventional carrier in the 50,000-ton class. Soviet officials
cite the advantages of such a carrier despite the overriding budgetary
priority that such a ship would entail. Soviet Vice Admiral K. Stalbo's
well-publicized words state: "It has been calculated that the combat
capabilities of large carriers compensate for the expense of their design
and construction. . . . A carrier with a 50,000-ton displacement can carry
twice the aircraft of a 35,000-ton carrier, while construction costs are
only 25% more."[38]

The aircraft carriers currently deployed by the Soviet navy are
enhanced by the introduction of the nuclear-powered, guided-missile
cruiser *Kirov*. Constructed in the Baltic Yard at Leningrad, the first unit
joined the fleet in 1980, with a second expected to be launched some time
in 1981. The addition of this cruiser to the Soviet navy represents a
significant landmark, as it is their first operational nuclear-propelled
surface ship and is reported to be capable of massive self-defense.

The *Kirov* has an impressive array of advanced armament and
sophisticated sensors (including a new type of large variable-depth sonar),
giving it ASW, antisurface warfare, and antiair warfare capabilities.
Included in the main armament are two innovations: twenty new type
cruise missiles, which are believed to be improvements over the SS-N-
3/SS-N-12 family, and a new SAM system (twelve launchers), which
may be a seaborne derivation of the yet-to-be-deployed ground-based SA-
10 missile system. Additional weaponry consists of two twin SA-N-4
SAM launchers, two twin SS-N-14 ASW missile launchers with reloads,

---

[37]"Soviets Planning Advances in Maritime Capabilities," *Aviation Week and Space
Technology* 114, no. 11 (16 March 1981): 18.

[38]"Soviets May Be Building a Large-deck Nuclear Carrier," *Proceedings* 105, no. 11
(November 1979): 126. Admiral Gorshkov himself has reportedly confirmed the con-
struction of such an aircraft carrier to U.S. diplomats. See William H. J. Manthorpe, Jr.,
"The Soviet Navy in 1979: Part I," *Proceedings* 106, no. 4 (April 1980): 114.

two single 100mm. dual purpose gun mounts, and eight single 30mm. Gatling guns. With an elevator and hangar aft, the *Kirov* also has the capacity to handle several *Hormone* helicopters.[39]

Two additional *Kirov* class cruisers are expected to be constructed by the end of the decade. Despite its obvious formidability and overall usefulness to the Soviet navy, production of this class in any significant numbers is likely to be hampered by its great construction and operational costs.[40] Yet, even with a limited number of this class deployed over the next few years, the power and effectiveness of the Soviet navy will have been considerably enhanced. As James Kehoe has observed:

> The *Kirov* is a formidable addition to the Soviet Navy's growing capability to conduct world wide operations at sea. Her technological sophistication and innovative combination of capabilities—and the cost that these represent—are unmistakable indications of the Soviets' attitude towards seapower and their growing ability to project that power.[41]

The *Kirov* is joined by an operational contingent of twenty-five guided-missile cruisers all armed with SAMs; some additionally are armed with SSMs. The current deployment of the CG class cruisers includes seven *Kara*, four *Kresta I*, ten *Kresta II*, and four *Kynda* class ships. All production of these units seems to have been completed with the possible exception of one *Kara* class cruiser currently under construction, although a follow-up design to *Kresta II* is expected to undergo construction throughout the 1980s. Of the older *Sverdlov* class, built during the 1950s, twelve remain in active service.[42]

Presently, the Soviet navy maintains a fleet of sixty-six destroyers: thirty-six DDG class guided-missile destroyers armed with SAMs and/or SSMs, and thirty DD class destroyers. Of special note, however, is the

---

[39] *Understanding Soviet Naval Developments*, p. 101. For a detailed analysis of the *Kirov*, including a review of weapons and electronics systems, see James W. Kehoe, "Their New Cruiser," *Proceedings* 106, no. 12 (December 1980): 121–26.

[40] On this point, Polmar makes the following observation: "Obviously, a one for one replacement of the *Kirov*-type ships for cruisers of earlier classes is unlikely if not impossible because of the nuclear ship's enhanced capabilities and, more important, the *Kirov*'s greater costs to construct and operate. In particular, the crew requirements for the *Kirov* [estimated by Kehoe at 800] must include a large number of nuclear-trained personnel, a particularly high-cost factor for any navy. And, there is competition for these 'nucs' to go into the increasing Soviet nuclear submarine force (160+ units) and growing civilian nuclear power industry." Polmar, *Proceedings* 107, no. 1 (January 1981): 83.

[41] Kehoe, "Their New Cruiser," p. 126.

[42] "One *Sverdlov* class cruiser has a 'refitted' twin launcher for medium-range anti-aircraft missiles in place of a six-inch gun turret, while two others have been converted to 'command ship' configurations. . . . Several other *Sverdlovs* have been modernized as well, so the class is expected to remain in service for some years to come." *Understanding Soviet Naval Developments*, p. 35.

introduction of the conventionally powered vessel, *Sovremenny*. This destroyer is expected to be in series production in the Zhdanov Shipyards (Leningrad) throughout the 1980s. The first unit has been undergoing sea trials and is expected to join the fleet in 1981. A recent report on the *Sovremenny* indicated that it will be armed with both SSM and SAM systems as well as ASW weapons, including two twin 21-inch torpedo tubes and two RBU-1000 launchers. It is also fitted for two twin 130mm. guns and four 30mm. Gatling guns. The helicopter deck aft makes it possible to hold one *Hormone*.[43]

In addition to the new *Sovremenny* class, the Soviet navy has added yet another class to the ranks of its destroyers. The new *Udalov* class guided-missile destroyer is designed primarily for ASW use and is armed with SS-N-14 cruise missiles, two RBU-6000 rocket launchers, two rapid-fire 100mm. guns, and four 30mm. Gatling guns. This 8,000-ton gas turbine-powered ship is also equipped with a twin helicopter hangar and flight deck to accommodate two ASW helicopters.

As a major component of both its antisubmarine and coastal defense force, Soviet frigates are currently at a level of 135 ships with several units expected to continue in production for the foreseeable future. Built at a rate of three to four ships per year, the *Krivak* class is armed with a four-tube launcher for the SS-N-14 ASW missiles and two twin reloadable launchers for the SA-N-4 SAM missile. Additionally, these ships have four 76mm. guns and eight 21-inch torpedo tubes.[44] Of the smaller frigates only the *Koni* and *Grisha* classes remain in production. At present, two *Koni* class ships are operational, and while it is uncertain exactly how many will be produced for the navy, construction is continuing at the Zelenodolsk Yard. As the most advanced in its class, the *Grisha III* is expected to be built at a rate of three units a year at the Petrovsky Yard.

A complement of approximately 940 ships makes up the small combatant fleet of the Soviet navy. Current estimates of force levels by general category include: 145 missiles craft, 395 patrol/ASW/torpedo boats, and 400 minesweepers (fleet, coastal, and inshore).[45] Moreover, data concerning naval construction programs indicate that production of the more advanced designs in the various classes that comprise these forces will likely stay at the present rate.[46] Among others, series production continues for such light craft as the *Nanuchka* class patrol guided-missile craft, *Matka* class missile attack craft, *Turya* class hydrofoil

---

[43]For a review of the *Sovremenny* see J. W. Kehoe and K. S. Brower, "One of Their New Destroyers: Sovremenny," *Proceedings* 107, no. 6 (June 1981): 121–25.

[44]*Krivak I* is in production at the Kamysh-Burun Yard (Kerch) while the *Krivak II* is constructed at the Kaliningrad Yard. Moore, *Jane's Fighting Ships*, p. 535.

[45]*Understanding Soviet Naval Developments*, p. 83.

[46]See, for example, Moore, *Jane's Fighting Ships*, pp. 541–48.

torpedo boats, *Zhuk* class patrol boats, and *Tarintul* class missile corvettes. Also, the ongoing production of the *Natya*, *Andryush*, and *Sonya*
class minesweepers attests to the interest in mine warfare long held by
Soviet naval planners.[47]

The introduction of the gas turbine-powered *Ivan Rogov* class LPD
to the amphibious forces of the Soviet navy is yet another illustration of
the continuing effort of the USSR to modernize and add versatility to its
already powerful surface fleet. As the largest high seas combatant of its
type in the world, this amphibious transport has given added dimension to
Soviet assault forces. First, it is capable of carrying air-cushioned vehicles
as well as conventional landing craft; a total of three *Lebed* class medium
landing craft can be carried in this ship's well. Second, estimates are that
the *Ivan Rogov* can transport a Soviet naval infantry battalion with one
company of tanks and other combat support equipment. That load would
total approximately 550 troops, thirty armored personnel carriers, and ten
tanks.[48] Third, it is the first Soviet amphibious ship able to carry a
helicopter, as it includes a hangar and two landing decks. Finally, this
LPD is capable of both launching landing craft or driving its bow up to the
beach for a direct landing.[49]

The vast size and growing potential of the navy heightens the
essential need for a large fleet of auxiliary ships. Currently, those ships
designed to serve a myriad of functions in support of the main fleet total
approximately 760 units.[50] Yet, despite this sizable force a persistent
criticism of the Soviet navy as a global force relates to its lack of effective
support for major vessels underway for sustained periods. The absence of
a suitable number of modern replenishment ships is still cited by western
analysts as a major problem.[51] However, the ongoing production of such

---

[47]These specific construction programs are cited in Daniel, "Navy (VMF)," p. 214.
For a review of the importance placed on mine warfare by the Soviet navy see also Mathew
J. Whelan, "Soviet Mine Warfare: Intent and Capability," *Proceedings* 106, no. 9 (Septem-
ber 1980): 109–14.

[48]*Understanding Soviet Naval Developments*, p. 118.

[49]The main armament included on the *Ivan Rogov* includes one twin 76mm. DP gun
mount, one twin SA-N-4 SAM launcher, four single 30mm. Gatling guns, one 122mm.
multiple barrage bombardment, and one rocket launcher. Ibid. According to one source, a
second *Ivan Rogov* class ship has been produced. See Moore, *Jane's Fighting Ships*, p. 548.

[50]This figure includes such ships as submarine tenders, command and general
maintenance ships, water transports, missile tenders, repair ships, tugs, and stores ships. It
does not include the wide variety of surveillance, intelligence, and communications ships that
also play an important supportive role. As with other ship types, in recent years, the
aforementioned specialized units of the Soviet navy have been characterized by both an
increase in their numbers as well as qualitative improvements in their ability to perform
complex tasks.

[51]At the present time, out of eighty-five Soviet replenishment ships only about twenty
are capable of alongside fueling.

formidable support vessels as the *Berezina, Chilikin,* and *Dubna* replenishment oiler (AOR) classes indicates that the Soviet navy is moving to rectify this limitation to its ocean-going potential.

Of particular significance is the building of the *Berezina* AOR. This large multipurpose replenishment ship is equipped to transfer various liquids as well as solid stores like missiles while underway. Other equipment includes two helicopters for vertical replenishment and armament such as a twin launcher SA-N-4 SAM and two twin 57mm. guns. While there is only one of these ships in active service, the expectation is that the Soviets will continue to build additional units of the *Berezina* class. Doubtless, there also will be incremental progress in the development and improvement of other types of auxiliary ships. In the meantime, a good deal of at-sea support for Soviet combatant ships remains one of the functions of an impressively large and active Soviet merchant marine fleet.[52]

CONCLUSION

There can be no denying both the quantitative and qualitative growth of the Soviet navy in recent years. Ongoing production programs of major surface ships also indicate that emphasis is being placed on larger sized ships designed for global use. Not only will this trend continue into the foreseeable future, but it also seems reasonable to assume that as the Soviet navy modernizes so, too, will the other navies of the Warsaw Pact, but proportionally. The Soviet desire for a balanced fleet notwithstanding, regional defense requirements will obviously retain the highest priority.[53]

---

[52]For further analyses concerning the role and importance of the merchant marine fleet as part of overall Soviet naval objectives see John Baker White, "The Soviet Merchant Navy Challenge," *Soviet Analyst* 10, no. 8 (15 April 1981): 5–7; and James Ellis, "Expansion of Soviet Merchant Fleet—Implications for the West," *NATO Review* 27, no. 3 (June 1979): 21–24.

[53]As a recent example of the formidable array of forces that can be employed in one of the Warsaw Pact regional waters, see Richard Halloran, "Soviet Ships in Baltic Mass for Amphibious Games," *New York Times*, 5 August 1981.

Military Management and Modernization Within the Warsaw Pact

However stridently NATO and the Warsaw Pact may proclaim their fundamental differences, each staunchly taking up their positions as sole guardians of the peace and imputing base designs to the other, both systems share at least one common trait, namely, the vexatious, frustrating, and divisive issue of the economics of collective defense. Such tensions and dissatisfactions have been well aired within the NATO camp, indeed to the point of becoming a constant theme heavily larded with beguiling euphemisms such as "burden-sharing" and solutions held out under the guise of the "two-way street" for U.S.-European military-industrial reciprocity. The arguments are at once abstract and expansive yet narrowly mean and parsimonious, even penny-pinching; the apparent generosity arises from considering defense a pure public good with no one excluded from consumption and, thus, not open to specific charge for the goods they consume, so other means must be devised for assigning the costs of such provision. This, paradoxically, furnishes a nonmarket situation, but to change the context slightly, intensifies much marketplace haggling.[1]

When comparing NATO and the Warsaw Pact the western observer has been conditioned to presentations of gross inventories, tallies of tanks, aircraft, and missiles as well as disparities in manpower. All of this has a certain pictorial relevance, but it scarcely goes to the heart of the matter with respect to alliance cohesion and effectiveness; it may have propagandistic value in presenting the Warsaw Pact as some vast, looming military monolith, but closer inspection of the military-economic affairs of the Pact shows that this is patently not the case. Let us take a simple instance, that of standardization and modernization within the Pact. There is much breast-beating within NATO about the lack of standardization and much admiration for the superstandardization of the Pact. Yet, that aspect is

---

[1]See Lawrence S. Kaplan and Robert W. Clawson, eds., *NATO After Thirty Years* (Wilmington, DE: Scholarly Resources, 1981); Colin Gordon, *The Atlantic Alliance: A Bibliography* (New York: Nichols Publishing, 1978); and Gavin Kennedy, *Burden Sharing in NATO* (London: Duckworth, 1979). Professor Kennedy also most generously allowed me to consult his unpublished research paper, "The Economics of Collective Defense."

213

open to a great deal of questioning. There is also the intriguing feature within the Pact that standardization can actually impede modernization, as can be shown by an analysis of the military economics of Pact weapons production. A rare hint of these tensions and dilemmas was provided not long ago in a commentary on CMEA (COMECON) and the defense burden by Oldrich Běhounek, who stressed the leading role of the USSR, which shoulders 80 percent of the burden, but also cautioned against pressing new defense demands that may be as inappropriate as minimizing defense commitments.[2]

Thus, the commonly held vision of military robots of the Warsaw Pact, armed to the teeth with the latest fully interchangeable and compatible weapons systems is very far from reality, and while there is much talk about reliability, or the lack of reliability, among the non-Soviet Pact troops, a more pressing and relevant aspect for investigation may be the management of the Pact's military-economic resources. First, however, it is necessary to look at its military-economic system *in toto*, with a brief review of its past developments leading to a survey of its present problems, for problems there are in abundance.

ARMAMENTS AND ECONOMICS IN THE COMECON/PACT SYSTEM

There is no great revelation in pointing to the fact that the Soviet Union is the predominant element in the Pact/COMECON system. By the same token the USSR pays heavily for the privilege, if it be that; the sum amounts to between five and ten times the defense contribution of other participants, hence Běhounek's figure of 80 percent for the total Soviet contribution to the defense burden. In the harsh days of Stalinism the Soviet Union used its power and position in brute fashion simply to impose armament quotas and investment requirements on non-Soviet countries, with military production assuming the highest priority. There is now belated recognition of the distortions that this Soviet effort produced, not only in the field of economic organization but also in military systems as such that lead to the total suppression of any indigenous "national" defense interest. Yet, the consequences of the post-Stalin period did not lead to greater independence on the part of the East European nations; rather, their dependence on the USSR actually increased due in no small part to their reliance on Soviet industrial equipment and machine tools.

---

[2]Oldrich Běhounek, "RVHP a obranyschopnost Socialismu," *Historie a Vojenstvi*, no. 1 (1980). This is quite a singular article, though Běhounek has contributed numerous studies on defense and war economics; for example, "K historii ekonomického zabezpečovani obrany sovetského státu," *Historie a Vojenstvi*, no. 5 (1977).

Additionally, hopes and plans for collaborative production foundered badly, introducing instead a marked competitive element. A new twist was added after 1967 by demands on the part of the Soviet Union that the East European nations also should meet commitments to the Arab nations for the supply of military equipment and support, a move that had been preceded by Soviet negotiations a decade before.[3]

A third stage, begun in the early 1970s, envisaged a form of military-industrial specialization, though that was essentially impeded by what amounted to a Soviet ban on particular types of indigenous military production, not least military aircraft. It could be that the German Democratic Republic did not perform too brilliantly in this field, but that was sufficient to foreclose further possibilities. Thus, competition in what might be called main weapons systems was eliminated and a form of division of labor introduced, leaving the field of standard armament to the USSR alone and assuring Soviet domination of the Warsaw Pact arms cartel. This predominance also extended into the field of licensing, where Soviet R&D costs can be included in the price of tooling and machinery furnished to produce weapons and equipment which themselves emanate from Soviet designs. If this is what is meant by "standardization," then it is an accomplished fact in the sense that main weapons systems are duly aligned with Soviet designs and requirements and that no non-Soviet main weapons system has ever been introduced into the inventory of all Warsaw military establishments.[4]

Soviet secrecy also impedes a more rational approach to modernization. In general, it might be said that non-Soviet military establishments are obliged to trail somewhat behind Soviet modernization plans, lacking as they do expansive information on Soviet investment plans and intentions. It is here that the jiggery-pokery begins with arbitrary Soviet adjustment of the prices charged for particular weapons. A small order from an East European state may well be accompanied by an increase in the price charged by the Soviet Union on the grounds that should domestic production begin, the unit cost inevitably will rise. The net effect is to produce common pressure to withdraw such a small order. All this obviously affects the profitability of indigenous (non-Soviet) arms production.[5]

---

[3]For this background see Uri Ra'anan, *The USSR Arms the Third World* (Cambridge, MA: MIT Press, 1969).

[4]On the COMECON armament market and its organization see Michael Checiński, *The Costs of Armament Production and the Profitability of Armament Exports in COMECON Countries*. Research Paper No. 10, Soviet/East European Research Center.

[5]Checiński, *The Costs of Armament Production*, pp. 28–29. Checiński also cites the abortive attempt in the early 1960s to become an "arms supplier" via an agreement to furnish rifles to Bulgaria, circumvented by the USSR supplying an entire plant to Bulgaria, excess capacity notwithstanding. Hebrew University of Jerusalem (1974). See also *Osteuropawirtschaft* 2 (June 1975): 117–42.

None of this has gone unnoticed in East European circles and much commentary has been produced on the problem of defense economics within the Pact's system, including Ciastoń's *Ekonomiczne aspekty obronności* and other affirmations of "Socialist military-economic thought." They have been discreet but sometimes pointed with respect to the Soviet monopoly position, though it was left to the Czechs in 1968 to break all these tacit rules.[6] Czech objections highlighted dissatisfaction with the entire gamut of the politics and economics of Soviet coalition warfare doctrines, with a military division of labor condemning the non-Soviet states to maintain bloated conventional forces, which inevitably sucked in scarce resources and which in no way corresponded to indigenous defense requirements. Heavy costs thus have impeded modernization, with 70 percent of the military budget gulped down by general requirements, leaving only 30 percent for modernization, which is further hampered by cumbersome arms negotiating procedures with the USSR and the supply of spare parts.[7]

A case in point seems to have been Czech dissatisfaction with the Su-7BKL *Fitter A* aircraft and its problems related to avionics and spares. Here, doctrine, organization, and procurement procedures all combined to add to Czech, as well as others, discomfiture. And here, Soviet domination of the Warsaw Pact machinery made itself known, as it does today. Much credence is lent in some quarters to the significance of the national military budgets (the percentage game), though it is arguable that apart from a certain political symbolism these figures have little real meaning. Indeed, that very point was conveyed to the author by a number of East European economists who recognized no reality in them. The major decisions bearing on armament program and production are made by the collectivity of the Pact itself, which is to say generally by Soviet decision, leaving the indigenous East European military with no direct influence on budgetary allocations. The Joint Command and the Military Council of the Pact will decide on all issues of modernization, with the higher national political levels left to argue it out, as was presumably the case with Poland a short while ago when it obtained relief from an

[6]See S. Ciastoń, *Ekonomiczne aspekty obronności* (Warsaw: MON, 1969), esp diagrams pp. 202–3; W. Stankiewicz, *Socjalistyczna myśl wojennoekonomiczna* (Warsaw: MON, 1972) and an earlier work, *Ekonomika wojenna* (Warsaw: MON, 1970); and Edward Sitek, *Ekonomika a obronność* (Warsaw: MON, 1970). See also a Hungarian essay, G. Ungvár, "A szocialista gazdasági rendszer és a szovjet állam védelmi képessége" [(Socialist) Soviet system and defense capability] *Honvédelem* (1978).

[7]These detailed observations were made by Srovnal in *A Revue* (Prague), 17 May 1968. The wider implications, including the case for indigenous Czech defense requirements, are discussed expertly in Robin Alison Remington, *The Warsaw Pact* (Cambridge, MA: MIT Press, 1971), pp. 101–3. See also A. Ross Johnson, Robert W. Dean, and Alexander Alexiev, *East European Military Establishments: The Warsaw Pact Northern Tier* (RAND/R-2417/1-AF/FF, December 1980), pp. 137–42.

obligatory increase in expenditures. The military departments of the various national planning bodies then take up the issue, arranging, at least in theory, types and rates of production within each national industry. Here, pricing and profitability enter the picture.

According to Michael Cheçiński, Soviet prices dominate the COMECON-Warsaw Pact arms market, even where the product is domestically manufactured.[8] That price factor is even more pronounced where military products do not have an accepted world price, as might be the case with other goods where there is general comparability. This process, as Cheçiński affirms, is particularly painful when there is a generation shift in weapons, particularly combat aircraft. This point was confirmed by the author in discussing the introduction of newer MiG models into East European air forces, with more than a hint of resentment vis-à-vis NATO, which was blamed for having forced this move. The same qualified observation might be made with respect to non-Soviet choices of main battle tanks (MBT), particularly skipping the T-62 for series production, with Poland jumping, as it were, from the T-55 with modifications to the license-produced T-72. Manufacture of the T-62 MBT probably would have been an expensive mistake from the Polish point of view; not only did it not suit Polish tactical purposes, but it also would have involved Poland in producing ammunition at three times the cost of the standard T-55 main gun round.

This and other observations tend to bear out the contention that there is no purpose in trying to identify true cost and pricing within the COMECON-Warsaw Pact area, least of all by the dollar comparison technique. It is certainly true from personal observation that East European economists find great difficulty in explaining the cost/price aspect of armaments programs, if only because these are artificially manipulated and subject much more to an intricate bookkeeping process rather than staid economics. The burden on the gross national product (GNP), though much bewailed, is simply impossible to determine, leaving aside all arguments about opportunity cost. This is also to say that East European armament concerns embark on specific enterprises with a high risk factor, since the lack of any knowledge of true costs constitutes a hazard that only can be partially compensated by the bookkeeping sleight of hand. Due to differences in labor costs and other factors, including smaller production runs, tank factories can only expect to reach profitability after the third year of production runs, with a gap always looming between the selling price and the planned cost of the vehicle or weapon. Here, there is a certain elision between military and civilian production in East Europe, where capacity is intermixed for engines, instrumentation, and even

---

[8]On pricing, trade, and barter arrangements as well as the absence of "stop prices" in the field of weapons, see Cheçiński, *The Costs of Armament Production*, pp. 30–34.

alternative production using military production facilities for civilian consumer goods. Whatever the provision of subsidies and any book-keeping adjustment, the issue of profitability is further complicated by Soviet pricing arrangements, which relate to NATO pricing for similar equipment as well as special increments for various types of weaponry.

Although they lack any immediate control over budgetary alloca-tions, it is now possible to understand why modernization has become such an issue for the East European military. What should be bought? Indeed, what can be bought? Clearly, it is impossible for modernization to be managed through indigenous resources even if the requisite expensive R&D is undertaken, because then it is a question of the Soviets' putting the weapon or the product into serial production. On the contrary, East European R&D is promoted in the interests of Soviet military efficiency; for example, Czech research on advanced radar, which well may be incorporated for Soviet Voiska PVO purposes. On the whole, East Euro-pean military establishments must suffer from an overall lack of reliable information on modern military technology and weapons development that can be translated into investment planning and profitable armament ventures. It would appear that joint non-Soviet ventures have had only limited success for the simple reason that the Soviet Union dominates the market for main weapons systems, leaving only a small margin of the market within the Pact for military equipment produced from non-Soviet sources.

WEAPONS PROCUREMENT, STANDARDIZATION, AND MODERNIZATION

In November 1978 at a meeting of the Political Consultative Com-mittee of the Warsaw Pact, the Soviet Union called for a 5 percent increase in defense expenditures from its Pact partners. Accordingly, the Soviet Union leads substantially in the proportion of defense expenditure to GNP (12 to 13 percent), followed by the German Democratic Republic (6.3 percent) and the remainder hovering at about 2.4 to 2.8 percent, with Romania providing the obvious and deliberately blatant exception of 1.4 percent.[9] This is assuming that these figures really mean anything at all, affected and influenced as they are by the general economic difficulties

---

[9]See table (p. 187) on defense expenditures valid to 1979 in Edwina Moreton's paper in K. Dawisha and P. Hanson, eds., *Soviet-East European Dilemmas* (London: Heine-mann/RIIA, 1981). There is also the aspect of "offset/support costs," both in cash and kind, for Soviet forces stationed in Eastern Europe.

prevailing in East Europe.[10] Understandably, the Soviet proposal met with little enthusiasm; Poland was officially excused from the increase and Romania deliberately snubbed the idea. There was small consolation that manpower levels had stabilized, because it is machines rather than men that consume money and scarce resources in the armed forces of the Warsaw Pact.

Modernization is by no means new within the Pact, though the present stage is marked by increasing sophistication of weapons and generation jumps, particularly in combat aircraft. In the modernization of frontline air forces, both for air defense and ground forces support, the non-Soviet nations seem to have had little choice but to accede to Soviet requirements, with the MiG-23 *Flogger B* appearing in East German, Czech, and Hungarian squadrons. Poland alone deploys the Su-20 *Fitter B*, which now equips three squadrons for a total of thirty-five aircraft, while Bulgaria has for some time—strangely enough in advance of other states—incorporated some twenty MiG-23 *Flogger B*s in its air units. It is conceivable that these latter aircraft were prepositioned Soviet air force elements. Otherwise, East European air forces make extensive use of the MiG-21, Su-7, and even retain the MiG-17, but it might be assumed that the non-Soviet air forces during the coming decade will take further deliveries of multirole fighter aircraft, the expense notwithstanding. By the same token, the modernization of the air defense systems (ground-based and air, including early warning) will presumably take place at Soviet behest, since the Warsaw Pact air defense systems come under the direct control of the Soviet air defense command.

Perhaps the modernization of air capability is an extreme case, particularly in view of the lack of an indigenous design and manufacturing capacity, save for Polish and Czech light aircraft (including trainers). The same absolute Soviet monopoly applies to civilian aircraft, with only Romania breaking out of this constraint with its BAC-111 production through an Anglo-Romanian coproduction arrangement. Equipment for the ground forces displays less complexity, but it must be emphasized again that main weapons systems are of Soviet origin, either in design or actual production. In the past it appears that a form of selective modernization predominated, probably out of a mix of economic and political motives. For example, the Polish army received the new 122mm. self-propelled gun well before it appeared in the East German army, while the Czechs recently have displayed their own version of a 152mm. self-propelled gun mounted on a wheeled rather than a Soviet-style tracked vehicle, using a modified *Tatra* 813 chassis. This singular Czech casemated gun could be a compromise solution to investing in the expensive

---

[10]Economics/Information Directorates, *Economics Reforms in Eastern Europe and Prospects for the 1980s*, NATO 1980 Colloquium (New York: Pergamon Press, 1980).

and complicated Soviet heavy self-propelled gun proper, while still retaining good cross-country capability.

There is unequivocally an uneven distribution of modern weapons within the Warsaw Pact and here the much vaunted mass of the Pact militates against both standardization and modernization, for satisfaction of both requirements would mean nothing less than full-scale mobilization of the Pact economies. Consider, for example, the distribution of MBTs. Including the aged T-34/85s (held in storage) and the latest T-72, the Pact deploys five types of battle tank (six, if one includes the few T-10Ms), though for all practical purposes there are three types, the T-54/55, T-62, and T-72 (the latter just entering licensed production in Poland and Czechoslovakia). Inevitably, this produces three classes of tank gun, the 100mm., 115mm., and 125mm., respectively, without interchangeability of ammunition. While the T-54/55 and the T-62 were not very different machines save for gun changes, with mere uprating of engine and essentially the same running gear, the T-72 is a "generation jump" and is a new system in terms of tank design and production.[11] The Polish Katowice tank plant thus will have to adapt substantially, and the Polish army presumably will have to fill any immediate first-line requirement by direct purchase from the Soviet Union. The same also will apply to Czechoslovakia. Though the Soviet Union produces the bulk of all Pact tanks, Polish and Czech versions equip not only their national armies but are also supplied to East Germany and Hungary. Polish-built T-55s with the East German army can be picked out by the large stowage bins on the left of the turret.

As pointed out earlier the non-Soviet Pact armies skipped the T-62, with cost no doubt a factor, but also its general unsuitability for East European tactical purposes bearing on this decision. In any event, with the later T-64/T-72 in the offing, the optimum choice would appear to have been to wait for the newer Soviet model, which presumably will offer a long production run, lower unit costs, and a degree of profitability. At least with the T-72 the East European armies, like the Soviet army, will acquire a battle tank that can keep pace on the battlefield with the newer BMP-1 infantry combat vehicle, which entered service in East Germany and Poland in 1970 (designated the BWP in Poland) and used by the Czechs as the BVP. Noteworthy about the BMP-1 is its high cost and complexity, though this should not conceal its drawbacks, most notably the slow time to target of the round from its 73mm. gun. Reportedly, the Poles have rectified this shortcoming with a gun of smaller caliber of their own design.

The inventory of light combat vehicles provides an even greater

---

[11]For full technical details see Steven J. Zaloga, *Modern Soviet Armour: Combat Vehicles of the USSR and Warsaw Pact Today* (London: Arms and Armour Press, 1979), esp. "Battle Tanks."

diversity, with the development within the Czech and Polish armies of the SKOT (OT-64) medium-armored wheeled transporter, a substitute for the Soviet-built BTR-60 (BTR-60PB), which suffered from the drawback of having its troop exits on the roof or the sides, thereby increasing personnel vulnerability. The Czech prototype was completed in 1961, followed by Polish participation in joint testing and production; the SKOT was brought into public view in 1964. The OT-64 has been produced in at least six versions, with Czech and Polish variants (the OT-64B being used only in Poland). The Czech-Polish product, when compared with the Soviet BTR-60P, employed different wheel spacing, propulsion by propeller in water, and a single air-cooled diesel engine, the *Tatra* 928.

Hungarian designers and industry, though prohibited from tank production, also developed a light-wheeled armored reconnaissance vehicle that went into service with the Hungarian army, was bought by the Czechs, and is also utilized in small numbers by the Polish amphibious assault formation. Called the FUG, it is not unlike the Soviet BRDM, though without a turret, and is powered by license-built Hungarian diesel engines. An improved version of the FUG appeared in 1970 equipped with a small turret. In turn, the Czechoslovak army adopted a special version of the FUG with a turret mounting an 81mm. recoilless T-21 gun.[12]

Further detail apart, the advent of new infantry combat vehicles, reconnaissance vehicles, and scout cars has undoubtedly improved tactical mobility and effectiveness but at the cost of standardization, involving different engines, varied armament, and variation in tire sizes, not to mention a considerable range of turrets. Supply, maintenance, and repair under battlefield conditions would not be so easy. Gone also are the days of simple interchangeability of ammunition between tank guns and field artillery. While the smoothbore 100mm. antitank gun, the T-12, fires fin-stabilized, nonrotating projectiles similar to those used in the 115mm. smoothbore gun of the T-62 tank, there is no interchangeability. The Czechoslovak 100mm. M53 rifled gun was designed to use the same ammunition as the Soviet M1944 dual purpose (field/antitank) gun, but the M1944 in the antitank role has been superseded by the T-12.[13] Even on the later BMP interchangeability is limited, as the 73mm. 2A28 smoothbore gun has a round similar to but not entirely identical with the PG-9 round used in the standard infantry RPG-7 antitank launcher or the newer SPG-9, the projectile being the same but the propellant charges differing.

---

[12]Ibid. On the FUG and its derivatives see also Czechoslovak developments, pp. 63–66.

[13]For extensive details on tank guns, field, and antitank artillery see David C. Isby, *Weapons and Tactics of the Soviet Army* (London: Jane's, 1981), chaps. 7, 9, 10.

A singular example of nonconformity is provided by the Czech small arms industry, rightly famed as it is. The Czechoslovak army adopted standard Soviet small arms caliber ammunition, introducing the M58 series of assault rifles that fire the Czech version of the Soviet M1943 intermediate cartridge. But in spite of the weapon's bearing a close resemblance to the Soviet Kalashnikov assault rifle, the M58 differs mechanically and has noninterchangeable magazines. Czechoslovakia has persisted with assault rifles and machine guns of native design and production. While the Soviet Union produced the PK/PKS general purpose machine gun, the Czechs developed their own weapon in two versions, one using standard Soviet ammunition and the other the M59N, firing 7.62mm. NATO ammunition and designed for export.

Once out of the field of actual weaponry and into support equipment, thin-skinned vehicles, trucks, trailers, prime movers for artillery, decontamination trucks, tank trucks, and tank transporters, then all semblance of standardization vanishes.[14] While Soviet vehicles are widely employed, the development of native automotive industries has meant a proliferation of multipurpose and specialist vehicles, with Czechoslovakia not only supplying its own needs from home production but also exporting generously to other Pact countries. This line includes highly specialized vehicles of Czech origin such as the metal road-laying vehicle that uses the *Tatra* 813, an 8x8 heavy-duty truck with a platform for two cassettes holding forty linked steel plates. In addition, Czechoslovakia produces a formidable mutiple rocket launcher with a rapid reload capability that has been purchased by East Germany, though significantly ignored by the Soviet Union. East Germany places some considerable reliance on Soviet trucks, but its own G-5 was for a long while a standard vehicle employed as a prime mover for artillery, a decontamination truck, and a tank truck. It has been replaced by the Soviet *Ural*-375D and the improved East German W50 LA/A, a 4x4 truck produced for both military and civilian use and also available for export. Hungary has steadily developed its automotive industry, moving away from heavy reliance on Soviet vehicles and developing extensive western contacts, particularly with the West German firm MAN. This latter set of connections has resulted in the Hungarian export of MAN engines to Romania and further cooperation with Romanian firms producing MAN trucks. East German trucks are exchanged for Hungarian buses and the Hungarian military also imports vehicles from Czechoslovakia in order to equip combat engineer units.

---

[14]See details and tables in Lawrence L. Whetten and James L. Waddell, "Motor Vehicle Standardisation in the Warsaw Pact: Problems and Limitations," *RUSI Journal* (March 1979): 55–60; also Stefan Brudny and Jerzy Cebulski, *Współczesne pojazdy terenowe* (Warsaw: MON, 1975). For technical details and line drawings/Pact wheeled vehicles see English translation of Friedrich Wiener and William J. Lewis, *The Warsaw Pact Armies* (Vienna, 1977) and subsequent editions: pt. 4/E "Wheeled Vehicles"; also Section F, Engineer Equipment.

Poland continues to develop its own industry, replacing the unsatisfactory *Zubr* heavy trucks with the improved *Jelcz* series that uses a water-cooled diesel engine built under license from British Leyland. The *Jelcz* 640 dump truck is license built from Steyr-Daimler-Puch and uses a 240hp. British-designed, Polish-manufactured engine.

While the Soviet Union has latterly produced excellent examples of field engineering equipment, such as tactical floating bridges and battle-field engineer tractors, excavators, and trench diggers, East European states also have developed their own models, notably the Czech MT-55 bridgelayer built on a T-55A tank chassis with its bridge launched hydraulically by an electrohydraulic control system for dry-gap launching. Such was the performance of the Czech MT-55 that it was adopted by the Soviet army, the only example of the USSR adopting non-Soviet equipment on any scale. The Polish army also uses the East German BLG-67 tank-launched bridge, while East German, Polish, and Czech forces use their own equipment for tank-launched or truck-launched, dry-gap bridging. In the Polish army the PP-64 heavy folding pontoon bridge was developed to provide a Polish equivalent of the Soviet PMP. This resulted in a bridge that can be built faster than the Soviet one, though its capacity is only forty tons as opposed to the sixty tons of the PMP. Soviet assault bridging is generally judged to be excellent, but for other field engineer equipment East German and Czech hydraulic cranes and engineer tractors are reckoned superior to Soviet items and have come into service with other Pact armies.

In one respect—chemical warfare equipment—non-Soviet Warsaw Pact establishments appear to have a very free hand, developing their own dosimeters, protective clothing, chemical simulators, and protective masks. The same variation is displayed in communications equipment and the provision for mine warfare, but none of this compares with the freedom that Romania has extracted from the Pact system in pursuing an independent military policy. Romania maintains close relations with two nations outside the Soviet orbit, Yugoslavia and China, with Romanian-Yugoslav military links expanding into close coproduction as with the *Orao* fighter design. At the same time close contacts have been nurtured with Austria and Switzerland.

Romania has become the true maverick, even to the point of contemplating the purchase of U.S. military equipment starting with military helicopter engines and reaching toward the F-5 fighter. Whatever the aggravation caused to the Soviet Union by Romanian contacts with China, including a possible deal over missile patrol boats, this must have been greatly increased by Romanian-Israeli exchanges, whereby Romania acquired some modern Soviet military stock via Israeli holdings of captured Soviet weapons. There is at least photographic evidence of Romanian pragmatism, or eclecticism, with the T-55 tank using a British Centurion-type armored skirt protecting the running gear, which itself is of

Vickers pattern and has an extra roller. The hybrid is further complicated by the addition of Israeli-type improvements. The Anglo-Romanian BAC-111 project has resulted in extensive coproduction and products reportedly of a high standard, while Romanian armament seems to be taking a widely divergent course, including the adoption of the Yugoslav M-48 76mm. "Tito gun" to provide fire support for mountain troops and a Romanian development of an internal security vehicle with a turret-mounted 12.7mm. machine gun.[15]

MODERNIZATION, PROFESSIONALISM, AND EFFECTIVENESS

In general, it might be argued that so-called "weapons packaging"—selective modernization suited to the particular tactical tasks of particular non-Soviet ground and air units—has now given way to overall modernization within the Pact, especially the Northern Tier forces and latterly East Germany, which has taken a leading place in the Soviet/Pact order of battle. Standardization in armor, infantry combat vehicles, and self-propelled guns seems to be the order of the day, even being pressed upon reluctant Hungarians and embracing the Romanians as well, at least in principle. The most prominent feature is the forced pace of modernization in combat aircraft, where a growing number of types have been in service for less than five years and not only have an all-weather capability but also advanced weapons delivery systems. It has been estimated that the Pact air arms will take up to 25 percent of new Soviet aircraft production in the coming decade. This will be accompanied by the Soviet Union making heavy demands on East European high technology, notably Hungarian high-speed computer printers and Czech electronics. It represents something of an aggravation, particularly for the Hungarians who must pay in hard currency (West German marks) for their components, yet sell, or are forced to sell, at a soft ruble price to the USSR. No doubt the USSR will continue to press for a unified computer system involving all East European states to a considerable degree. And all the while the East European nations will continue to pay into the secret common fund, lending aid to the Soviet program to assist national liberation struggles in the Third World.

---

[15]On Romanian policies see Alexander Alexiev, "Romania and the Warsaw Pact: The Defense Policy of a Reluctant Ally," *Journal of Strategic Studies* 4 (March 1981): 5–18. See also his *Party-Military Relations in Eastern Europe: The Case of Romania*, University of California, ACIS Working Paper No. 15 (January 1979).

Tabulation. Warsaw Pact Vehicle Types or Series†

Type or series	Tanks* (incl. stored T-34 and PT-76)	APCs, Infantry combat vehicles	Scout cars	Wheeled vehicle types (non-Soviet)	Half-track APCs	Wheeled tractor types (non-Soviet)	Bridging equipment types (non-Soviet)
Poland	3	2	2***	9	—	1	3
East Germany	3	2	2***	8–9	—	4	3
Czechoslovakia	3	2	2***	12	1 OT-810 antitank	8	7
Hungary	3	1 FUG series**	2***	8	—	4 Dutra series	—
Bulgaria	4	2	1	2 1 Soviet-based 1 Czech-based	—	—	—
Romania	3 western mod. to T-55s	2	1	7	—	—	1

†This tabulation is inevitably approximate and is simply an indicator of diversity and not a complete identification. Note, for example, further diversification in T-54/55 models as well as artillery and small arms. The reader's attention is drawn to a very recent and significant study by M. Checiński. *A Comparison of the Polish and Soviet Armaments Decision Making Systems*, Report R-2662-AF (RAND Corporation, 1981).

*T-54/55 as one type

**FUG-70

***1 Soviet, 1 non-Soviet type

CONCLUSIONS

It is obvious that the form and pace of modernization must remain consistent with Soviet operational designs and that equipment inflows will substantially influence Pact training programs. Even more importantly, with greater complexity of equipment and advanced weaponry, the question of command and control will submerge doctrinal questions. National programs will perforce become increasingly involved in the technical operation of the Pact, though this will not solve the problems of tactical handling, nor will it erase the hauteur with which Soviet commanders annoy their non-Soviet counterparts. Thus, nationalism and national resentments, which up until this time have been the bane of Pact politics, will assume a more pronounced form. Modernization, meant to ease the transition of the Pact into the 1980s, may only contribute to exacerbating attitudes of antagonism and deeply felt subservience on the part of the frustrated professionals within all the military-economic establishments in East Europe. That will be a singular form of standardization.

DOCTRINE
AND
CAPABILITIES

Warsaw Pact Ground Forces:
Formations, Combat Doctrine,
and Capabilities

JOHN J. BINDER and ROBERT W. CLAWSON

In the dark of early morning on 16 April 1945 the Soviet 1st Byelorussian Front began the most intense preparatory barrage in history against what remained of the German armies in the East. Twenty thousand guns and rocket launchers of all calibers fired along a line of fifty kilometers with an almost incredible density of approximately 350 guns per kilometer. After thirty-five minutes the fire was lifted, searchlights turned on, and in the north and south, Red Army soldiers began crossing the rivers, with some actually swimming and others floating on an astonishing variety of bizarre assault craft including logs and doors. From the Oder and Neisse the Soviet armies stormed forward into the smoke and dust, accompanied by hundreds of heavy and medium tanks.[1]

Although it is no longer accurate to portray the modern Soviet Ground Forces as they were then, a makeshift army of peasants and newly urbanized workers, the lessons learned from the war still play a key role in Soviet military doctrine. The principle of massive and long artillery and rocket preparation for the battlefield is standard procedure. Use of the tank in conventional and even nuclear warfare is central to Soviet battle plans. The infantry, which in 1945 moved into battle packed aboard Soviet tanks and self-propelled artillery, is now completely motorized to maximize mobility while continuing in its traditional role as a shock

---

[1]Marshal Georgy K. Zhukov, *Vospominania i razmyshlenia* [Reminiscences and reflections] (Moscow: Novosti, 1969). Citations refer to English versions, *The Memoirs of Marshal Zhukov* (New York: Delacorte Press, 1971), pp. 585–620. Zhukov claims that 1,236 shells and rockets were fired by the 1st Byelorussian Front, using 2,450 railway carloads, almost 98,000 tons of metal, p. 604. See also Erich Kuby, *The Russians and Berlin, 1945* (New York: Ballantine Books, 1969), p. 41; and Cornelius Ryan, *The Last Battle* (New York: Simon & Schuster, 1966), pp. 331–36. Actually, the artillery preparation for the neighboring 1st Ukrainian Front's assault across the Neisse involved a longer, if somewhat less dense, preparation followed by a dawn attack. For details of this latter offensive, see Marshal I. S. Konev, *Sorok pyaty* [Forty-five] (Moscow: Voyenizdat, 1969). English version, *Year of Victory* (Moscow: Progress Publishers, 1969), pp. 89–94.

force.[2] These are all principles which, with few exceptions, have been incorporated into the combat doctrine of the allied Warsaw Pact armies of Eastern Europe.

However, there has been little opportunity to observe these modern armies on the field of battle. Between the occupation of Manchuria and the intervention in Afghanistan, Soviet Ground Forces and allied troops have had only limited and mostly irregular experience in such places as Hungary and Czechoslovakia. Warsaw Pact weapons and tactics have been tested by proxy in the Arab-Israeli wars, but that at best has afforded only modest insight into the potential future performance of the East European and Soviet armies themselves. Thus, observers have to rely primarily on training patterns, exercises, and military texts.

In the first section of this study the major formations and tactical principles that Soviet Ground Forces and their Warsaw Pact allies would employ in an engagement with NATO forces on a European battlefield will be examined. For a detailed analysis of the Soviet and East European orders of battle, the reader may refer to the essays by James T. Reitz and Thomas O. Cason included in this volume. Here, the primary concern is to present an overview of tactical expectations and a summary of the strengths and weaknesses of Pact doctrine. It should be noted at the outset that the Warsaw Pact ground forces combat doctrine is primarily standardized to the Soviet model.

FORMATIONS AND THEIR ROLE IN BATTLE

The Front

Warsaw Pact ground forces are normally organized in military districts and groups. In combat they would be immediately reorganized into fronts. A front has no set structure but has tactical, administrative, and logistical capability and is therefore self-sufficient. The zone of action of the front is approximately 200 kilometers wide and 180 kilometers in depth. It has the planned capability to seize strategic objectives as far as 550 kilometers away and then advance an additional 500 kilometers. The width of the zone is the same in a nuclear or nonnuclear environment, but it is probable that additional combat power would be employed in a

---

[2]The conventional Soviet army, especially the armored forces, passed through a period of partial deemphasis during Khrushchev's tenure but since has been restored to a key position in Soviet military planning. The cycle is comprehensively summarized in Jeffrey Record, *Sizing Up the Soviet Army* (Washington, DC: Brookings Institution, 1975).

nonnuclear situation. A strategic offensive operation in a large theater like North and Central Europe might consist of several fronts as it did during World War II. In addition to motorized rifle, tank, and airborne divisions, the front would include varying numbers of missile, artillery, combat engineer, signal, chemical, transportation, supply, and medical units.

To emphasize the planned capability of the front in terms of both destructive force and rapidity of movement, it may be useful to note that Soviet and Pact doctrine posits the following timetable for a major offensive operation:

Phase I: Penetration (intermediate objective); days 3 through 5; 250–80 kilometers. Purpose: to encircle and destroy enemy combat units.

Phase II: Exploitation (long-range objective); days 7 through 13. Purpose: to destroy enemy strategic reserves and advance an additional 250–80 kilometers.

Phase III: Pursuit of enemy remnants (final objective); days 15 through 21. Purpose: to advance an additional 500 kilometers.

Thus the front, despite its massive size and relatively complex configuration, is a dynamic force, containing highly maneuverable units within its command.[3]

The Army

An army is a tactical and administrative grouping, presently designated with flexible organization for various missions. There are two types of Soviet and East European armies: tank and combined arms. The main difference is that the tank army has a preponderance of tank divisions in its complement, while a combined arms army normally has a preponderance of motorized rifle divisions. When tailored for combat an army will have anywhere from three to seven divisions. In support of the fighting division will be field artillery, antiaircraft artillery, and surface-to-surface and surface-to-air missile units as well as signal, engineer, assault-crossing, transport, supply, and medical detachments. The allocation of support formations and the basic army structure are flexible and may change significantly during the course of an operation.[4]

[3]A description and analysis of the contemporary Soviet front is included in *Military Operations of the Soviet Army,* prepared by U.S. Army Intelligence and Threat Analysis Center, Report No. 14–U–76 (Arlington, VA, 1979), pp. 79–89.
[4]See U.S. Intelligence and Threat Analysis Center, *Soviet Army Operations,* Report No. IAG–13–U–78 (Arlington, VA, 1978), pp. 2–7, 2–8.

The Division

A division forms the basic battle formation of the modern Warsaw Pact ground forces.[5] The motorized rifle division is designed to attack enemy defensive positions as part of a combined arms army. It consists of three motorized rifle regiments and one tank regiment; an independent tank battalion is provided to assist the commander in influencing the battle and exploiting opportunities.[6]

The tank division, which usually is made up of three tank regiments and one motorized rifle regiment, can both attack the enemy defensive position and exploit gaps in enemy defensive configurations. It is the primary maneuver element of the combined arms army and possesses shock potential, mobility, and firepower. It is designed to penetrate rapidly into enemy territory, destroy continuity of the defense, and assist in securing the army's objectives.[7]

A Warsaw Pact airborne division is designed to seize, disrupt, or destroy important rear area targets such as headquarters, communications centers, or airfields. It is also capable of seizing and holding river crossings and motor routes as well as conducting sabotage against enemy nuclear delivery means and assisting in partisan and guerrilla operations.[8]

Artillery divisions and other large gun and rocket formations constitute one of the primary means of influencing the battle. Soviet artillery combat doctrine, more or less dominant throughout the Warsaw Pact, continues to stress detailed planning particularly in the preparation of the

---

[5]Detailed organizational materials on Soviet tank and motorized rifle divisions and subunits are included in *The Threat—Organization, Tactics and Equipment*, prepared by U.S. Army Field Artillery School, Report No. TC6–4–2 (Fort Sill, OK, 1976), pp. A–2 to A–10.

[6]For an in-depth analysis of Soviet rifle forces see Robert M. Frasche, *The Soviet Motorized Rifle Battalion*, prepared by Soviet/Warsaw Pact Division, U.S. Defense Intelligence Agency, Report No. DDB–1100–197–78 (Washington, DC, 1978). See also the recent short article by LTC Artemenko, "Ognyom i manyovrom" [With fire and maneuver], *Krasnaya zvezda*, 4 July 1980.

[7]A recent western study of Soviet tank forces may be found in Richard E. Simkin, *Tank Warfare: An Analysis of Soviet and NATO Tank Philosophy* (London: Brassey's Publishers, 1979). See also Edward H. Cabaniss, IV, "The Soviet Tank Battalion in the Offensive," in David R. Jones, ed., *Soviet Armed Forces Review Annual 3* (Gulf Breeze, FL: Academic International Press, 1979): 239–51 (hereafter cited as *SAFRA*). The Soviet journal *Soviet Military Review* concentrates heavily on historical and contemporary short studies of tactical armor use. An exceptionally informative, if somewhat dated, Soviet volume is A. Kh. Babdzhanyan, ed., *Tank i tankovye voiska* [Tanks and tank troops] (Moscow: Voyenizdat, 1970).

[8]"Vozdushno-desantnie voiske" [Airborne troops] in A. D. Aristov, N. E. Stasenko, and E. A. Udovichenko, *Sluzbu Sovetskomu Soyuzu* [In service to the Soviet Union] (Moscow: Voyenizdat, 1978), pp. 68–71. For a popularized but informative memoir by a long-serving Soviet airborne general see I. I. Lisov, *Zemlya-nebo-zemlya* [Earth-sky-earth] (Moscow: Izdatelstvo DOSAAF, 1973).

assault phase of operations. Artillery fire in an offensive, following traditional Soviet philosophy, should proceed through three phrases:

Phase I: Preparatory fire designed to destroy enemy defense and disorganize any subsequent resistance efforts.

Phase II: Fire in support of the actual assault.

Phase III: Fire to accompany motorized rifle and tank units through enemy defenses.

Conventional fire from Warsaw Pact batteries includes that from towed and self-propelled artillery and truck-mounted multiple rocket launchers. In the Soviet army much of the towed artillery is being replaced by the new generation of self-propelled artillery, with priority going to support the tank divisions. Such a trend may be expected to continue at a steady pace through at least the major Warsaw Pact allies. Normal preparatory fire can last as long as one hour in a nonnuclear environment and twenty to thirty minutes in preparation for a nuclear attack.[9] After the preparatory phase, artillery becomes attached to the division and may fire upon preplanned targets or targets of opportunity. To achieve rapid deployment, artillery batteries fire from open positions, but this technique may have been modified because of the low survival rates of such positions during the 1973 Yom Kippur War.[10]

DOMINANT COMBAT DOCTRINE

In the years following World War II, the U.S. Army developed training manuals with imaginary order of battle information, using a fictional country and a fictional enemy force known as "aggressor." Many of the scenarios presented were patterned after an army in Central and Eastern Europe. This thinly disguised force was the Soviet Red Army of the Great Patriotic War. These scenarios included carefully constructed deep defensive zones and an aggressor army heavy in tanks and able to mount strong counterattacks with massive armor, a capability

---

[9]The historic role of prolonged artillery bombardment is well established in the Soviet military mind. A. A. Sidorenko reports that the Soviets' longest artillery preparation of World War II took place on the Karelian Front in June 1944 and lasted three hours and thirty-two minutes. Sidorenko, *Nastuplenie* [The offensive] (Moscow: Voyenizdat, 1970), translated and published as *The Offensive* (Washington, DC: Government Printing Office, 1970), p. 24.

[10]Christopher Donnelly, "The Soviet Ground Forces," in Ray Bonds, ed., *The Soviet War Machine: An Encyclopedia of Russian Military Equipment and Strategy* (New York: Chartwell Books, 1976), p. 159.

combined with artillery and a seemingly endless supply of infantry soldiers.[11]

By the late 1950s Soviet leaders, especially First Party Secretary Nikita Khrushchev, raised questions about the ability of ground forces in their Great Patriotic War mold to fight a modern nuclear war. Under Khrushchev's direction, substantial demobilization of the conventional army accompanied Soviet development of first-class strategic rocket forces. Marshal Rodion Malinovsky, then minister of defense, urged military writers to publish what he called "information" explaining the nature of war in a nuclear environment. A prolonged debate ensued which, in fact, outlasted Khrushchev. The culmination, representing a return to prominence by the modernized Soviet Ground Forces, was celebrated by the publication of several book-length studies. Perhaps the best known of these was by Colonel A. A. Sidorenko, translated and widely read in the West under the title *The Offensive*.[12] His study placed Soviet Ground Forces in their newly regained context of an essential and central element in any modern military effort. As his prewar philosophical predecessors had, he stressed the offensive. However, Sidorenko's Soviet armed forces, unlike the prewar Red Army, now had the wherewithal to make good on their preferences: "Only the offensive leads to the attainment of victory over the enemy. The offensive is the only type of combat action of the troops, the employment of which attains the complete route of the enemy and the seizure of important objectives and areas."[13] Certainly even the largest and most powerful army in the world must employ defensive operations, or the counterattack, but in modern Soviet Ground Forces and most other Warsaw Pact armies the offensive is paramount. Defensive or delaying tactics are considered unusual temporary measures to be undertaken only until the offensive can be resumed.[14]

Today's Pact doctrine requires that ground forces fight from the advantage of numerical superiority. On the main axis of an attack, to be masked by a broad frontal assault, tactical doctrine calls for an ideal ratio of 6:1 in personnel, 8:1 in tanks, 10:1 in artillery, and 4 to 5:1 for combat maneuver battalions. The minimum force for any successful attack suggests a ratio of 2 to 3:1 in personnel, 4:1 in tanks, 5:1 in artillery, and 3:1 for combat maneuver battalions. Warsaw Pact military writing has little to say if these ratios cannot be reached, which again is reminiscent of prewar thinking.

---

[11]Present U.S. Army training doctrine deals directly with undisguised Soviet and Warsaw Pact tactical doctrine and equipment. However, Pact forces are sometimes referred to as "opposing forces" or "the threat."

[12]Sidorenko, *Nastuplenie*.

[13]Sidorenko, *The Offensive*, p. 1.

[14]William P. Baxter, "Soviet Defense Tactics: Tenacity, Aggressiveness the Key," *Army* 31, no. 2 (February 1981): 37–39.

In strategic doctrine, ratios do not usually take into account support troops, the use of special weapons, or how long hostilities will be sustained. John Erickson recently estimated that in a westward assault by the Central and Southern groups of Warsaw Pact forces, using at least two Soviet airborne divisions with Czechoslovak divisions assigned to the Central Group, an unreinforced offensive would encounter eighteen NATO divisions resulting in a 2:1 ratio in favor of the USSR. That would be far from satisfactory from the Soviet viewpoint.[15] In a general world context where the Soviet Union is likely to be able to choose the time and place for any attack on NATO, it seems clear that in the absence of optimum numbers an offensive would be deemed inappropriate by the traditionally cautious and conservative Soviet leadership, unless the provocation were overwhelming. However, should a situation arise where Soviets feel that hostilities are inevitable, they are committed by doctrine to hit first, and with maximum strength available. Under such conditions Warsaw Pact ground forces most likely would launch a massive attack westward into Central Europe following standard assault doctrine.

Soviet Ground Forces and their Warsaw Pact allies are to attack in several echelons, with at least two in any attack and perhaps even three. The first echelon is the principal attack force and carries the preponderance of the force; it includes about two-thirds of the total assault including tank support and most of the artillery available. The second wave is to be used to maintain the momentum of the attack. It also may be directed to exploit the successes of the first, be ordered to attack in a new direction, or be employed to destroy bypassed enemy elements, fight off counterattacks, neutralize air mobile or airborne attacks, or replace first echelon units that have lost combat effectiveness. The second echelon has no NATO counterpart and should not be interpreted as a reserve force. An actual Warsaw Pact designated reserve force is likely to seem very small in comparison with western practice. A reinforced battalion may serve as the reserve for an entire division, while a battalion reserve may be no larger than a platoon. However, under the authority of a forward commander these units are formed and trained for maximum impact at crucial moments.[16] While some NATO tacticians still might perceive it as unorthodox if a first assault wave were to bypass an enemy strongpoint, it is a standard tactic according to Soviet doctrine.[17]

The second echelon's mission is to be assigned at the same time it is given to the first, but it is usually allotted a more general task. In major

[15]John Erickson, "The European Military Balance," *The Soviet Threat: Myths and Realities* (New York: Academy of Political Science, 1978), p. 117.

[16]S. Pemirbiev, "Ispolzuya reservy" [Utilizing reserves], *Krasnaya zvezda*, 22 August 1980. The Soviets seem to use the term "reserve" with modifiers to indicate the same range of groups and people that the English word connotes.

[17]Simkin, *Tank Warfare*, pp. 51–57.

maneuvers, Pact commanders are often given a "mission of the day" that provides a timetable with which the commander operates; it may be assigned from the front down to the battalion.[18] The immediate objective for the army would be considered a division's mission of the day and would be the objective that the first echelon divisions would secure within the first twenty-four to forty-eight hours and might extend to a depth of thirty to fifty kilometers. The mission of the day provides flexibility for the commander, while addressing the overall objectives of the offensive action.

The Meeting Engagement

Soviet tacticians have concentrated on perfecting Pact doctrine especially on three main offensive actions, based upon their perception of the nature of modern war, the capabilities of Soviet and other Warsaw Pact ground forces, and the historical perspective of previous wars.[19] First, Soviet and allied forces have placed special significance in their training on the "meeting engagement," which occurs when two opposing forces encounter each other either intentionally or by surprise and neither is in a position to go on the defensive. It might happen at the beginning of a war, during a reconnaissance in force, following a breakthrough, during pursuit, or at the time of an enemy counterattack.[20] This results in a forced decision by both sides, often when still in march column, to go into the attack. The objective for Warsaw Pact forces in a meeting engagement is to achieve and maintain the initiative by swift and violent action. Soviet doctrine assumes that Pact forces will be able to react and deploy quicker than any opponent and that it is better to have an uncoordinated attack than an enemy with time to prepare. The meeting engagement is characterized by immediate changes in the situation, fluid operations on a wide front, rapid changes in combat formations, and open flanks for both forces. It is the aggressive domination of the meeting engagement and of the shifting maneuver that will best disrupt the enemy's formations and lead to his confusion and inability to sustain his own attack.[21]

---

[18]V. Goltsev, *Bolshie manyovry* [Large-scale maneuvers] (Moscow: Izdatelstvo DOSAAF, 1974), pp. 69–89.

[19]An excellent example of this genre is Y. Novikov and F. Sverdlov, *Manyovr v obshchevoiskovom boyu* [Maneuver in combined-arms combat] (Moscow: Voyenizdat, 1972). English version, *Maneuver in Modern Land Warfare* (Moscow: Progress Publishers, 1972).

[20]V. Moroz, "V bronirovankom boyevom poryadke" [In armored battle order], *Krasnaya zvezda*, 3 January 1980. See also Joseph D. Douglass, Jr., *Soviet Military Strategy in Europe* (New York: Pergamon Press, 1980), pp. 99–100; and *Soviet Army Operations* (April 1978), pp. 3–35 to 3–44.

[21]Novikov and Sverdlov, *Manyovr* (English version), pp. 62–68.

The Breakthrough

The second form of offensive action most heavily emphasized—the breakthrough—is one that evokes more distinct memories of Great Patriotic War victories.[22] When the enemy has established either a hasty or deliberate defensive line, Soviet and Warsaw Pact tactics would place primary emphasis on breaking through it to carry the battle to the enemy rear rather than seizing or consolidating terrain objectives. It is anticipated that the breakthrough might even occur at a single rupture of the line that would have to be rapidly exploited and widened. Breakthrough operations would utilize at least two, and perhaps three, echelons of attacking forces. The first would be designed to breach the enemy line and destroy his frontal defenses; the second echelon would then move quickly through the gaps and begin exploitation operations deep in the enemy rear. In hostilities the Soviets are willing to accept a much higher rate of attrition among first echelon units than would be acceptable under NATO doctrine. First echelon units are expected to attack until they are rendered ineffective; they then would be replaced by preplanned movements of relief formations.

The Pursuit

The third form of offensive action is designed to destroy the enemy completely through pursuit.[23] Although the pursuit might appear to be spontaneous, it in fact would be well planned and rehearsed while determining possible enemy routes of withdrawal. Tank and motorized units would move rapidly along parallel routes, outdistancing and then blocking escape. Ground forces might be assisted by airborne units in cutting off the enemy or capturing key terrain objectives.[24] Pursuit is to be initiated by units of regimental size and larger and to be terminated when the enemy is destroyed or a logistical support problem arises.

All of these actions should be viewed against the dominant Soviet offensive assumption that an attack by a reinforced battalion or combat team will begin off the line of march with massive artillery and close air support. An attack by larger units would entail more conventional patterns.

---

[22]See especially the recent book by A. I. Radziyevsky, *Proryv* [Breakthrough] (Moscow: Voyenizdat, 1979), which includes historical material from the Russo-Japanese War, First World War, Civil War, and the Great Patriotic War.

[23]Novikov and Sverdlov, *Manyovr*, pp. 68–71.

[24]Yu. Chernyshov, "A Tactical Airborne Landing," in *Soviet Military Review*, no. 5 (May 1980): 27–29. See also Douglass, *Soviet Military Strategy*, pp. 96–98.

COMBAT SUPPORT: FORCES, DOCTRINE, AND CAPABILITIES

As a supplement to Warsaw Pact offensive tactical doctrine, it is appropriate to review combat support practices, including those known as "special operations." The focus is primarily on the role of nuclear, biological, and chemical weapons (NBC), river-crossing/amphibious capabilities, and air-delivered assault. In addition, a brief review is provided on Pact rear services.

NBC Weapons

Perhaps the most striking characteristic of the Soviet military attention devoted to the use of tactical nuclear weapons is the seemingly common assumption that they in fact will be used. Tank and motorized infantry units, while having to take special mechanical and tactical measures in the nuclear blast "environment," nevertheless will push through.[25] The clear Soviet military consensus seems to be that someone will use them and they will be answered in kind. The Soviets build equipment and Pact members train with that in mind.[26] Although it may be unlikely and presently perhaps unnecessary for the Soviets to initiate use of tactical nuclear weapons in Europe (no other Warsaw Pact army has any), the temptation to employ various forms of chemical weapons would be more difficult to resist. Toxic and nontoxic gases, herbicides, and other chemical agents are available to complement a Pact commander's conventional weapons. An initial massive surprise use of gases delivered at long range, especially to neutralize enemy aviation and tactical nuclear resources, appears to be a regular feature of Warsaw Pact planning.[27]

Much less is known about Soviet biological weapons doctrine, but it seems reasonable to assume that the very unstable nature of the material would make it appropriate mainly for attacking the far rear of the enemy. Targets there might include strategic reserves, supply depots, and in

---

[25]See Novikov and Sverdlov, *Manyovr*, pp. 70–71, 111–17. See also Babdzhanyan, *Tanki i tankovye voiska*, pp. 210–14. In the section devoted to the tank in a nuclear blast environment battlefield, sketches illustrate dozens of Soviet tanks charging around and between tiny mushroom clouds.

[26]Many earlier versions of these Soviet assumptions are illustrated in William R. Kintner and Harriet F. Scott, *The Nuclear Revolution in Soviet Military Affairs* (Norman: University of Oklahoma, 1968). See also S. T. Cohen and W. C. Lyons, "A Comparison of U.S.-Allied and Soviet Tactical Nuclear Force Capabilities and Policies," *Orbis* 19, no. 1 (Spring 1975): 72–92; and *Theater Nuclear/Conventional Warfare*, prepared by the Air University, USAF, Maxwell Air Force Base (Alabama, 1978).

[27]Jacquelyn K. Davis and Robert L. Pfaltzgraff, Jr., *Soviet Theater Strategy: Implications for NATO*, Report No. 78–1 (Washington, DC: Strategic Institute, 1978), pp. 21–22.

Western Europe, prepositioned weapons storage facilities and reception centers for trans-Atlantic reinforcements.[28]

River-Crossing/Amphibious Capabilities

Warsaw Pact emphasis on hyperrapid and continuous advance has had to take into account the formidable numbers of south-north rivers flowing through North and Central Europe. The result has been a concentration of technical and tactical resources on offensive river crossings to a degree unparalleled outside Eastern Europe. A Pact army in battle will be equipped with assault vehicles and armored personnel carriers that are authentically amphibious and actually capable of firing most of their heavy armament while in midstream. Main battle tanks too heavy to swim rivers are designed to be winched across or to snorkel, both extremely difficult tasks. All of these dazzling characteristics would be effective only if suitable river banks, bottoms, and depths could be located. Thus, reconnaissance engineers are charged with the formidable task of locating the numerous possible crossing points necessary to allow the broad front attack required by Pact doctrine.

Alternatives such as ferrying and bridging are mainly designed to follow and exploit initial successful amphibious assaults, but they also have continued to be the subject of extensive technical innovation and intensive practice. Bridging and other river assault engineer troops are available in substantial numbers in each major attack formation from division on up. Given the Soviet preoccupation with rapid and aggressive advance, there is also a substantial expectation that many conventional enemy bridges would be taken intact, either by the advancing forward reconnaissance forces or by special helicopter or airborne commandos.[29]

Although their amphibious exercises in the Baltic have attracted western publicity, the relatively small numbers of Soviet and Warsaw

---

[28]The USSR is a signatory to international agreements that not only prohibit the use of biological weapons but also require the destruction of any existing stocks. Whether or not the Soviets have been violating the agreement on manufacture and testing of biological warfare pathogens recently has been the subject of a great deal of controversy in the West, following a 1980 outbreak of an anthrax epidemic in the Urals. See Charles H. Bay, "An Update on the Other Gas Crisis," *Parameters* 10, no. 4 (December 1980): 27–35. The article covers both Soviet gas and germ warfare capabilities and doctrine in detail.

[29]Friedrich Wiener, *The Armies of the Warsaw Pact* (Vienna: Carl Veberreuter, 1978), pp. 143–49. West European analysts like Wiener have found many Warsaw Pact fording and bridging claims hard to credit, pointing out that there are considerable differences between the rivers of East and West Europe; they feel that much of the Pact's film and printed versions of river crossings are heavily edited smoke screens, if not outright deceptions. See also the encyclopedic *Soviet and Warsaw Pact River Crossing: Doctrine and Capabilities*, prepared by Soviet/Warsaw Pact Division, U.S. Defense Intelligence Agency, Report No. DDB-1100—197-78 (Washington, DC, 1976). Official U.S. Army policy apparently is to adopt a "worst case" attitude.

Pact marines and dedicated landing craft up to this point have restricted sea-launched ground forces operations to areas close to suitable naval bases.[30] Primary targets would include the narrow entrances to the Baltic and Black seas.

Air-Delivered Assault

Soviet and Pact troops and equipment in impressively large numbers can now be transported by air to almost any spot on the globe. This rapidly evolving capability takes several major forms: heliborne assault long-range conventional air delivery of motorized rifle divisions, and air drops and airlandings of specially trained, equipped, and independently organized airborne paratroops.[31]

The Afghan invasion of December 1979 provided a major opportunity for western analysts to observe Soviet airborne and air-delivered infantry troops. Their operations were reported in some detail before more effective security measures could be established. Unlike most of the other major Afghan deployments, the air-delivered operations provided information appropriate to the European theater.[32]

Soviet and other Warsaw Pact airborne forces are trained and equipped to fulfill strategic long-distance tasks as well as shorter range operational responsibilities, and they are also assigned certain kinds of special purpose roles.[33] Strategic operations might include seizure of seaports, enemy air facilities, and perhaps most importantly, enemy theater nuclear weapons launch sites. In addition, the strategic concept would encompass long-range power projection. Within the Pact, only the USSR has the ability to carry out strategic missions. Operational assaults

---

[30]P. Suchy, "Amphibious Forces: A Mechanized Future," *Ground Forces International* 7, no. 61 (February 1980): 47–52. See also Peter Hertel Rasmussan, "Naval Infantry," *SAFRA* 4 (1980): 228–38. The most authoritative sources place the size of the Soviet naval infantry at 12,000 men. International Institute for Strategic Studies, *The Military Balance: 1980–81* (New York: Facts on File, 1980), p. 12. The Polish amphibious force is apparently a reinforced brigade of between 5,000 and 6,000 men. The German Democratic Republic possesses one motorized rifle regiment, trained for beach landings. For a useful and informative, if dated, Soviet work on the naval infantry, see P. V. Kukushkin, *Batalon v morskom desante* [The battalion in amphibious landing] (Moscow: Voyenizdat, 1972).

[31]The use of Soviet tactical air support and helicopter gun ships is covered in Robert W. Clawson's article on Warsaw Pact air power included in this volume.

[32]Graham H. Turbiville, Jr., "Airborne Troops," *SAFRA* 4 (1980): 253–63.

[33]A. Pinchuk, "Desant v tyl 'protivnika' " [Landing in the rear of the enemy], *Krasnaya zvezda*, 15 July 1980. See also K. Kurochkin, "V tylu protivnika" [In the rear of the enemy], *Krasnaya zvezda*, 15 July 1980. General Kurochkin is deputy commander of airborne troops. Also, General Lisov wrote a historically based book in the late 1960s: *Desantniki* [Paratroops] (Moscow, Voyenizdat, 1968). For an English language article on long-distance use see Kenneth Allard, "Soviet Airborne Forces and Preemptive Power Projection," *Parameters* 10, no. 4 (December 1980): 42–51.

would be made at short distances from Warsaw Pact airfields, would generally involve up to division-sized forces, and most likely would be in support of a front offensive. Targets not only might include river crossings, airlanding facilities, or other such objectives but also might involve delivering forces on the far side of nuclear strikes or enveloping cutoff enemy forces and ground supply bases. Poland and Czechoslovakia have airborne forces capable of operational missions but must rely on the USSR for transport. A special purpose landing by paratroops most likely would be at company strength or smaller. Such a unit might operate at any range from friendly forces and could be assigned missions out of a broad selection of special tasks, from reconnaissance to irregular warfare. These might also be accomplished by special heliborne infantry forces.

Airlift services provided to selected drop zones for strategic and operational missions would be by aircraft of the Military Transport Aviation, an arm of the Soviet Air Forces.[34] Should the pressure of events so dictate, aircraft from *Aeroflot* and East European state airlines also would be employed.[35]

Airborne doctrine is grounded in concepts normally associated with similar operations in the West: surprise, flexibility, small-unit initiative, high security, and tough, realistic training. It stresses the use of specially designed equipment, particularly the small airborne fighting vehicle known as the BMD, and self-propelled airborne artillery. Despite the emphasis on aggressive tactics, actual combat use of the eight Soviet airborne divisions and other Warsaw Pact airborne formations would be relatively conservative, avoiding battle situations where these elite troops might stand a chance of suffering unacceptable casualties.

Soviet and Warsaw Pact heliborne infantry capabilities and doctrine only recently have been developed. Although their heliborne operations are partly the result of close study of American practice in Vietnam, Pact forces have not created special air assault units but rather rely on the regular motorized rifle troops, most of which appear to receive some training in helicopter landing operations.[36] The typical helicopter assault in the European theater is apt to be a special tactical operation designed to seize and hold river crossings and unique terrain objectives or to reconnoiter nuclear battlefields, probably no more than fifty kilometers ahead of

---

[34]Harriet Fast Scott and William F. Scott, *The Armed Forces of the USSR* (Boulder, CO: Westview Press, 1979), pp. 158–59.

[35]*Aeroflot* aircraft have played central roles in Soviet deployment of forces during such operations as the Cuban air lifts to Angola and Ethiopia but do not appear to have played a major part in the invasion of Afghanistan. Other East European airlines have often delivered weapons and advisers overseas.

[36]Yu. Romanov, "Krylya motostrelkov" [Wings of the motorized rifle troops], *Krasnaya zvezda*, 29 April 1980. See also "Soviets Deploying Helicopter Assault Forces," *Aviation Week and Space Technology* 103, no. 13 (29 September 1975): 57; and Graham Turbiville, "A Soviet View of Heliborne Assault Operations," *Military Review* 55, no. 10 (October 1975): 3–15.

the Warsaw Pact's forward line. Helicopters would be made available from the local front's tactical air support.[37] Unlike airborne units operating at greater distances from friendly forces, heliborne troops would not carry significant offensive resources with them. Once a target was seized, the force would go on the defensive to await the arrival of the advancing front.[38] As a variation on this theme, it does appear that something like "search and destroy" missions have been carried out in the Afghan conflict; Soviet troops are brought in by helicopter and then lifted out following the conclusion of a mission. This mode undoubtedly would have its place in a European conflict as well.

Rear Services

The highest priority battlefield function provided by rear services is the supply of missiles, ammunition, and fuel to forward combat forces. Fuel is transported by truck, pipeline, and rail, all run by specially trained military forces operating a broad range of mission-designed equipment.[39]

Removal and repair of battle-damaged Warsaw Pact combat vehicles is not considered as important as in western armies. Tank and other fighting equipment designs are purposely kept uncomplicated to facilitate ordinary maintenance by crews; in combat, a piece of equipment in need of major repair would be cast aside to be collected later and brought to assembly points. The crew would pick up a replacement or go on to another combat assignment, while the original piece eventually would be attended to by roving repair teams capable of more complex tasks. Expecting a land war in Europe to be short, the Pact forces plan that only moderate problems would be repaired, hoping to get as much lightly damaged equipment immediately back into battle as possible. Badly damaged weapons systems either would be cannibalized for spares or eventually sent to rear areas where more comprehensive repair services would be available.[40]

The major military combat transportation mission is carried out by army trucks, railroads, helicopters, and a variety of other specialized, and often tracked, vehicles. However, in the event of full mobilization it is still likely that a large number of trucks would have to be mobilized from the civilian sector. Truck design is highly standardized in the USSR and Eastern Europe. The civilian economies use the same types of vehicles

[37]Peter M. Wargo, "The Evolution of Soviet Airmobility," *Military Review* 55, no. 11 (November 1975): 3–13. See also Thomas J. McNamara, "An Analysis of the Soviet Helicopter Threat," *U.S. Army Aviation Digest* 27, no. 1 (January 1981): 45–46.

[38]*Soviet Army Operations*, pp. 7–6 to 7–8.

[39]Christopher Donnelly, "The Modern Soviet Ground Forces," in Ray Bond, ed., *Russian Military Power* (New York: St. Martens Press, 1980), pp. 194–95.

[40]*Soviet Army Operations*, pp. 6–9 to 6–13.

found in the armed forces, thus presenting no significant new repair problems other than the generally lower rate of preventive maintenance practiced in civilian enterprises.[41]

Medical care in the field is regulated by much the same philosophy as that governing the repair of equipment. Emphasis is on getting the lightly wounded back into battle as soon as possible while evacuating the more severe cases to specialized facilities farther to the rear.[42]

Pact troops, particularly the Soviet Ground Forces, are still encouraged to exploit local resources, although Soviet writers emphasize that plans are not designed to depend entirely on such foraging. However, given the inflexibility of the ammunition and fuel supply mission, it is likely that some Pact troops would be expected to live off the land at least for food and basic living supplies.

POSSIBLE VULNERABILITIES

It would be difficult to dispute that the Soviet Union possesses in both quality and quantity one of the finest conventional ground forces in existence today. Sustained emphasis on vigorous offensive action, deep objectives, echelon attack on a massive scale, and the employment of thoroughy modernized combined arms forces have made the Soviet army ideally suited for unlimited war on a continental level. Continued build-up of long-range capabilities makes force projection and even full-scale intervention at distances far from the Soviet homeland increasingly available as a foreign policy option. Soviet military writers claim that their ground force commanders possess strident confidence in their ability to win a war in Europe. This is probably more than simple propaganda to inspire faith in friends and fear in enemies. Much of that confidence is undoubtedly authentic and represents an element of morale essential to the kind of warfare the Soviets clearly intend to fight, if the time comes. The East European Pact armies, to the degree they augment this confidence, play another important role.

In 1976 then U.S. Army Secretary Martin Hoffman, reflecting on a popular image, asked if the Soviet soldier were really ten feet tall. The secretary concluded that he was 5'6" and still growing. Soviet Ground Force capabilities have grown considerably in the last five years, but they remain unevenly proportioned and continue to exhibit weaknesses of some probable consequence.

---

[41]Ibid., pp. 6–13 to 6–14.
[42]Donnelly, "Modern Soviet Ground Forces," p. 194.

Perhaps the most glaring vulnerability relates to the confusion that is likely to result from emphasis on high speed and mobility in enemy territory. Simkin suggests:

> [that] the advance will lose momentum quite simply because the spearhead companies will get lost. Take any arm of any army any-where—think how often you see a tank commander desperately comparing the map with the signpost or village sign. I wonder if the Russians are any different; and vehicle navigation systems, like dictionaries, are only of real use if you know the answer beforehand.[43]

It is ironic that the army with the finest assault rifle and armored personnel carrier in the world still usually issues only four maps per motorized rifle company.

Similarly, Pact emphasis on attacking off the line of march may not stand the test of real war, as Simkin explains:

> If a combat team attacking off the line of march has to deploy and fight, specially if it has to dismount its infantry, it will most probably either take the wrong objective or fail to take the right one. The confusion of war has to be experienced to be believed; there is no reason to believe the Russians are immune to it.[44]

The meeting engagement, which also can occur in situations other than off the line of march, would certainly suffer from inevitable confusion. Only after years of the pressure exerted by war were the Soviets able to blend a degree of discipline with true local initiative in order to produce effective spontaneous battle behavior against the Nazis. They may be able to simulate comparable pressure through what are assuredly the most realistic, and dangerous, combat training programs in the world today, but it is unlikely. Training is just that, and the conscript knows it. Experience in Afghanistan is also unlikely to yield much in-depth familiarity with this problem due to the peculiar nature of that conflict.

Other features of their enormous scale and rapid continuous attack doctrine also might prove troublesome for Warsaw Pact forces. Preparations for a first-shot offensive in Europe would be very difficult to hide, especially from satellite and other electronic observation.[45] The USSR cannot keep its entire western army permanently poised for a jump-off in Eastern Europe; massive movement would be required and, inevitably, observed. Too many things would be revealed to allow them both to get in the first lick, as they so strongly advocate, and to do it in the kinds of numbers that they know are necessary. Even if the ratio needed for

---

[43]Simkin, *Tank Warfare*, p. 57.
[44]Ibid., p. 58.
[45]The Soviets are now capable of destroying most U.S. and NATO hardware in space, but the very act would be interpreted as an initial step toward the deployment of full Soviet strength in East Europe.

breakthrough were concentrated in only a small sector, they still would need great mass within which to hide the point of attack and to exploit immediately any possible successes.

There can be little doubt that in the process they would generate damaging transportation bottlenecks.[46] And once an offensive got underway, should the Soviet and Pact forces stick to their doctrinal assumptions, it seems probable that the spearhead tanks and BMPs would soon outrun their supplies. Again, Simkin states:

> The logistic quantities an armored force of this kind needs are much too large even for modern airlift and it would be physically impossible to superimpose intensive logistic traffic on the main forward move . . . and logistic vehicles and even aircraft may have considerable difficulty in finding and getting through to roving combat teams and scattered remnants of subunits, which may themselves be none too clear where they are.[47]

In short, the Warsaw Pact offensive system, which plans on a partial live-off-the-land policy for logistical backup, may be very vulnerable to a carefully coordinated enemy policy of denial.

In addition, it may be important to examine briefly the Soviet attitude toward the defensive. While it is certainly inaccurate to suggest that Warsaw Pact armies are untrained and unprepared to assume a strong defensive if necessary, it is clear that the bulk of contemporary Soviet and East European military doctrine and training is devoted to the frontal attack and advance.[48] The continuing tide of Soviet military training literature, whose principles are grounded in the experience of the Great Patriotic War, rarely speaks of Soviet wartime defensive operations. Perhaps this is because the first year and one-half of the war is still an extremely distressing period for most who lived through it, especially today's Soviet military leadership. Nevertheless, about all one can usually learn, even from material devoted to the first days and months of the

---

[46]It has been suggested by western observers that many improvements have been made in Soviet European deployment capabilities since the Czech occupation in 1968 when the system seems to have broken down in important respects. Nevertheless, should the USSR feel the need to bring troops up from the Far East, for example, it would still face massive transportation problems including changes of rail gauge. There are other bothersome transportation problems. Despite significant growth there is presently insufficient air transport to move all Soviet airborne divisions at one time. Near border areas Soviet forces still show amazingly poor light discipline during night operations, and their wheeled vehicles are especially heavy noise producers.

[47]Simkin, *Tank Warfare*, p. 59.

[48]Defense is rehearsed as a purely temporary measure and mainly at the battalion level. For example, see V. Kruk, "Batalon perekhodit k oborone" [The battalion goes over to the defensive], *Krasnaya zvezda*, 14 March 1981. See also Dale D. Best, "Soviet Motorized Rifle Battalion (Reinforced) in the Defense," *Air Defense Magazine* (January–March 1981): 6–9.

German invasion, is that the border guards fought to the last bullet. But
they failed to keep out the invasion. Clearly, they do not intend to let that
happen again; surely, they had not intended to let it happen then.

There are also certain aspects of Soviet and, to a lesser extent, other
Pact personnel policies that deserve attention. For example, despite recent
corrective measures, the Soviet army still lacks a true professional noncommissioned officer corps.[49] This must be considered a lingering weakness that very quickly would become evident if the ground forces of the
Warsaw Pact were required to make rapid adjustments to new situations
and to rely on the ingenuity of small groups to cope with changes in
tactical conditions. Although some of the other Pact forces do have career
noncommissioned officers, they could hardly make up for the Soviet
deficiency.

Another personnel problem, and one shared by most of the major
armed forces of the world, is that the Warsaw Pact cannot adequately
train its conscripts in the use of advanced electronics and other highly
complex equipment essential to the operation of modern weapons systems
before it loses them back to the civilian population. Nor can it hope to
keep them operationally knowledgeable about changes in technology
during their reserve status period. Those few that it can retain as career
soldiers almost inevitably become warrant or commissioned officers and
are often taken away from direct interface with the equipment.

With regard to the capabilities of the individual soldier, some
western sources, citing what they believe is convincing evidence from two
world wars, contend that the kind of combat envisaged by doctrine
corresponds unconvincingly with the mentality of most Warsaw Pact
soldiers; there seems to be an assumption that it is appropriate perhaps
only for the forces of the German Democratic Republic.[50] However,
another body of history suggests that this form of spontaneous movement
may be rather well represented, for instance, in past Russian and Soviet
battle experience, particularly on somewhat predictable occasions during
World War II.[51] It is also obvious that the Soviet and East European

---

[49]An editorial in the Soviet ministry of defense newspaper presents an update on
recent Soviet efforts to reinstitute and broaden the ranks of the noncommissioned *prapor-
shchik* [ensign] and *michman* [midshipman]. See "Praporshchiki i michmani," *Krasnaya
zvezda*, 17 March 1981.

[50]This assumption is relatively widespread, appearing frequently in U.S. and
European military handbooks. For example see *Handbook on Soviet Ground Forces*,
compiled by the Department of Army, Report No. FM 30–40 (Washington, DC: Government Printing Office, 1975); and Wiener, *Armies of the Warsaw Pact Nations*, p. 130.

[51]A particularly informative source of data on Soviet military innovation during the
1941–45 war is the U.S. Air Force series on the German Air Force in World War II
produced by the USAF Historical Division, Air University, and published in the early
1960s. See esp. Klaus Uebe, *Russian Reactions to German Air Power in World War II*
(New York: Arno Press, 1964); and Karl Drum, *Airpower and Russian Partisan Warfare*
(New York: Arno Press, 1962).

armies of today are made up of men considerably different from those who fought in 1945.[52] Decades of rigid and astonishingly strenuous tactical training have been designed to prepare the army for this kind of flexible warfare; its success, however, is still unproven.

Finally, the question of equipment standardization should be considered. There is a great variety of equipment dispersed throughout the Warsaw Pact and even within the Soviet Ground Forces themselves, and that would inevitably complicate repair and replacement in wartime. This is at least in part because equipment throughout the Pact varies by generation due to a hierarchical policy of distribution. Warsaw Pact officers in the Balkans grumble that they are at the end of the long Soviet distribution cycle and therefore are using military equipment two generations behind those in the NATO arsenal. Also, due to the Soviet penchant for exceptionally long production runs of relatively untested equipment, as well as the Warsaw Pact's reluctance to take anything out of service, large amounts of permanently troublesome equipment soldier on. Thus, although the Warsaw Pact has carried standardization and interoperability further than the NATO alliance can ever hope to, it does not quite yield the absolute advantage with which it is sometimes credited.

UNLIKELY VULNERABILITIES

There are other existing and potential problems continually stressed by western, particularly European, sources which should not be omitted in any study that includes a consideration of Warsaw Pact military capability. Neither, however, should they give much comfort to any potential adversary. There is, for instance, much western attention given to the sharply increasing percentage of non-Europeans in the Soviet annual drafts. The implication is that somehow the Soviet military system will be unable to handle the various associated social problems that will arise.

Although adjusting to major changes in racial composition does not appear to be particularly easy for any social organization, military ones seem less vulnerable than most. The postwar Soviet army long has had a very effective system of folding the numerous and highly diverse Soviet ethnic groups into its fabric, and although the process obviously does not

---

[52]A controversial study by Richard A. Gabriel used a panel of recently serving former Soviet troops now outside the USSR to assess morale, fighting spirit, and even combat effectiveness. The author's conclusions paint a less-than-rosy picture of life in the ranks of the Soviet armed forces and call into question some of the more common assumptions about the high ideological motivation and willing volunteerism of the Soviet soldier. See Gabriel, *The New Red Legions: An Attitudinal Portrait of the Soviet Soldier* (Westport, CT: Greenwood Press, 1980), esp. pp. 151–226.

quite produce the harmonious "brotherhood of the peoples" portrayed in the group photos of *Krasnaya zvezda*, it certainly does work. The lessons taught by massive World War II defections have formed the basis for a system of integration that ensures a broad distribution of non-Slavic soldiers, mainly throughout the Ground Forces. This dilution, along with the careful use of ethnic cadres, helps ensure the necessary Russianization and socialization of non-Slavic and non-European recruits. In the context of superpower military competition, the United States surely faces at least an equally difficult set of problems resulting from changes in its own army's racial composition.

Similarly, the Warsaw Pact's obvious manpower shortages, already having an impact on military planning, are easily matched by American and British reluctance to reinstitute a system of peacetime national service. Also, although the Warsaw Pact armed forces are certainly more labor-intensive than their NATO competition, the pressure of a shrinking manpower tool is likely to result in additional efforts to increase the effective technological capital of the armed forces, thus resulting in an even more accelerated effort to narrow the quality gap between NATO and Warsaw Pact equipment.

Another seemingly critical national security weakness often identified, particularly by Americans, is the unimpressive performance of particularly the Soviet economy. The argument seems to be that at some point the Soviet population will force a halt to the steady increase in national wealth devoted to the defense sector. Even given the remote possibility that the Soviet consumer can ever learn the true extent of the military budget, historical experience—Soviet as well as Imperial—hardly leaves any doubt as to the willingness of the average citizen to shoulder a defense cost far beyond that acceptable to the West European or North American. As Simkin concludes, the USSR is probably the last remaining major industrial power willing to assume this kind of burden, but assume it they will. While East European states have been less enthusiastic, their reluctance is not likely to be critical.

Finally, the problem of alcohol abuse must be considered. Anyone visiting the German Democratic Republic can watch entire convoys of elite soldiers from the Soviet Group of Forces in Germany pulled off at rest stops to drink their lunch. There is a serious alcohol problem in the Soviet army, as well as in other Warsaw Pact forces, and there can be little doubt that the seemingly endless consumption of vodka will have an impact on combat effectiveness. But can there be any doubt that the Soviet Red Army of the Great Patriotic War defeated the Nazis on the same fuel? And is it not possible to draw a balance with the American military drug and alcohol problem, particularly in Germany?

Suffice it to say that the Warsaw Pact armed forces do have vulnerabilities. However, before a recitation of them can be useful, an evaluation of their relative importance needs to be made. It is this latter that all too often seems to elude western commentary. It does not require blind adherence to "worst-case" analysis to conclude that most Warsaw Pact vulnerabilities are likely to be of minor consequence if the Soviets are able to choose the time and place for ground force combat in Europe. To expect any one or a combination of those vulnerabilities to come to the rescue of inadequately equipped and manned NATO forces in a future struggle would be optimism stretched beyond the credible. Soviet and East European capabilities can be accurately estimated only by a realistic evaluation of the complex world of the Warsaw Pact, not by simplistic analysis and wishful thinking.

OTHER PACT MEMBERS AND SOVIET OPERATIONS: CONCLUSIONS

While the Soviets have imposed and nurtured an alliance of its East European neighbors, their reliability as wartime allies never has been taken for granted. Were there a truly free choice, it can hardly be doubted that most of the East European members, even under Communist governments, would withdraw, or at least renegotiate the terms of their association. And there are certainly responsible Czechs, Poles, and Romanians who privately view NATO not so much as an aggressive threat but as a bulwark against further Soviet expansion in Europe.[53] Whether the Soviet commitment to dominate the East European buffer is offensive or defensive in nature is purely an academic question for most of the people living there. Thus, the Soviets have had to produce a system of military alliance designed to assign other Pact ground forces a fairly rigid series of battlefield tasks within the framework of a common Soviet tactical doctrine and command. Aside from the few East European airborne and marine units, their ground forces would fit into position with the Soviet fronts almost automatically.

While strictly subordinate to Soviet commanders and subject to tight Soviet control in the event of war, other Pact ground forces do vary slightly in their peacetime configurations. However, no matter what their domestic or regional roles until recently most have not been allowed even to look like national armies.[54] East European Pact officers are constantly

---

[53]This is certainly not meant to be an exclusive list, but merely the nationalities of representatives with which the authors have discussed the question.

[54]Recent changes in uniform, especially the return by both Poland and Romania to essentially prewar dress and helmets, is certainly a manifestation of national identity. Though Poland may well have received permission from the Soviets, it is doubtful that

being schooled and reschooled in the USSR in an atmosphere specially
structured to create shared values both between counterpart East Europeans (perhaps from traditionally enemy armies) and with brother Soviet
officers.[55] Frequent joint maneuvers involving the "fraternal" armies are
designed to accomplish not only the standardization of Pact operations to
the Soviet model but also to increase, at least to some modest extent, the
shared values between the ranks of the various Pact armies.[56] While
especially the latter task may be largely hopeless, the Soviets probably
have managed to assure that in the event of a general ground war in
Europe the other Pact armies would be initially propelled into it on the
Soviet side, and that they would be led by officers whose careers had been
augmented by the degree to which they had become "standardized" to the
Soviet model. Whether or not these other armies would support their
senior partner might ultimately depend, as much as on anything else,
on whether the patron is winning or losing, as it has in the last several
regional wars.[57]

Romania even asked. See Friedrich Wiener, *Uniforms of the Warsaw Pact* (London: Arms
and Armour Press, 1978).

[55]Christopher D. Jones, "The Warsaw Pact Directorate for Educational Exchanges"
(paper presented at the U.S. Air Force conference, "The Soviet Union: What Lies Ahead?",
held in Reston, VA, 27 September 1980).

[56]P. I. Yefimov et al., *Boyevoi soyuz bratskikh armiy* [The fighting alliance of the
fraternal armies] (Moscow: Voyenizdat, 1974), pp. 25–27. See also *Nash soyuz boyevoy: iz
opyta vospitatelnoy raboty molodyozhnykh organizatsiy bratskikh armiy* [Our fighting
alliance: from the experience of youth organization educational work in the fraternal armies]
(Moscow: Voyenizdat, 1975); and John M. Caravelli, "Soviet and Warsaw Pact Joint
Exercises: Functions and Utility" (paper presented at the U.S. Air Force conference, "The
Soviet Union: What Lies Ahead?," held in Reston, VA, 27 September 1980). Recent Soviet
articles of interest include G. Kashuba, Bogdanovsk, Ivanov, and V. Zhitarenko, "Druz-
heskie vstrechi" [Friendly meetings], *Krasnaya zvezda*, 7 September 1980. This article is a
typical example of Soviet reporting of contacts between troops of the various Pact armies
from the large-scale maneuver "Brothers in Arms, '80" held in East Germany and the Baltic
in fall 1980. For a particularly ironic piece see R. Zvyagelsky, "Sodruzhestvo: na polevom
zanyatim Sovietskikh i Polskikh voinov" [Cooperation: Soviet and Polish forces in the
field during joint operations], *Krasnaya zvezda*, 23 January 1981.

[57]Dale R. Herspring and Ivan Volges, "Political Reliability in the Eastern European
Warsaw Pact Armies," *Armed Forces and Society* 6, no. 2 (Winter 1980): 270–96.

Warsaw Pact Air Forces:
Organization and Combat Doctrine

ROBERT W. CLAWSON

Although Soviet military air power inherited a significant, if heavily damaged, prerevolutionary aviation industry, it was definitively forged only during the difficult days of the counteroffensive against the Nazis. A postwar international environment fundamentally different from the earlier wartime experience forced the USSR to develop in the unfamiliar and sometimes uncomfortable directions of strategic aerial defense and offense. But the net fundamental emphasis of postwar Soviet air power, reflected also in the organization and training of the allied East European Warsaw Pact air forces, has been on what aviation could contribute to success on the battlefield— tactical air support. Soviet aircraft design, only rarely out of touch with the main world trends, has made impressive qualitative and quantitative improvements especially in the last decade, allowing all of the various Soviet and East European air arms to participate in a comprehensive program to upgrade capabilities, with a continuing emphasis on tactical aviation.

The major Soviet air services include: the Air Defense Forces, the Military Air Forces (including Frontal Aviation, Military Transport Aviation, and a strategic bomber component), and Naval Aviation. The organization and combat doctrine of each of these branches, as well as of the East European counterparts to the Air Defense Forces and Frontal Aviation, form the subject of this study.

Before proceeding further it is essential to note that major changes are now taking place in the organizational framework of Soviet combat aviation. These reforms are typical of the Soviet defense establishment in that they appear to be a blend of both structural redesign and transfers, either of operational or administrative control. The complex implications of these changes are far from clear at the time this volume goes to press; the following analysis has attempted to take into consideration what is presently known from public sources.

251

AIR DEFENSE FORCES

Detached from army artillery in 1948, established as a separate command in 1954, and subsequently evolved into an independent service, the Soviet National Air Defense Forces, known until recently by the abbreviation of its Russian name PVO Strany (now evidently called Voiska PVO), were created and developed in response to the Soviet view of the western threat.[1] The Air Defense Forces originally were designed to defend Soviet airspace primarily against the manned bomber fleets of the U.S. Strategic Air Command and British Bomber Command. Massive infusions of capital and personnel resources eventually resulted in a complex in-depth system of radar, interceptor, rocket, and artillery protection, forming an air defense capability more costly and more comprehensive than any other in the world.[2] Since the danger from manned bombers has decreased in relation to other strategic weapons, Voiska PVO has been the focus of a multifaceted effort to create an effective antiballistic missile system as well as to meet the cruise missile threat.[3]

Voiska PVO units are organized territorially into air defense districts in the USSR and in Eastern Europe.[4] They are directly linked with the tactical air defense units of Frontal Aviation in the Soviet groups of forces stationed in other Warsaw Pact countries as well as with air defense units of allied Warsaw Pact air forces.[5] The system is designed to give priority protection to large industrial cities in the western portion of the USSR; the most highly valued area is controlled by headquarters in Moscow.[6]

The personnel strength of the Voiska PVO stands at about 550,000, larger than the Strategic Rocket Forces (385,000), the navy (433,000), or the Military Air Forces (475,000).[7] Enlisted men start as conscripts, while the officers are generally career pilots or technical specialists. Conscripts are given individualized basic training with the unit to which they are

[1]M. A. Anaymanovich et al., *Voiska protivovozdushnoi oborony strany* [National air defense forces] (Moscow: Voyenizdat, 1968), p. 337–40. The volume was under the editorial supervision of a collective headed by General P. F. Batitsky, PVO Strany commander in chief, 1966–78. Soviet sources list Batitsky as the editor.

[2]M. O. Norby, *Soviet Aerospace Handbook* (Washington, DC: Government Printing Office, 1978), pp. 62–63. The handbook is Air Force Pamphlet 200–21 of May 1978.

[3]S. A. Tyushkevich et al., *Sovetskie vooruzhonnye sily: istoria stroitelstvo* [The Soviet armed forces: a history of their development] (Moscow: Voyenizdat, 1978), pp. 460–61.

[4]Air Vice-Marshal S. W. B. Menaul, "The Defense of Soviet Airspace," in Ray Bonds, ed., *Russian Military Power* (New York: St. Martin's Press, 1980), pp. 50–59.

[5]*Handbook on the Soviet Armed Forces*, prepared by the Department of Defense Intelligence, Defense Intelligence Agency, Report No. DDB–2680–40–78 (Washington, DC, 1978), p. 11–3 (hereafter cited as *HSAF*). See also Robert P. Berman, *Soviet Airpower in Transition* (Washington, DC: Brookings Institution, 1978), p. 14.

[6]Norby, *Soviet Aerospace Handbook*, p. 66.

[7]See the essay by James T. Reitz in this volume.

assigned. The particularly heavy emphasis on mathematics and electronics in the assignments, even of enlisted personnel, has resulted in the
use of a complex system of selection for specific jobs within the service;
testing of all kinds is an important part of the early basic training period.
There are a number of higher military schools that commission officers
trained in one of the major Voiska PVO specialties.[8]

The air defense service, like the Strategic Rocket Forces, has no
distinctive uniform. Interceptor pilots wear the regular Air Forces uniform
and specialty badges; antiaircraft missile and artillery troops wear regular
army clothing with artillery badges and colors; radar troops wear army
uniforms and army radiotechnical badges and colors. There is now a
distinct Voiska PVO badge given after long service and substantial contributions to performance effectiveness, but as yet its award is a relatively
rare event. As in the Strategic Rocket Forces, Communist Party political
work receives a priority, and high political motivation (often interpreted as
refraining from asking awkward questions) is an important factor in a
Voiska PVO officer's career.[9]

The Voiska PVO combat arms include Fighter-Interceptor Aviation, Antiaircraft Rocket Troops, and Radiotechnical Troops.[10] In addition, a special antispace weapons defense element (PKO) apparently
was established in the early 1960s.[11] Voiska PVO organization and
doctrine by combat arm will be examined in the following portions.

Fighter-Interceptor Aviation

Soviet fighter-interceptor forces of the 1980s suffer from an
inglorious past. Their World War II service was weak, unimpressive, and
largely unnecessary. Nazi Germany's decision not to develop a long-range
bomber force—and a similar decision by Japan—meant that neither
dedicated high performance interceptors nor workable early warning
systems were essential to the Soviet war effort.[12]

---

[8]*HSAF*, pp. 11–5 to 11–6. See also A. Lazarenko, "Shkola vospitania" [Training
school], *Krasnaya zvezda*, 3 February 1981.

[9]*HSAF*, p. 11–5. On party work see the typical "V nebe – raketnye boi" [Rocket
combat in the sky], *Krasnaya zvezda*, 19 February 1981.

[10]S. S. Lototskiy et al., *Armia Sovetskaya* [The Soviet Army] (Moscow: Izdat. Pol.
Lit., 1969), pp. 423–24.

[11]David R. Jones, "National Air Defense Forces," in David R. Jones, ed., *Soviet
Armed Forces Review Annual* (Gulf Breeze, Fl: Academic International Press, 1977), 1:
40–47 (hereafter cited as *SAFRA*). See also the *Sovetskaya voyennaya entsiklopedia* [The
Soviet military encyclopedia], 8 vols. (Moscow: Voyenizdat, 1978), pp. 594–95 (hereafter
cited as *SVE*). Evidently, an antiballistic missile command (PRO) was established at about
the same time. See *SVE*, 6:603–4.

[12]Asher Lee, *The Soviet Air Force* (New York: John Day Company, 1962), pp. 109–
13. Lee claims that for most of World War II the Soviets maintained not much more than
one division of fighter-interceptor—between 250–350 aircraft—for strategic air defense. See

The awesome reality of a postwar Anglo-American long-range bomber threat concentrated Soviet efforts on the development of an aerial defense, almost to the exclusion of other aviation projects. However, for many years the results were disappointing, despite Soviet possession of data, hardware, and even personnel from the formidable Reich air defense system. Airborne interceptor radar, ground controlled intercept equipment and knowhow, and appropriate fighter tactics took an exceptionally long time to become effective. In fact, it may be said that Soviet fighter defenses were not truly credible until after the manned bomber had been replaced by the intercontinental ballistic missile as the principal strategic threat to the USSR.[13] Only by then had the East European allies been effectively integrated into a Warsaw Pact interceptor defense in the West. However, the continued U.S. and NATO maintenance of a force of strategic nuclear armed aircraft and the development of the relatively slow cruise missile, as well as the perceived threat from China, have prolonged the importance of the interceptor: new resources for Voiska PVO fighter aviation have continued to be allocated over the last decade.[14]

Voiska PVO's Fighter-Interceptor Aviation is organized operationally around the air regiment. The regiment, with a strength of about forty aircraft, is made up of squadrons, links, and sections, the latter being the smallest air element consisting of two aircraft. Although in theory the Voiska PVO control center can decide to attack invading forces with any of the weapons at its disposal, past practice has been to meet an enemy air attack at very long distance with fighter-interceptors in vectored sections.

Voiska PVO air interception doctrine and tactics have been the subject of intense discussion in the West since the 1976 defection of Lieutenant Victor Belenko with his PVO MiG-25.[15] Belenko's various accounts of interceptor operations portray the pilot/crew as encased in a rigid system of discipline and subject to a doctrine, which in its most extreme form (e.g., the MiG-25 system), delegates virtually all phases of interception to the ground controllers. Belenko seems to say that the pilot

also John T. Greenwood's comprehensive historical study of wartime Soviet air power titled "The Great Patriotic War," in Robin Higham and Jacob W. Kipp, eds., *Soviet Aviation and Air Power: A Historical View* (Boulder, CO: Westview Press, 1977), pp. 69–136 (hereafter cited as *Soviet Aviation*). The Soviet viewpoint of the role of fighter-interceptor forces is well displayed in I. V. Timokhovich, *Operativnoye iskusstvo: Sovetskikh VVS v Velikoi Otechestvennoi voine* [Operational art: the Soviet air forces in the Great Patriotic War] (Moscow: Voyenizdat, 1976), esp. pp. 301–41.

    [13]Lee, *Soviet Air Force*, pp. 114–25.

    [14]Jones, *SAFRA* 3 (1979): 24–44. For the contemporary Voiska PVO mission from the Soviet viewpoint, see Ye. Yurasov, "Chasovye neba rodiny" [Sentinels of the homeland sky], *Krasnaya zvezda*, 12 April 1981, in celebration of Voiska PVO day, 1981.

    [15]For example, see various issues of *Aviation Week and Space Technology*, particularly the 16 October and 6 November 1978 issues. See also Jones, *SAFRA* 2 (1978) and 3 (1979). Belenko's story is told in greater depth but sensationalized form in John Barron, *MiG Pilot: The Final Escape of Lieutenant Belenko* (New York: McGraw Hill, 1980).

is allowed to do little more than take off and land. Infractions of these rules are dealt with severely. This certainly fits with a great deal of Soviet literature on the subject, and the use of draconian punishments for deviations also conforms with past Russian and Soviet military practice.[16]

Such a system has been judged necessary for relatively clear-cut reasons related to the psychology of individual behavior in Russian and subsequent Soviet society. Just below the regimented and seemingly apathetic surface of the Slavic Soviet system there is a persistent personal, often highly irrational, anarchism, probably resulting mainly from entrenched traditional Russian child rearing patterns. Russian and Soviet military leaderships have always dealt with this very real potential problem of disastrously idiosyncratic behavior with some kind of disciplinary overkill, particularly the threat of physical harm. It has always included heavy verbal abuse and endless rule making. However, Soviet interceptor pilots certainly are expected to mature in their personal capabilities to the point where true initiative and what they call "free hunting" can be exercised where appropriate.

At this time there is increasing evidence that the Soviet doctrine on individual effort is undergoing steady change. Soviet interceptor pilots, like their counterparts in other air defense forces, are still taught to work as closely and effectively as possible with their ground-controlled intercept (GCI) crew during a mission. However, should the GCI people lose track of a target or in some other way be unable to vector the aircraft into a suitable contact, the pilot or crewman is increasingly being urged to conduct an independent free hunting search, to obtain his own radar, or even make visual contact with the target and go into the attack as quickly as possible.[17] In language reminiscent of the army's doctrine on the meeting engagement, the interceptor pilot is instructed to plan alternative actions carefully before a mission in case standard procedures have to be abandoned; then, if necessary, he is to meet the enemy with only his own resources. He is to go over to the attack immediately without any time-consuming analysis, using the alternate plan that best suits the occasion. With as much surprise as possible, the interceptor pilot is to press home his attack with vigor, giving the enemy no time to retreat or set up an active new set of defenses.[18] It also seems clear that a hard and fast rule still

---

[16]An excellent example of the Soviet "iron discipline" genre can be found in G. Mikhaylov, "Ditsiplina lyotchika perekhvatchika" [Interceptor pilot discipline], *Vestnik protivovozdushnoi oborony*, no. 1 (January 1980): 30–33.

[17]G. Federyakov, "Boytsovskaya initsiativa" [The fighting man's initiative], *Aviatsia i kosmonavtika*, no. 6 (June 1979): 4–6.

[18]Mikhaylov, the disciplinarian, also has written a plain speaking article on independent search—"free hunting"—and the relatively underemphasized need for individual initiative even in the days of virtually automated GCI. "Samostoyatelny poisk vozdushno tseli" [The independent sweep for an airborne target], *Vestnik protivovozdushnoi oborny*, no. 8 (August 1979): 34–38. See also Ye. Chumakov, "Perekhvatchiki deistvuyut nochyu" [Interceptors operating at night], *Krylya rodiny*, no. 1 (January 1980): 8–9.

requires pilots to break off and return to their base or to a preselected alternate field following complete loss of contact with the GCI.[19] It is unlikely that this procedure could long survive the opening of major hostilities.

While Soviet tactics for some time have emphasized the use of salvoed rockets of different homing types, trouble with the original group of operational air-to-air rockets and the possibility of prolonged aerial chases posed by enemy low-level strategic attack aircraft and the cruise missile have resulted in a return to the supplementary use of airframe-mounted rapid fire guns. Newer models of interceptors are being fitted with automatic cannons in addition to their missile pylons.[20]

Although many western observers are still skeptical of the quality of Soviet pilot training, interceptor tactics, and the hardware provided to the average fighter-interceptor, there is little doubt that the force is competent to engage an enemy flying strategic missions in manned bombers. They probably will soon have the look-down, shoot-down capability to send up their high performance aircraft armed with appropriate anticruise missile ordnance to attack incoming targets with reasonable accuracy.[21]

Antiaircraft Rocket Troops

Voiska PVO Antiaircraft Rocket Troops are organized into regiments, missile battalions, batteries, sections, and teams. They form the second major system for active air defense, after the interceptor force. While the fighters are still expected to engage the enemy at long range, the rocket batteries are responsible for the destruction of enemy intruders at sufficient distance to prevent the launching of air-to-surface missiles. In addition, the rocket force provides site defense for the most important industrial and defense complexes.[22]

There are more than 10,000 surface-to-air missiles (SAMs) deployed along the Soviet frontier and in carefully located in-depth deployments deep inside the USSR. Moscow and Leningrad, the two largest Soviet cities, are especially well protected by dense SAM rings; in fact, Moscow has a double ring of conventional SAMs, plus the aging and antiquated antiballistic missile system.[23]

Antiaircraft Rocket Troop conscripts are integrated immediately

---

[19]Barron, *MiG Pilot.*

[20]Jones, *SAFRA* 4 (1980): 108–74.

[21]Menaul, "Defense of Soviet Airspace"; Jones, *SAFRA* 4 (1980).

[22]Tyushkevich, *Sovetskie vooruzhennye sily,* p. 461; Anaymanovich, *Voiska protivovozdushnoi oborny,* pp. 364–66.

[23]*HSAF,* pp. 11–4 to 11–5. Western analysts have expressed substantial doubt concerning the effectiveness of the Soviet ABM system to do anything more than add to the total destruction of a nuclear exchange.

into regularly functioning crews for practical training, along with their basic military indoctrination and classroom work. Soviet authors claim that this simultaneous system allows troops to achieve operational proficiency earlier than under the sequential method, thus making more effective use of the conscripts' limited time on active duty.[24] Continual SAM strategic air attack drills and simulations persist for all units. Antiaircraft Rocket Troops are also trained to defend against airborne assault as well as nuclear, chemical, and biological attack. To operate in those environments, crews are drilled in the use of personal protective gear, decontamination equipment, and other responses to catastrophic attack.

Rocket troops long have been trained to operate high- and middle-altitude rockets and are now manning systems augmented to attack low-level targets. Evidently, the new Mach 6 SA-10 has been specifically designed to deal with low-level bomber penetration; it also may well be part of the anticruise missile arsenal.[25] Until the advent of the SA-10 on a fully operational basis, probably no sooner than the mid-1980s, part of Voiska PVO's defensive plan apparently involves the use of battlefield air defense SAMs, whose principal liabilities are their restricted speed and range.[26]

Radiotechnical Troops

The mission of Soviet Radiotechnical Troops, the third major component of the Voiska PVO, is to detect approaching air intruders at long range. They must then identify them quickly and accurately, track them, and direct appropriate aircraft and missiles to intercept the enemy.[27]

The Soviet system of strategic air defense radar is a three-line set of early warning belts that is far more complex than anything comparable in the West. The first-priority, northward-looking portion runs from offshore in the Arctic Ocean down through Warsaw, over to Moscow, and out along the route of the Trans-Siberian Railway to Vladivostok. In the east a line stretches from the Bering Sea southwest to the Korean border (looking east), then turns and continues along looking south at the Chinese, and ends near the Afghan border. Directed toward the southwest a third early

[24]*HSAF*, p. 11-7. Six of the Voiska PVO higher military schools are assigned to train Antiaircraft Rocket Troops. See Jones, *SAFRA* 2 (1978):79-128. A tactical rocket exercise is summarized by A. Polyakov, "Sentinels of the Sky," *Soviet Military Review*, no. 4 (April 1981): 19-20.

[25]Jones, *SAFRA* 3 (1979): 24-44. Jones notes rumors that the Soviets would construct a picket line of ships armed with SA-10s or another similar system to stand at some distance off Soviet shores, deployed to intercept the proposed U.S. wide-bodied cruise missile carrier-aircraft should the United States develop an air-launched fleet.

[26]Jones, in *SAFRA* 4 (1980).

[27]"Radio tekhnicheskie voiska" [Radio technical troops], *SVE*, 7:25.

warning system runs from the Caspian Sea across the Caucasus Mountains, along the Black Sea coast, and into Bulgaria and Romania. In addition to these three lines, there is an incredibly dense westward-looking Warsaw Pact system designed to alert the alliance of any airspace penetration from NATO. This latter system, manned by both Soviet and other Warsaw Pact forces, is linked to the central Voiska PVO operations center in Moscow, as are the three central belts.[28] The Soviet equipment includes more than 7,000 surveillance radars.[29]

The Radiotechnical Troops recently have put into operation an over-the-horizon detection capability and have had an airborne warning and control system (AWACS) aircraft flying for some years. A newer model AWACS is presently being produced, reportedly with an authentic look-down capability. Additionally, they are now deploying phased array systems, replacing their older units.[30] Although much time and effort has been committed to data processing, inadequate and temperamental computer operation still remains the principal weakness of the Warsaw Pact's early warning system; the solution is really not yet in sight. However, despite their long and slow evolution and their relatively simple design, today's Soviet-made conventional radar equipment does form an adequate early warning system, mainly because of its power and the density with which units are sited.[31]

Space and High Energy Responsibilities

Various Soviet claims to having created and deployed a successful ABM missile have not been particularly convincing to western analysts, and the antiballistic missile command (PRO) evidently has not been discussed in the Soviet military press for some years. However, the antispace weapons element (PKO) has been more visible. It apparently has been responsible for the formidable Soviet killer satellite program and has achieved considerable success in its efforts to develop systems designed to blind U.S. space reconnaissance vehicles.[32]

The PKO also has been identified as the military command involved in research on laser and particle beam weapons. If these weapons

[28]HSAF, p. 11–4.
[29]Jones, SAFRA 4 (1980).
[30]Menaul, "Defense of Soviet Airspace."
[31]The density partly results from typical Soviet reluctance to retire obsolete equipment after the next generation has been deployed. In this case, older radar units are kept in service, providing added depth and redundancy. Harriet Fast Scott and William F. Scott, The Armed Forces of the USSR (Boulder, CO: Westview Press, 1979), pp. 150–51.
[32]Various rumors persist that the Soviets are continuing to work on hyper-sprint ABMs. If so, their development may be the responsibility of the PRO. The killer satellite program has been the subject of extensive western coverage, particularly in journals such as Aviation Week and Space Technology and Armed Forces Journal. See Jones's summary, SAFRA 4 (1980).

are developed, their principal application evidently would be as satellite-mounted, antiballistic missile rays.[33] While the feasibility of such systems is still a matter of heated debate in the West, there can be little doubt that the Soviets long have been committed to significant and costly laser and charged particle beam weapons research. Deployment of these weapons certainly would be more than consistent with standard Soviet air defense philosophy of meeting the enemy as far from Soviet territory as possible, in this case moving the focus of conflict to outer space. However, the future of these devices is far from certain, and speculation about space combat doctrine undoubtedly soon would be proven foolish at best.

Voiska PVO: Conclusions

Although there is disagreement in the West over the likely future of Soviet air defense forces, particularly the manned fighter branch, there can be little doubt that the defense of East Europe and the USSR against attack from the air or from space will continue to have a high priority.[34] Manifestly, the Soviets do not intend to be caught off guard again; they also hope that being prepared to absorb punishment will serve as deterrence.

However, while Soviet leaders may believe that the correlation of forces has now shifted in their favor, they also fear that an increasingly desperate West might try to reverse the tide of history in an insane gamble on a first strike. While Chinese nuclear capability does constitute a kind of strategic threat, it is the continuing U.S. and NATO technological superiority, combined with their menacing role in the Soviet view of history, that causes the USSR to respond with such an energetic defense program. To meet this possible challenge during the decade of the 1970s, the Soviets spent about half of their strategic forces budget on defense. This compares with a U.S. expenditure of about 15 percent of its strategic budget.[35] By 1977 Voiska PVO was allocated approximately 12 percent of total

---

[33]For an extensive review of Soviet and U.S. particle beam weapons research see *Particle Beam Weapons* (New York: McGraw Hill, 1978), a collection of articles reprinted from *Aviation Week and Space Technology*. The material includes data on the Soviet program.

[34]Jones has earlier argued that all branches of Voiska PVO retain high priorities for funds, personnel, and new equipment, *SAFRA* 4 (1980). The editors of the British aviation magazine *Air International* claim that the fighter-interceptor force is losing resources to the tactical air arm, Frontal Aviation. They argue that the Voiska PVO fighter component has been reduced by 30 percent over the last decade and that between two-thirds and 75 percent of the aircraft are now ten to fifteen years old. *Air International* 20, no. 6 (June 1981): 273–83. Today there is general agreement that the manned fighter branch is being trimmed back.

[35]Central Intelligence Agency, *Soviet and U.S. Defense Activities, 1970–79: A Dollar Cost Comparison*, Report No. SR80–10005 (January 1980), pp. 8–9, cited in Jones, *SAFRA* 4 (1980).

military spending, while Soviet strategic rocket forces received only about 8 percent.[36]

This formidable defense effort is interpreted in the West as an attempt to assure Soviet national survival in the event of a world war. That certainly is an accurate, if elementary and hardly ominous, conclusion. But having made that judgment, many analysts then assume that it also must mean that the Soviets are preparing to launch an unprovoked survivable surprise attack on the West; in short, that so much Soviet defense is dangerous to world peace.[37] This latter set of conclusions is virtually incomprehensible to Soviet leaders, all of whom clearly can remember the events of summer 1941 when the USSR came perilously close to being wiped out as a nation.

At the same time the American and NATO defense posture of nuclear deterrence, along with its subsequent manifestations, have depended on a maximum effort to develop punishing strategic offensive forces—to hold up the West's responsibilities to mutually assured destruction—and a minimum program to build an actual and effective defense. This has posed what the Soviets have concluded is a clearly comprehensible aggressive threat. To them it is especially dangerous in the hands of what they consider reactionary western leaders who see their cause losing out to the forces of history.[38]

The perceived likelihood of that last desperate gamble on the part of the West undoubtedly helps keep such enormous resources flowing into Soviet strategic defense and will continue to make research and development for new defense weapons a central priority for Soviet strategic planners. They evidently have concluded that their massive defense establishment might actually deter the West through denial of victory, and as long as there persists the possibility of an actual showdown, the USSR plans to lose less than its enemies because of the protection afforded by a more than adequate defense capability. Soviet efforts to provide a significant civil defense, though almost impossible to achieve convincingly, are surely carried out in the same spirit.

In this strategic defense effort the East European air defense component of the Warsaw Pact is designed mainly to protect the western

[36]Central Intelligence Agency, *Estimated Soviet Defense Spending: Trends and Prospects*, Report No. SR–78–10121 (June 1978), p. 3, cited in Jones, ibid.

[37]For an excellent example of this style of analysis see "Soviet Buildup in North Exceeds Protection Level," *Aviation Week and Space Technology* 114, no. 24 (15 June 1981): 101–7.

[38]The Soviet perception is nowhere more clearly stated than in Tyushkevich, *Sovetskie vooruzhennye sily*, pp. 440–54. For a comprehensive western review of the strategic perceptions and misperceptions see John Baylis and Gerald Segal, eds., *Soviet Strategy* (Montclair, NJ: Allanheld and Osman, 1981).

approaches to the USSR. To the extent that their contribution is undermined by divisive events in individual Pact countries, the West is encouraged. Comprehensive Soviet integration of East European air defense systems with that of the USSR has been designed to deny that comfort.

MILITARY AIR FORCES

While the Military Air Forces of the East European Warsaw Pact nations are not integrated into a single Soviet-directed system as are the strategic air defense units, they do operate Soviet aircraft and adhere to Soviet air combat doctrine in all but a few relatively insignificant cases.[39] They also are all organized on almost exactly the same lines, with only the USSR possessing a strategic air arm and substantial heavy air transport. Because it is the most comprehensive, the Soviet model will serve as the framework for this analysis. Soviet Military Air Forces have been organized into three principal operational arms: Frontal Aviation, Military Transport Aviation (VTA), and until recently, Long-Range Aviation.

The Soviet Air Forces include some 475,000 men. The vast majority of enlisted personnel are conscripts, while the officer corps is made up mainly of career pilots, navigators, and technical specialists. Like the other services, the Military Air Forces maintain a complex system of higher education and training. The majority of pilot and navigator candidates, most likely with DOSAAF experience, study at what they call "higher flying schools," which combine a basic engineering course, actual flight training, and military theory. This four-year curriculum results in an engineering degree, a junior lieutenant's commission, and basic flying or navigation certification. Once assigned to an operational unit, the officer continues his training until fully qualified in the unit's tasks. Perquisites, which accrue to the air force officer, are important but not substantially different from those available to other services within the Warsaw Pact.[40]

Frontal Aviation

The Soviet decision in the mid-1960s to build modernized Ground Forces able to win at any level, from conventional to nuclear, carried with

[39]The East European air forces are reviewed briefly in A. S. Schevchenko et al., *Boyevoi soyuz bratskikh armii* [The fighting alliance of the fraternal armies] (Moscow: Voyenizdat, 1974), pp. 45, 72, 104, 143, 172. For a review of the East European air forces see Bill Sweetman and Bill Gunston, *Soviet Air Power* (New York: Crescent Books, 1978), pp. 38–69.

[40]*The Military Balance 1980–81* (London: IISS, 1980), p. 12. On training, see *HSAF*, pp. 10–9 to 10–10.

it the necessity to revive and upgrade their tactical air power in order to
assure air superiority over the battlefield and to influence the course of
ground combat. This tactical branch, known in the USSR as Frontal
Aviation, alone among the Soviet air services can lay claim to meaningful
wartime achievements against both the Germans and the Japanese.[41]
Today it is considered to be the most important Soviet Air Forces
component. It is organized into sixteen air armies: four in the groups of
Soviet forces in Eastern Europe and one in each of twelve military
districts in the USSR. East European combat aircraft in the past have
been mainly assigned to tactical roles and were to be integrated into the
operational frameworks of the Soviet fronts in the event of war.[42] This
aspect of Pact cooperation is presently the subject of extensive redesign;
the precise dimensions of this reform are not clear at this time.

The Soviet air army is designed ideally to consist of three air
divisions of about 350 aircraft each. The air division is divided into three
air regiments made up of three squadrons of about twelve to fifteen
aircraft. The basic unit is the link, which contains four aircraft. In fact,
these all vary significantly in number of subunits and aircraft, depending
on their theater. For example, the elite Sixteenth Air Army with the Soviet
Group of Forces in Germany may have 750 tactical aircraft, while a
Central Asian military district may be allotted as few as 200.[43]

Frontal Aviation has been assigned five principal roles. It is to
provide: 1) fighter top cover, air defense, and air superiority over the
battlefield, 2) close air support for Soviet Ground Forces, 3) deep interdiction behind enemy lines, 4) reconnaissance of the battle area and
enemy rear, and 5) electronic countermeasures and warfare in the battle
zone. These tasks represent a substantial expansion of the tactical air
force's responsibilities, now made possible by the availability of appropriate mission-designed, high-performance aircraft and equipment.[44]

Fighter top cover and air superiority were probably among the least

---

[41]Editors, *Air International* 20, no. 6 (June 1981): 33–43. See also Tyushkevich,
Sovetskie vooruzhonnye sily, p. 469; and Joseph D. Douglass, Jr., *Soviet Military
Strategy in Europe* (New York: Pergamon Press, 1980), p. 178. For historical background
see the official history of Soviet air operations during World War II in S. I. Rudenko et al.,
Sovetskie voyenno-vozdushnye sily v velikoi otechestvennoi voine 1941–1945 gg. [Soviet
air forces in the Great Patriotic War, 1941–45] (Moscow: Voyenizdat, 1968), esp. pp. 134–
414. See also Timokhovich, *Operativnoye iskusstvo,* and Robert A. Kilmarx, *A History of
Soviet Airpower* (New York: Praeger, 1962), pp. 171–200. Soviet Frontal Aviation forces
also engaged Japanese aircraft and tanks of Nomonhan in 1939. For a detailed study of the
engagement see Edward J. Drea, *Nomonhan: Japanese-Soviet Tactical Combat* (Fort
Leavenworth: U.S. Army Command and General Staff College, 1981). This monograph is
no. 2 of the *Leavenworth Papers.*
        [42]*HSAF,* p. 10–6.
        [43]S. W. B. Menaul, "The Modern Soviet Air Force," in Ray Bonds, ed., *Russian
Military Power* (New York: St. Martin's Press, 1980), pp. 60–71.
        [44]*HSAF,* p. 10–7; Berman, *Soviet Airpower,* pp. 27–34; Tyushkevich, *Sovetskie
vooruzhennye sily,* p. 461.

effectively performed roles of all those assigned to Frontal Aviation during World War II. Soviet fighters showed great reluctance to escort their own fighter-bombers effectively or to intercept German air strikes against Soviet forces. In fact, these roles were not viewed as crucial by Soviet tacticians; the heavily armored Ilyushin IL-2 *Shturmovik* ground attack aircraft was regarded as capable of sufficient self-defense and was to attack with or without escort whether or not they were engaged by German fighters.[45] Likewise, until perhaps as late as mid-1944, Soviet Ground Forces were almost solely responsible for their own air defense. They developed an exceptionally fierce system of local flak, but for the whole war had to do without any kind of reliable early warning system no matter how far behind the forward edge of battle.

Today the recent and continuing addition of massive numbers of high-performance, all-weather interceptors has given Frontal Aviation and its East European counterparts the equipment needed both to provide air cover and to exclude the enemy air force from the battle area.[46] About 40 percent of all Soviet Frontal Aviation aircraft are assigned to tactical air defense. However, they still do feel that effective tactical air offensive operations against the enemy can be carried out before air superiority has been gained; aircrew motivation and well-armored aircraft are thought to be the key.[47]

Close air support, the most successful form of Soviet air combat during the war, was neglected during the period in which strategic nuclear rocket forces dominated Soviet military thinking. Following the reemphasis of tank and motorized infantry forces and conventional war capabilities, the Soviet aviation industry began to supply Frontal Aviation and the East European allies with formidable numbers of new high-quality fighter-bombers and armed helicopters to provide effective support for Ground Forces operations.[48] Close air support missions are designed to attack enemy forward edge positions with heavily armed and armored attack helicopters (under army control), while striking at tactical and operational depth with high performance fighter-bombers. Targets such as enemy control posts, artillery positions, reserve forces, communications and command centers, and especially tactical nuclear missile launch sites would be attacked in carefully planned multiple sorties.[49]

[45]An in-depth German evaluation is provided in Walter Schwabedissen, *The Russian Air Force in the Eyes of German Commanders* (New York: Arno Press, 1968), esp. pp. 12–14, 107–24, 213–29, 332–48.

[46]Editors, *Air International*; Alfred L. Monks, "Air Forces (VVS)," *SAFRA* 4 (1980): 174–96.

[47]*Soviet Army Operations*, prepared by the U.S. Intelligence and Threat Analysis Center, Report No. IAG–13–U–78 (Arlington, VA, 1978), p. 5–33.

[48]Kenneth R. Whiting, "The Peacetime Air Force at Home and Abroad 1945–76," *Soviet Aviation*, pp. 289–313. See also editors, *Air International*.

[49]*Soviet Army Operations*, p. 5–34. A typical Soviet close air support exercise against Voiska PVO "enemy" interceptors is reported in Yu. Onufritzov, "Vnezapnyi

Tactical interdiction, isolating the enemy's front lines from supply bases and deeply held reinforcements, was never seriously undertaken by the Soviets during most of World War II, much to the surprise of their German opponents. Although the USSR did seek to remedy its weakness in the postwar years, specially designed deep-strike, all-weather interdiction aircraft only recently have been available to Soviet commanders. Interdiction doctrine now stresses the importance of mass attack on a broad front, shutting down all access through the employment of a carefully drawn plan that concentrates on the most important targets.[50] In special cases, tactical interdiction sorties still may be assigned to heavier bomber aircraft, but this is becoming much less necessary because of the broad deployment of new generation dedicated interdiction fighters.

Tactical air reconnaissance units are to be employed immediately prior to the opening of hostilities to locate and assess troop concentrations, air base facilities, and most importantly, tactical nuclear aviation and missile sites. Following the outbreak of war, visual, photographic, electronic, and other forms of surveillance would be available to the Soviet tactical reconnaissance fighter forces for continuous and comprehensive surveillance. Armed reconnaissance, which takes advantage of targets of opportunity, is mainly viewed as a potential waste of assets. However, it does find a limited place in Soviet air combat doctrine.[51]

Until recently it was thought that Frontal Aviation had been designated as the principal manager for combat helicopter forces. However, these assets now appear to be under direct control of the army. Modern Soviet attack helicopters, heavily armored against conventional ground fire and even against air attack, provide ideal platforms for the employment of antitank, anti-APC, and counterhelicopter weapons, including a variety of missiles and heavy automatic weapons. All Soviet combat helicopters also have an air assault troop-carrying capacity, providing Soviet forces with especially effective special operations capabilities.[52]

bomboyvi udar" [Surprise bombing attack], *Krasnaya zvezda*, 16 June 1981. See also B. Makarevich, "Lyotchik-snaiper" [Sniper-pilot], *Krasnaya zvezda*, 1 April 1981. By the end of the 1970s the Soviets still did not possess sophisticated bomb ordnance such as that used by U.S. forces in Southeast Asia. Deployment of Soviet "smart bombs" is anticipated for the first half of the 1980s. Scott and Scott, *Armed Forces of the USSR*, p. 158.

[50]*Soviet Army Operations*, pp. 5–34 to 5–40.

[51]Douglass, *Soviet Military Strategy*, pp. 101–4. See also "Razvyedyvatelnaya aviatsia" [Reconnaissance aviation], *SVE*, 7: 35.

[52]Lynn M. Hansen, "Soviet Airpower: Behind the Buildup," *Air Force Magazine* 64, no. 3 (March 1981): 68–72. See also G. Ivanov, "Vertolyoti vysazhivayut desant" [Helicopters deliver a landing force], *Krasnaya zvezda*, 2 August 1978. Hansen suggests that the reconstituted prewar Army Aviation arm may now be assuming direct control of all combat helicopters, thus handing ground commanders decentralized operational direction of this increasingly potent set of weapons.

WARSAW PACT AIR FORCES

These have been widely used for counterinsurgency operations in Afghanistan.[53]

Frontal Aviation's role in air-mounted electronic countermeasures and warfare generally has been confined to tactical battlefield operations. However, increasing numbers of specially equipped high-performance aircraft have added an exceptional new dimension to Soviet front line capabilities.[54] Inevitably, in wartime that would mean continually deeper penetration on medium and probably eventually on long-range missions.

In addition to direct tactical combat assignments, Frontal Aviation is committed to a number of auxiliary tasks, including short-range troop and air cargo transport, especially medical evacuation as well as reinforcement of strategic aviation and Voiska PVO as the need might arise. Aircraft also would be made available for tactical nuclear deliveries, and helicopters would be employed for immediate follow-up. In fact, Soviet doctrine shows a distinct preference for air delivery of initial nuclear strikes.[55]

The massive and ongoing additions to the aircraft stock of Soviet Frontal Aviation, combined with the present Warsaw Pact policy of upgrading most of the East European tactical air arms in an across the board program, should result in a substantially modernized Pact tactical air capability by the mid-1980s. This force, able to perform general and specialized tasks on a comprehensive basis, perhaps represents the most fundamental and sweeping change in the nature of air power in Central Europe since the end of World War II.

Military Transport Aviation

The Soviet air transport arm, known by its Russian initials VTA, has not been a high-priority service. Equipped for many years with relatively small, short-range aircraft, the VTA was seen as performing strictly local theater-related tasks. As new longer range and more capable aircraft began to fill the VTA inventory in the early 1960s, Soviet doctrine continued to stress theater-related tasks. Only since the early 1970s has

---

[53]The Soviets have been publishing a steady selection of politically slanted, but militarily informative, articles on helicopter operations in Afghanistan. For example, see B. Budnikov, "Gory ne proshchayut oshibok" [The mountains do not forgive mistakes], *Aviatsia i kosmonavtika*, no. 9 (September 1980): 8–9; and A. Khrobrykh, "Za perevalom pereval—iz Afganskoi tetradi" [From one mountain pass to another—from an Afghan notebook], *Aviatsia i kosmonavtika*, no. 10 (October 1980): 8–9.

[54]See "Radioelektronnaya borba" [Electronic war], *SVE* 7: 29–30; and "Radioelektronnaya zashchita" [Electronic defense], *SVE* 7: 30.

[55]*Soviet Army Operations*, pp. 5–39 to 5–40.

long-range, heavy-lift transport of troops and equipment for political-strategic purposes become one of the VTA's central missions.[56]

Today the military air transport service is charged with the following tasks: 1) moving combat troops, especially airborne units, to immediate operations areas, 2) support of ground combat forces through airlift of supplies and equipment and air drop operations, and 3) overseas or domestic delivery of supplies or personnel for disaster relief or foreign military assistance.[57] In the last decade the VTA's force of conventional transport aircraft has been supplemented by the addition of only modest numbers of newer transport helicopters. Also, while the USSR is the only Warsaw Pact member with heavy strategic airlift capabilities, the civilian airlines of both the Soviet Union and the East European members of the Warsaw Pact are linked to the VTA or regional command and can be made available at extremely short notice. Especially large numbers of medium and heavy civilian transport aircraft serving with the Soviet airline *Aeroflot* are available. Internally configured for military transport, they lack only the external defensive armament characteristic of many VTA planes.[58]

The VTA is organized into regular air regiments and also maintains some degree of control over transport aircraft assigned to other branches of the armed forces. The latter would be released to VTA operational command should the need arise. The military airlift capacity of the Soviet VTA is now estimated to be as many as three airborne divisions, depending upon the distance of an operation and the accompanying equipment stock. At long distance with full equipment it is likely that the Soviets can transport no more than two airborne divisions at a time.[59]

Despite its apparently continuing low priority, the Soviet VTA has proved crucial to any number of Soviet foreign ventures. In particular, the air resupply of the USSR's Arab clients during the 1973 Yom Kippur War was probably essential to the survival of Soviet interests in the area. Later operations to Angola, Ethiopia, and Afghanistan, for example, have depended heavily on VTA and *Aeroflot* support.[60] In addition, Soviet

---

[56]G. N. Pakilev, *Sovetskaya voyenno-transportnaya aviatsia* [Soviet military transport aviation] (Moscow: Izdatelsvto *DOSAAF*, 1974). General Pakilev served as commander of the Soviet VTA and deputy commander in chief of the Soviet Air Forces.

[57]Berman, *Soviet Airpower*, pp. 34–36. See aso V. Nagorny, "Krylya dlya voisk: voyenno-transportnoi aviatsii – 50 lyet" [Wings for the troops: 50 years of military transport aviation], *Krasnaya zvezda*, 31 May 1981.

[58]Scott and Scott, *Armed Forces of the USSR*, pp. 158–59. See also Ralph Ostrich, "Aeroflot," *Armed Forces Journal International* 118, no. 9 (May 1981): 38–59.

[59]*HSAF*, p. 10–8. In the Czech occupation of 1968, two Soviet divisions were air landed at Prague airport in one effort lasting slightly more than sixteen hours. This was a relatively short-distance operation. Since then total lift capacity has been increased somewhat, though the number of aircraft has been reduced.

[60]Menaul, "Modern Soviet Air Force."

Military Transport Aviation performs regular domestic airlift tasks, particularly in Siberia and the Far East, in assisting geological and scientific efforts as well as economic operations.[61]

Strategic Aviation

Soviet strategic air power, known until recently as Long-Range Aviation, is organized into three groups. Approximately three-quarters of Soviet strategic aircraft assets are assigned to the Northwest and Southwest Bomber Corps directed at NATO targets, including those in North America. About one-quarter of the force is deployed with the Far East Bomber Corps at bases located near the Chinese border. Though nominally under the Military Air Forces high command, Long-Range Aviation actually operated for many years as a semi-independent arm, with its commanding general reporting directly to the Soviet ministry of defense.[62] No East European air force possesses a strategic air capability. As part of the general reorganization of the air forces, the strategic aviation service recently has been downgraded to a much less independent status.

With no serious World War II long-range bombing experience, the Soviets began a rapid building program in the mid-1940s based on the design of the American B-29, several examples of which had made forced landings in the Soviet Far East after damage was sustained in raids over Japan. Although the Soviets subsequently produced modern jet and turboprop long-range bombers in the late 1950s and throughout the 1960s, neither the number of planes nor their weapons loads ever constituted a formidable intercontinental challenge to North America. Soviet strategic doctrine, focusing mainly on land- and sea-based ballistic rockets, has never accepted the long-range bomber as anything but a helpful secondary weapon.[63]

In the event of hostilities, bombers are expected to attack enemy nuclear weapons sites, strategic naval facilities, bomber bases, and war industries, but all such raids would be in cooperation with a combined arms offensive. In addition, strategic aviation might be called upon to deliver first strikes in the opening days of a European or Asian theater war. Increasingly, strategic aviation also has been charged with major intercontinental and peripheral reconnaissance missions.[64]

---

[61]V. Izgarshev, "V nebye – VTA" [In the sky—the VTA], *Pravda*, 4 January 1979.
[62]Editors, *Air International*. See also Alfred L. Monks, "Air Forces," *SAFRA* 1 (1977): 48–64.
[63]Alfred L. Monks, "The Soviet Strategic Air Force and Civil Defense," *Soviet Aviation*, pp. 213–38.
[64]*Soviet Army Operations*, pp. 5–39 to 5–40. See also Norby, *Soviet Aerospace Handbook*, pp. 46–51.

While the long-range bombing mission underwent only a modest revival of importance following the decline of Khrushchev's missile philosophy, the development of the controversial Tupolev *Backfire* intermediate-range bomber has given Soviet strategic aviation something of a new lease on life.[65] Nevertheless, the fact that production is being shared evenly with Naval Aviation, as well as that their strength in other long-range bomber types remains static, argues strongly against any fundamental change in Soviet strategic delivery assumptions.

In an attempt to compensate for its marginal strength and limited weapons load capability, Long-Range Aviation invested heavily and with reasonable success in electronic countermeasures and electronic warfare. In addition, they armed a high percentage of their bombers with standoff air-to-surface missiles and have maintained a modest fleet of airborne tankers to help extend the range of their aircraft. This latter capability is especially important if the *Backfire* is to play any truly strategic role.[66]

Although the western aviation press still makes much of the *Backfire*'s possible key strategic role, the United States apparently has appreciated the Soviet long-range bomber threat for what it is. It was recently reported that all of the strategic defense Nike-Hercules SAM batteries are being decommissioned, with the exception of those in Florida and Alaska, and that the U.S. fighter-interceptor force would be reduced to less than 150 aircraft.[67]

Military Air Forces: Conclusions

The loose Soviet air power confederation, clustered under the Military Air Forces rubric, is a diverse multirole group of personnel and weapons. The strict hierarchy into which each group falls has assured that tactical Frontal Aviation and its East European counterparts receive by far the largest portion of the new aircraft and equipment, while the other Soviet military air services get a kind of maintenance ration of new assets. This obviously fits Soviet strategic and tactical assumptions. However, it must be assumed that at some point the VTA will begin to receive an accelerating share of the new air power investment. It stands to reason that as tactical European needs permit, additions to power projection capabilities, such as those afforded by long-range air transport aircraft, will become increasingly attractive to the Soviet leadership. The future of the strategic air arm is much less certain.

[65] Editors, *Air International.*
[66] Norby, *Soviet Aerospace Handbook*, p. 50.
[67] Menaul, "Modern Soviet Air Force."

NAVAL AVIATION

While the East European members of the Warsaw Pact do not maintain significant naval air arms, the Soviet Union—the inheritor of a meaningful naval air tradition from tsarist days—has consistently operated a formidable number of naval fighters and bombers. Flying from shore-based facilities, this force provided an important maritime strike force during World War II and has continued to play an important role in Soviet national defense plans in the postwar era, particularly in the anticarrier, antisubmarine, and long-range reconnaissance roles.[68]

Though under navy operational control, Naval Aviation often uses the air force supply system, administrative network, and even base facilities. Naval aviation personnel wear regular air force uniforms and have air force ranks.[69] In most cases, their aircraft are the same basic types as those provided to the Military Air Forces but are specially modified and equipped for useful maritime missions.[70] Naval Aviation technical and flying personnel receive their training in the air force's educational system, followed usually by a year's orientation at the Nikolayev Naval Air Base. Later in their careers, officers may be assigned to the naval or air force academies for postgraduate education. The naval air arm includes some 59,000 men.[71]

Soviet Naval Aviation units are operationally assigned to fleet commands. The basic fleet aviation unit is the air division, directly subordinate to the fleet commander of Naval Aviation, who reports to the fleet chief of staff. The naval air regiment forms the fundamental combat unit.[72] Although each fleet has approximately the same number of aircraft, some hold more modern assets than others. For example, the Northern fleet, with important long-range Atlantic tasks, has perhaps the most modern aircraft, including a regiment of *Backfire B* bombers configured for the maritime reconnaissance strike role. The Black Sea fleet, with Turkish Straits and Mediterranean responsibilities, possesses similar holdings.[73] On the other hand, the Baltic fleet, with less comprehensive missions, has a somewhat smaller, less powerful inventory.[74] The Pacific

---

[68]Jacob W. Kipp, "The Development of Naval Aviation 1908–75," *Soviet Aviation*, pp. 137–65.

[69]Whiting, "The Peacetime Air Force pp. 289–313."

[70]Menaul, "Modern Soviet Air Force."

[71]*HSAF*, p. 9–12; *Military Balance 1980–81*, p. 11.

[72]*HSAF*, p. 9–4.

[73]Editors, *Air International*. Black Sea fleet air units maintain a regular periodic reconnaissance patrol to South Yemen for surveillance of western naval operations in the Persian Gulf and its approaches.

[74]Recently, *Backfire B*'s have been observed operating with the Baltic fleet in tactical support of joint Warsaw Pact amphibious assault exercises in East German waters. It has

fleet until recently has maintained only a modest aviation force; now its air assets have been substantially upgraded, especially by the addition of a *Backfire B* regiment.[75]

Today's Soviet Naval Aviation units are assigned the following primary missions: 1) maritime surveillance and reconnaissance, 2) antisubmarine warfare, 3) destruction of enemy surface forces, 4) destruction of enemy ports and harbors, 5) minelaying, and 6) support of amphibious assaults. In addition, in wartime Naval Aviation units would be assigned a number of other utility missions as the need arose, including air transport and evacuation of wounded.[76]

Trends in Soviet Naval Aviation

Perhaps the most fundamental new feature of Soviet Naval Aviation has been the forward deployment of VTOL fighter aircraft and antisubmarine warfare (ASW) helicopters aboard dedicated carrier-cruisers, including the *Moskva* and *Kiev* class ships. The Soviet decision to meet the then rapidly expanding U.S. and NATO nuclear missile submarine threat with an air-sea, hunter-killer force patrolling on a global basis represented an important reversal of earlier Soviet assumptions about the vulnerability of the aircraft carrier.[77]

The present Soviet naval building program apparently will produce at least several more *Kiev*-type carrier-cruisers; subsequent classes are likely to be much larger, possibly nuclear-powered, conventional aircraft carriers capable of carrying high-performance strike aircraft as well as ASW helicopters. Naturally, this global ASW force will involve Naval Aviation in other tasks at great distances from Soviet shores, including force projection, protection of Soviet nuclear submarines, and similar operations.[78] At the same time the addition of the *Backfire B* to the navy's

been reported that the Baltic fleet is now assigned forty to forty-five *Backfires*. David R. Griffiths, "Backfires Spotted in New Role," *Aviation Week and Space Technology* 114, no. 23 (8 June 1981): 57–58.

[75]Editors, *Air International*.

[76]Norby, *Soviet Aerospace Handbook*, p. 73. An excellent, if dated, Soviet review of airborne ASW is provided in I. M. Sotnikov and N. A. Brusentsev, *Aviatsia protiv podvodnykh lodok* [Aviation against submarines] (Moscow: Voyenizdat, 1970).

[77]Jacob W. Kipp, "Naval Aviation," *SAFRA* 4 (1980): 239–52. The massive defensive capabilities built into the present generation of Soviet carrier-cruisers and their escorts is a determined attempt to reduce a vulnerability that few can deny. See also Jan S. Breemer, "The New Soviet Carrier," *Proceedings of the U.S. Naval Institute* 107, no. 8 (August 1981): 30–35. For an interesting Soviet work on the possible uses of naval aircraft, including carrier-based planes, see N. A. Brusentsev, *Voyenno-morskaya aviatsia* [Naval aviation] (Moscow: Voyenizdat, 1976). Brusentsev uses data primarily from western navies but provides a concluding chapter that is more general in nature.

[78]Editors, *Air International*.

aging bomber force represents a substantial improvement of Soviet long-range reconnaissance and strike capabilities, while continuing the basic program of arming maritime bombers with increasingly more effective antishipping cruise missiles.[79]

While this Soviet naval air capability is still dwarfed by U.S and European naval air forces, these mission-specific air regiments and carrier forces have helped to transform the Soviet navy from a coastal defense force to an effective and continually growing strategic sea denial combat arm. Not as spectacular as the growth of Frontal Aviation in the last decade, the increased and changed capabilities of Soviet Naval Aviation still reflects a fundamental shift in the direction of Soviet naval air power development. Whether or not this trend continues will certainly depend heavily on the operational success of the next generation of Soviet carrier vessels and the aircraft supplied to them.

WARSAW PACT AIR POWER: CONCLUSIONS

Important and meaningful contributions to strategic air defense and tactical air-ground support capabilities are increasingly being made under close Soviet supervision, by the highly integrated and standardized air forces of the East European Pact members. Soviet deployment of modern interceptors and fighter-bombers within the alliance is upgrading the East European air forces at almost the same pace as the USSR's own impressive air modernization program.

Given the Soviet version of deterrence as the ability to absorb high levels of punishment and still be able to fight back, there can be no doubt that continued support for strategic Air Defense Forces and tactical Frontal Aviation will persist through the 1980s. If these forces, both Soviet and East European, can be brought to what they feel are adequate levels, then military airlift undoubtedly will be the subject of stepped up development. Certain aspects of long-range strategic aviation, particularly reconnaissance and electronic warfare, probably also will receive increased attention. The East European Pact nations are unlikely to participate in these latter programs.

In conformity with Soviet policy governing the combat roles of East European armed forces, allied air units are structured and trained to perform only certain specific and limited tasks within the European theater. They do not have any important offensive, strategic, or power projection capabilities. From the Soviet standpoint this makes good sense,

---

[79]Menaul, "Modern Soviet Air Force."

and East European combat aviation commanders surely must be gratified by the increasingly important, if still strictly supplementary, roles they at last are now performing with first-rate equipment. But the cost of even this limited participation must be relatively high for each of the East European allies, so it is difficult to imagine their demanding a significantly greater role in long-range aviation or military air transport within the framework of the Pact. On the other hand, the frustrated aviation industries, particularly of Czechoslovakia, Poland, and Romania, surely resent the Soviet injunction against their entry into the major combat aircraft business.

While recognition of the expanding role of the Pact's junior partners is important for a balanced assessment of Warsaw Pact air power, it also must be noted that only Soviet Voiska PVO and possibly Frontal Aviation interceptor personnel have had significant post-World War II air combat experience. Flying mainly against American pilots in Korea and later in Southeast Asia, limited numbers of career interceptor pilots gained invaluable experience opposite formidable western forces. Also, particularly during the period between 1967 and 1973, Soviet pilots flew combat missions against Israeli crews who were operating French and U.S. aircraft. In addition to this flying experience, Soviet Antiaircraft Rocket and Radiotechnical Troops have gained exceptional combat skills in identifying, tracking, and attacking a broad selection of American- and European-made aircraft, from fighters to strategic bombers. Some East European allies may have participated in selected combat operations, but it is clear that they did not do so in significant numbers and that such experiences would have been accomplished on a bilateral basis outside the provisions of the Warsaw Pact. Subsequent Soviet joint training operations undoubtedly have been designed to pass on the results of first-hand experience, but that inevitably must be an unsatisfactory process.

It seems clear that Warsaw Pact air forces' operational concepts and combat doctrine are presently undergoing important modifications accompanying the massive deployment of their new and significantly more capable aircraft. Tight integration of Pact command and control, long the hallmark of strategic air defense in East Europe and the western USSR, is becoming increasingly characteristic of East European and Soviet cooperation in tactical air power operations as well. In contrast to this operational centralization, Soviet air combat doctrine is increasingly emphasizing individual initiative and flexibility as the capabilities of Soviet aircraft are expanding. Such a willingness to rely more on the experienced pilot's skill at "free hunting" is an unmistakable sign of the maturation of today's Soviet air combat forces as well as of a leadership judgment that major combat aircraft and equipment, especially avionics and combat electronics, are at last becoming competitive with NATO assets.

Finally, various organizational changes within the Soviet air forces and their Pact counterparts, portions of which are just becoming perceptible in the West, may yet prove to be fundamental. Rumors that the recently renamed Voiska PVO strategic Air Defense Forces have increased their jurisdiction to cover virtually all air defense systems persist alongside equally intriguing reports that Voiska PVO is being eliminated as a separate service. Similarly interesting suppositions about the other branches and services abound, particularly the revived Soviet Army Aviation.[80] If past practice is any guide, the complete picture of Warsaw Pact air forces' organization and configuration for the 1980s will be a long time emerging.

---

[80]In what has become a highly controversial article, Phillip A. Petersen alludes to some of these changes, particularly those affecting Frontal Aviation assets and Army Aviation. See Petersen's "The Soviet Conceptual Framework for the Application of Military Power," *Naval War College Review* 34, no. 3 (May–June 1981): 15–25.

The Navies of the Warsaw Pact*

STEVE F. KIME

The Soviet Union . . . is a continental power with interior lines of communication and operation and with the contiguous geography that would enable it to move forces and equipment by land to probable theaters of wars. Thus, Warsaw Pact strategy essentially entails *sea denial*, as against NATO's requirement for *sea control* and *force projection* strategies.[1]

The non-Soviet navies of the Warsaw Pact have important missions. They do not, however, bear the responsibility for the life or death of the alliance in war, nor do they act as vital instruments of peacetime policy. These navies, after all, are peripheral forces of a continental alliance that is dominated by a great continental and intercontinental nuclear super-power. Only the Soviet navy has global pretensions, and its global roles are not much related to the missions of the other navies of the Warsaw Pact.

It is important to place the Warsaw Pact navies in perspective. Too often western analyses of Soviet and East European military forces are conducted in a vacuum. Soviet and Warsaw Pact military doctrine and forces cannot be intelligently discussed separately from domestic and foreign sociopolitical and economic considerations. Further, specific Soviet and Warsaw Pact forces, like navies, cannot be sensibly viewed separately from broader doctrinal and force posture considerations.

THE POLITICO-MILITARY CONTEXT

The Soviet view of peace is as important to consider as the Soviet view of war.[2] The Warsaw Pact is attuned to political as well as military

---

*The views expressed herein are those of the author. They should not be taken to represent those of the U.S. Navy or the Department of Defense.

[1]Ihsan Gurkan, *NATO, Turkey, and the Southern Flank* (New York: National Strategy Information Center, 1980), p. 56.

[2]Steve F. Kime, "The Soviet View of War," *Comparative Strategy* 2, no. 3 (1980): 205–21.

realities. Political facts of life governing military doctrine and construction apply both in peacetime or in war, and the Soviet Union has been attentive to the need for the Pact to serve not only as a political integrating instrument in peacetime but also as "a highly integrated body capable of fielding modern conventional military forces in the vital Central European theater. . . ."[3]

A military alliance, dominated by Soviet power, is a necessity for political control in East Europe even in peacetime. Therefore, the political reliability of Pact allies in the event of war is questionable. Soviet military planners see missions that can be served by their junior military partners, but individual Pact nations will not have armies or navies designed and built to serve the needs of each separate nation's defense. In terms of navies, East European forces are relegated to supportive and peripheral roles. Only the Soviet navy is tailored in a comprehensive way to serve the needs of an individual nation's political and military doctrine.

In situations short of war with the West, non-Soviet Warsaw Pact forces are supposed to help cement an alliance with woefully weak political legitimacy. From the Soviet point of view, it is hoped that they are indoctrinated, trained, and positioned so that they will at best be helpers and at worst be weak opponents if military power must be brought to bear to ensure or restore a Soviet-dominated political order. Obviously, in peacetime such forces are not going to be instruments of foreign political expression or individual national pride. Non-Soviet Warsaw Pact navies do not share the large international political role that has been served increasingly in the last two decades by the Soviet navy.

Political considerations extend ominously into the realm of war.[4] If the reliability of its allies is in question, the Soviet Union must develop a military doctrine that minimizes the options of those allies. Non-Soviet Warsaw Pact forces must be tied to doctrine and force postures in such a way that the only viable option is to join the Soviet juggernaut and serve, rather than disrupt, its lines of communication. Soviet military doctrine and Warsaw Pact military posture are designed so that incipient political dissidence in Eastern Europe, along with the military and naval forces of the non-Soviet Warsaw Pact countries, would be sucked into the slipstream of a massive military machine moving westward.

It is not the author's intent to suggest that Soviet military plans and policies to deal with the political realities in Eastern Europe will work; they may not be effective in either peace or war. Elsewhere it has been

---

[3]Dale R. Herspring, "The Warsaw Pact at 25," *Problems of Communism* 29, no. 5 (September–October 1980): 6.

[4]A good summary of these political considerations is in Peter Vigor, "Doubts and Difficulties Confronting a Would-Be Soviet Attacker," *RUSI* (June 1980): 32–38.

suggested that political realities impose much rigidity, and probably weakness, upon Soviet military doctrine.[5] For the purposes of this study, the point is that the postures of East European military forces can be expected to reflect the politico-military facts of life governing the Pact. They will not be designed and disposed for nationalistic political purposes. Instead, they will be designed and disposed to be folded into a Soviet-led and Soviet-dominated westward offensive, and for little else. Non-Soviet Warsaw Pact navies reflect these realities and are not intended to operate very far from their shores; even in war they will perform tasks close to home or in the wake of their senior ally.

NUCLEAR GEOPOLITICS AND MILITARY DOCTRINE

Soviet military doctrine is characterized by preoccupations and orientations that reinforce the tendency to prepare for a massive westward offensive on the Eurasian landmass. This is an offensive that must incorporate East European land and air capacities as well as fruitfully occupy maritime forces at the periphery. It must be understood, however, that the Soviet Union is not a traditional sea power. Russia long has been a Eurasian land power. The Soviet Union has become the dominant Eurasian land and air power. In addition, the USSR has become an *intercontinental* nuclear superpower on at least a par with its major adversary. The Soviet Union's intercontinental adversary is a great, natural sea power that has successfully participated in two massive continental conflagrations.

The nuclear age, and especially the rise of the USSR to equal intercontinental nuclear superpower status with the United States, has altered the familiar asymmetries between continental and sea powers, but it has not eliminated those differences. The prospects of an immediate devastating attack on American home territory affects the ability of the United States to counter natural Soviet power on the ground and at the periphery of Eurasia. On the other hand, in the nuclear age the Soviet navy has found new room to maneuver and new license for expression.[6] There is in the Soviet Union a new appreciation of the importance of maritime missions and, in fact, an ever greater understanding that the

---

[5]These ideas are more fully developed in Kime, "Is the Warsaw Pact in Disarray?," *Defense 81* (February 1981): 10–13.

[6]Again, these geopolitical and military policy transformations can only be mentioned in passing in this paper. See Kime, "A Soviet Navy for the Nuclear Age," *Parameters* 10, no. 1 (March 1980): 58–70, for a more complete discussion.

intercontinental element now present in military strategy carries with it a new range of naval missions. But the USSR reserves these new nuclear age missions to itself and relegates the navies of its Warsaw Pact allies to subordinate roles associated with dominating the Baltic and Black seas, and if progress in the land campaign in Europe permits, gaining control of the straits that determine access to and from those seas.

At bottom, the Soviet view of potential war is a continental view. Who controls Eurasia is the ultimate postwar question that must be posed by the Soviet military thinker. In the Soviet view, the war between East and West, if it occurs, no doubt will be a huge one and almost certainly a nuclear one. The nuclear phase probably will be decisive to the outcome, but it will not be the only determining element. Masses of people and conventional military equipment will play important roles in determining who controls whatever might be left in Eurasia. Domination of the periphery of Eurasia and isolation of the Continent from outside support and supply is an important element of that control.

The rapid seizure of West Europe would help shift the battlefield away from the USSR and would help if any postwar recovery is possible. It puts the onus of nuclear escalation on the West and could move the focus of some western nuclear weapons, if they are used, away from the USSR. A decisive westward offensive at the outset of East-West conflict also fits well within Russian and Soviet doctrinal preferences for mass, mobility, and surprise. And, as suggested, it provides a logical way of managing potential unenthusiastic allies while at the same time attacking the enemy.

The nuclear age has not removed the threat of a massive westward Warsaw Pact offensive. Therefore, it makes sense for Soviet military planners to prepare for such an offensive that would be dominated by the Soviet military machine and would thoroughly determine the options for non-Soviet Warsaw Pact force. While Soviet units might be used for lesser contingencies away from Soviet borders in the proper circumstances, non-Soviet Warsaw Pact troops are subordinated to Soviet forces and doctrine for continental conflict and disposed with internal control and major war in mind.[7]

THE PACT AND SOVIET NAVAL POLICY

Since the Soviet navy reserves strategic nuclear missions, high seas offensive and defensive roles, and global political presence to itself, it is in many ways more distinct from non-Soviet Warsaw Pact navies than it is

---

[7]An attempt to deal with the limited application of Soviet military power is in Kime, "Power Projection, Soviet Style," *Air Force Magazine* 63, no. 12 (December 1980): 50–54.

linked to them. East European navies are not likely to be built with the "legs" that would permit them the freedom to range as far as Soviet units. Moreover, the Soviet Union is not disposed to assign naval missions to junior partners that are vital to the maintenance of supremacy in the Baltic or Black seas, or that might determine the success or failure of gaining control of the Dardanelles or the Danish Narrows. There is an interesting difference between the way that East European armies and air forces relate to the Soviet army and air force and the way East European navies relate to the Soviet navy.

As illustrated in the essays on ground and air power elsewhere in this volume, the armies and air forces of East European countries are structured along the same lines as those of the Soviet Union, and they adhere to Soviet indoctrination and training methods. In wartime they are to operate alongside Soviet forces. This is not so of non-Soviet Warsaw Pact navies.[8] Even though there is some training of East Europeans in Soviet naval schools and some talk of "joint exercises, voyages and meetings of representatives of the fraternal navies,"[9] the non-Soviet Warsaw Pact navies have relatively few points of contact with the Soviet navy and only supplementary, and somewhat separate, roles in Soviet naval strategy:

> The fact that they have no place in Soviet naval strategy has led to the anomalous situation that these nations, which have imposing armies, very large, well-trained air forces and very modern armament generally, have few ships most of which are obsolete and not particularly well-armed or seaworthy.[10]

For example, the Polish and German Democratic Republic (GDR) navies together comprise less than half of the surface ships available to the Pact in the Baltic, even though those two countries have most of the Pact's Baltic coastline. The Soviet Baltic fleet has more than half of the surface ships, virtually all of the submarines, and the vast majority of naval aircraft. The Soviet Baltic fleet very importantly furnishes the heavier, more critical units. Polish and GDR naval forces primarily provide medium-sized amphibious craft and lighter surface vessels. All Warsaw Pact units in the Baltic are under the command of the Soviet headquarters in Kaliningrad. Polish headquarters at Gdynia and GDR headquarters at Rostock are assigned subordinate level command functions; they are separate ones and are not integrated into mixed formations with Soviet units.[11]

---

[8]Vittorio Gabaglio, "Eastern Navies," *Aviation and Marine* 5, no. 44 (July–August 1977): 56.

[9]For example, see Fleet Admiral V. A. Kasatonov (Soviet navy), *Sovietskaya Estonia*, 30 July 1972.

[10]Gabaglio, "Eastern Navies," p. 56.

[11]Klaus Jancke and Ulrich Weisser, "The Problems in the Baltic—Threat and Response," *NATO's Fifteen Nations* 23, no. 2 (April–May 1978): 55.

The Soviets have tried to perpetuate the notion that the Black Sea is a Russian lake. The Bulgarian and Romanian navies are fit for little more than coastal defense in support of the Soviet fleet. Control of the Black Sea in wartime is viewed as a vital interest in Moscow; denial of NATO's maritime control of the Mediterranean is important throughout any major East-West conflict, and the ability to seize control of the Turkish Straits at the appropriate point in a major conflict on the ground in Europe is important to Soviet military planners. But none of these highly significant tasks relies critically on capacities of non-Soviet navies.

THE NAVIES OF THE WARSAW PACT

Because the Soviet Union clearly sees other navies in the Pact as best kept separate and unequal, even in the limited theaters where those navies operate, it is useful to address the navies separately.[12]

Poland

Next to the USSR, Poland probably has the most significant of the Warsaw Pact navies. Poland's 141 ships and 75 naval aircraft compare with the 545 ships and 260 naval aircraft maintained by the Soviet Baltic fleet. The nature of Polish naval missions is revealed by the preponderance of mine warfare ships and craft, medium and light amphibious vessels, and coastal craft. Forty-nine ships, or about one-third of the Polish navy, are dedicated to mine warfare. Twenty-three ships, or approximately one-sixth of the Polish navy, are amphibious ships that would assist the Soviet navy in landings aimed at dominating the Baltic littoral or seizing the Straits. Fifty of Poland's 141 ships are only small coastal patrol craft.

Poland has just one warship that can be called a principal surface combatant—the SAM *Kotlin* class destroyer, a 2,850-ton ship fitted with surface-to-air missiles and transferred from the USSR in 1970. Four old submarines, also Soviet hand-me-downs, are in the Polish inventory. There are no ships for underway replenishment, only five ships for fleet support, and nine auxiliary vessels.

If Poland were independent, it might well see the need for a better balanced navy. There is no question that Poland could build a navy with larger more impressive units, and it might be expected not to concentrate

---

[12]All order-of-battle information in the text of this section is from the *Unclassified Communist Naval Orders of Battle*, Report No. DDB–1200–124A–80 (Washington, DC: Defense Inteligence Agency, 1980).

on the kinds of amphibious units now maintained in the Polish navy. Polish shipbuilding is certainly capable of producing a more credible navy if one were demanded of it. *Polnochny* class landing ships and most of Poland's light surface forces are built in Polish shipyards.

German Democratic Republic

The GDR navy actually has a few more ships than the Polish navy, but there are no East German naval aircraft. About one-half, or 82 of the 175 ships in the GDR navy, are small coastal patrol craft. There are 12 small amphibious ships, 33 mine warfare craft, 4 underway replenishment ships, 2 fleet support ships, and 28 auxiliaries of various types. Only 2 ships, by any stretch of the imagination, can be considered principal surface combatants. These are old Soviet *Riga* class frigates.

It is probable that East Germany, if the USSR were disposed to tolerate longer reins on its German ally, could build and maintain a more formidable navy. One source cogently sums up the naval situation of the GDR as follows: "It is anomalous and a little sad that a nation which, in its original entirety, relied so heavily on the seas, is now reduced to being a mere onlooker."[13]

Bulgaria

Bulgaria has a minor navy. It has a total of 65 ships and no naval aircraft. Bulgaria has been entrusted with 4 used Soviet submarines (2 *Romeo* and 2 *Whiskey* class) and 4 frigate-sized transfers from the Soviet inventory. Reflecting the importance of coastal defense to the Bulgarian navy, there are 26 mine warfare ships and craft and 27 coastal patrol craft.

Romania

When considering Romania, the least enthusiastic of all Pact members, it is always important to entertain the possibility that this country might consider its potential enemy to come as likely from the East as from the West. In any case, the Romanian navy is vengefully defensive in character. Its 104 ships are mostly coastal patrol vessels and mine warfare ships and craft. There are no amphibious warships with which to help the Soviets dominate the Black Sea coast or take the Straits. On the other hand, there are no major ships or submarines that might get in the way of the Soviet Black Sea fleet. It is interesting that several Romanian craft are transfers from the People's Republic of China.

---

[13]Gabaglio, "Eastern Navies," p. 62.

Table 1. Navies of the Warsaw Pact[14]

	Bulgaria	German Democratic Republic	Poland	Romania	Soviet Northern fleet	Soviet Baltic fleet	Soviet Black Sea fleet & Caspian Sea flotilla	Soviet Pacific fleet	Total Soviet navy units
Submarines	4	0	4	0	about 186	about 37	about 30	about 119	372*
Aircraft carriers	0	0	0	0	1	0	2	1	4**
Principal surface combatants	2	2	1	0	71	46	74	78	269***
Patrol combatants	3	12	0	3	†	†	†	†	120†
Amphibious warfare ships	0	12	23	0	‡	‡	‡	‡	86‡
Mine warfare ships	2	0	24	4	40	40	35	50	165
Mine warfare craft	24	33	25	28	40	90	55	50	235
Coastal patrol river/ roadstead craft	27	82	50	66	35	125	120	140	420
Underway replenishment ships	0	4	0	0	20	15	20	25	80
Material support ships	0	0	0	0	30	10	10	20	70
Fleet support ships	1	2	5	2	40	25	35	35	135
Other auxiliaries	2	28	9	1	110	115	105	145	475
Total ships	65	175	141	104	about 621	about 545	about 545	about 720	2,431
Naval aircraft	0	0	75	0	380	260	390	400	1,430
Naval personnel strengths	10,000	16,000	22,500	10,500	118,000	105,000	99,000	121,000	443,000

*About 170 Soviet submarines are nuclear powered; 215 Soviet submarines are nonmissile-carrying submarines of both nuclear and nonnuclear types; 70 Soviet submarines are missile-carrying attack submarines, and most of these are nuclear powered; and 87 Soviet submarines carry ballistic missiles, 33 of which are the newer *Delta* class SSBN and 29 are *Yankee* class SSBN.

**Two of the four aircraft carriers listed here are the *Moskva* class guided-missile aviation cruisers in the Black Sea fleet. The other two are *Kiev* class guided-missile V/STOL aircraft carriers.

***The principal surface combatants include ships as big as the single nuclear-powered, guided-missile cruiser in the Soviet Baltic fleet and as small as the 140 frigates and light frigates dispersed throughout the four Soviet fleets.

† The 120 patrol combatants in the Soviet navy are dispersed variously between the four fleets and the Caspian Sea flotilla.

‡ Sixty of the 86 Soviet amphibious warfare ships are smaller MP-4 and *Polnochny* classes. These are distributed variously between the fleets. There is only one large new *Ivan Rogov* class LPD and it is in the Pacific fleet. There are 25 *Alligator* and *Ropucha* class LSTs. Ten of these are in the Pacific fleet and the other three fleets have five each.

14All information from Table 1 was condensed and derived from the *Unclassified Communist Naval Orders of Battle*. In that publication a more complete breakdown of the various categories can be found with explanations of types of ships.

The Soviet Union

The Soviet navy has been the subject of much study by others as well as by this writer. There is no need here to describe thoroughly either Soviet naval strategy or Soviet naval force posture. There are, however, some general observations to be made about the Soviet navy, not as one of two superpower navies in the world but as the dominating navy of a continental alliance—the Warsaw Pact.

The Soviet navy and naval strategy are different from past great navies and traditional naval strategies in some fundamental ways. The Soviet navy is the follow on to a limited peripheral navy of a vast land power that has taken on intercontinental missions in the nuclear age. As an instrument of an intercontinental nuclear superpower, it is able to operate beyond the closed seas and choke points that traditionally determined the effective range of Russian navies in both peace and war. In the nuclear age the Soviet navy thus has become a credible political tool and a viable threat to western naval power in limited conflict situations. But the Soviet Union did not become an equal sea power with the United States simply because it was an equal intercontinental nuclear superpower any more than the United States has become equal to the Soviet Union as a European land and air power simply because U.S. nuclear weapons can strike Russia.

In any attempt to understand Soviet and Warsaw Pact naval power, it is inappropriate to look for the kinds of missions and capabilities that have characterized traditional sea powers whose national survival has depended on sea communications and on the necessity to control or command the seas. It is necessary to understand the political significance of a global Soviet navy as well as the military fact that the capacity to interpose lesser naval forces in the path of greater naval forces has a deterrent effect, given the probability of escalation to nuclear war if actual shooting begins. It is also crucial to understand that the combat capabilities of the Soviet navy are always connected with military events in Eurasia. Either intercontinental nuclear strikes and defense from such strikes, or a major conflict on the ground in Eurasia, or both will be the context of Soviet naval combat operations. Simply stated, Soviet naval strategy is not aimed at war at sea independent of events affecting Eurasia. Neither is it aimed at combating western power directly at long distances from the Eurasian landmass.

The primary preoccupation of the Soviet navy has been the prospect of nuclear war with the United States. Strategic offensive and defensive missions have been the Soviet navy's best arguments for resources. Table 1 reveals how much investment has been placed in the huge Soviet submarine fleet, and most of this has been deployed in the two strategic fleets—the Pacific and Northern. Much of the Soviet investment in naval surface combatants has been justified in terms of strategic, that is, inter-continental nuclear offensive and defensive missions. It is clear that the Soviet Union reserves to itself the tasks associated with attacking the territory of the United States and coping with the naval strategic offense and defense of the United States. For these purposes the Soviet navy maintains the two strategic fleets and disposes forces outside their restricted seas, particularly in the Mediterranean Sea and the Indian Ocean.

The Soviet naval forces noted above are not detached from the primary Warsaw Pact concerns that are associated with massive continental conflict as well as with nuclear war. It must be remembered that Soviet doctrine considers such a conflict in Eurasia as highly unlikely separate from nuclear war. Also, and very significantly, there are important missions for the Soviet navy on the high seas in connection with isolating Europe from America and with attacking NATO directly, especially its southern and northern flanks. Not all open-ocean Soviet naval missions are involved with intercontinental nuclear offense and defense.

SOVIET AND PACT NAVIES: CONCLUSIONS

When considering the Soviet navy as a Warsaw Pact threat to the flanks of NATO, it is important to avoid the trap of considering Soviet maritime operations against the flanks as secondary or support operations. Indeed, the Soviets perceive such operations as vital ones, thoroughly integrated into a complex alliance strategy for subduing and controlling Western Europe. Moreover, Soviet military strategists do not envision a separate attack against NATO on one of the flanks but rather coordinated attacks in the context of a major war between the two blocs. The Soviet navy is not intended to operate in a limited war, either in terms of geography or in terms of weapons employed.[15]

It is also important to note that the Soviet navy would have a critical role in maintaining control of NATO territory after a westward Warsaw Pact offensive succeeded, whether or not the conflict has become nuclear in Europe and/or escalated to intercontinental nuclear exchanges. Dominating sea lines of communications to isolate Europe from America and the Middle East and controlling ingress and egress from the Baltic and Black seas, along with nuclear attack missions and the conduct of the

---

[15]These points are made and amplified in Marian K. Leighton, *The Soviet Threat to NATO's Northern Flank* (New York: National Strategy Information Center, 1979), pp. 87–89.

westward offensive itself, are the major strategic missions of the Warsaw Pact.

These missions require forces capable of operating effectively on the high seas in a hostile environment. Gone are the days when the Soviet navy could be accurately described as a coastal defensive navy.[16] To be sure, a large number of Soviet naval units, quite logically for a traditionally continental power, are built for the defense of the Eurasian periphery and its restricted seas. But so much of the Soviet navy is now dedicated to the global strategic missions of the Warsaw Pact, both nuclear and nonnuclear, that it is no longer sensible to view that navy in continental terms. Therefore, even though analyzing a continental alliance dominated by a traditionally continental power with a fixation upon major war, whose nature will be determined by events and outcomes in Eurasia, it is important to remember that the senior partner now possesses a navy with global capacities. That superpower navy is assisted in limited ways by limited navies in the Baltic and the Black seas.

---

[16]It is significant that both the U.S. Pacific fleet commander and the U.S. Atlantic fleet commander recently told a Senate subcommittee about the increased Soviet threat to sea lines of communications. See *Washington Star*, 17 February 1981.

INDEX

Norway, 103
  Storting, 71
Novotny, Antonin, 32, 39, 148
Nuclear, biological, and chemical (NBC)
  protection, 127–28, 132, 168, 171,
  174–76, 238, 257
Nuclear-powered ballistic missile submarine
  (SSBN), 201–02, 203

O

Oder River, 29, 31, 73, 229
Odessa, 58
The Offensive (Sidorenko), 234
Ogaden, 59
Ollenhauer, Erich, 85
Organization of Petroleum Exporting Coun-
  tries (OPEC), 62
Ostpolitik, 42
Ottoman rule, 54

P

"Pact on Friendship, Cooperation, and Mu-
  tual Aid," 28, 68
Pan-Slavic entente, 30
Paris, 78, 87, 89
Paris agreements (1954),8, 14, 68–72, 75–
  77
Pavlovsky, Ivan, 56
Pearson, Lester, 67, 84
Peking, 36
People's Militia (GDR), 30
Petrovsky Yard, 209
Pfaff, William, 78
Plzeň, 29
Poland, 3–6, 9, 12, 14–15, 18–19, 21–24,
  31–32, 34–35, 39, 42–44, 46–47, 49,
  68, 82, 95, 104–06, 141, 154, 156–
  57, 160, 175, 195, 198, 216–17, 219,
  220, 223, 241, 272, 280
Polish Communist Party, 22, 23, 29, 157
Polish military forces, 150, 154–57, 173,
  176
Polish Navy, 195–97, 279–81
Polish People's Army, 141
Polish People's Republic, 30
"Polish spring in October," 31

Political Consultative Committee (PCC) *see*
  Warsaw Pact
Potsdam conference, 9
Poznan workers' strike, 31
Prague, 23, 28–29, 31, 36, 39, 41, 43
Prague Spring uprising (1968), 20, 31, 40–
  41, 83–84, 146–48
Prussia, 151

R

Radar, 121
Radom, 43
Rakosi, Matyas, 52
Rapacki, Adam, 36, 87
Rapacki Plan, 14, 84
Reagan, Ronald, 105
Reith radio lectures, 86–87
Reitz, James T., 230
Republican Women's National Conference,
  80
Reston, James, 72
Rhine River, 178
Rokosovsky, K. K., 29
Romania, 3, 6, 9–11, 14, 17, 19–22, 24, 39,
  49–50, 52, 54–58, 60–63, 68, 74, 89,
  95, 145, 154, 158–59, 168, 195,
  218–19, 222–23, 258, 272, 281
Romanian Communist Party, 55, 58, 158
Romanian-Israeli exchanges, 223
Romanian military forces, 158–60
Romanian Navy, 195, 198, 280–81
Rostock, 279
Royal Military Academy Sandhurst, 152
Royal United Service Institution, 69
Russia, 152, 157

S

Salisbury, Harrison, 70, 71
Salt I agreement, 15, 104, 113
Salt II agreement, 104
Saseno Island, 55
Scharnhorst, David Gerhard Johann von, 43
Sea lines of communication (SLOC), 201
Sea Power of the State (Gorshkov), 202
Self-propelled (SP) artillery, 131, 175–76,
  219–20, 229, 233